Hollywood and Anti-Semitism

Hollywood and Anti-Semitism: A Cultural History up to World War II examines how the public perceived American Jews in the entertainment industry from the turn of the century to the outbreak of World War II. Eastern European Jewish immigrants are often credited with building a film industry during the first decade of the twentieth century and dominating it by the 1920s. In this study, Steven Carr reconceptualizes Jewish participation in Hollywood by examining prevalent attitudes toward Jews among American audiences. Analogous to the Jewish Question of the nineteenth century, which was concerned with the full participation of Jews within the sphere of public life, the Hollywood Question of the twenties, thirties, and forties addressed the Jewish population within mass media. This ground-breaking study reveals the powerful set of assumptions about ethnicity and media influence as it related to the role of the Jew in the motion picture industry.

Steven Alan Carr is associate professor of communication at Indiana University–Purdue University Fort Wayne. He has contributed to *Shared Differences: Multicultural Media and Practical Pedagogy* and *Jewish Women in America*, among other publications.

Cambridge Studies in the History of Mass Communication

General Editors

Kenneth Short, University of Houston
Garth Jowett, University of Houston
David Culbert, Louisiana State University

Cambridge Studies in the History of Mass Communication includes books that examine the communications processes and communications systems within social, cultural, and political contexts. Inclusive of empirical, effects-based research, works in this series proceed from the basis that the histories of various media are an important means to understanding their role and function in society. The history of a medium – its pattern of introduction, diffusion, acceptance, and effects – varies in each society, interacting with, and in turn shaping, its culture. Moreover, each society reacts differently to the introduction of a medium, and regulatory policies are shaped by both political and cultural forces. The detailed study of various communications forms and their complex message systems is now understood to be the key to unraveling the evolution of modern society and its culture.

Other books in the Series:

U.S. Television News and Cold War Propaganda, 1947–1960
by Nancy Bernhard

South Africa's Alternative Press by Les Switzer

Propaganda and Democracy by J. Michael Sproule

Hollywood's Overseas Campaign: The North Atlantic Movie Trade, 1920–1950 by Ian Jarvie

Ronald Reagan in Hollywood: Movies and Politics by Stephen Vaughn

Hollywood Censored: Morality Codes, Catholics, and the Movies
by Gregory Black

Children and the Movies: Media Influence and the Payne Fund Controversy
by Garth Jowett, Ian Jarvie, and Kathryn Fuller

The Making of American Audiences by Richard Butsch

HOLLYWOOD AND ANTI-SEMITISM

A CULTURAL HISTORY UP TO WORLD WAR II

Steven Alan Carr

Indiana University–
Purdue University Fort Wayne

CAMBRIDGE
UNIVERSITY PRESS

Watkins College
of Art & Design

PUBLISHED BY THE PRESS SYNDICATE OF THE UNIVERSITY OF CAMBRIDGE
The Pitt Building, Trumpington Street, Cambridge, United Kingdom

CAMBRIDGE UNIVERSITY PRESS
The Edinburgh Building, Cambridge CB2 2RU, UK
40 West 20th Street, New York, NY 10011-4211, USA
10 Stamford Road, Oakleigh, VIC 3166, Australia
Ruiz de Alarcón 13, 28014 Madrid, Spain
Dock House, The Waterfront, Cape Town 8001, South Africa

http://www.cambridge.org

First published 2001

Printed in the United States of America

Typeface Goudy 10/13 pt.   *System* DeskTopPro$_{/UX}$ [BV]

A catalog record for this book is available from the British Library.

Library of Congress Cataloging in Publication Data
Carr, Steven Alan, 1964–
Hollywood and anti-semitism : a cultural history up to World War II / Steven Alan Carr.
p. cm. – (Cambridge studies in the history of mass communications)
Revision of the author's thesis (doctoral – University of Texas at Austin, 1994) presented
under the title The Hollywood question.
Includes bibliographical references and index.
ISBN 0-521-57118-9 – ISBN 0-521-79854-X (pbk.)
1. Motion picture industry – California – Los Angeles – History.   2. Jews in the motion
picture industry – United States.   3. Antisemitism – United States.   I. Title.   II. Series.
PN1993.5.U65 C37 2001
384'.8'089924073–dc21   00-058532

ISBN 0 521 57118 9 hardback
ISBN 0 521 79854 X paperback

For Nancy, Maxine, and William

Contents

Illustrations

Acknowledgments

This work has some of its own history, characterized in large part by my good fortune and the generosity of those around me. It was originally a dissertation, and numerous individuals mentioned in that document have had a formative influence. I owe certain people, however, my redundant gratitude. Much of the dissertation came together through the generosity and patience of Kimberly Jones, who offered both compassion and living quarters in those final weeks as I prepared to deposit a document for my doctoral degree from the University of Texas at Austin. Only in retrospect do I truly recognize the immense debt of gratitude I owe my dissertation committee and my advisor, Charles Ramìrez-Berg. In particular, committee member Thomas Schatz has played a lasting role as both mentor and editor in giving me sage advice. In terms of both the dissertation as well as early stages of the revision, he remained key to the shape of the work.

Since I deposited my dissertation, new encounters and opportunities have greatly aided the reformulation of this work. Yossi Khen, a fellow compatriot from the now defunct New Jewish Agenda, generously opened his home to me on numerous occasions while I did research in Los Angeles. Faye Thompson and especially Barbara Hall of the Margaret Herrick Library in Los Angeles proved invaluable sources of information. Bob Marshall, Tony Gardner, and the other archivists at Urban Archives Center on the campus of California State University–Northridge managed to survive both my visit and an earthquake. That archive remains a veritable and relatively overlooked treasure trove of California history.

I am incredibly fortunate to work at Indiana University–Purdue University Fort Wayne (IPFW). Here, I have received a great deal of institutional, collegial, and academic support. An Indiana University–Purdue University Fort Wayne (IPFW) Summer Faculty Research Grant helped defray research and writing expenses in 1996. The Document Delivery Service at IPFW has spent countless hours tracking down obscure materials – Cheryl Truesdell and Chris Smith were particularly diligent and patient with my requests. My colleague Rodney Farnsworth generously shared his library carrel, away from the diversionary allure of telephone and Internet. The collegiality of my department members – Jane Banks, Jeanne Barone, Marcia Dixson, Richard Hess, Mary Anne Higgins, Claudia McCalman, Dave Switzer, and Jonathan Tankel – helped to sustain me throughout the project. Department chair John Parrish-Sprowl expertly mentored me, patiently but insistently prodding completion of the work (and yes, I have finally finished the book). I am also grateful to the students at IPFW, who have taught me how to be a better teacher and scholar. The fall 1996 COM 316 Controversy in America class especially inspired many new insights and observations. That class helped me to think about new ways of explaining culture and provided me with one of the most moving and rewarding teaching experiences of my career.

Although I had to make a difficult choice between publishers, I am grateful to those associated with Cambridge University Press. Professor Garth Jowett first encouraged me to submit the work to the History of Mass Communication series. Beatrice Rehl has patiently guided me through the publication process – so patiently, in fact, that she had time to leave, take another job, and then return to Cambridge as my editor while I was working on the book. Professor K. R. M. Short has also demonstrated his patience. Working closely with me on a major overhaul of this manuscript, he has provided his indispensable advice and insight. His wisdom extends well beyond his scholarship. He has proven an excellent mentor and friend as well. Designer and production editor Holly Johnson and copyeditor Barbara Folsom have expertly guided me through the publication process. Their hard work, patience, and professionalism greatly improved the manuscript, making this stage more enjoyable than it should have been.

Finally, a series of loving, close, and supportive relationships have carried me further than I deserve. My aunt, Gladys Justin Carr, freely offered her wealth of experience as Vice-President/Associate Publisher for HarperCollins. My parents, William and Maxine, as well as my brothers, Jackie and Daniel, continue to prove an inspiration in my life. My parents' love of books and learning, plus my father's talent as a writer, first planted the seed in my six-year-old mind. My career as an author began with magic-markered tomes consisting solely of a list of upcoming (and yet to be written) works. Thirty-five years of others' nurturing, love, and faith in me has allowed actual achievement, as opposed to my own empty ambitions. More recently, I have somehow managed to meet someone willing to put up with me on a day-to-day basis. Between tolerating my writing anxiety, Nancy Virtue provided me with countless suggestions, insights, and ways of explaining a difficult topic. Modest to a fault, she is a first-rate teacher, scholar, and editor. Our conversations on her work as well as mine – plus her true genius for rendering complex ideas accessible – account for the clearer passages of this book. I would be lost without her friendship, although she is so much more than just a friend.

Introduction: What Is the Hollywood Question?

GABLER'S PARADOX

The end of an era in American history has brought a remarkable degree of cultural ferment, no doubt the result of large-scale shifts taking place in national and international affairs. One finds this ferment imbuing discussions of both internal domestic affairs and the nation's role in a shifting global order. In 1990, Germany completed its reunification as the Soviet Union crumbled. Amid the biggest bank failures and bailouts in United States history, American conservatives cast this successive chain of international events as a victory for Western capitalism over communism. With the purported fall of communism, however, American political discourse lost one of its most potent, influential images. The specter of communism – the so-called Red Menace that had haunted American popular consciousness since World War I and that had structured the virtual entirety of United States post–World War II foreign policy – was suddenly gone. The very raison d'être for blacklisting, national security, "police actions," missile crises, Vietnam, arms races, and nuclear holocausts had seemingly crumbled into powdery oblivion.

As one demon corroded from public consciousness, others quickly took shape. Iraq moved its troops across the Kuwaiti border in the summer of 1990, triggering a series of events that helped redefine post–Cold War American foreign policy in terms of ready access to the world's petroleum resources. Meanwhile, Operation Desert Storm coincided with what Evan Carton has dubbed Operation Campus Storm. As a still undisclosed body count continued to rise in Iraq, American popular culture fretted over didactic campus leftists. That Campus Storm in fact had no name is significant. Instead, it gave a name to what it fought: political correctness, or PC for short. Concealing its own form of correctness, it thus made attacks upon diversity, affirmative action, and curricular reform seem "normal," perhaps even a bit modish.[1]

New paradigms such as multiculturalism – deemed the penultimate example of campus correctness by its opponents – emerged in stark contrast to earlier pluralist models celebrating America as a cohesive "melting pot." Multiculturalism argued, among other things, for a critical re-visioning of the canon and other accepted bodies of work. Part of this project involved the privileging of voices that had spoken heretofore from the margins. Not surprisingly, when some of those voices from the margins gained a chance to speak, they failed to hew along consensus lines. In fall 1990, a *New York Times* feature by author Neal Gabler detailed recent publicized tensions between blacks and Jews. "Jews, Blacks and Trouble in Hollywood" recounts how various high-profile figures within the black community had charged Hollywood with "Jewish racism." Gabler brought his own unique perspective to this controversy. His 1988 book, *An Empire of Their Own: How the Jews Invented Hollywood*, had told a compelling, bittersweet story of Jewish success in America. Well-received by the popular press, the book shows how American Jews, marginalized by Protestant America, found solace "within the studios and on the screen," where they could fashion their own influential vision of what America meant to them.[2]

The thesis that a special symbiosis emerged out of the relationship between immigrant Jews and Hollywood success retained an especially high degree of relevance to eighties-era shifts in American demonology. Hollywood Jews, Gabler argued, were neither the subversive Communists nor the greedy capitalists that had appeared in so much anti-Semitica of yore. Indeed, with the alleged triumph of the free market over Communism, such images appeared somewhat anachronistic. Instead, Hollywood Jews were semitragic figures, immigrants who desperately yearned for acceptance from the very culture that ultimately rejected them but accepted their vision of America. As the Berlin Wall crumbled, the image of the Jew that had once embodied both Communist threat and capitalist maleficence now appeared as a bittersweet harbinger of the American Dream. The semitragedy, semicomedy of Jewish assimilation also remained especially compatible with debates over political correctness. Appearing in a Sunday *New York Times* section whose feature story decried America's "new tribalism," Gabler's article renders the deterioration of black–Jewish relations as evidence of yet another tear in a culture placing too much stock in cultural difference. Such emphasis had borne the fruit of racial discord. In this particularly emblematic case, one minority was not only begrudging the success of another one, but also invoking invidious stereotypes in doing so.

A curious contradiction emerges from these observations of racial discord. According to an old story, expertly refurbished by Gabler, Jews had acted as Jews in "inventing" an empire of their own and in the process helped fashion a twentieth-century American national identity. Nevertheless, when the empire left blacks "virtually unrepresented in the top echelons of production," Gabler argues that Jews had acted no differently than Gentiles – namely, other whites. Why did Jews act as Jews in one instance, but no differently than whites in the other? How could one excoriate Legrand Clegg for black anti-Semitism when at a National Association for the Advancement of Colored People convention he observed that "Jewish racism in Hollywood" kept blacks from decision-making positions? In discussing Hollywood, how did notions of Jewish "invention" achieve acceptance while accusations of Jewish "racism" met with opprobrium?[3]

These parallel commentaries, so powerfully divergent yet feeding into the same deeply felt tributaries of racial, religious, and ethnic identities, hint at something larger and deeper than just a debate over the connotation of "Jewish Hollywood." At least two profound fears have threaded their way through American history: fear of the Other and fear of potentate. Stereotypes of Jews could accommodate both.

A fundamental set of tensions has historically pitted white Protestants against a host of Others. In 1845, Congregationalist minister John L. Sullivan coined the term "Manifest Destiny" in his *United States Magazine and Democratic Review*. The term describes the natural and eventual process in which whites would "overspread the continent allotted by Providence for the free development of our yearly multiplying millions."[4] As a sexual and immoral savage, the Jew remained closer to Others who might threaten the taming of the wild frontier. Manifest Destiny often depicted a struggle between the civilizing forces of Western superiority and the violent, savage threat of the wild man – even if this concept could justify genocide, slavery, and large-scale displacement of indigenous peoples.

The stereotyped Jew could also embody the threat of assimilation. Unable to curb his voracious appetite and lust for power, the Jew allegedly channeled his savage impulses toward the socially acceptable. Ultimately a counterfeit, the assimilated Jew supposedly hollowed out the core of civilized society as the unruly hordes threatened to storm its gates. Racism directed toward blacks and Native Americans has traditionally located nonwhites outside the walls, displacing the actual brutality and violence meted out to these groups as an imagined, projected savagery of an uncivilized Other. American anti-Semitism, however, conjured a different kind of projection. Recalling the myth of the Trojan Horse, traditional anti-

Semitism envisioned the Jew inside the walls, abusing the rules of assimilation to amass greater power and special privileges, much to the detriment of communal welfare.

In an era of relative prosperity and enlightenment, one might easily lose perspective on the historical manifestation of anti-Semitism. On the one hand, anti-Semitism did not have the same economic and political ramifications embodied by the racism of Manifest Destiny and its structuring gaze toward various perceived Others. Yet, this racism of Manifest Destiny did not have the same *moral* ramifications that anti-Semitism had. Before World War I, the white Anglo-Saxon Protestant elite – that is to say, its churches, schools, government, banks, and virtually every major business concern – considered the United States to be not only Anglo-Saxon but Christian as well. Immigration threatened this vision of America, but it did not automatically threaten control over these institutions by the Protestant elite. Indeed, these institutions created barriers – both explicit and implicit – keeping immigrants at the margins of employment and culture.

Imposition of such barriers, however, presumed a static culture – something America was decidedly not. Jews – and later, Catholics – found easy access to marginal culture, and the cultural margins were quickly migrating toward the center of popularity. Once a novelty, motion pictures emerged at the rising crest of a new mass – not marginal – culture. When the shift caught Protestant elites by surprise, most rearticulated a Manifest Destiny–like prognostication. Having lost control of the American small town to the invading marauders of mass immigrant-Jewish counterculture, Protestant elites hoped to refashion America into the vision of the small town these elites saw themselves as once having controlled. When the Catholic church flexed its audience muscle in the 1930s, ultimately wedging its way into the moviemaking process, Protestants had clearly lost both their chance and their clout.

If Manifest Destiny could maintain outsider status for Jews, even as the rise of mass culture could bring this marginal status into the center of the mainstream, overt hatred of Jews did not necessarily receive a warm welcome in America. A hatred as old as it was international, overt anti-Semitism emigrated from the foreign lands, a product of immigrant ignorance. Anti-Semitism was one thing shared by all nations and cultures, but in a land where any uncolored person deserved a fresh start and a fair chance, such shared bonds were not necessarily welcome. For these hatreds and prejudices, America served more as a series of land mines than as a melting pot.

What separates blacks from Jews – at least, in terms of skirting land mines – is that Jews have a powerful narrative that speaks on their behalf. According to this narrative, Eastern European Jewish immigrants built the film industry in the first decade of this century and dominated it by the second. As the industry grew and attracted others to its ranks, Jews "favored their own." The Jewish movie moguls proceeded to craft a particular vision of America. That this vision reflected "a powerful wish fulfillment that idealized America and sanctified its values" is not entirely incompatible with the complaints of various black leaders. Indeed, an idealized America for many Americans has meant the relative invisibility of black roles and experience upon the screen. One might even argue that if the only roles accessible to blacks are maids, buffoons, and shiftless darkies, these stereotypes could reflect a certain set of values fulfilling the vision of this idealized America.[5]

Of course, the anti-Semitic charge of Jewish control is nothing new. Protestant reformers advocating federal censorship of the movies had begun to enunciate the charge shortly after World War I. Throughout the 1930s, the charge electrified the formation of such pressure groups as the Catholic Legion of Decency and, in the early 1940s, the isolationist America First. More recently, the Reverend Donald Wildmon of the American Family Association wrote to Sidney J. Sheinberg, president of MCA/Universal. In protesting the 1988 film *The Last Temptation of Christ*, Wildmon asked Sheinberg, "How many Christians are in the top positions of MCA/Universal?" Dolly Parton explained her unsuccessful bid to launch a TV series about a country star turned gospel singer as having to face "people [in Hollywood who] are Jewish. And it's a frightening thing for them to promote Christianity." William Cash, correspondent to the conservative British magazine *The Spectator*, used *An Empire of Their Own* in 1994 to characterize a "Jewish cabal" behind the "21st Century Entertainment Superhighway." Moreover, in April 1996, Marlon Brando blamed a Rodney King–style beating of Mexican migrant workers administered by the Riverside Police Department on cinematic stereotypes perpetuated by Hollywood Jews.[6]

There is a reason why stories of ethnic invention and maleficence could say essentially the same thing yet come to such radically different conclusions. Accusations of Jewish control *over* Hollywood (anti-Semitic or otherwise) and philo-Semitic explanations of a Jewish presence and contribution *in* Hollywood are in fact part of the same discussion. The "discussion," of course, has remained protracted, frustrating, at cross-purposes, difficult, obtuse, ill informed, and disjointed. The discussion has privileged some voices but not others. Nonetheless, the discussion has taken place. It has taken place, not in an interpersonal sense, but in a mediated one, through the country's newspapers, magazines, nonfiction, popular and marginal fiction, children's literature, pamphlets, broadsheets, and cartoons. The discussion has taken place through the stories, characters, and images that emerged from Hollywood films. But the discussion remains just as present in what did not emerge from these films: the censored stories, the rewritten characters, the haggling and negotiating between film personnel, studio administration, and the Production Code Administration (PCA), Hollywood's own self-censorship cum marketing arm extraordinaire. The discussion has taken place in letters from the PCA files, in memos between production personnel, and in veiled and not so veiled congressional testimony. Neal Gabler, William Cash, Legrand Clegg, and Spike Lee continue a discussion that began a long time ago, but the discussion infrequently calls attention to the fact that there *is* a discussion. However lopsided, the discussion is as much an exchange *between* speakers as it is a catechism *for* an audience, working out deeply held assumptions about race, ethnicity, power, mass media, modernity, and national identity.

The above-named sources used in this book represent more than a meticulous or idiosyncratic history. They evidence the extent to which the discussion has operated within the liminal and sometimes not so liminal spaces of culture. The discussion has heretofore gone unnamed, and like charges of political correctness, it accumulates its power to structure popular consciousness from its anonymity. Yet, unlike charges of political correctness, which arguably emanated from a handful of well-funded conservative think tanks during the early 1990s, this discussion over Jews and Hollywood is much older, more profound and has greater implications for the way in which society interrogates ethnicity, race, mass media, even itself. Competing voices have struggled within the terms of its discussion to attain dominance. Importantly, the struggle over who gets to explain ethnic instrumentality has spoken to a distinct set of concerns for a modernizing, urbanizing, heterogeneous America. Having taken place for most of the twentieth century, the discussion served as a bulwark of provincial American values against the more liberal, cosmopolitan values of urban ethnics. It has provided commentary – both positive and negative – on the American Dream myth through its emphasis upon the meteoric rise of immigrant Jews. It has appropriated antitrust rhetoric to express concerns over the workings of capitalism. It has attacked New Deal liberalism by conflating it with communism. In addition, it augured the downfall of isolationism, whose proponents tried and failed to capitalize upon this debate by using it to attack the increasing power and presence of the United States in world affairs. And now, approximately fifty years after its last great appearance on the eve of the United States's entry into World War II, a renewed articulation has once again proven its resilience by manifesting itself in other discussions concerning black–Jewish relations, Mexican immigrants, and the information superhighway.

THE HOLLYWOOD QUESTION

While both powerful and resonant, this discussion possesses an ephemeral quality as well. Like accusations of political correctness, allegations of Jewish control operate most effectively unnamed, in the background with their attendant assumptions implicit. In order to talk about this discussion, then, one must talk about something that in its most effective state and under normal circumstances one should not see. Understanding this discussion, as opposed to giving it added momentum, not only means foregrounding it. Understanding this discussion means taking a different perspective from the ones normally taken in this ongoing conversation, talking *about* the discussion rather than talking *within* or *through* it. Moving this discussion from background to foreground also means making its attendant assumptions explicit. All of these activities require taking a certain perspective. To understand this powerful, resonant, and yet ephemeral discussion, this perspective seeks neither to embrace nor to denounce the discussion, but to engage critically with it.

Consider an analogy initially proposed by the newspaper of automobile magnate Henry Ford, who – as Chapter 3 shows – built a publishing empire based on his allegation of Jewish control. A 1921 editorial from Ford's *Dearborn Independent* expresses longing for the ability to map out a "community mind." Such mapping would "trace the impressions of American people, American habits and American standards which those mind-groups hold."[7] This yearning to plot American consciousness appears somewhat naïve. However, the statement's operative metaphor – a map – seems rather prescient. Maps, after all, represent physical space in a way that helps to make sense of the world. The *Dearborn Independent* editorial desires to map out cultural space so that it can make sense of perceived cultural shifts taking place in American intellect and morality. Yet the editorial's obsession with both Jewish control as well as mind-effect is itself significant. From a historical perspective, by tracing this obsession one can learn much about a phenomenon that has suffused American cultural history. Thus, while much scholarship has demonized the *Dearborn Independent*'s anti-Semitism, one can use these editorials to chart out a certain cultural topography.

Rather than chart out American mind groups as *The Dearborn Independent* proposes, then, I am proposing that recorded allegations of Jewish control themselves require mapping as significant reference points within American culture and ideology. These allegations do not map out an American mind per se – few statements have such power and rarely are minds so cohesive or gullible. Nevertheless, these allegations do help chart the larger set of rules, beliefs, and guidelines that for over a hundred years have structured American cultural thought and lived experience. Just as the geographic map depicts the space within which people reside – as opposed to depicting the people who reside within space – so the cultural map shows allegations of Jewish control over Hollywood in a particular manner. This map does not try to show what people thought per se, but rather the cultural space within which such thought took place. The sources listed above – the memos, letters, fiction, nonfiction, testimony, and the like – remain vital because their statements occupy cultural space in a significant way. These sources and the statements they embody, like the features depicted on a map, offer tangible evidence to help make sense of a cultural landscape. Thus the term "The Hollywood Question" describes not so much a way of thinking as the landscape, structured by a key set of historical and discursive features, within which such thought takes place.

Calling this debate the Hollywood Question refers to an earlier, better-known discursive landmark: the Jewish Question. Achieving its currency in the late nineteenth and early twentieth century, the Jewish Question really articulated a problem: given their cultural and religious difference, should Jews enjoy the same basic rights as everyone else? For example, should Jews have the right to own land and vote? In making this emphasis, the Jewish Question (also, significantly, called the Jewish Problem) invokes a whole set of assumptions. The Hollywood Question built upon this already predetermined set of answers to structure its own deep-seated assumptions concerning Jewishness, mass media, audiences, and America.

In the United States, the Jewish Question operated within a distinctly American context. German Jews had emigrated to the United States mostly in the 1830s following a period of political turmoil and repression in their native country. Relatively small in number, German Jewish immigrants remained indistinct from other Germans who arrived in this country. By the end of the century, large waves of Russian Jews were arriving. Markedly different in appearance and demeanor from their Russian counterparts,

German Jews had already been assimilated into American culture. Russian Jewish immigration, however, belonged to a general increase in immigration to this country. New populations transported traditional cultural values. Truly international, anti-Semitism was one of the few cultural similarities that could bind together disparate groups.

These assumptions construct a particular version of what it means to be Jewish. Like most attempts to construct ethnicity, the Question cum Problem has very little to do with ethnicity itself. As Stephen Jay Gould has shown, the whole concept of race remained founded upon totally arbitrary distinctions. Defined by nineteenth-century white Anglo scientists who manipulated their experiments, race science found what it presumed: that one could determine the mental inferiority of other people through a certain set of perceived physical characteristics. Not surprisingly, these scientists ranked Jews above blacks but below "white" whites in intelligence. To these men, Jews looked similar to whites although Jews maintained a culturally distinct identity. Science ascribed this difference to racial inferiority.[8]

The people the scientists deemed racially inferior, of course, had very little say in the matter. In this way, science could construct race in a way that maintained certain power relations. This scientific perspective – a perspective that constructed its "objectivity" along a highly subjective set of criteria – included nothing of the subjectivity of the people it racialized. The scientific perspective did not consider the diversity and complexity of what being Jewish meant. It did not consider Jewish identity from the perspective of the Jew. It did not consider Judaism's long and rich cultural heritage. It flattened Jewishness into something simply different – superior to other nonwhite "races" but inferior to the white one. In some ways, this flattening treated Jews no differently than it treated blacks, Asians, or Southern Europeans. The very act of grouping, naming, and calling by race was an act that maintained power. Science, making whiteness invisible and thus a position of power and authority, could naturalize the cultural and economic forces that had privileged its own voice and perspective, while quelling the voice and perspective of those it presumed to study.

The Hollywood Question simply updates the Jewish Question and its attendant set of assumptions. Instead of overtly asking whether Jews can participate in the regular affairs of daily life, the Hollywood Question asks whether Jews, given their quasi-racialized difference, should participate in the regular affairs of mediated life. The Question does not attempt to understand the complex, contradictory relationship between ethnicity and social identity. Rather, it constructs Jewishness for Jews. Like its antecedent tradition, the Hollywood Question is concerned with how Jews see themselves as Jews only insofar as its racialized perspective explains the impact and influence Jews have had on American culture. Jews, both questions presume, perennially act *as Jews*. Yet this construction can never explain who a Jew is, or what being Jewish means. Jews just are. Whatever a Jew is, the assumption goes, a Jew will always behave like a Jew. Ethnicity serves as one of many motivating factors for Jews – as well as for anyone else. Obsessive attempts to locate ethnicity as the driving force behind individual action fail to distinguish the important role that *talk* about ethnicity has in constructing ethnic identity.

Obviously, there were people who identified themselves as Jews and who worked in Hollywood. Unfortunately, there is no easy or accurate way to account for who these people were. In his 1941 treatise on American anti-Semitism, Donald S. Strong went through the eighty thousand names listed in Poor's *Register of Directors*. After finding that only 4.7 percent had what appeared to be Jewish names, Strong argued that any omission of Jews with "names common to other peoples" would be offset "by the inclusion of non-Jews with 'Jewish-sounding' names."[9] Since the task of determining who could be identified as a Jew is nearly impossible, consider untangling – at least for the time being – the discourse on Jewish control and Jewish participation from the phenomena of Jewish participation in Hollywood and American life. In other words, this project asks that the reader contemplate the Hollywood Question as a phenomenon in its own right, not just a phenomenon justified by what it seeks to find.

To make this separation affords a new set of possibilities for understanding the tremendous impact that the Hollywood Question has had on American culture. One can, for example, heed Robert Sklar's observation that focusing upon *who* controlled the movies was probably far less daunting than attempting to understand the awesome power of the movies themselves. Rather than arguing that the Question was a function of the number of Jews in Hollywood, Sklar suggests that elusive explanations of something as powerful as media influence generated a kind of anthropomorphism. This study seeks to move away from the anthropomorphism that Robert Sklar recounts. It does not even seek to counter such notions with alternative explanations of media power. Rather, this study argues that discussions concerning film and the power of this medium could generate their own kind of authority.

In reframing and "mapping out" the discussion concerning Jews and Hollywood that has already taken place, I do not mean to squelch debate. To the contrary, the influence of ethnicity at both individual and collective levels remains a vital concern, however difficult it is to ascertain its extent. In his recent *Celluloid Soldiers: Warner Bros. Campaign against Nazism* (NYU Press, 1999), for example, historian Michael E. Birdwell seeks to explain the interventionist efforts of the studio. Birdwell sees these efforts as more than just a function of Harry and Jack Warner's Jewishness. He seeks to explain the studio's support of interventionism within the cultural context of 1930s America.[10] Nonetheless, I hope to accomplish a different task. While allegations of Jewish control over Hollywood remain relevant to this cultural context, no scholarship has focused on how these allegations helped to structure a whole way of looking at American culture. This study is not about ethnic instrumentality per se; rather, it begins to think about how such instrumentality – both real and imagined – gets discussed within culture. Such a "meta" discussion only means there is more than one way to examine this issue.

If anything, reframing the discussion in terms of the Hollywood Question should broaden and enrich our understanding of ethnic motivation. Ethnicity, like most other socially defined identities, does not occur in a vacuum. Just as Birdwell connects the ethnicity of Harry and Jack Warner to Warner Bros's output of socially conscious films, so company memos from other film studios of the 1930s reveal the significance of talk about ethnicity among Jewish and non-Jewish personnel. David O. Selznick and others continually negotiated their own ethnic identity in terms of how they believed others perceived this ethnicity, and often acted because of these beliefs. While my examination of ethnic instrumentality is far from exhaustive – I have made a conscious effort to focus on how this instrumentality was discussed rather than how it functioned – my research suggests that the Hollywood Question ultimately structured a position of *non*-Jewish Jewishness for some studio personnel.

One might argue, however, that, while I may not intend to stifle debate, I have nonetheless engaged in my own version of political correctness, supplanting an orthodoxy of pluralist assumptions with a Marxist-tinged orthodoxy of cultural studies and critical theory. To some extent, this is true. As Stanley Fish notes, one always engages in some form of correctness, although some forms of correctness may be more apparent than others. Fish finds an error of perspective in charges of political correctness, however. The correctness behind charges of political correctness means to stifle certain voices, according to Fish, by suggesting that some discussions are "politically" motivated and organized, and that some discussions insert politics where politics do not belong. Fish asks why one would single out "political" correctness when other kinds of correctness – like the correctness of banishing any voices deemed too political – are always operating. If one chooses to think in terms of "correctness," then the "correctness" of cultural studies and critical theory is one that opens up and enriches debate through examination of fundamental assumptions. In using cultural studies and critical theory to approach the Hollywood Question, this study does not suggest that we should or should not arrest talk about Jews and Hollywood. If one chooses to think in terms of competing correctnesses, then the "correctness" of the approach I take here simply asks for a certain acknowledgment. Although they may have not had the same name for it, people already have been talking about the Hollywood Question for a very, very long time.[11]

GETTING TO THE HOLLYWOOD QUESTION

If one could locate the Hollywood Question within a cultural topography, one would need directions on how to "get to" the site of this question. Just as streets and highways allow travel through space, so a particular set of ideas organizes the Hollywood Question, connecting its assumptions to the rest of the cultural landscape. Some of these ideological connectors – questions of race, modernity, isolationism, national identity, and the like – have carried more "traffic" over the years than others. Issues of race, for example, have become a kind of rhetorical superhighway today. Roads carrying attacks upon modernity and internationalism, while still bustling, no longer carry the kind of traffic that they once did.

These roads function as a set of discourses, transporting bodies of statements laden with deeply felt beliefs and ideas. The Hollywood Question serves as a site at which these discourses meet, compete, and reveal their assumptions. The site of the Question redirects these statements, giving renewed impetus to the discourses that intersect and pass through it. In this way, the site of the Question could infuse allegations of Jewish control with disparate beliefs concerning morality, the New Deal, and isolationism. In doing so, the Question propelled a variety of fears and desires to other destinations. Nevertheless, the Hollywood Question could also generate its own discourse: a discourse that speaks directly about a Jewish presence in Hollywood. As this study will show, the Hollywood Question took its most overt discursive shape in popular literature of the 1930s. Meanwhile, the site of the Question, with its attendant assumptions of Jewish control, inflected opposition to the New Deal, anti-Communism, isolationism, even the very writing of film history.

The Hollywood Question remains closely linked to the process described by Edward Said in the eponymously titled *Orientalism* (1978). Orientalism, as he notes, is "a way of coming to terms with the Orient that is based on the Orient's special place in European Western experience." Since both the Orient and Hollywood are partly "imaginative" and partly "material" (in terms of its "supporting institutions, vocabulary, scholarship, imagery," and the like), the study of Orientalism reveals many of the same operative processes that support the Hollywood Question. Employing Foucault's notion of discourse, Said argues that "texts" within discourse "*create*" their own body of knowledge, from which they draw. Along with and from this knowledge, a discourse also creates "the very reality" which it appears to "transcribe." The "material presence or weight" of a discourse produces its texts and statements, rather than the "originality" of individual authors. In similar fashion, the Hollywood Question has been able to produce and reproduce a body of statements concerning Jewish presence in Hollywood. These statements have emerged textually, graphically, ideologically, politically, and imaginatively in the United States, at least since World War I and well into the present.[12]

In reproducing a certain image of a Jewish presence in Hollywood, these statements serve an ideological function that, in the word of Althusser, "hails" a variety of subjects. By hailing or interpellating an individual, these statements work to catch one's attention. If successfully hailed, the individual subject takes an assumed position or perspective. Richard Dyer, for example, has described the phenomenon of "whiteness," which, while not very apparent, nonetheless assumes a certain ideological position for the subject that is predominantly white, male, and Christian.

From this dominant position of whiteness, the Hollywood Question engages a crude though powerful set of mental representations or stereotypes. Sander Gilman argues that, in stereotyping, an essential dichotomy exists between the self and the Other. The Other constitutes a projection of a group's "own insecurities concerning its potential loss of power onto the world." This projection takes the "shape of that Other through which it imagines itself threatened." The Other becomes an alien and cohesive power, its ascribed difference menacing ideological negotiations of reality – another way of describing what Gilman calls "society's communal sense of control over its world."[13]

Gilman considers language a force that helps to define and structure difference. Stereotyping and the construction of difference exert what Gilman calls the "double bind." The process of assimilation entreats an ethnic group to accede to a standard way of speaking, thinking, and expressing the self. When a member of an ethnic group is shown trying to speak within these constraints, however, he or she is mocked and the person's attempts labeled superficial or a disguise. Their accent and original tongue become the marks of inferior difference. Thus, in novels and caricatures, one often finds the belief in Jewish control expressed as a Jewish mogul stereotype speaking in dialect or pidgin. The humor of such dialogue conceals a deeper antagonism toward the social mobility of a perceived ethnic inferior.[14]

Concepts of difference and Otherness do not fully explain the Holly-wood Question, however, for the belief in Jewish control is not just about difference, but a difference that occurs along a perceived dynamic of power. Like other ethnic stereotypes, the Hollywood Question shows the Jew alternately as powerful and as inferior to white Christian culture. Similarly, white Christians appear as both powerless and as superior in the Hollywood Question. Their eventual ascendance to the Hollywood throne of power, only a matter of time, will thereby displace un-Christian Jews. The Holly-wood Question crudely represents this perceived disparity by employing a stock set of rhetorical props describing wealth, participation in conspiracy, licentious activity, and the like. The Hollywood Question is thus a double stereotype: it oversimplifies ethnic difference as well as the meanings of power and powerlessness.

One can also apply the notion of difference and stereotyping to a definition of national identity. The stereotype of the ethnic conspirator and controller drew from antitrust rhetoric in a way that helped define Protes-tant-Catholic, white America against an increasingly diverse urban and immigrant population. This national identity formed out of a fear of sexu-alized, radicalized Others – not just Jews, but blacks, Native Americans, Asians, and others. Race science, virulent nationalism, opposition to im-migration, and eventually fear of Communist subversion all helped to define who were Americans and what being an American meant. Even the supposed sexual and moral degradation of starlets, conjured by the Holly-wood Question, took on political meaning in its analogy to the perceived degradation and humiliation of American culture. Locating national iden-tity within a collective public mind, the Question showed the movie mo-guls enjoying an insidious access to this once-protected sanctum through the films their studios produced.

There is a particular irony to these fears. Such agitations and their attendant stereotypes were themselves mass-mediated cultural products. Yet as an integral part of the Hollywood Question, they responded as much to the phenomenal rise of mass culture as they did to perceived ethnic differ-ence. While the Hollywood Question invoked an implicit critique and fear of an emergent mass-mediated culture, as a discourse it ultimately relied upon print, radio, and other mass-mediated forms to reach its audience. Henry Ford's publishing empire, for example, promoted a uniquely American articulation of the Question. Eventually known as *The International Jew*, this articulation did more to propel the Hollywood Question into worldwide circulation than any other discursive form.

The success of *The International Jew* in articulating a perceived Jewish threat to culture lay in its racializing the Jew. Configured by race discourse, Ford's publication drew upon a predetermined body of statements, texts, images, and other communicative forms that constituted anti-Semitism. The term "anti-Semitism" itself, with or without the hyphen and capital S, is a term laden with meaning. Allegedly coined in the late 1870s by Wilhelm Marr, the term served as a standard for Marr's political group and its opposition to granting German Jews full citizenship. The hyphen and capital revealed their distinctive perception of Jews. The capitalized S marked off the word "Semite," a reference to the perception of Jews as a race. The reference also linked Jews to another perceived inferior: the Arab. Thus, the term "anti-Semitism" shows how opposition to assimilation perceived Jews *as a race of Semites*, thus providing the crucial link between Jews and race.

By racializing the Jew, the discursive site of the Hollywood Question could channel a variety of other discourses, giving them added impetus. Through this process, the Hollywood Question could speak to and through a set of relatively autonomous discourses, including its own. The Question served as a bulwark of provincial American values, commented upon the myth of the American Dream, appropriated antitrust rhetoric, attacked New Deal liberalism, and denounced the United States's increasing participation in global affairs. Well into the 1990s, the Hollywood Question has continued to inflect and redirect a variety of powerful statements, invigorating a new set of discourses on black–Jewish relations, migrant workers, and the information superhighway. In channeling these diverse discourses, the Hollywood Question has remained highly flexible and interactive. As a Question, it conceals and naturalizes a constructed subject position – white, male, and Christian. The Question, in essence, does not simply tell people *what* to think about Jews, Hollywood, and control, but simply reminds people that they should think *about* these things from a particular vantage point.[15]

Although the Hollywood Question works to gain the consent of the populace from a particular vantage point, it achieves its greatest resonance in times of crisis. The Question was *so* powerful and *so* influential precisely because it remained so flexible in channeling powerful, influential and often contradictory forces that emerged in times of social upheaval like the Great Depression. In a very limited sense, the Hollywood Question did unmask the process of consent, interrogating the role of the film industry as one of many mass media serving dominant elite interests. However, the Question also ultimately rearticulated its concealed, constructed position of whiteness. In concealing whiteness as its vantage point, the Hollywood Question discourse was, and is, able to ally a broad range of competing concerns and interests. The Question was able to "contain" Jews within an "ideological space" when it could not, like Nazi Germany, "subordinate" them. In the midst of an economic depression and on the eve of the United States's entry into war, the Question achieved its greatest circulation during a time of fundamental change in the structure of American life. When it resurfaces in tensions between blacks and Jews, concern over immigration, or fear of the information superhighway, it similarly works to contain Jews within an ideological space emphasizing assimilation rather than separation. Moreover, because such containment serves broad ideological interests, the Question can indeed make for strange bedfellows.[16]

As both a site and a discourse, the Question could explain mass media and its influence in compelling fashion. The Question succeeded in inflecting its own and other discourses with ideological assumptions of ethnic instrumentality – both individual and collective – that emerged as a powerful interpretive framework for twentieth-century America. For many this framework provided a potent explanation of how the motion picture industry worked. Unquestioned, it became crucial to a larger ongoing process masking powerful, complex corporate and institutional forces operating within society. Instead of unmasking these more diffuse and concealed forces as part of a complex web of social and institutional relations, the Hollywood Question ethnicized – and ultimately racialized – individuals, constructing people rather than institutions as the dominant elites. By concealing powerful social forces behind a mask of racial difference, this process sought to gain and maintain a particular kind of consent of the populace. Despite its protests against the emergence of an urban, industrial, ethnically diverse and globally significant America, the Hollywood Question served this process well. Using individual and collective ethnic instrumentality, the Question offers a crude explanation of the way in which mass media function within modern urban-industrial capitalist society.[17]

This study, then, addresses how the Hollywood Question took its modern shape – a shape that, for the most part, still holds to this day – during the Great Depression of the 1930s. Using ethnic motivation to explain a broad series of cultural shifts, the Question could respond in compelling fashion to a series of depression-era social crises. This book addresses the emergence, circulation, and transformation of the Question in three parts. Part 1 examines the initial formation of the Question leading up to the depression. Chapter 1 seeks to locate the Hollywood Question within emergent and residual images of American Jews at the turn of the century. In this chapter, I argue that long-standing stereotypes, Populist sentiments, the fear of conspiracy, antitrust rhetoric, opposition to immigration, and a heightened nationalism converged upon the discursive site that would eventually form the Hollywood Question. Articulating the fear of a Jewish conspiracy, the discourses channeled through this site would chart the subsequent "roads" connecting the Question to the New Deal, anti-Communism, and isolationism after World War I. The chapter locates this fear of a Jewish conspiracy – a fear that would help drive the Question into modernity – within the contest of three reactions to crises of late nineteenth- and early twentieth-century America. These reactions include a heightened nationalism, protests against the changing face of American drama, and the convergence of anti-Semitism and anti-Communism.

Chapter 2 addresses the earliest articulations of the Hollywood Question. The Question's emphasis upon morality throughout the 1920s served as a way to come to terms with the changing face of America. The chapter considers the diverse efforts of Protestant, Catholic, and even Jewish groups to impose some form of censorship on the motion picture industry. The Question drove such efforts, rendering a particular vision of America that, while remarkably consistent, could still articulate divergent, nuanced explanations of what constituted a nation. A single, rural American small town served as the predominant Protestant metaphor for national identity, justifying federal censorship of motion pictures as a way to protect Main Street from the urban Sodomites. The Question could also speak to Catholic efforts, which found in the Question an emergent vision of America as a series of networked, local communities. This chapter also examines how both the motion picture industry's own self-censorship and Jewish groups ultimately acceded to the terms of the Question.

Amid such efforts to pose the Hollywood Question in terms of morality, Henry Ford's newspaper *The Dearborn Independent* and subsequent book *The International Jew* had rendered the Question in a powerful new manifestation by the end of the 1920s. These collected editorials blended older stereotypes, concerns over the changing face of America, and fear of Communism in a profound and compelling manner. They spoke in particularly adept fashion to a perceived crisis: a crumbling, older, more rural and diffuse order facing an onslaught of unwelcome internationalism. Bringing together a discourse on morality with an emergent discourse on anti-Communism, *The International Jew* marked a potent convergence that would help propel the Hollywood Question into the Great Depression.

Part 2 considers the powerful ways in which the Hollywood Question could respond to the Great Depression, Communism, and World War II. Chapter 3 addresses how various organizations and individuals tried to use the Hollywood Question to help make sense of the New Deal, the Roosevelt administration's bold package of economic and social reforms. Opponents of block booking and·blind bidding used the Question's antitrust inflection to push for the breakup of the industry's vertical integration. The Hollywood Question also functioned as a way to make sense of depression-era anti-Semitism. Just as the New Deal tried to address an economic crisis, so too did various groups use the Hollywood Question to define a moral and political crisis. Ultimately, this chapter suggests that the motion picture industry's own Production Code emerged from powerful invocations of both New Deal and Hollywood Question discourses.

Chapter 4 examines the breadth of circulation the Question had achieved in the popular literature of the time. Fiction, nonfiction, children's literature, movies, and other popular forms all articulated a remarkably consistent invocation of the Question. These forms consistently employed ethnic stereotypes, such as the Shylock and the parvenu, to represent Jewish movie moguls. The texts, hailing an assumed position of whiteness, reveal how the Hollywood Question worked to contain, not just Jews, but a variety of disenfranchised groups including blacks, Hispanics, and women.

Chapter 5 addresses the way in which the Hollywood Question could drive both anti-Communism and isolationism. The first part of this chapter considers how the Question could draw upon earlier perceptions linking Jews to Communism. In making this association, the Question helped structure subsequent investigations into the motion picture industry by the House Un-American Activities Committee. The chapter also examines the way in which the Hollywood Question drove opposition to United States involvement in World War II. In doing so, the Question set the stage for a 1941 showdown between isolationism and an emergent internationalism.

Various attempts to respond to the Hollywood Question, as Chapter 6 argues, acceded to the Question's powerful terms. Creating a space of ideological containment, the Question provided a structural framework for Jews themselves to talk about the Holocaust, ethnic instrumentality, America, and their role in Hollywood. Before World War II, many, like Archibald MacLeish, tended to dismiss the seriousness and import of anti-Semitism. Furthermore, such dismissals chided American Jews for overreacting. Meanwhile, those working in Hollywood articulated a variety of responses toward both anti-Semitism and Jewish identity. As the second half of the chapter shows, the American Jewish response to anti-Semitism remained anything but cohesive.

A cultural shift preceding United States's entry into World War II constitutes the third and final section of this book. As Chapter 7 shows, the tenor and style with which some responded to the Question changed substantially. With Nathanael West's *Day of the Locust*, F. Scott Fitzgerald's *The Last Tycoon*, Budd Schulberg's *What Makes Sammy Run?* and Leo Rosten's *Hollywood: The Movie Colony, The Movie Makers*, the Hollywood Question demonstrated its discursive flexibility by inverting its stereotype of the Jew. Instead of using its stereotype of the Hollywood Jew to represent the Other, the Question universalized this stereotype to criticize a core set of American values. Turning the stereotype of the Hollywood Jew "inside-out," the Question fashioned a powerful commentary upon American society at large.

This inversion of the Question – one in which the Hollywood Jew came to stand for an emergent vision of modern America – drove a newer discourse toward its impending collision with an older articulation of the Question. As Chapter 8 discusses, this collision took place during the 1941 Senate investigation into motion picture propaganda. At these hearings, the Hollywood Question spoke through and from competing visions of America. An older articulation of the Question tried to reassert its definition of America as an isolated, loosely knit confederation of smaller communities threatened by a foreign, Jewish Other. This articulation, however, ultimately capitulated to the Question's newer articulation, which universalized the Hollywood Jew and envisioned a more cohesive, centralized America active in global affairs. The films cited by the committee especially demonstrated a powerful new vision of America and the end of isolationism.

Although isolationist reliance upon the Hollywood Question ultimately brought about its downfall as a viable political movement, the Question had hardly stalled, but went on to drive a new set of emergent discourses. The final chapter of the book suggests ways in which film scholarship can begin to examine the Hollywood Question. In particular, this chapter considers how the Question has structured the body of "common knowledge" constituting this scholarship. This chapter argues that film scholarship needs to reexamine Hollywood blacklists, the breakup of the studio system, and postwar Hollywood imagery of the Jew in light of the Hollywood Question. Hardly conclusive, this chapter begins to chart just how profoundly the Question has contributed to shaping an entire way of looking at Jews and film history against the backdrops of the Cold War and modern America.

This book examines the discussion of ethnic motivation because what this discussion reveals about cultural assumptions says a lot about American lived experience – in the ideological mainstream as well as at the margins. The sources from which this book draws show the extent to which this discussion has operated, revealing not just the power of this discussion but its incredibly protean nature as well. If ethnic motivation does exist – a phenomenon neither proven nor disproven here – then one must surely address how discussion of this instrumentality has imbued a whole way of seeing modern America. Investigating this discussion by looking at *how* one poses the Question can reveal much about the nature of media, their function, even the very way in which culture itself works.

PART I

The Hollywood Question and American Anti-Semitism, 1880–1929

I

Anti-Semitism and the American Jewish Question

FROM INDIVIDUAL DEVIANCY TO COLLECTIVE INSTRUMENTALITY

After World War I, the Hollywood Question began making its specific allegations of Jewish control over the motion picture industry. It drew from a confluence of other discussions that had already "mapped out" a particular way of linking American Jews, ethnicity, and agency. This "mapping out" charted the route along which one could invoke the Hollywood Question. The Question circulated amid a field of stock images and assumptions. Through these images and assumptions, the Question could respond to an increasingly urban, modern, diverse, and globally significant America. Moreover, through these images and assumptions, the Question could resonate with a certain dissatisfaction over this changing America. Many of these stock images and assumptions had been circulating for centuries, well before the emergence of the Hollywood Question. The way in which they spoke through the Hollywood Question, however, marked a profound shift in American prejudice during the Gilded Age.

Prior to the twentieth century, most of these stereotypes worked to justify, maintain, and repair the marginal status – often codified into European law – that Jews held within Christian culture. For example, both Germany and Russia had historically denied Jews property and voting rights. By even interrogating the ability of Jews to coexist with Christians in a presumably Christian society, the Jewish Question used certain stereotypes to justify this denial. In most cases, these stereotypes emphasized that the individual deviancy of the Jew was at odds with the rest of the Christian community. In its most extreme form, these stereotypes could activate the blood libel. This libel accused Jews of absconding with Christian children and then using their blood in various religious rituals. In alleging the most extreme form of deviancy, the blood libel thus worked to create and justify an ideological space that could contain and marginalize Jews.

In the United States, allegations of individual deviant behavior contin-ued to play a central role in the Hollywood Question, although not to the extent that these allegations played in either the blood libel or European civil law. The United States, of course, has never codified overt anti-Semitism to the extent that European governments have codified it. None-theless, the Question's most potent manifestation, the Jewish movie mogul stereotype, could embody both the figurative and tangible deviance that had been articulated throughout Europe. As the mogul figuratively mur-dered Christian culture, using film immorality to poison the minds of the young, he was in his office, ravaging the Gentile maiden atop the casting couch.

While these figurative and tangible depictions of deviance played a central role in the Hollywood Question, the way in which the Question updated and articulated such deviance marked an important shift in em-phasis. Throughout the nineteenth century, most American articulations of anti-Semitism relied upon stereotypes of individual deviance. In 1862, for example, General Ulysses S. Grant issued orders expelling every Jew from his military jurisdiction. As historian John Higham suggests, Grant's action presumed that culturally inborn greed drove Jews to profit from the war. Although never codified into law, anti-Semitism frequently justified a kind of informal yet recurrent prohibition. In the late nineteenth century, the public sphere simply forbade Jews from participation in many sectors. In 1877, a leading Saratoga Springs resort refused to admit financier Joseph Seligmann, a decision ostensibly based upon a certain prevailing wisdom that all Jews were uncouth, ill mannered, and too loud.[18] Anti-immigrant bias certainly underpinned such observations, but similar practices occurred overseas to a greater and more extreme extent. There, religious anti-Semitism drove a whole host of institutionalized discriminations.

The blood libel, as perhaps the most extreme indictment of alleged Jewish deviancy, could withstand neither modernity nor increasingly global ranges of scrutiny. As the 1911 trial of Mendel Beiliss in Russia had demonstrated, this libel could not exert the same kind of influence that it had exercised in more parochial settings. Beiliss, accused of ritually tortur-ing and murdering a Russian boy, languished in jail without a trial for nearly two years. Only after intense international pressure did the Russian Supreme Court eventually acquit him. Four years later, America demon-strated its own brand of the blood libel in Atlanta. Leo Frank, the supervi-sor of a pencil factory, was charged with raping and murdering a young girl who worked for him. Evidence submitted during the trial emphasized Frank's Jewishness as the motive. Like the Beiliss trial, the potency of this articulation diminished as its range of circulation increased. After pressure from Jewish organizations and intense scrutiny from the press, Georgia State Governor Frank Talmadge commuted Frank's sentence. While the blood libel dissipated at the state and national level, its local adherents formed a lynch mob, forcibly removed Frank from prison and hanged him themselves.

Although alleged individual Jewish deviancy still drove the Hollywood Question, the Question ultimately operated on a much grander scale than these earlier stereotypes. Explaining and responding to large, substantial shifts taking place in American daily life, the Question offered up an explanation of emergent mass society in terms of older notions of individual Jewish deviancy. Primarily rendering a perceived threat to society in terms of deviant behavior, the Hollywood Question could rearticulate these older stereotypes when responding to a changing cultural and economic landscape. It updated older stereotypes such as those of Judas, Shylock, and the Wanderer in ways that could respond to an emergent modernity. In a sense, the Hollywood Question "bridged" well-defined depictions of individual deviancy with a more diffuse, fearsome image of the city, industrialism, diversity, and internationalism. As the face of America changed, so too did various versions of the Jewish Question change. Discourses on race and immigration, the American theater, and a Jewish conspiracy all connected an embodiment of discrete Jewish deviancy with something much larger, more profound, and ultimately more insidious. In using older Jewish stereotypes to respond to newer shifts within culture, these highly flexible articulations of Jewish control over culture were charting the ideological terrain out of which the Hollywood Question could emerge.

The Judas stereotype, for example, originally came from New Testament doctrine, but easily merged with concerns over alleged Jewish control. Just as Judas had betrayed Jesus Christ in exchange for money – a betrayal that ultimately led to the Crucifixion – so the newer form of this stereotype showed Jews "killing" Christian beliefs and morals by pandering to society's base instincts through art, literature, poetry, and philosophy. Other catechisms refused to believe that Romans had killed Jesus, blaming not just Judas but Jews in general for the crucifixion. The image of the Jew as Judas – a greedy betrayer and a threat to Christianity – remained popular in America throughout the mid-nineteenth and early twentieth centuries. The stereotype expressed a fear that the changing cultural, political, and economic landscape posed a threat to churches and other religious institutions, and that these changes were the result of Jewish influences.

Another popular image of the Jew, Shylock, has its origin in the villainous moneylender in William Shakespeare's play *The Merchant of Venice* (1600). In the play, the "rich Jew" Shylock threatens to exact a "pound of flesh" from the "merchant of Venice" when the merchant is unable to pay back a loan. While this was technically an agreed-to pact, the play portrays the Jew as pursuing the letter of the law to enact a vicious, animal-like revenge. Although the character of Shylock had appeared well before Shakespeare's time, its Elizabethan incarnation readily translated into Jewish viciousness, greed, and amorality for turn-of-the-century America. Like the character of Judas, the Shylock stereotype ultimately symbolized a threat to culture, religion, morality, and economic competition.[19]

Almost as old as the Shylock stereotype, the image of the Wandering Jew shows the Jew as rootless and dispossessed from his homeland by Arabs. Based not on the New Testament but on aspects of Synoptic Gospel, the Wandering Jew's sad tale first appeared – at least in print – in *The Chronicles of St. Albans* (1228). According to legend, Jesus of Nazareth was struck as he bore the cross to his crucifixion. He condemned the man who struck him to wander the earth until Jesus' Second Coming.[20] The implications of this rootlessness paralleled the amorality of both Judas and Shylock. Like these two stereotypes, the image of the Wandering Jew hints at a dispossessed morality that could resonate with fears of a sexual other.

The stereotype of the Wandering Jew remained unique, however, in capturing the literary imagination of the nineteenth century. This cultural fascination indexes a larger set of preoccupations concerning emergent discourses on race and nationality. Inspiring pity, the Jew lacked allegiance to any nation or ruler. Yet this pity effectively questioned whether Jews could ever become citizens of the country in which they resided and was therefore in keeping with political movements intended to deny Jews basic civil rights. The stereotype of the Wandering Jew also depicted Jews as trespassers who belonged elsewhere – namely, the Orient. By tying Jews to a particular geographic area, the stereotype linked Jews to Arabs, thus speaking to the way in which nineteenth-century race science positioned both groups as "Semites" within a constructed racial hierarchy.

While the stereotypes of Judas, Shylock, and the Wanderer could speak within a newer context, they could also justify and generate additional images. During the late nineteenth century, for example, the image of the Jew as parvenu gained currency. An outsider like Judas, Shylock, and the Wanderer, the Jewish parvenu appeared as the undeserving stranger, rapidly ascending the ranks of social status by devious and cunning means yet never completely able to shed uncouth mannerisms and the mother tongue. For some, the parvenu took on a darker cast. The Rothschild family, for example, epitomized the Jewish éminence grise upon the throne. Others, like author and future British Prime Minister Benjamin Disraeli in *Tancred* (1847), suggest that what appears so threatening about Jews in fact represents the finest that Western culture has to offer. Disraeli's Semitism, of course, could also justify the expansion of British imperialism.

Unlike Shylock or Judas, however, the parvenu could just as easily represent other immigrants coming to the United States. Jews appeared no different from Eastern and Southern Europeans, all of whom were deemed racially inferior to Northern and Western Europeans. In one sense, the image of the Jewish parvenu was less a Jewish stereotype than a stereotype representing Jewish and non-Jewish immigrants alike. In another sense, however, the Jewish parvenu retained a great deal of ethnic and racial specificity. Scientists grouped Jews together with blacks, Asians, Italians, and Russians – in part because of the belief that Jews had intermarried with nonwhites, but also because of the belief that Jews retained certain physical characteristics: long noses, oily visages, tentacle-like fingers, and the like. That Jews could *appear* white yet be scientifically classified along with other so-called inferior races made the Jewish parvenu seem all the more unworthy, as well as threatening.

After World War I, another more protean representation subsumed individual images of Judas, Shylock, Wanderer, and the Jewish parvenu. The image of the Jew as conspirator recalled older threats emphasizing viciousness, greed, amorality, and rootlessness. Yet whereas Shylock and Judas existed as individual characters, and the Wanderer and parvenu retained individual characteristics, the image of the conspirator achieved its rhetorical power through collective rather than individual agency. Individual stereotypes, of course, did not totally disappear. But they did begin to serve a different function, explaining and justifying the ethnically based motivation of unseen manipulators working behind the scenes.

These images of the Jew – as Judas, Shylock, Wanderer, parvenu, and conspirator – existed more or less independently of the Hollywood Question. The belief in Jewish control was also not solely concerned with Jews running Hollywood. Jews supposedly controlled banking, the press, theater, and politics. This presumption of ethnic control was hardly unique in singling out Jews, either. While Jewish stereotypes had certain distinct characteristics, accusations of control demonized Jews in much the same fashion as they did other ethnic and religious groups. Throughout the late 1800s, Catholics had been criticized for their alleged control over the press, money, and politics. After World War I, the word "Jew" literally supplanted "Catholic" in allegations of ethnic conspiracy and control. Even by the

1920s, some people still maintained that Catholic control had spread to Hollywood.

In many ways, however, the Hollywood Question and its implicit reliance upon stock ethnic characters constitutes a unique phenomenon in American history. Though one might diagnose the Question as a garden variety of American anti-Semitism, or simply as yet another instance of demonizing an ethnic group, such a diagnosis falls short of understanding the full impact of the Question. The stock set of images through which the Hollywood Question spoke included a profound set of social and cultural issues. Although the Question had briefly and marginally been a Catholic Question, the Hollywood Question achieved its greatest currency by transforming Jewish stereotypes into powerful commentaries on the rise of mass media, power, and shifts within American culture. In ways that more general Jewish and Catholic Questions could not address, the stereotypes of the Hollywood Question drew from a variety of discourses. The subjects ranged from widespread immigration, through the rise of the city and to the increasing prominence of the mass media, to the changing role of America within world affairs. The Hollywood Question could respond to these discourses with a ferocity and passion unlike anything that had existed before it.

"100 PERCENT AMERICANS"

Just as the Hollywood Question could not have emerged without an underlying stock set of assumptions concerning Jews, both the Question and its stock set of assumptions could not have emerged outside of a broader debate over immigration, race, and national identity. Opposition to immigration in the United States had already begun as early as 1798, although most of its restrictions either expired or were repealed.[21] During the 1850s, a number of secret anti-immigrant organizations joined to form the American Party, an anti-Catholic vigilante group opposed to German and Irish immigration. Popularly called the Know-Nothing Party because its members "knew nothing" when asked about their affiliation, the party's constituents worked on two fronts. Pushing for legislation restricting immigration, the Know-Nothing Party was also not above using more expedient methods, such as inflicting violence upon immigrants and their advocates.[22]

Adherents of immigration, on the other hand, extolled the virtues of an unlimited supply of low-cost labor. During the Civil War, Congress allowed employers to pay for travel and bind the services of prospective immigrants. After the Civil War, as blacks migrated to the Northern states, Southern politicians saw immigration as a way to fill the void in the work force. Some Southern states even set up immigration recruiting boards. Immigrants could provide labor for the westward expansion and fill positions formerly occupied by slaves.[23]

Ironically, annual figures for immigration between 1881 and 1910 – the largest in this country's history – never accounted for more than 1 to 2 percent of the entire U.S. population. In fact, after a devastating economic depression in 1897, immigration had dropped from 790,000 in 1882 to below 230,000 in 1898. Of course, annual immigration continued to rise in successive years, reaching 1.3 million by 1907. Even this figure, however, never amounted to more than a few percent of the total population.[24] Nonetheless, many believed an immigrant flood was washing over the land, and that this flood was decidedly Jewish. The 1910 United States Census shows that between 1899 and 1910, when the census counted Jews as Jews, total Jewish immigration reached only 1.5 million, or roughly 1.6 percent of the entire population. The perception that most immigrants were Jews, while somewhat off in perspective, did explain a phenomenon. The percentage of Jews coming from certain areas, such as Russia, was disproportionately high – 91.6 percent of all Russian immigrants in 1891, for example. From year to year, Jewish immigration steadily increased and even doubled. Unlike other immigrants, Jews also tended to stay in America once they had arrived. And as statistician Samuel Joseph found, Jewish organizations themselves even overinflated these figures. Widely cited statistics listed in *American Jewish Year Book* exceeded federal numbers for Jewish immigration by several hundred thousand.[25]

Because powerful elites encouraged increased immigration to serve their own interests, some politicians, labor organizations, and newspapers saw immigrants as unwelcome harbingers of big business, the increasing centralization of government, and the rise of the urban-industrial society. Presumably speaking on behalf of small farmers and the working class, opposition to immigration could respond to these economic and cultural changes. John Higham has described immigrants as appearing to be "both symbols and agents of the widening gulf between capital and labor." By 1891, *The National Economist*, the official organ for the populist National Farmers Alliance and Industrial Union, was arguing that "charity begins at home." The newspaper stated that the "American press and people" were wasting too much "time and sympathy" on the plight of "the Russian Jews" and too little on "bettering the condition of the American pauper."[26]

Such attitudes reveal at least a tacit distinction between the Eastern European Jewish immigrant and the Eastern and Southern European Catholic immigrant. Knowledge of pogroms could explain the large numbers of Jews fleeing their homelands. Before World War I, however, Roman Catholic immigration induced fears of a protean, faceless organization sending its minions to invade the United States. All immigrants, however, represented a potential threat to jobs and wages. During the Pennsylvania coal strikes of the 1870s, recent immigrants were brought in to replace striking workers. A 1913 letter to *Harper's Weekly* claimed that immigration bureaus were "a scheme of the mill men to keep down the price of cotton" and "an effort to lower wages and to prolong hours of employment." The letter argued that immigration was no better than slavery, not because of the way immigrants were treated, but because it subjected "less well-to-do farmers . . . to ruinous competition."

As Daniel De Leon, founder and leader of the Socialist Labor Party and cofounder of the Industrial Workers of the World, noted, anti-immigration could actually serve dominant interests by perpetuating worker exploitation as well as maintaining a divided working class. He called such opposition "the anti-Immigration howl."[27] Race science ideologues tried to capitalize upon these resentments. Monroe Royce found an analogue between how the Southern "colored man" had "driven the poor white man to the wall" and how the "alien" had harmed "the New Englander."[28] As Royce and others argue, nonwhites stood in the way of the inevitable Manifest Destiny. In order to fulfill that destiny, the White Anglo-Saxon Protestant male needed to overcome this resistance and seize the birthright that was his due.

Many saw immigration not only as a labor problem but as an urban and cultural one as well. By 1940, the number of Americans living in rural areas had dropped from 71.8 percent, in 1880, to 43.5 percent. As Will Herberg notes, white Protestantism was ill prepared for the rapid social change that took place during the latter half of the nineteenth century. Given this lack of preparation, an emergent discourse configured the city as a place of squalor, amorality, and the passing of a traditional way of life. The cultural and religious emphasis of Protestantism tried to explain urban social problems arising from modernity in terms of a failure in individual morality. For American traditionalists, urban problems did not arise until immigrants settled there. Consequently, immigration must be the root problem. This "city problem" in turn crystallized a broader intellectual and cultural crisis within traditional American Protestant values. As John Higham notes, many observed the high concentration of immigrants in urban areas and inferred that an invasion had spread to the culture at large. According to

Higham, "enraged traditionalists" blamed immigrants for "mongrelizing language, literature and society."[29] These accusations often implicated immigrant Jews, most of whom had emigrated from an urban area and so tended to settle in American cities. Thus, when Henry Ford's *Dearborn Independent* assessed the situation in 1920, the newspaper could define the "Jewish Problem" as "essentially a city problem."[30]

What historian Arnold Rose has called "city hatred," then, resulted from a convergence of social forces, including responses to modernity and opposition to immigration. Nostalgia for a mythical, bygone America – predominantly rural and free of the complications, frustrations, and complexities of modernity – drove much of what would become the Hollywood Question. But not exclusively. In articulating this nostalgia in response to modernity and urbanity, anti-immigration forces successfully projected their fears and desires upon immigrant bodies by drawing from an emergent and powerful discourse on race. A particular way of speaking about the immigrant arose, essentializing ethnicity and nationality in terms of biology and anthropology. In racializing the immigrant, anti-immigration discourse could respond in yet another way to profound cultural shifts taking place in American life. Codified into law, the race-based quota system that by 1920 had severely curtailed immigration still exists in much the same form today.

Although racism had informed institutions like slavery and colonialism before the nineteenth century, its scientific and cultural justifications flowered during the Industrial Revolution. After World War I, ideologues blended both a scientific and a romanticized notion of race into a new definition of national identity. Both notions were readily accepted without question. Immigration officials, for example, began to consider Jews a race in 1899. The president of Harvard, Abbott Lawrence Lowell, even instituted a quota system in 1922, limiting the number of Jewish students who could attend the school.[31] During the 1930s, the Roosevelt administration asked Lowell to head the Code of Fair Competition for the Motion Picture Industry, presumably to quell Lowell's vocal objections to Hollywood. Unlike the later Production Code Administration (PCA), which served as the motion picture industry's self-regulatory response to accusations of film immorality, the Code of Fair Competition originated from Roosevelt's National Recovery Administration (NRA), the latter attempting to reform American industry in general. As Gregory Black notes, however, the NRA Code of Fair Competition for the Motion Picture Industry included the only government-stipulated morals clause out of all of the codes the NRA

had drafted for virtually every American industry. Lowell nonetheless refused the invitation, not objecting specifically to Jews or Catholics but to
unspecified Hollywood "business methods."[32]

Despite its widespread acceptance as biological fact, the concept of race
originated in faulty scientific assumptions and an abstract mythology of
Anglo-Saxon superiority. The reliance upon race was a response both to
recent developments in science and to an increasing cultural diversity.
Peter Pulzer has described the study of race as an "anti-science" that drew
from a "bewildering eclecticism" of "biology, anthropology, theology and
psychology." Race science ranked different groups of people according to
genera and sub-genera, much like a scientist would classify animals and
plants. There was little in the way of an established scientific method to
define such categorization. Often, nationality, religion, and race were inter-
changeable concepts. Thus, Jews, along with blacks, Italians, Spaniards,
and even the French, could be classified as a separate race.

Within race science, elaborate hierarchies defined difference. "Evidence"
of Anglo-Saxon superiority was obtained through a battery of tests, all of
which reified intelligence and ability into physical appearance. Craniome-
try, the science of inferring intelligence from skull capacity and brain
weight, was arguably the most influential of these methods. Yet, as Stephen
Gould has shown, when data conflicted with the hypothesis that allegedly
inferior races had smaller and lighter brains, scientists were not above
simply fudging the numbers to prove their point.[33]

Theories of evolution proposed by Charles Darwin and Herbert Spencer
ultimately proved useful for race science. Darwinian theories that human-
kind had evolved from apes particularly rankled Creationists, who believed
the story of the origins of men and women could be found in Genesis. At
first opposed by race science adherents, Darwinism could inspire bowdler-
ized explanations of evolution and survival of the fittest. According to race
science adherents, Anglo-Saxons were at war with the rest of the world's
races. But because the Anglo-Saxon race was inherently superior (and, as
some would later argue, the lost tribe of Israel that was God's true chosen
people), Aryans would eventually prevail.[34] Anglo-Saxonism, this heady
amalgam of theology, philosophy, science, nationalism, and ethnocentrism,
was the ideological descendant of measuring skull and brain sizes. Infusing
race science with a more overt nationalism, it defined American national
identity as decidedly Protestant. Race was no longer just a mere physical
attribute, but a particular state of mind and set of beliefs constituting an
entire culture.

That Anglo-Saxonism could define itself as both inherently superior and under siege worked to justify a battery of measures Michael Rogin has defined as countersubversion. Countersubversion took tangible steps to marginalize various groups within the culture. As Rogin notes, its targets shifted between "reds and blacks of frontier, agrarian America to the working-class 'savages' and alien 'Reds' of urban, industrializing America." At its core, countersubversion justified colonialist expansion, political and working-class repression, and racial, ethnic, and religious discrimination by demonizing racial, ethnic, and religious Others. Nevertheless, it achieved predominance, not so much in what it did, but in how it could justify its measures. By intimating that a social group was anything less than 100 percent American, countersubversion could inspire a wholesale revocation of civil liberties.[35]

Catholicism served as a primary target of countersubversive rhetoric. During the late eighteenth and nineteenth centuries, accusations of a Catholic conspiracy targeted French, Irish, Germans, Italians, Poles, and Slovaks. Nativist organizations like the American Protective Association blamed the depression of 1893 on a pope-inspired Catholic run on the banks, replete with a forged document entitled "Instructions to Catholics." The same year, a forged encyclical from Pope Leo XIII appeared, absolving Catholics from U.S. nationality and urging them to kill non-Catholics. The anti-Catholic magazine *The Menace* published an open letter to President Taft in 1912, alleging Catholic control of the press.[36]

Although far less prevalent than nineteenth-century anti-Catholicism, countersubversive attacks upon Jews before World War I mirrored allegations of a Catholic conspiracy. Grass-roots political movements like the Populist Party emerged as a viable political force during the 1890s, amid one of the country's worst economic depressions. In one 1891 editorial, *The National Economist* linked Russian Jews to cornering the world supply of gold. If the United States would adopt the "free coinage of silver," the newspaper reasoned, it could avoid a situation like that in Russia, where "Jews are being expelled from that nation for crimes very similar."[37] By 1892, the Populist National Farmers Alliance and Industrial Union platform included planks restricting immigration and remonetizing U.S. currency from a gold to a silver economic standard. In this opposition to the gold standard, Silverites argued that the Rothschilds and other London-based international Jewish banking concerns had hoarded the world's gold. Gordon Clark, Mary Elizabeth Lease, and others personified international banking in terms of a Shylock. A common refrain was the necessity to drive the money changers from the temple.[38]

This powerful, flexible notion of an international Jewish conspiracy would serve as a keystone to the countersubversive imagination. While Jewish capitalists squeezed the middle and lower classes, the anarchist Jew threw bombs, the journalist Jew printed lies and half-truths, and the entertainment Jew polluted high culture. Of course, these particular manifestations of a perceived Jewish threat were not unique to Populism. Many political tracts reflected the belief in Jewish control over banks and the press. Magazines like *Life* railed against a supposed Jewish theatrical trust. *The Talmud Jew* (1892) even coveted what it saw as an inherently Jewish ability to "form a secret society for their mutual advancement to the detriment of their fellow-citizens." "Any nationality or race," the tract argued, could be "as successful as the Jews" if they were willing to take such measures. That Populist rhetoric reflected some of these statements and images merely demonstrated the growing prevalence of these attitudes within American society.[39]

At the beginning of the twentieth century, countersubversion began to subsume overt appeals to anti-immigration and racial nationalism. It was not, for example, "to any party or race spirit" that Monroe Royce appealed in *The Passing of the American* (1911). Instead, he called for "a broad and deep patriotism, a patriotism that shall seek to direct this vast democratic nation in the true spirit of its founders; and the true interests of all the people." Royce acknowledged that anyone should be allowed to become an American citizen, "without regard to race or descent." But Americans "who inherit the blood, the traditions, and the ideals of the founders of the Republic, have a fiduciary responsibility" to stem the flow of those who continually arrive later "on these ever hospitable shores."[40]

William T. Hornaday, an American naturalist who wrote on subjects ranging from camping to the extermination of the American bison, applied his knowledge of nature to immigration, patriotism and Socialism (Fig. 1). He warned the "patriotic Jews of New York" to "protect their race from the parasites who live by preying" and "disgracing" them: mentally unfit, Socialist "Russian Jews." To Hornaday, "the continuous inflow of alien races" had made America "the dumping ground for the ashes and the cinders of all nations." Having "flung aside nearly all considerations making for quality," America had "welcomed the lame and the lazy, the ignorant, the vicious, the veneered criminal and the 'assisted' immigrant with envy in his eye, greed in his heart, and a knife inside his shirt, all coming to exploit America for their own benefit."[41] Emerson Hough, also an American naturalist and novelist, imbued immigration with sinister, conspiratorial overtones. One passage in *The Web* (1919) shows immigrants as "sinister figures" passing "day by day, in ghostly silhouette," plotting "against America all

FIGURE I. W. T. Hornaday, New York Zoological Park, 1910.
Library of Congress, Ruthven Deane Collection.

the deeds that can come from base and sordid motives, from low, degenerate and perverted minds; all the misguided phenomena of human avarice and hate and eagerness to destroy and kill."[42]

Countersubversion, however, did not just depict immigrants as a threat; it also constructed an idealized version of national identity. Between 1915 and 1916, the term "100 percent American" came into play, demanding total, unquestioning loyalty to the U.S. Taking on a punitive tenor, "100 percent Americanism" pushed for legislation increasing the power of federal government over immigrant aliens. President Woodrow Wilson made vague reference to "some Americans [who] need hyphens in their names." In one beguilingly compact turn of phrase, Wilson evoked a powerful connection between patriotism and ethnicity. His hyphen symbolized dual allegiance;

a reminder that "only part of" the immigrant had "come over." The immigrant would become an American "when the whole man has come over, heart and thought and all." Only then would the hyphen drop "of its own weight out of his name." The heart and thought of this idealized immigrant would be "centered nowhere but in the emotions and the purposes and the policies of the United States." Patriotism equaled assimilation and rejection of the home country. After the United States entered World War I, the hyphen's iconicity represented not only the potential disloyalty of the German-American but the potential disloyalty of any perceived foreigner. Former President Theodore Roosevelt explained its importance quite succinctly in 1916: "the hyphen," he wrote, "is incompatible with patriotism." Roosevelt struck a powerful chord. A hero of the Spanish-American War in 1898, he served two terms of office as president. Roosevelt discussed the threat of immigration in many of the same terms he used to describe the large, powerful trusts like the railroad monopolies he had opposed while in office. [43]

Fear of the hyphenated American sprang from a number of factors. Federal legislation began to regulate seemingly large numbers of immigrants entering this country. Films like D. W. Griffith's *The Birth of a Nation* (1915) expressed an outburst of racist sentiment. The film, in turn, helped spur the revival of the Ku Klux Klan one week before its theatrical opening. With labor unrest widespread, a burgeoning movement of antiradicalism and especially anti-Communism took root. Through its linguistic analogy, the hyphen came to symbolize what many feared: an encroaching foreign influence, incomplete assimilation, and loss of a pure American character and identity.

Two qualitatively different concepts emerged out of this fear of the hyphenated. The concept of the melting pot suggested not so much a residual foreign allegiance as a blended, cohesive whole. The melting pot analogy appeared more benevolent than the hyphenation metaphor; and in some ways it was. Unlike the notion of the hyphen, the melting pot blandished the promise of assimilation. The price of such assimilation, however, often entailed a rabid and unquestioning allegiance to American nationalism. As John W. Baer points out, the National Education Association helped to institute the Pledge of Allegiance in the public school system in 1892, in conjunction with the establishment of Columbus Day the same year. Students recited the pledge while "giving a stiff, uplifted right hand salute." Instead of supporting a pledge of loyalty to core documents like the Declaration of Independence, organizations lobbied to have the pledge of allegiance to the flag recited in classrooms because they viewed this practice as an acceptable means of indoctrinating immigrant children.[44]

Countersubversion could allow vigilantism to operate under the imprimatur of the United States government. The American Protective League (APL), whose name was suspiciously close to the older, anti-Catholic American Protective Association (APA), enjoyed the sanction of the Federal Justice Department's "authorization" in 1917. Its activities included harassment and the tar-and-feathering of labor and political activists. The APL even forcibly removed families from their homes. Beginning in 1919, the Justice Department began rounding up thousands of legal immigrant aliens and accused them of being Communists, anarchists, or revolutionaries. Some were detained for weeks without trial. The U.S. government shipped 556 people back to Russia, many of them Jews.[45] The oath of allegiance for U.S. citizenship, given to this day, reveals its countersubversive origins. Federal loyalty oaths date back to the 1790s, and requiring renunciation of foreign allegiances dates back to 1802. The emphasis upon repudiating "domestic" enemies, however, appeared more recently. Applicants must "renounce absolutely and forever all allegiance and fidelity to any foreign . . . State or Sovereignty" as well as swear to "support and defend the Constitution and law of the United States of America against all enemies, foreign and domestic."[46]

Defined as an immigrant, a racial Other, and a subversive, this image of the Jew led to successive critiques of the press, theater and, eventually, Hollywood. As the perceived threat to national identity shifted from a fear of individual deviancy to a fear of collective ethnic subversion, the Hollywood Question emerged from a powerful set of discourses implicating the Jew as both non- and un-American. Employing older and more traditional stereotypes, relatively newer accusations of Jewish control protested against mass-mediated communication. These accusations relied upon an image of an older, more traditional and moral America under siege. Galvanizing what would eventually become the Hollywood Question, the accusation of Jewish control marked an important ideological shift. Deviant behavior, in and of itself, no longer constituted the alleged threat Jews posed to culture. Rather, this explanation of deviant individual agency was now marshaled to explain a broader, more insidious and fearsome collective agency. Bridging nostalgia for rural, agrarian America with resistance to a more modern urban and industrial America, the Hollywood Question constructed a particular image of the Jew. In doing so, this image managed to capture the very quintessence of an alienated American cultural identity.

"A PECULIAR JEWISH MONOPOLY"

The accusation of Jewish control is not unique to the Hollywood Question. In this country, accusations of Jewish control over the press and theater and its deleterious influence upon culture presaged accusations of Jewish control over the film industry by nearly forty years. Relatively obscure tracts such as The Talmud Jew (1892) and Telemachus Timayenis's The American Jew (1888) and The Original Mr. Jacobs (1888) all allege Jewish control over the press. To the anonymous author of The Talmud Jew, Jews ruled "the world through the press" and committed such atrocities as assigning Jewish criminals "some other nationality, so that the Jewish name will not be discredited by the many crimes perpetrated by Hebrews." Not unlike The Protocols of the Elders of Zion that appeared in this country shortly after World War I, The Talmud Jew envisions centralized Jewish control. A central Jewish organization supposedly gives orders "to the Jewish press and their allies, to sustain such movements and such statesmen in power that will help the cause of the Jews, or, if adversary, to fight them."[47] Timayenis ultimately perceives the Jewish journalist along racial lines, seeing him as part of a "Jewish race." To Timayenis, race itself becomes a useful metaphor to describe the decline of journalism. "Metropolitan journalism," he argues, was "sickened and deteriorated with the injection of Semitic blood."[48]

In such tracts, the individual deviance of the Jew speaks to a more general perceived decline in journalism and culture. "It is the part of Jew editors," The Original Mr. Jacobs argues, "to wilfully [sic] degrade the profession of journalism. They give way knowingly to the lowest instincts of animal life. They are reckless of private character and are promoters of private scandal. They neither regard truth, nor respect public opinion."[49] Meanwhile, "materialistic doctrines openly advocated by the Jewish press" caused a "constantly increasing immorality" within society. The Jewish-owned press propagated "anarchical doctrines" that would "embitter the working man," encourage labor strikes, and cause social upheaval.[50] Moral reform sentiment gives Timayenis's accusations added impetus. He suggests that Anthony Comstock, a reformer who worked to ban birth control information from the mails, focus attention upon "Jew editors that disgrace public morals by their filthy articles." Such action would garner the applause of "the entire Christian community."[51]

While such tracts often held marginal status within American culture, the beliefs they espoused often appeared in a variety of discursive communities. Images of Jewish control had long served as a mainstay of Populist rhetoric. For example, on the sale of the *New York Times* in 1894, *The Representative* – the official organ of the Populist Minnesota State Farmers' Alliance – took the opportunity to connect Jewish control over the press to other evils of capitalism. "In these evil conditions, made by bad laws, the Jews alone thrive," wrote Ignatius Donnelly, the paper's editor. "The reason is they deal only in money; they have no belief in farming, manufacturing or any other industry; they are money-mongerers." The Spanish Inquisition had been a rebellion against usury. Now, Jewish "cunning" and "the folly of mud-headed Christians" had made "man, industry, property, wealth" all "slaves of an artificial thing called money." Jews were said to be behind "the great Trusts and Combines," hoarded gold, and opposed the remonetization of silver. Talk about Jews had become a powerful way to oppose fin-de-siècle industrialism.[52]

The charge of Jewish control ultimately used ethnic stereotypes to protest power. As Donnelly explained in a subsequent retraction, the newspaper did not mean to "persecute the Jews." Rather, he hoped that Jews would humbly assimilate into "the great body of the white race" once their persecution ceased. For Donnelly, Jews had "become conspicuous, as types of the Plutocrat, because they excel all the other people in the capacity to accumulate wealth. We are fighting Plutocracy not because it is Jewish or Christian, but because it is Plutocracy."[53] This claim reveals the central purpose of the Jewish image, not to understand Jews, but as a vehicle of protest.

The image of the Jew and control over the press could also serve as satirical protest. In the midst of the Spanish-American War, an 1898 cartoon from humor magazine *Life* – published by Harvard alumni and unrelated to the Time-Life photojournal of the 1930s and 1940s – shows a bespectacled, bearded gentleman with a large nose hawking a newspaper (Fig. 2). This spectacle is so reprehensible that it drives away even Spaniards, who run holding their noses. "If nothing else will conquer the Spaniard," the caption reads, "let us try this." Harvard graduates Edward Lanford Martin and Andrew Miller served as editors for the magazine, first published in January 1883 by John Ames Mitchell.[54] Having achieved a circulation of 150,000 by 1916, the Harvard-inspired *Life* strove to be an American version of the popular British satirical magazine *Punch*. As a satirical magazine caricaturing Jews, *Life* was also not alone. Between 1880 and 1906, *Puck* magazine caricatured Jewish merchants and immigrants.[55] Unlike *Punch*, however, *Puck* lacked the social and literary satirical savvy of the British publication. Whereas *Punch* engaged its audience with gentle irony, both *Life* and *Puck* favored a harsher form of caricature.

IF NOTHING ELSE WILL CONQUER THE SPANIARD, LET US TRY THIS.

FIGURE 2. Cartoon referring to coverage of the Spanish-American War. *Life*, 28 April 1898, 366.

Accusations of Jewish control over the press were also not fodder solely for the marginal and the satirical. The highly publicized 1913 trial of Leo Frank served in part as a lightning rod for these kinds of allegations. Tom Watson, a newspaper publisher and political hopeful who later became a U.S. senator, exploited anti-Jewish sentiment by running a number of inflammatory editorials during the trial. Watson's newspaper had been noted for its virulent anti-Catholicism, but his invective was easily tailored to fit hostility toward another ethnic group. During Frank's trial and appeal, Watson's newspaper tied Frank to a Jewish conspiracy. When major urban newspapers began to denounce the court proceedings of the Frank case, and a popular backlash against the press developed, Watson took full advantage of the situation, accusing Jews of using the newspapers to manipulate public opinion. "It is a peculiar and portentious [sic] thing," wrote Watson, "that one race of men – and one, only, – should be able to convulse the world, by a system of newspaper agitation and suppression, when a member of that race is convicted of a capital crime against another race." *The Atlanta Journal* later claimed that its circulation suffered when it criticized the Frank case proceedings. Some accused the paper of being "bought with Jew money." Leonard Dinnerstein writes in his study of the case: "many Georgians considered the pro-Frank editorials as the product of a press servile to Jewish interests."[56]

Jews were aware of invidious associations between Jew and journalist. In fund-raising for Leo Frank's appeals, men like Albert D. Lasker avoided any appearance of a connection between Jews and the press, so that "their work can do no harm, but only good." As Dinnerstein notes, "the Southerners who feared and resented aliens could not have been expected to heed the pleas of Northern, urban, Jewish-owned newspapers." Ten years later, prominent Jews even approached *The Atlanta Constitution*, requesting that the paper not run new information regarding Frank's innocence. According to Pierre Van Passen, these Jews feared repercussions if another story on Frank ran.[57]

Of course, others could just as easily single out any perceived foreigner as controlling the press. Not only did this opposition evince anti-Semitism, but anti-Catholicism as well. Many assumed that Catholicism precluded patriotism, as all Catholics presumably owed sole allegiance to the pope. Evangelists like Bob Shuler had warned, in a 1917 article, of Rome – a code word for Catholicism – "coming with her ideals, hostile and inimicable to free and untrammeled government." Ever hungry for "the vitals of our government," Rome would inflict such horrors as stilling "the voice of free speech and stay[ing] the hum of the printing press." Well into the 1920s, Shuler had accused Catholics of "virtually control[ling] the press in America." Singling out Hearst-owned newspapers and *The Literary Digest*, Shuler claimed that these publications were "known to be dominated by the Roman Church."[58]

Yet Shuler, like Watson, could easily transfer the accusation of Catholic control to the accusation of a Jewish one. This demonization served a number of purposes. It provided a conduit to criticize the power of a mass medium like the press, although the criticism usually accompanied the belief that Protestant power would or should supplant Jewish or Catholic power. It evinced a profound will to retain strict divisions along class and racial lines. The demonization of ethnic control over the press also held out hope for what Gordon Clark called the small "country press" when the "metropolitan press" threatened to "degrade" and "prostitute" American journalism.[59] Whether employing demon imagery to protest the changing cultural landscape or exploiting disenchantment over these changes to bolster its points, the accusation of Jewish control over the media rebelled against a modernizing America.

Whereas charges of Jewish control over the press rendered Jews as distinctly foreign, emanating from the city, and holding key financial interests, accusations of Jewish control over the theater contained a certain moral outrage that would come to characterize the Hollywood Question.

Jews supposedly stood ready to ravage the theater in a crassly commercial frenzy. The demonization of Jewish control over the theater generated a powerful set of images that, along with accusations of collective ethnic instrumentality, helped to clear discursive inroads leading the Hollywood Question to depression-era America. This demonization succeeded through a unique blend of racial caricature, stereotypical associations with money and parvenu status, and the perceived threat of a sexual Other.

Despite its distinctly American inflection, anti-Semitism and its aspirations for a culture free from Jews emanated abundantly from Europe. As both Sander Gilman and Carol Ockman show, European theater criticism of the late nineteenth century freely deployed anti-Semitic stereotypes and disease metaphors when referring to such stars as Sarah Bernhardt.[60] Such instances played upon fears of infestation, locating the threat at the site of the Jewish body. While these images also appeared in *Life*, the American humor magazine connected this threat to a fear of ethnic power and control.

Sharing many of the concerns for the well-being of the press, accusations of Jewish control over the American theater vociferously protested a changing cultural climate. In their attacks on both the press and the theater, critics singled out the Jewish immigrant arriviste, valorized rural North America, excoriated the city, capitalized upon antitrust sentiment, and lamented what they perceived to be a threat to North American cultural capital. The accusation of Jewish control over the theater, however, articulated a unique perspective. To those who feared Jewish control, the press held political power. Jewish control over the theater, on the other hand, menaced the very moral fiber of the nation. Not only did salacious material degrade public morals and taste; any North American woman hoping to land on the stage had to fend off lascivious Jewish parvenus. Ultimately, the representation of the female Protestant body in these accusations served two purposes. First, it emphasized the sexual threat of the racialized Jewish Other. Second, it became a metaphor for what Jews allegedly did to culture, ravaging it racially as they ravaged a body corporeally.

Life magazine ostensibly attacked what it called trusts, like the New York Theatrical Syndicate and the Klaw and Erlanger chain of legitimate theaters. Yet *Life* also seamlessly blended a belief in conspiracy with sexualized images of culture and traditional Shylock stereotypes. "The entire control of the theatrical business in America," trumpeted James Metcalfe in one of *Life*'s 1898 theater reviews, "rests in the hands of a few Jewish gentlemen, who have decided what the American people want." The theatrical wasteland, according to Metcalfe, "can easily be traced to this peculiar Jewish monopoly. The gentlemen who compose it take no chances. . . . Everything must have an absolute commercial rating." Not only did this monopoly "cause the dearth of dramatic novelty"; it kept the theater "closed to everything and everybody that they do not feel sure will return a profit." Antitrust rhetoric and appeals to high art appeared alongside this evocation of the greedy Jew. Referring to the "Theatrical Trust," for example, Metcalfe roundly criticized a feeble attempt "to cajole or coerce" the producer of *The Merchant of Venice*.[61]

In criticizing the theater, Metcalfe exploited stereotypes of Jews and money. "With a few men using their peculiar Jewish judgment to determine what is and what is not art (paying art)," Metcalfe wrote, "it is not strange that few attractions should please their fancy and fit their financial schemes." With such a link established, Metcalfe explained everything that he found wrong with the theater: "This is a large public and the few attractions which please the Jewish gentlemen are not enough to go around. Hence the short theatrical season, the closing of the theatres, and the unreasonable crowding of playhouses where there are what our Jewish theatrical mentors call 'success.' "[62]

Like others who decried alleged Jewish control, Metcalfe called upon his readers to take a more active role in reclaiming the theater. He warned that, if "the American people are content" with what "these Jewish gentlemen" give the public, then "the American people have no right to complain." Like journalism's rural deliverance, Metcalfe suggested that the only salvation for Western drama lay in the hands of stock companies across the country and "outside the purely mercantile and Jewish control" of New York. Metcalfe would tailor his accusation to suit the pages of the *Atlantic Monthly*. Nowhere in this 1905 article does he mention ethnicity. Instead, he discreetly complains of "the men to-day in charge of the business interests of the theatre" who were "far from representative of the best, even in American business life."[63]

Like those who demonized the allegedly Jewish-owned American press, Metcalfe betrayed elitism concerning the stock of those involved in American culture:

The men who find their occupation on the business side of theatre have been recruited, with few exceptions, from those who have no education, no association with the finer things in life, and no social standing to lose. Success means to them the money return, a position of authority over others, and place in the public eye – all attractive to a certain class of persons who hold these as the most desirable things in life. . . . The theatre is to-day in the hands of men unfitted to direct its destinies upward instead of downward.[64]

By no means unique in linking elitism, anti-Semitism, and aesthetics, Metcalfe had belonged to a stable of writers and artists who worked for *Life* during the late 1800s and early 1900s. *Life*'s editors and staff had fashioned a consistent outpouring of anti-Semitic accusations through images and text. When attacking the Gentile parvenu, whom Joseph Smith calls a "Deadhead," Smith refers to "a class of persons who have made inveracity a fine art and a permanent investment." He defines this "class" as "the merry persons with crescent noses who pillage the public at the box-office," or simply "the Nose Trust." The "Deadhead's" mission, Smith confides, was to convince Jews of his "influence in moulding public opinion," and to "imbed" his views "in the gray matter of the nasal exiles of Poland and Pomeranis."[65]

During the late nineteenth and early twentieth centuries, *Life*'s caricatures augmented these observations. The magazine's cartoons drew heavily from a set code when referring to Jews and Jewish control. These images, in turn, helped to lay the ideological and discursive foundations for the later demonization of Jewish control of Hollywood. Four main features made up the caricature's code – physiognomy, appearance (or dress), money, and sexuality. The stereotyped image of the Jew exploited popular perceptions of physiognomy, particularly in exaggerated depictions of noses, heads, facial hair, and bodies. In extreme cases, the image showed the Jew as beastlike, his hideous appearance inconsistent with the signs of his assimilated position. The Jew also appeared as well dressed. In one sense, the code reinforced the traditional explanation that Jews could dress well because they were all in the garment trade. But the code also pointed to the Jew's parvenu status. To reinforce this meaning, artists drew shiny diamond cufflinks or tie clasps, representing the parvenu's ostentatious display of wealth.

Traditional associations with Jews and money articulated protests against the commercialization and debasement of high culture: Jews polluted the theater through their commercial influence. One cartoon shows two Jewish entertainers beating a theatergoer for his last nickel. Another shows the stars of the day as mere puppets who would dance for a mere $2.50. Three globes – the universal symbol for pawnbroker – appear throughout these cartoons, reinforcing the common associations between usury and Jews.

By their very symbol, albeit somewhat implicitly, the three globes also

FIGURE 3. "American Drama as Leading Lady," shackled and garlanded.
Life, 14 November 1901, 391.

invoke the link between Jews and licentiousness. The three globes refer to three sisters. According to legend, Saint Nicholas saved these sisters from prostitution by secretly giving them gifts. (The custom of secret gift giving in the name of Santa Claus developed out of this story.) Ironically, what first appeared as an example of Christian virtue eventually served as a metaphor for Shylockian proprietorship over Gentile sexuality.

Other symbols depicted Jews as a sexual threat more overtly. One caricature showed Drama – personified as a woman – turning away her Jewish suitors in favor of Andrew Carnegie, a wealthy industrialist of the day. Another showed Jews holding Drama – once again in the form of a woman – bound and encircled by a string of garlands. Another carried the implication that a cigar-chomping impresario had a rather prurient interest in seeing an aspiring actress in tights (see Fig. 9).

In a 1901 cartoon entitled "Puzzle," a group of bearded, large-nosed men assemble in the lobby of the Knickerbocker Theater under the three-globed lamp. The caption implores the reader to "find the Christian." Such images effectively wed Shylock imagery with physiognomic caricatures. The cartoon's depiction of the Jew follows a well-honed code. The Jews appear

FIGURE 4. Three globes help solve the "puzzle."
Life, 24 October 1901, 332.

with large noses, beards, potbellies, and misshapen heads. Their suits serve a double purpose, reinforcing their status as both parvenu and tailor. The three-globed lamp hovers above the entire group, just in case *Life*'s readers might miss the point (Fig. 4).

When *Life* received word that theaters were pulling ads from publications whose critics gave their productions bad reviews, the magazine published an article critical of such behavior without mentioning Jews. Instead, a small caricature accompanied the text (Fig. 5). A balding man, with a large nose and a triangulated beard (shaped like the bottom of a Jewish star) and wearing diamonds, holds an assortment of actors and actresses in his palms. The word "THEATRE" fills the inside of his mouth, drawn as a leering grin. This caricature often accompanied Metcalfe's theater reviews.

An Impertinence.

FIGURE 5. Cartoon of theater producer. *Life*, 7 November 1901, 374.
Note the triangulated beard.

Stereotypes of Jewish venality and stinginess could also decry the commercialism of the theater. A caricature of Weber and Fields (Fig. 6) shows the vaudevillians standing before a mound of coins, beating a "theatregoer" in search of his last nickel, thus reinforcing an association between Jewish control over the arts and Jewish control over money. Another cartoon exploited the image of the Jew as a behind-the-scenes manipulator (Fig. 7). Here, a well-dressed man turns a crank to a stagelike contraption, jiggling the stars of the day as mere mechanical puppets if one drops "$2.50 in the slot."

Other cartoons played upon fears of the sexual threat of Jews to demure femininity. In "Hasten the Day," Andrew Carnegie courts the womanly ideal of Drama away from the "Theatrical Syndicate of the Jews" (Fig. 8). To the extreme right, a banner depicting an overweight Jewish woman counterposes the artist's rendering of Hellenic-Aryan womanhood. Some cartoons expressed this fear more subtly. As we have seen, in Figure 3 a band of overweight Jewish men lead a feminized "American Drama," bound by a string of garlands. Another shows a well-dressed impresario with the requisite beard and large nose, smoking a cigar as he leers at his female charge (Fig. 9). "I wish to go on stage," the woman says, "and would like your opinion as to my chances of success." "Well," answers the man, "did you bring your tights?"

The impresario is clearly meant to be Jewish. On the page preceding this cartoon, one of James Metcalfe's reviews rails against the "Jewish syndicate." In addition to the impresario's physiognomy, facial hair, and well-

FIGURE 6. Weber and Fields pummel the Gentile
patron. *Life*, 21 November 1901.

FIGURE 7. Jewish control over actors and actresses. *Life*, 31 October 1901, 353.

FIGURE 8. Andrew Carnegie "hastens the day" when American theater will no longer be beholden to Jewish control. *Life*, 12 September 1901.

tailored appearance, he smokes a cigar. As in later Hollywood novels, the cigar not only emphasizes the Jew's position as parvenu: through its phallic shape, it indexes male Jewish power over women. The image of the cigar, its signal of a sexual threat, and its demarcation of power reappeared years later in the Hollywood novel.

Images of Jewish power, commercialism, and sexuality surfaced, not just in *Life*, but in other elitist magazines as well. The December 1895 cover of *M'lle New York*, an arts magazine, shows a nude maiden lying before the Jewish sphinx of commercialism (Fig. 10). Not only did this caricature exploit sexual fears through its depiction of a female nude prostrate before a leering Jew, but by picturing the Jew as a sphinx the image links Jewish commercialism to Orientalist stereotypes of Semitic inferiority. The image also suggests that Jewish ambition would lead to Christian servitude before the idol of commercialism.

Life's readers, some of whom were presumably Jewish, protested these images. These readers nonetheless appeared to respond to the magazine's campaign on principle rather than in self-interest. "You owe the American public, which stands for freedom and fair play, an apology for so gross and

THE DRAMA IN NEW YORK.

"I WISH TO GO ON THE STAGE, AND WOULD LIKE YOUR OPINION AS TO MY CHANCES OF SUCCESS."
" WELL, DID YOU BRING YOUR TIGHTS ? "

FIGURE 9. The Jew as Impresario. *Life*, 12 May 1898, 405.

contemptible an attack upon a whole people," Henry Berkowitz wrote in a letter to *Life*'s editor. In particular, Berkowitz objected to "the sweeping charge that 'the Jew has contaminated everything in American life that he has touched.' " As Berkowitz noted, *Life* itself had praised David Warfield, a Jewish actor and impresario, in the article making the condemnation. "Why do you attack a religion which surely possesses many bright names and deeds in all the Arts, including the Dramatic?" asked Richard Scheiner. "Is it right and fair and just to maliciously emphasize the religion of men when attacking their unworthy deeds? If, perchance, our theatrical manag-

FIGURE 10. Christian Art prostrate before Jewish Commerce.
M'lle New York 1.9 (1895).

ers belonged to the Protestant or the Catholic race, would you speak of them as the 'Protestant Syndicate,' or the 'Catholic Syndicate?' "[66]

Life's editors responded by sympathizing with "intelligent, intellectual and refined [Jews] in their suffering from the acts of the great majority of their race" and by blaming those "other" Jews for bringing anti-Semitism upon the entire group. Politicians and evangelists subsequently employed this strategy during the 1920s and 1930s, calling upon Hollywood Jews to denounce their so-called Communist brethren. Taking a cue from race science, *Life* informed its readers that it "never criticised the Jews for their religion, but for their racial characteristics."[67]

Magazines like *Life* were important arbiters for urban Protestant manners, morals, and behavior that the publication saw as "distinct from those of the rest of the world." When *Life* could locate "Catholic or Protestant codes of business morals and social manners distinct from those of the rest of the world," it assured readers that it would "criticise them as Catholic and Protestant, just as it now does those that are distinctly and exclusively Jewish." *Life* and even Scheiner had failed to mention that other groups and publications *had* singled out Catholics only a few years before. In addition, neither *Life* nor Scheiner noted that urban Protestants would never be singled out for their business morals and social manners. While muckrakers may have attacked Christian robber-baron industrialists like Andrew Carnegie, they never attacked Carnegie for being *Christian*, or Anglo-Saxon. Nor did they ever attempted to explain Carnegie's actions in terms of the Christian religion or a Christian race.[68]

Whereas *Life* had failed to acknowledge the country's rampant anti-Catholicism when defending the magazine's anti-Semitism, most protests against the magazine had accepted a basic presumption: a few men controlled the purse strings of theater. This view ultimately worked to cement and naturalize the ideological bond between *Life*'s editorial obsession with morality and its antitrust rhetoric. The success of this rhetoric is evident, even in some of the letters protesting the magazine's attitudes toward Jews. "That you go hammer and tongs for the Theatrical Syndicate is, in my opinion, highly just and praiseworthy," writes Scheiner. "The managers, in question, are a sordid lot who ignominiously drag the Drama down to the dollar and cent basis."[69]

As long as cultural disdain for the popular art persisted, disguised as objections to greed and defense of aesthetics, *Life* continued to justify its attacks on Jews. In response to Berkowitz, *Life* defended its "assertion that the Jew is a contaminating influence in American life." One need only look at "such cases in point as what the Theatrical Syndicate has done to debase dramatic art in America, what Mr. Pulitzer has done for American journalism by the discovery of yellow methods, and what Mr. Andrew Freedman has done" for baseball, "the national game." "One Jewish actor," the editors of *Life* maintained, "proves nothing for or against" the Jews. The magazine defended the stereotype of "greed for money, no matter how vulgarly or immorally to be obtained" as "the leading racial characteristic of [Warfield's] people."[70]

Another reader challenged, not just the way in which *Life* demonized

Jews, but its assertion that so-called racial characteristics drove the theatrical "trust":

> Has the Jew lowered the standard of commercial honor in this country? Was he concerned in any of the infamous deals that have brought destruction upon the orphan and the widow, that have debauched the Court and corrupted the Legislature? Does his name often figure among the numerous lists of embezzlers and other betrayers of trusts? Do the activities with which he is commonly connected depend upon deceit, manipulation of news and courts, and the defiance of law, the circulation of lying rumors and the cornering of necessities of life?[71]

Noting the irony of a magazine Jew-baiting a newspaper, the anonymous author of this letter asked if journalism was "less reliable, or as prolific in fakers and vile cartoons as other papers that may be easily mentioned?" The answers to these questions, the author notes, "will show that for a race that is popularly believed to have such a large capacity for evil, the Jew has sadly neglected his opportunities. Perhaps he hasn't had a fair show, because the field for mischief seems to have been pre-empted." *Life's* editors refrained from responding to these observations.[72]

One of many publications venting frustration and anxiety over the mass media, *Life* and its editors, writers, and artists used Jewish stereotypes to protest mass culture. The code *Life* employed – stereotypes invoking physiognomy, usury, ostentation, and sexual threat – provided a foundation for subsequent attacks upon the American film industry. Although *Life's* readers challenged such representations, few challenged the assumption that a small, cohesive group could exert control over the theater – or any mediated form. This belief in conspiracy and its control over the media, for the most part undisputed, would achieve even greater currency after World War I.

THE PROTOCOLS OF THE ELDERS OF ZION

More than any other single publication in the United States, the *Protocols of the Elders of Zion* propelled the demonization of Jewish control into mass culture. Despite barely mentioning the movies, the *Protocols* nonetheless explained the mass media, and particularly Hollywood, in terms of an encroaching pluralism and modernity. The text of the *Protocols* arrived in the United States shortly after World War I, imported by Czarist army officers fleeing from the newly formed Soviet Union. By circulating this document, the officers hoped to gain American sympathy for reinstalling a monarchy.

Originally appearing in Europe in the late nineteenth century, the *Protocols* purported to expose Jewish plans for world domination. Extreme nationalist groups in the United States, like the National Civic Federation and the American Defense Society, reprinted the *Protocols*, at the height of 1920s anti-immigrant fervor, and distributed them for free to Congress. Partly on the basis of this tract, a 1934 United States Chamber of Commerce publication cited Jews as the group "of foreign origin" with the greatest "communist membership." A trial held in Berne, Switzerland, that same year proved the *Protocols* to be an obvious forgery. Supposedly Jewish, the *Protocols*'s author or authors had actually plagiarized a number of earlier texts, including one liberal political tract that had nothing to do with Judaism.[73]

In the words of one of the *Protocols*'s own ideologues, the forgery appealed to those alienated from "social, political and economic developments" of the late 1800s. Recent technological developments had the potential to shift national identity from one of isolation and domestic concerns to an awareness of nationhood within a global community. "Nations remote from one another," Boris Brasol had written in 1921, "were brought into close contact." Railroads, telephones, telegraphs, and radio communication, while potentially increasing communication, all pushed the West toward what Brasol and others feared was a dangerous infusion of foreign ideas.[74]

In *The World at the Crossroads* (1921), Brasol characterizes these ideas as "philosophical skepticism, biological and economic materialism, irreligious rationalism, idealistic anarchism, together with all the extreme deductions of free thought and positivism." Perceiving them "the consequence of . . . radical changes," Brasol fixes upon freethinking as the harbinger to the decline of the realm. "The destruction of the four empires," he writes, referring to Russia, Germany, Austro-Hungary, and Turkey, "has almost predestined the destruction of the fifth and last empire, that of Great Britain. At present humanity witnesses its gradual dissolution." For Brasol, however, this was no cause for celebration. Rather, these challenges to Western imperialism were the beginning of a never-ending coda of conspiracy apocalyptic:

Ireland is no longer ruled by the British crown; the Jacobin cap has taken its place. England has lost Egypt, while she proved unable to win Palestine. India is in revolt. The battle which is being fought there at any time may be turned into a British Waterloo. That will be the hour of triumph for the Montagus and the Gandhis. That will be the epilogue to the world drama, the prologue to which was the revolution in Russia.

Who was the group responsible for this "slow but inevitable . . . gangrenous process; . . . the poison of the disease . . . worming its way to the very heart of the English nation?" No less than "a handful of Semitic agitators from Moscow [who] have already succeeded in imposing their will upon the British people."[75]

For Brasol, only one nation "stood firm and has not yielded to the cancer of international Bolshevism and moral degradation": the United States. Yet this country, according to Brasol, remained vulnerable. "On these shores, too," he writes, "the enemy of civilization is at work, trying to spread the germs of the plague, endeavoring to undermine the stable foundations of America's political and social structure. Great is the desire of the Demon of destruction to tear down the last stronghold of stability and wealth."[76]

The *Protocols* supposedly evidenced this process of destruction. In fact, it voiced frustration with the mass media, particularly the press. Written as if Jews themselves had betrayed their intentions, the *Protocols* revealed unhappy sentiments for journalism: "What is the present rôle of the press? It serves to arouse furious passions or egotistic party dissensions which may be necessary for our purpose. It is empty, unjust, inaccurate, and most people do not understand what end it serves." More than any other medium, the press poses a danger because of its accessibility to both popular and divergent views. "*There is one great force in the hands of modern states which arouses thought movements among people,*" the second protocol states. "*That is the press.* The rôle of the press is to indicate necessary demands, to register complaints of the people, and to express and foment dissatisfaction."[77]

In the world of the *Protocols*, Jews work for Jewish control while setting up fronts to attack Jewish control. "Organs," established by Jews, would "attack exclusively those points which we plan to change." Through maintaining this kind of semblance of opposition, Jews could solidify Jewish control. Jewish periodicals would "seem to be of contradictory views and opinions, inviting trust in us, thus attracting to us unsuspecting enemies." Even criticism of alleged Jewish control, "although always superficially" asserted, would only allow Jews "an opportunity to express [themselves] in greater detail."[78]

For the *Protocols*, free speech was yet another way of camouflaging so-called Jewish thought. Fabricated attacks upon Jews would "*convince the people that complete liberty of the press still exists*," giving Jewish agents "*the opportunity to declare that the papers opposing us are mere wind-bags*, since they are unable to find any real ground to refute our orders." The *Protocols* abhors diversity of opinion, even though it also attacks monolithic control. "All our newspapers will represent different tendencies," the *Protocols* confesses, "namely, aristocratic, republican, revolutionary, even anarchistic, so long of course as the constitution lasts." But according to the *Protocols*, this was only a temporary phenomenon.

> Like the Indian God VISHNU, these periodicals will have one hundred arms, each of which will reach the pulse of every group of public opinion. When the pulse beats faster, these arms will guide opinion toward our aims, since the excited person loses the power of reasoning and is easily led. Those fools who believe that they repeat the opinions expressed by the newspapers of their party will be repeating our opinions or those which we desire them to have.[79]

In the world of the *Protocols*, free speech is a Jewish means to an end. Once Jews reached "*the phase of the new régime*," they would prevent the press from exposing "*social corruption. It must be thought that the new régime has satisfied everybody to such an extent that even criminality has stopped.*" Thus the press posed two threats: one, as a present source of confusion, and two, as a potential site of censorship. The *Protocols* criticized democratic forms of media because democracy allegedly created confusion, which in turn paved the way for Jewish control and greed. "The triumph of free babbling is incarnated in the press," the *Protocols* notes; "but governments were unable to profit by this power *and it has fallen into our hands*. Through it we have attained influence, while remaining in the background. Thanks to the press, we have gathered gold in our hands."[80]

The power of the *Protocols* rested upon fears of persuasion, confusion, and diversity. The so-called Jewish press, according to the *Protocols*, sometimes printed "the truth, sometimes lies, referring to facts or contradicting them according to the way they are received by the public." In particular, a sense of disenfranchisement manifests itself in the *Protocols*'s fears. The Jews would "*surely conquer [their] enemies because [the Jews' enemies] will not have the press at their disposal.*"[81]

The *Protocols* also finds that Jews divert public consciousness with their "*amusements, games, pastimes, passions, and cultural centers for the people.*" Jews were responsible for creating "*insane, dirty, and disgusting literature.*" For the *Protocols*, these forms of mass media represented a loss of consciousness and identity. "By losing more and more the custom of independent thought," the public would "begin to talk in unison" with Jewish conspirators.[82]

A whole cottage industry of quasi-scholarship emerged from the *Protocols*, interpreting the forgery's sometimes incoherent passages on financial control, conspiracy, religious hatred, and fear of mass culture and modern thought with a fervor ironically worthy of Talmudic exegesis. If the *Protocols* uncovered anything, it revealed an audience highly conversant with the demonization of Jewish control. As Chapter 3 will show, automobile magnate Henry Ford played a crucial role throughout the 1920s in further popularizing this discourse. But by 1920, the British-published *Jewish Peril* had already found "the Press, the theatre, stock exchange speculations, science, law itself . . . in the hands that hold all the gold." This Jewish conspiracy had at its disposal "so many means of procuring a deliberate confusion and bewilderment of public opinion, demoralization of the young, and encouragement of the vices of the adult." Rather than simply decry an alleged Jewish conspiracy, the *Protocols* and its various adherents emphasized the effects of Jewish control upon Christian consciousness. With a Jewish conspiracy in place, "the idealistic aspiration of Christian culture" would soon yield to such undesirable results as " 'cash basis' " and "a neutrality of materialistic scepticism [and] cynical lust for pleasure." This same basic fear of a vulnerable Christian morality would reappear in later anxieties over a defenseless public mind.[83]

The *Protocols* evinces a fear of modernity and the diversity perceived to accompany it. Like the earliest accusations of Jewish control over the press, the *Protocols*'s anti-Semitism reacts, at least in part, to a changing political, cultural, social, and ideological landscape. It fears diversity of thought, speech, and ideology, as these choices supposedly would only confuse the public. But the *Protocols* did not fear diversity in and of itself. Rather, it saw diversity and its attendant confusion as a means to an end. This attendant confusion, in its view, would ultimately lead to monolithic Jewish control. Given the choice, adherents of the *Protocols* would rather choose monolithic Christian control over diversity, particularly when that diversity – *any* diversity – appeared only as a way to impose another form of monolithic control.

The *Protocols* unites conspiracy fears with the sense of moral outrage that had appeared in magazines such as *Life*. Omitting overt reference to the anti-Semitic code depicting Jews as racial freaks, parvenus, usurers, and sexual threats – in short, as Shylocks – the *Protocols* perceives the Jewish threat to morality in far more insidious terms. Jews undo Christian virtue through their control over the media. Diverting the Christian mind from an alleged Jewish threat, the invisible Jew encourages moral and intellectual lapses into licentiousness and radicalism.

Jews and non-Jews alike criticized the *Protocols*. Louis Marshall, then president of the American Jewish Committee, wrote to publisher George H. Putnam in 1920, protesting Putnam's decision to print Brasol's *The Cause of World Unrest* and the *Protocols*. After Marshall refused Putnam's offer to write a rebuttal, Putnam decided to delay publication of a new edition of the *Protocols*. Subsequent volumes and articles appeared refuting the *Protocols* and its growing body of sympathetic interpretations. These *Protocols* "exposés" include Lucien Wolf's *The Jewish Bogey and the Forged Protocols of the Learned Elders of Zion* (1920), Israel Zangwill's essay on "The Legend of the Conquering Jew" (1920), John Spargo's *The Jew and American Ideals* (1921), and Herman Bernstein's *The History of a Lie* (1921). Many of these works show line by line the plagiarism and incoherence extant in the *Protocols*. And in 1920, the American Jewish Committee and other Jewish organizations denounced the *Protocols* as an inauthentic attempt to link Jews to Bolshevism.[84]

Such protests and proofs could not overcome several legacies of the *Protocols*, however. The pall of American anti-Semitism continued to strengthen xenophobia and anti-Communism. The arrest and eventual execution of Nicola Sacco and Bartolomeo Vanzetti for a payroll holdup in Braintree, Massachusetts, attested to a fear of radicalism and anarchy that extended to almost any foreigner, but especially Jewish immigrants. Often associated with anarchy, radicalism, and Communism, Jews carried the brunt of countersubversive opprobrium after World War II. Six of the Hollywood Ten – motion picture personnel accused by Congress of harboring Communist sympathies in 1947 – were Jewish. This anti-Communist fervor climaxed in 1953, when the United States executed Julius and Ethel Rosenberg for trading secret nuclear details with the Soviet Union – an action many believed to represent incipient American anti-Semitism.

In addition to its charge of Jewish conspiracy and its demonization of the racialized Jew, *The Protocols of the Elders of Zion* propelled one more concept into the arena of conspiracy discourse: the notion of a public mind or intellect. According to this concept, a delicate public mind remained vulnerable to media influence. Whoever maintained control of the mass media could induce the fragile public mind to babble "in unison" along with the rest of a bereft and brainwashed mass culture. Articles appearing in Henry Ford's newspaper *The Dearborn Independent* and the subsequent

International Jew develop this assumption even further. Mapping out a so-called community mind became a way of shoring up mental and cultural defenses. As this discursive strategy reveals, charting the public mind remained a bulwark of whiteness against an alleged Jewish conspiracy. Along with the belief in conspiracy and a racialized image of ethnic agency, this faith in a singular, mappable mind helped to make sense of mass media and an emergent modernity. In its attempt to render a changing America in fathomable terms, the notion of the vulnerability of a public mind gave the Hollywood Question its added urgency and charge. Propelled by both fear of and faith in this mind, the Hollywood Question emerged as a powerful justification for censorship and, later, allegations of propaganda.

2

Religion, Race, and Morality in the Hollywood Question

INTRODUCTION

The Hollywood Question was clearly more than just itself. It functioned as both a site and a discursive route in its own right. Remarkably versatile, it could channel other discourses, redirecting and reinvigorating these ideas and statements in ways that responded in powerful fashion to the changing face of America. The movies were but one feature of this evolving face of modernity, but as the enormous popularity of storefront nickelodeons had demonstrated, its mass-mediated visage was a feature of modernity with which to reckon. As historians John Kasson, Robert Sklar, and Garth Jowett have noted, the popularity of the movies marked a decided shift in the ideological control of culture. Just as Gutenberg's printing press wrenched literacy from the sole domains of nobility and the church, so the movies echoed this process of democratization for mass culture. Movies, however, only represented one facet of this shift. Compulsory education also helped to facilitate greater literacy. The mass press, and in particular the explosion of the multilingual ethnic press, created a new textual bridge to a new culture. Once out of the hands of Protestant elites, mass culture in America became increasingly accessible to greater numbers of people – and ultimately more threatening to those who advocated greater control over it. As the movies grew more popular, the desire to exert some level of ideological control over them assumed heightened urgency. Concerns over the moral influence of motion pictures on the country, particularly its youth, became a powerful vehicle to exert this control.

This moral indignation had already been well rehearsed within a variety of contexts. In many cases, the assumptions of collective ethnic agency, the demonizing images of Jewish greed and sexuality, and the starkly contrasting images of a chaste yet vulnerable Christian culture simply shifted wholesale from one discourse on entertainment to another. Staying largely intact, this stock set of images and statements moved from the accusation of Jewish control over the legitimate theater to one of Jewish control over the not-so-legitimate movie theater. Similarly, allegations of collective ethnic agency easily moved from a Catholic peril to a Jewish one. Thus, the Hollywood Question could successfully redirect and vivify an already powerful set of discourses. In doing so, the Question responded in potent fashion to a nascent American modernity.

In addition to operating as a kind discursive depot linking and feeding into a compelling set of old and new ideological "routes," the "morality" of the Hollywood Question also forged a powerful consensus among competing groups vying for cultural control. As Protestant elites worked to maintain control over the movies, pushing for national legislation that would implement federal censorship, the Catholic Church organized millions of members to engage in protests, such as a threatened boycott of the movies. In asserting their moral agenda, these religious groups ultimately "mapped" out their response to a changing America in very different ways. While Protestants moved within the halls of state and federal legislatures, the Catholic response spoke through its ethnic press to an informal network outside Protestant domains of power. This response became a way of speaking both to and from smaller, localized and integral communities. By the end of the 1920s and the dawn of the Great Depression, the Hollywood Question had unified these competing efforts, forging a powerful consensus between these divergent religious interests.

Explicitly, this consensus articulated a concern for morality. Implicitly, however, this concern marginalized ethnicity by equating it with immorality. Unlike discussions concerning other industries and their business leaders, the Hollywood Question assumed that Jews behaved *as Jews*. In achieving this consensus through assertion of morality and a demonization of the Other, this explanation ultimately set the stage for subsequent protests over propaganda and the New Deal. No longer just about the movies, the morality of the Hollywood Question indeed charted a course for prewar isolationism and postwar anti-Communism.

"A BUSINESS, PURE AND SIMPLE"

Ironically, the scandals of the Protestant elite first helped to initiate motion picture censorship in the United States. On June 25, 1906, as nickelodeons were beginning to achieve phenomenal popularity, Pittsburgh millionaire Harry K. Thaw walked into Madison Square Garden's rooftop restaurant and shot architect Stanford White to death. Thaw had discovered that before he married his wife, Evelyn Nesbit Thaw, she and White had been having an affair. Throughout the trial, many embarrassing details emerged in the press. In 1909, by the time a jury acquitted Thaw for reason of insanity, Canon William Sheafe Chase of Christ Church, Brooklyn, alleged that nickelodeons were projecting scandalous films related to the case. Chase pressured the mayor of New York to hold a public meeting on the movies. Mayor George B. McClellan subsequently ordered all movie theaters to close on Christmas Eve. The incident launched Chase's crusade against the movies, which lasted well into the thirties. And while theater owners were able to reopen the day after Christmas, the action set a precedent defining film, not as speech or expression, but as a form of commerce inimical to morality.[85]

Indeed, at the time a variety of economic interests were vying for the very high commercial stakes of this nascent industry. During this same period, the Motion Picture Patents Company (MPPC) dominated the film industry. Headed by the Edison Company and American Mutoscope and Biograph, the company set up exclusive licensing arrangements among producers, distributors, and exhibitors. In exchange for MPPC films, exhibitors had to pay a special fee to the Patents Company. In April 1909, a few months before McClellan shut down New York City theaters, distributor Carl Laemmle bolted from the MPPC and began the Independent Motion Picture Corporation, thus sounding a clarion for dozens of other independent concerns. By 1914, independent producers were able to gain prominence within the industry. As Patricia Erens notes, many of these independent producers were Jewish. A year later, the Supreme Court ruled against the MPPC, arguing that the company had illegally constrained fair trade and competition.[86]

Defining films as a form of commerce threatening morality allowed more overtly ideological controls like censorship to gain foothold. The first legally recognized censorship board began in Ohio in 1913, organized under the state's Industrial Commission.[87] William I. Swoope, deputy attorney general for the State of Pennsylvania, claims to have prosecuted hundreds of people under the state's 1915 "picture show law."[88] In Connecticut, *Fox Film Corp.* v. *Turnbull* reaffirmed the right of a commissioner to revoke of the registration "of any motion picture which he finds immoral or liable to offend racial or religious feelings."[89] Many local communities successfully moved to prohibit Sunday exhibitions on religious grounds. Some Christian leaders dutifully informed Jews of their place in these matters. One Birmingham, Alabama, pastor warned the city's Jews not to vote on a 1918 Sunday ordinance, reasoning that such matters did not concern them.[90] Between 1921 and 1922, thirty-six states were seriously considering censorship legislation. By 1926, thirty-five cities and seven states – New York, Pennsylvania, Maryland, Kansas, Ohio, Florida, and Virginia – had censorship boards. [91]

By conceiving of the film industry as a form of commerce, judicial and congressional activity could justify intervention and regulation at the federal level as well. Beginning in 1915, a series of congressional hearings investigated films as a type of interstate commerce. Regulation of transportation, particularly of the railroads, provided the model. Just like mass transportation, films could cut across state lines, knitting heretofore isolated communities into a national, more tightly woven fabric. By 1916, the Supreme Court reasoned that motion pictures were "a business, pure and simple," and not eligible for the same protections afforded the press. In *Weber* v. *Freed* (239 U.S. 325), the Supreme Court ruled that motion pictures were a form of interstate commerce, and therefore not subject to local police power but under the jurisdiction of Congress.[92] By 1926, Swoope, now a Pennsylvania Representative, had sponsored four separate bills to regulate the film industry via Congress and used the *Weber* v. *Freed* decision to justify his efforts.[93] A whole way of thinking and speaking about the film industry emerged. Rendering movies as a form of commerce traversing state lines, this influential view generated regulatory efforts at least up until the eve of World War II. Indeed, in 1941, when isolationists tried to mount an attack upon Roosevelt administration foreign policy via the film industry, they did so through a Senate Subcommittee of the Interstate Commerce Committee.

Defining the film industry in terms of commerce also helped justify charges of propaganda. During World War I, a number of studios promoted rabidly anti-German films. George Creel, who had headed the Wilson administration's Committee on Public Information, later publicized the apocryphal nature of some of the more rabidly anti-German stories he had helped to promote. Investigations during the 1930s into the armaments industry, headed by North Dakota Senator Gerald P. Nye, uncovered an intensive public relations effort to fan anti-German sentiment, push the United States into war, and thus maximize arms industry profits.

Some also saw World War I as a watershed for a shift in public attitudes. "Few people will deny that since the war the market has been flooded with a great many very questionable pictures," the Municipal Committee of the Cleveland Chamber of Commerce observed in 1922. The increase in pictures dealing with what the chamber called "the sex problem" was due to "the inevitable backwash of war." The problem, the chamber reasoned, was that of big government. "During the war the government told us what to eat, when to turn out our lights, when not to drive our automobiles, when to do this and when not to do that. We were confronted by 'don'ts' on every hand." After the war, "the pendulum swung to the other extreme." The end of war, the chamber observed, had brought about an end to a certain degree of propriety within American life.[94]

While Senator Nye would later invoke the Hollywood Question to inveigh against the *a*morality of using the film industry to push the country into war, two scandals helped galvanize public opinion against a perceived *im*morality of the movie business. In 1922, police found director William Desmond Taylor mysteriously murdered in his home. Meanwhile, popular silent comedian Fatty Arbuckle was on trial for the rape and murder of actress Virginia Rappe. In fall 1921, Rappe had attended a party at Arbuckle's house. Bootleg liquor was served. The actress fell ill, her bladder ruptured, and she soon died. Suspect testimony placed Arbuckle with Rappe right before her death. Despite eventual exoneration of all charges against the silent film star, many believed that Arbuckle had crushed the woman with his immense weight as he violently raped her. Public outrage over the incident mobilized religious and moral groups to force Arbuckle's films off the screen.[95]

Wary of the myriad cries for federal censorship that arose amid these and other scandals, Congress left states, local communities, and the industry itself with the responsibility of policing motion picture morality. All four of Swoope's efforts for congressional regulation failed. Industry executives, however, responded to the outcry by forming their own trade group, the Motion Picture Producers and Distributors Association (MPPDA). Industry executives hoped that the MPPDA would serve to counteract efforts legislating motion picture censorship. In December 1921, Charles C. Pettijohn, an Indiana Democrat and lawyer representing the major studios, advised the MPPDA that it should approach William Harrison Hays. Pettijohn, a longtime associate of movie executive Lewis J. Selznick, knew Hays from their mutual experience in Indiana politics. As former chair of the Republican National Committee, a Presbyterian elder, and postmaster general under President Warren G. Harding, Hays seemed the perfect ambassador to represent an industry besieged by negative publicity.[96]

Through Hays's banking contacts, the MPPDA was legally and fiscally independent of studios and the later Production Code Administration. Unlike other industry trade organizations prosecuted in government antitrust litigation, the MPPDA was never named as a codefendant in litigation against the film industry.[97] As Lea Jacobs notes, the MPPDA was part of the institutional process of making films rather than simply censoring them.

FIGURE 11. Will H. Hays delivering the opening speech at the 17th Republican National Convention. Frame enlargement from *President Harding and Calvin Coolidge* (1920), Library of Congress Motion Picture, Broadcasting and Recorded Sound Division.

At this stage, Jacobs argues, "censorship as an institutional process did not simply reflect social pressures; it articulated a strategic response to them."[98]

Hays's connections thus remained critical to the success of the MPPDA. As the author of a 1941 National Recovery Act investigation politely put it, the former Presbyterian elder was not hired "solely because of his abilities as an administrator."[99] Hays was a high-profile member of a group of politicians known as the "Ohio Gang." This group had helped Harding achieve what was at that time the largest-ever presidential landslide in history. In return, Harding rewarded Hays by appointing him postmaster general.[100] Because Hays had played such an integral role in Harding's election and administration, Kenneth G. Crawford accused him of being tainted by Harding-era corruption. Hays, as chair of the Republican National Committee, had allegedly used " 'hot' tax-dodging bonds" to cover the party's deficit.[101] This and other evidence of corruption surfaced amid a series of congressional hearings conducted by Senator Burton K. Wheeler. One of the old-time progressives and a guiding hand in the 1941 Senate Propaganda Hearings, Wheeler was investigating the "Ohio Gang." By the time the Teapot Dome scandals of the Harding administration had surfaced, however, Hays was safely ensconced in his position as a paid industry lobbyist.

According to Crawford, that "Hays was not hired to clean up the movies . . . and isn't expected to clean up the movies" was no secret. By 1939, he deemed the MPPDA "one of the country's most elaborate and most effec-tive lobbies." To Crawford, Hays's success could be measured in terms of blocked legislation, vitiation of "extragovernmental attempts to raise the moral tone of the trade," and steps to allow "movies to defy the antitrust laws with impunity and impertinence."[102]

Film industry executives hoped that their heartland scion would defuse current hostility against the movies. And, in a sense, he did. The Holly-wood Question could depict Hays as ineffective – or even worse, as a Gentile dupe. "Mr. Hays will simply be the hired man of a bunch of rich Jews," the Reverend Bob Shuler wrote in 1923, "doing politics for them as so much per." Yet rarely did one pose the Hollywood Question quite so harshly. More often, the Question interrogated the ineffectiveness of self-regulation much more subtly. In 1926, as Representative W. B. Upshaw from Georgia introduced his bill for federal censorship of motion pictures, he quoted from the New Testament. His high expectations for Hays dashed, Upshaw drew a biblical comparison. Just as the disciples had hoped Jesus "would deliver Israel at this time," or disappointed Americans "had fondly hoped that Will Hays . . . would strike the shackles that bound the motion picture business to so much that was unclean."[103]

By depicting Hays, either explicitly or implicitly, as a Gentile dupe, the Hollywood Question could actually serve the interests of the film industry. Hays could go quietly about his business, lobbying Congress and other governmental organizations. Meanwhile, both Shuler and Upshaw could paint a relatively coherent picture of Gentile powerlessness. In doing so, both men could avoid looking at the broader context of monopoly capital-ism. Shuler easily wielded his anti-Catholic conspiracy rhetoric with the grace of a sledgehammer, while Upshaw subtly invoked parallels between moguls and Pharisees. A hired employee of "a bunch of rich Jews," accord-ing to Shuler, Hays was no more capable of surmounting the rampant commercialism of the film industry than Jesus had been able to deliver Israel from the Pharisees. By depicting Hays as hapless fool rather than as paid lobbyist, the Hollywood Question could actually serve industry inter-ests, concealing industrial behavior behind an accusation of ethnic moti-vation.

The willingness of the MPPDA to work with various reform agencies no doubt contributed to the somewhat sinister picture that emerged. Mrs. Robbins Gilman, general secretary of the Women's Cooperative Alliance (WCA) of Minneapolis, had at first cooperated with the MPPDA in opposing censorship efforts in Minnesota and Massachusetts. The WCA had espoused a position of "selection – not censorship." In 1925, however, Gilman and William Sheafe Chase formed the Federal Motion Picture Council with the backing of the liberal, mainstream Federal Council of the Churches of Christ. The Motion Picture Council, predominately Protestant, disapproved of "indirect measures for improving the tone of pictures," like working with "the Hays organization." Gilman would later profess "that efforts to bring about improvement in pictures through 'cooperation' with the industry were futile."[104]

Like Upshaw and Shuler, the Motion Picture Council doubted the effectiveness and even the integrity of Will Hays. "The frequent reference to Mr. Hays as a 'czar' of the industry is misleading," the council maintained.

> We found no ground for such a claim to power on his behalf, yet the circumstances of the creation of Mr. Hays' office were such as to encourage it, and Mr. Hays' assurances that the industry "stands at attention" to do the will of disinterested public groups, suggest some extraordinary power on his part. Thus, it has come about that critics of the industry have tended to draw one of two inferences: either the organization is impotent to do what Mr. Hays and his associates would like to accomplish or it is a "smoke screen" to deceive the public and to cover purposes of a narrowly selfish character.

The Motion Picture Council accused the MPPDA of never intending "to delegate to Mr. Hays arbitrary power." Rather, Hays was "to negotiate, so to speak, with an insistent public opinion." The so-called czar's sole purpose, the council ultimately argued, was "to accommodate the industry . . . with the least possible loss to a group of profit-making enterprises."[105]

Rather than work with the MPPDA, the Federal Motion Picture Council pushed for "federal legislation" that would "regulate the industry's trade practices and the quality of its product." In addition to lobbying Congress to enact federal censorship, the council distributed leaflets, held public hearings, and organized national conferences to gain public support for its cause. While this and other sustained efforts to justify federal censorship ultimately fell short of their goal, these labors were nonetheless remarkably successful in enunciating a national discourse that united assumptions of ethnic instrumentality with a sense of moral outrage and urgency.[106]

THE PROTESTANT PUSH FOR NATIONAL CENSORSHIP

As federal, state, local, and religious efforts had defined the motion picture industry as commerce inimical to morality, reformists advanced other arguments that would eventually form the bedrock of the Hollywood Question. Opposed to commercialism, war, big business, and immigration, these reformist arguments responded to the changing face of American life. In his 1910 *National Perils and Hopes*, Wilbur Fiske Crafts decried a "national ruling passion of commercialism" and the "growth of impersonal, and so irresponsible corporations."[107] Such rampant commercialism, according to Crafts, ultimately works to enslave children's minds. "Foul shows and corrupt literature" are the means "by which our youth are chiefly seduced." Crafts specifically calls motion pictures "attacks on [children's] innermost life" that just "fall short of the instinct of beasts."[108]

Crafts's opposition to militarism evoked similar cultural concerns. Predicting that the "hard-earned money of the poor" would pay for American military strength, Crafts was also opposed to war because of how it would harm the character of traditional American life. Wars, according to Crafts, increased "intemperance, impurity, Sabbath breaking and gambling, and lessens the sacredness of both life and property."[109] The Civil War, Crafts claimed, had brought about "the flood of foreign immigration that rolled in upon us in a practically unrestricted tide." These foreigners replaced the millions of war dead who, if alive, could have laid down the railroad lines.[110]

National Perils and Hopes does not make any specific accusations of Jewish control, over the movies or otherwise. But what it does do is articulate an influential, reformist agenda evident in subsequent articulations of the Hollywood Question. Crafts's biography gives some clues to certain shared characteristics of those who would later adhere to the Hollywood Question. Like so many later depression-era advocates of the Question, Crafts grew up in the proverbial American small town. A Methodist minister "of Puritan stock," Crafts was born in Fryburg, Maine. After serving as pastor for various churches throughout Massachusetts and New Hampshire, Crafts moved to Brooklyn, New York, where he founded the American Sabbath Union in 1889. The organization pushed for Sunday blue laws. Six years later, he founded the Reform Bureau, which later became the International Reform Bureau and served as one of the leading

Protestant voices calling for federal censorship and regulation of motion pictures.[111] According to the historian Charles Matthew Feldman, Crafts authored the original draft of a 1914 bill to create a Federal Motion Picture Commission. Together with the Reverend William Sheafe Chase, an Episcopalian and fellow Brooklyn minister who had pressed Mayor McClellan to shut down the nickelodeons back in 1909, the two frequently represented the Reform Bureau before Congress and were the guiding force behind the 1914 bill. [112]

These hearings, conducted before the House Committee on Education, represented a Protestant old-line approach to the Hollywood Question. Unlike later, largely Catholic grass-roots efforts to push for industry self-censorship, this approach vested its faith in government to legislate morality. Because the Supreme Court had established that motion pictures were "a business, pure and simple," Crafts, in his opening testimony before the committee, could argue that the Reform Bureau's efforts were one of "regulation" rather than "censorship." The proposed Federal Motion Picture Commission, Crafts argued, would treat film as a form of "interstate-commerce." Drawing a parallel to "pure-food" laws, Crafts explained why film required very different treatment from the small-town traveling theater troupe. "A motion-picture film is a tangible, finished product," Crafts told the committee, "which is intended for interstate commerce and can be judged once and for all. But a drama is in the memories of the traveling actors, who may give it very differently in different communities. The spoken drama should therefore be left to the mayor or some other local guardian of morals."[113]

In subsequent hearings, however, the push for federal regulation met with sustained resistance. In testimony before a 1916 hearing on proposed federal censorship, Rabbi A. H. Simon of Washington, D.C., spoke against the bill. When movies "first held us up to ridicule," Simon recalls, "we did not come to Congress." Instead, he claims, they organized B'nai B'rith.[114] Disapproving of using government to legislate morality, Simon notes that, under the proposed legislation, Jews would remain "compelled to bow and bend and scrape and humble ourselves, and come before the Federal board of Congress and say, 'Please, Mr. Congressman, do not let these movie men make fools of us and traduce our character.'"[115]

Simon's response, however, misrepresents the origins of both B'nai B'rith and its adjunct Anti-Defamation League. Formed in 1843, the B'nai B'rith functioned as a fraternal organization whose default constituency consisted of German-born Jews. The organization belonged to liberalizing nineteenth century trends in American Jewry, before the great waves of Eastern European immigration. The Reform Movement of American Judaism emphasized the importance of amending and revising Jewish tradition as a way to facilitate assimilation. B'nai B'rith offered a secular alternative to other brotherhoods and lodges that still allowed Jewish men to maintain a religious identity. Its later formation of the Anti-Defamation League in 1909 continued this interest in maintaining a Jewish presence within secular life. Unlike B'nai B'rith's initial mission, however, the Anti-Defamation League manifested a very different kind of Jewish presence in the public sphere. Rather than offering a secularized religious identity, the league actively sought to combat anti-Semitism in American public life. Such efforts remained consistent with the tenets of Reform Judaism, which strove for greater Jewish participation within the public sphere.

Opposition to Protestant censorship efforts was not unique to Reform Judaism. Even the Ku Klux Klan's newspaper *The Searchlight* belittled these efforts. "Censorship of the movies, of the drama and the stage in general already exists in sufficiency in the minds of the leaders of American thought," one 1922 editorial states. "The dispenser of salacious and immoral pictures will not be patronized, because the best people do not want this kind of a thing, and the best persons of a community are the leaders of thought."[116]

Whether or not Protestants supported federal censorship, though, they consistently criticized what they saw as an ethnically motivated cinematic attack upon traditional Christian values. "For a long time," the Klan newspaper claimed nearly a year later, "Protestant clergy and laity" have known of "a deliberate attempt" on the part of "certain Jew picture show magnates to send out pictures for the purpose of bringing into contempt and ridicule the Protestant ministry of the land."[117] The notion that movies were mocking Protestant leaders later sustained national censorship efforts. In a 1926 federal hearing, Georgia Representative W. B. Upshaw testified that "the god-fearing, law-abiding masses of America are getting righteously tired" of "insidious" cinematic "reflections on Christian ministers and on the essence and spirit of vital Christianity."[118]

Praised by *The Searchlight* for defending the Klan, William Sheafe Chase, like Crafts, was a leading voice within moral reform efforts to censor and regulate motion pictures. [119] Unlike Crafts, however, Chase overtly articulated an argument of ethnic agency and control that was highly compatible with Klan anti-Semitism. Superintendent of the International Reform Federation and president of the "aggressive, militant, moral reform organization," the New York Civic League, Chase was one of the founding members of the Federal Motion Picture Council.[120] In testimony given before Congress, he would often address his remarks to the "Patriotic Gentile Americans."[121] His 1922 *Catechism on Motion Pictures in Inter-State Commerce* is not simply an attack on Jews but a justification for moral reform of the movies based upon deep-seated assumptions concerning ethnic agency.

In it Chase characterizes the threat of motion pictures by defining them as a form of "inter-state business" that is "dangerous to morals and to politics" and is engaged in an "attack upon Free Government."[122] Film "exploits and commercializes the lowest vices" and "appeals to the baser passions of youth. It has an ignorant and unalterable conviction that motion pictures must be either vulgar or stupid." By making an "appeal, through indecency and immorality, to the baser passions and obsessions of the lower human nature," motion pictures ultimately produce a "sterility of genius, paucity of ideas and poverty of feeling on the part of authors and directors." This results "in an increasing number of low-grade motion pictures" that constitute "the grave-yard of dramatic art and business."[123]

Using antitrust rhetoric to justify federal intervention, Chase argues that an unregulated film industry is a much greater threat than federal regulation. "Uncontrolled big business, in the hands of a few unmoral men," he writes, constitutes "a new species of King." That film industry executives are seeking "monarchial power in the name of personal liberty" is, in fact, "the chief enemy of freedom." Chase calls upon "loyal patriots, trusting in liberty established by law," to "vigorously resist such insidious enemies of mankind and of established Government."[124]

By differentiating morality from an all-powerful commercial instinct, Chase can then easily characterize Jews as "enemies of mankind" and "established Government." The characterization is pure Hollywood Question; it is even posed as a question, with an already encoded answer. "What ground is there," he asks, "for thinking that the motion picture industry is in the despotic control of four or five Hebrews?" As he names names – Lasky, Loew, Fox, Zukor, and Laemmle – he has already answered his own question. By invoking the Hollywood Question, he has thus defined out the space within which to link ethnic agency to motion pictures.[125]

In subsequent editions of the book, Chase blamed Jewish movie moguls for the failure of a 1922 Massachusetts referendum calling for the creation of a state censorship board. Hays and the MPPDA were major forces in defeating this referendum by more than a two-to-one margin. Hays was later able to use this case to convince other states not to enact censorship legislation. [126] Chase was also able to capitalize upon this defeat, pasting an addendum into all of his books. The downfall of the referendum, according to this addendum, "demonstrated the political influence of the movie trust, composed of five or six New York Jews, over the Massachusetts voters, by the assistance of Mr. Hays's political experience, through the newspapers and the publicity power of the screen. It illustrates how the movies have entered politics."[127]

As Chase suggests, the industry requires federal regulation because it uses power in ethnically motivated ways. Noting that "the few producers who control the motion pictures are all Hebrews," Chase reasons that the film industry requires regulation, just like "the railroads, banks and meat businesses" are "supervised by a Federal Commission." Ethnic agency thus poses as great a threat to American society as vital safety, financial, and health concerns. Jews have behaved as Jews in using their power over motion pictures "for selfish commercial and unpatriotic purposes." According to Chase, Jews acting as Jews have "prostituted" the industry "to corrupt government, to demoralize youth, and break down the Christian religion." So deleterious, alleged Jewish control could even harm Jews themselves. "Conditions are such," Chase warns, "that all who love and believe in the Hebrews should expose and denounce the demoralizing conduct of some of their evil leaders, and should unite to deliver the Hebrews from the power and influence of certain conspicuous Jews who are doing much to betray and demoralize their race." Should Jews appeal to the federal government for regulation of their industry, they "might begin a movement which would minimize the anti-Jewish feeling which exists in the United States."[128]

Even when Chase professes that he "has absolutely no anti-Jewish spirit but a profound admiration for the real Hebrews," he still sees Jews behaving *as Jews*. For him, "Hebrews" can "occupy public offices and positions of power in the world," but only as long as they "are best qualified" for these positions. They must be "possessed by the spirit of righteousness, justice and universal brotherhood." In short, then, Jews must operate within a Christian-mandated ideal that both constructs and conceals their Jewishness.[129]

Of course, the direction of such overt anti-Semitism toward Hollywood only occasionally appeared within mass culture, at least until the early depression. But such allegations did take shape on a regular basis – and not just behind church walls. During a 1926 Congressional Hearing on a Proposed Federal Motion Picture Commission, certain leaders of Protestant reform organizations betrayed their assumptions of ethnically motivated cohesion and behavior. Mrs. Howard D. Bennett, president of the Citizens League of Maryland for Better Motion Pictures, read from an address by a Baltimore rabbi. The rabbi's speech makes reference to "our tactics" and warns that if these presumably Jewish tactics remain the same, the movies will destroy "all that humanity has valued." After finishing her recital, Bennett informed committee member Florence P. Kahn that reading the rabbi's address out loud was "for your benefit."[130]

In addition to such religiously inspired accommodation, allegations of Jewish control appeared in secular quarters as well. In 1923, mogul B. P. Schulberg complained to Adolph Zukor about a Harold Lloyd profile that had appeared in *Sunset Magazine*. The article refers to "one of the most important experiments the cinema has ever known" taking place at the Lloyd studios:

> Nowhere in the offices, on the stages or in the dressing rooms can be seen a Semitic countenance. As everybody knows, the lost tribe of Israel has turned up in the rich field of the movies. Where there is honey there are bees. But the bees buzzeth not on the Lloyd lot. Its [*sic*] just an experiment, like making cake without eggs.[131]

In his letter to Adolph Zukor, Schulberg suggests that the head of Famous Players–Lasky approach Will Hays about the matter, given Zukor's institutional clout. "We have enough antagonism from the outside and from the Crafts and Roachs of the pulpit," Schulberg writes, "without having a screen figure of importance authorizing or tolerating such views to be published."[132]

In responding to anti-Semitism, however, Hays served as only one venue. Schulberg's letter to Charles K. Field, president of *Sunset Magazine*, addresses the reference to "Israel" more directly:

> It was the so-called lost tribe of Israel that took the motion picture when it was a despised and lowly thing, and developed it and the industry surrounding it to its present high function as an art, an amusement and a business. It was the same lost tribe who represented the lost money in the early stages of development and who built the theatres throughout the country which today house pictures made by that tribe as well as Mr. Lloyd.[133]

Like the earlier manner in which *Life* had deflected charges of anti-Semitism, Field argued that there was no real cause for concern. In defending the story to the *Jewish Times and Observer*, the president of *Sunset Magazine* claimed that the reference in question was no more than an editorial oversight:

No one here realized that it would be taken as covering more than the frequent criticism of a type of men who have had much to do with the promotion of the motion picture industry and who have been considered unequal to the responsibility of making it realize its possibilities as an art. I understand "the lost tribe of Israel" to mean that particular group and not Jews as Jews.

I do not know anything about Mr. Lloyd's "experiment" further than the statement of our correspondent that he is conducting one, but I do know that none of us thought of that statement as a criticism of the Jewish people as such. I should have been the first to blue-pencil it had it struck me that way. And now that it has struck you so, I assure you I wish it had been blue-pencilled rather than even seem to suggest such a criticism. I must ask you to believe that I sincerely regret the printing of anything in *Sunset Magazine* that could fairly be taken as a "gratuitous insult at the Jewish people" or an attack upon any race or creed in general.[134]

Rather than talking solely about Jews in Hollywood, however, those who espoused the Hollywood Question more often articulated their fears in terms of the threat that movies held for a Protestant America. Georgia Representative W. B. Upshaw, who had hoped that Hays would "deliver" Hollywood from its Pharisees, testified that the movie "monopoly" had "nobody to blame but itself for arousing the militant decency of America." Upshaw claimed that in endeavoring to regulate the film industry "we are simply proposing to stand at the door of our homes, our churches, and our schools and fight back the wolves of immorality, that are crouching to destroy the hope and strength of the Nation." Using the metaphor of "seed corn" to refer to American children, Upshaw observed that only someone wanting "to produce and distribute unclean and degrading pictures" would oppose federal censorship.[135]

Such objections were clearly rooted within cultural shifts taking place at the time. Speaking in support of the 1926 measure, for example, the Reverend Dr. Clifford Gray Twombly of Lancaster, Pennsylvania, objects to "indecent, sensual dancing, and even open and lewd muscle dancing." Twombly describes the latter as "the imitation, the vile exaggerated imitation, of sexual intercourse on the part of the woman." Such dancing, according to Twombly, takes place "in the East, and that is what it is here on the motion-picture screen."[136]

Antitrust rhetoric could help frame these objections and thereby justify censorship and federal regulation. During the 1926 hearings, Dr. Charles

Scanlon, general director of the Department of Moral Welfare of the Presbyterian Church of the United States of America, read a pamphlet into the record calling for increased regulation. "We have agencies to supervise railroads, currency, banks, immigration, passports, food inspection, and many other things," Scanlon notes. "We require physicians, druggists, lawyers, teachers, ministers of the gospel, and others to have a certificate or license. Is the history of the motion picture and the character of those who are interested in it such that they are above the law or such as to warrant absolute freedom to do as they please without regard to private morals or public welfare?" Although Scanlon here omits any reference to ethnicity, he traces the threat of the movies, not to their influence, but to "a half dozen men who hold a controlling interest in one of the most, if not the most, influential enterprises in the world." The threat that they pose, like that of the Shylock Jew, is a presumably ethnic motivation "to influence and often debase the ideals and conduct of millions of people daily without restraint, regulation, or control."[137]

Such expressions of antitrust rhetoric did not go unchallenged. Lee F. Hamner, director of the Department of Recreation in the Russell Sage Foundation, noted that "the motion picture industry is not held tightly by any small group."[138] Toward the end of the hearings, Republican Representative John M. Robsion of Kentucky questioned Chase's use of the term "the Movie Trust." Asked if he had "introduced proof showing that it is a trust," Chase could only appeal to the authority of the Federal Trade Commission, claiming that it had first made the claim. "I hear you make the charge every few minutes," Robsion said, "and I wondered if you had submitted evidence establishing it as a fact."[139]

By 1934, in the midst of the Great Depression, such opposition still had not quelled the antitrust rhetoric attacking the motion picture industry – nor the Hollywood Question – friendly images of greedy, amoral movie moguls. In his opening address before the House Interstate and Foreign Commerce Committee, Wright Patman noted "the financial greed and lack of public spirit" that deceived industry leaders "into thinking that they have an inherent and artistic right to make and circulate pictures." Patman found this sense of entitlement responsible for pictures "which incite to crime and demoralize youth."[140] Drawing a parallel between the advent of the printing press and the development of motion pictures, Patman concluded, "the invention of printing quickly fell into the hands of educated people and religious people"; they consequently produced "the Gutenberg Bible and religious pamphlets." In contrast, "motion pictures early fell into the hands of those whose chief concern seems to have been to use it chiefly in the amusement field where the largest financial profit could be secured."[141]

Unlike earlier hearings, however, Jews played a more active role in supporting federal regulation and censorship efforts in these hearings. William Sheafe Chase once again testified, placing a copy of a *Christian Century* article by Fred Eastman, "Your Child and the Movies," at each committee member's desk. But the voice of Protestant reform was now also quoting Jews as one of the many religious denominations denouncing the movies. Baltimore Rabbi Edward L. Israel even spoke in support of the measure on behalf of the Maryland Citizens' League for Better Motion Pictures.[142]

If Protestant reform efforts had eschewed the overt anti-Semitism of Chase's *Catechism* in exchange for Jewish participation, these efforts nonetheless relied upon a legacy of Shylock imagery dating back to attacks upon the New York theater. The Hollywood Question, driven by an implicit anti-Semitism, was so flexible that one could even marshal the voice of Jews in support of protests against the changing visage of American culture. As the Hollywood Question began to suffuse popular culture, it also drove a metamorphosis of Protestant reform efforts. By the 1930s, these efforts were most clearly evident in a campaign against block booking and blind bidding. After World War II, the Justice Department realized these efforts in a consent decree that forced the major studios to sell off their exhibition holdings. But another religious denomination dealt the industry a much more immediate blow. The Hollywood Question not only drove Protestant calls for a federal, centralized solution to the threat of the movies; it could also be used to justify measures steeped, not in federal intervention, but in the power of smaller, more localized communities banding together under the banner of the Catholic press.

CATHOLIC WATCHDOGS

Since the early 1920s, the Catholic press had played a critical role in activating the Hollywood Question. An undated issue of the official publication of the Catholic Knights of Columbus claims that only "foreign-born Jews of the lowest sort" who controlled the film industry would stoop to "glorify crime and make heroes of seducers and heroines of prostitutes for a dollar." The editor of the Catholic *Brooklyn Tablet*, in a 9 April 1921 article, described leaders of the industry as nothing "more or less than alien ex-buttonhole makers and pressers" applying the principles of "the cloak and suit trade" to Hollywood.[143]

By 1927, these sentiments had reached a crisis point as a result of two

Hollywood films, Warner Bros.'s *Irish Hearts* and MGM's *The Callahans and the Murphys*. The Catholic press played a crucial role in articulating protests against these films within the terms of the Hollywood Question. Not only did the press use the Question to mobilize these protests; it used it to justify the violence that ensued.

Like the Protestant push for federal censorship, Catholic protests over *The Callahans and the Murphys* prompted accusations of a "Jewish Trust."[144] The film was a slapstick comedy about two feuding Irish families that relied upon numerous ethnic stereotypes. Objections to this comedy articulated two persistent themes: the victimization of the Christian woman (and by extension, society at large) and the association of Jewish control with "British propaganda."

The Gaelic American, an Irish-Catholic newspaper, vociferously objected to the Irish stereotypes in these films. Taking its cue from a 2 June 1927 negative review from a newspaper in Ireland, *The Gaelic American* called *Irish Hearts* a "vile play."[145] The article attacked Warner Bros. after it balked at withdrawing the film, instead proposing to make revisions. The newspaper noted that the "Warner Bros. are Jews" and asked if they would "caricature their own race in the atrocious manner in which they misrepresent the Irish?"[146] Objecting to stereotypes showing the Irish fighting and dancing, the newspaper accused Warner Bros. of lacking "taste or judgment" while at the same time taking "special care not to caricature their own people – the Jews."[147]

The *Gaelic American* consistently accused Jews of acting as Jews. "Jewish exploiters" were responsible for resurrecting "the stage Irishman." In its attack upon MGM's *The Callahans and the Murphys*, also released that year, the paper blamed "Jewish producers" for "specializing on plays which belittle the Irish" in a way that was "neither accidental nor spasmodic." James O'Gorman, a New York City attorney, wrote to *The Gaelic American*, announcing an all-Irish production. "It will be a great picture," the published letter states, "embodying the finest traditions of the Irish Race, in distinct contrast to the vulgar, burlesque pieces put out by Jewish producers."[148] Noting that Jews were responsible for both the MGM film and Warner Bros.'s *Irish Hearts*, the paper propounds upon Jewish–Irish relations in terms of racial motivation. "So far the Irish had no quarrel with the Jews. In fact, the two races have lived side by side in America in perfect harmony. This harmony will not survive if the theatres controlled by Jews specialize on caricaturing the Irish."[149] Jews, acting as Jews, in essence will "lose more than they will gain by caricaturing the Irish."[150]

In addition to repeatedly invoking the image of a racially motivated

"Jewish Trust," hell-bent on destroying the Irish, the Irish-American press could also link deep-seated notions concerning sex and gender to race. *The Irish World and Independent Liberator* suggested that Hollywood should confine itself to ridiculing "the Rebeccas and Marthas of their own families. If they want filth and stupidity and indecency, they needn't go out of the Ghetto to find it. If they want grotesque figures, Hester Street is full of them." The paper then promised that moviemakers were never "going to put their filthy hands on Irish women any more."[151]

The Motion Picture Producers and Distributors Association responded swiftly to such charges. Carl Milliken of the MPPDA set up a special screening of the film for an Irish delegation. The *Gaelic American*, however, did not relent in its attack. A headline condemned *The Callahans and the Murphys* as "the vilest production ever screened" and again noted that the producers for both this MGM film and Warner Bros.'s *Irish Hearts* were Jews.[152]

Protests against these films tapped into other antagonisms as well, in ways that linked a perceived Other to Jews. A reader in Boston complained of British propaganda in movies, such as shots of buildings, palaces, Houses of Parliament, Union Jack flags. "Why not have people write letters to your paper explaining what they have seen of the British propaganda in the movies," the reader asks. "This would make people more alert to the doings of the alien propagandist."[153]

Such protests could also respond, not just to movies, but to other forms of mass culture. Another reader from New York commended the paper for its "stand in bringing to the forefront the vile campaign of caricaturing our race practiced by certain movie film producers." The reader then called for a crusade against "phonographic records put on the market by the Columbia and other Companies, that have the effrontery to describe a lot of base trash as typical Irish folklore songs."[154]

As Frank Walsh has noted, the Catholic press played a critical role in inciting the public to violent anti-Semitism, using protests against Hollywood as the vehicle. One editorial even called for "direct action" against Jewish producers and theater owners. "Rotten-egg the Stage Irishman and punch the theatre manager who produces the vile thing," *The Gaelic American* inveighed. "It is the only way to get rid of him. Peaceful protests are unavailing. The theatre man and the playwright think the Irish can be insulted with impunity, and both must be taught that they are woefully mistaken."[155]

The newspaper could justify such violence by using racial discourse both to explain ethnic motivation and to link Jews to Great Britain. Accusing "rich Jews" of being "the chief supporters and purveyors of British propaganda," *The Gaelic American* capitalized on both traditional American anti-British sentiment and support for an independent Ireland. The alleged ties between Jews and the English could explain objectionable stereotypes as well. "The Stage Irishman is part of the English Propaganda, and its object is to hold the Irish Race up to contempt," the editorial continued. "No other race is treated in that way because the other races will not submit to it. If an attempt was [sic] made to hold the Jews up to contempt on the stage, every Jew in America would rise up in wrath and effectually [sic] put a stop to it. It is because the Irish take insult lying down that the brutal insults are continued." Ten years later, the charge of Jewish–British collusion would once again emerge for a very different purpose: to galvanize opposition to America entering World War II.[156]

Explaining alleged Jewish motivation in terms of race could reveal attitudes toward other perceived racial inferiors as well. After a series of violent riots took place at theaters screening *The Callahans and the Murphys*, Judge Elperin fined all nonviolent protesters and released others on bail. When one of the protesters refused to pay, Elperin reportedly had him handcuffed to a black prisoner. The judge, who was Jewish, was reviled in the Catholic press for this action, and, in Walsh's words, his Jewishness "touched on the darker side" of the controversy.[157]

By May 1928, however, *The Gaelic American* had to admit that Jews could also be offended by depictions of Jews. Widespread protests over Paramount's *King of Kings* (1927) revealed that Jews could just as easily activate the Hollywood Question as Protestants and Catholics. But few if any other religious groups protested against this film, which, having earned a domestic gross of $1.5 million, ranked as one of the all-time biggest money-makers in 1939.[158] As Patricia Erens notes, even before *King of Kings*, Hollywood films had portrayed many unflattering stereotypes of Jews, particularly throughout the teens and twenties, and despite Jewish participation within the industry.[159] And perhaps even more significant, at least by 1923 the B'nai B'rith Anti-Defamation League was active in protesting Jewish stereotypes in films. In the process, even Jews themselves could perpetuate the Hollywood Question. In a 1923 article for *Forum*, Joseph Levenson made passing reference to the fact that objectionable "Jewish pictures" were being made by "Jewish motion picture concerns."[160]

Especially in the silent era, one could look at Jewish images in radically different ways. While most Jews tended to live in or near urban areas, the German-Jewish community and Eastern European immigrants represented completely different demographics. An urban immigrant audience might appreciate the opportunity to laugh at stereotypes in a knowing and self-referential manner. Awareness that others were laughing *at* one's group, however, might result in a very different reading of a stereotype. If a slapstick series like *Potash and Perlmutter* remained phenomenally popular with Jewish audiences, why the sudden protest against Jewish stereotypes? Perhaps this rise in concern signified a greater awareness of audience diversity, a fear that unlearned others might misinterpret or misuse the humor. Since such protests occurred after Irish Catholic censure, this activity also remained consistent with religious concerns about participation within the secular public sphere. In other words, just the appearance of protest could, in fact, underscore assimilationist desires. Jews protesting Jewish stereotypes could do so on the basis of denying their own ethnic specificity, instead asserting the ideal of 100 percent Americanism.

If Jewish opinion appeared less than monolithic on the subject, the discourse on race that drove the Question could still remained intact. "The citizens of Jewish blood have also complained of plays insulting to their race," *The Gaelic American* stated. "The creations of the film producers have given insult to many races, with the result that the American moving pictures [sic] industry has been injured in several countries." If Jewish protests against *King of Kings* made ethnic motivation seem relatively divided, however, another issue would successfully mobilize Catholics against Hollywood and reinvigorate the Hollywood Question. "Besides racial insults," *The Gaelic American* noted, Hollywood "pictures are coarse, vulgar and salacious."[161]

Meanwhile, many in the film industry had hoped that Cecil B. DeMille's *King of Kings*, a film about the life of Jesus, might quell protests against the perceived sacrilege and prurience of a Jewish-dominated film industry. A calculated risk, the film had the potential to alienate those who might see it as the ultimate in Jewish Hollywood's cheapening of Christianity. The film did incur wrath, but not from Christian or Catholic groups. Like *The Callahans and the Murphys*, *King of Kings* appeared at a time of heightened ethnic intolerance. In the view of many Jews, recounting the story of Christ invited anti-Jewish hatred, as traditional religious anti-Semitism advanced the notion that Jews – not Romans – had killed Christ. Pathé, the film's distributor, made some attempt to defuse the potential anti-Semitism that many feared the film would arouse. A tacked-on foreword explained that the events portrayed took place when Judea was a Roman province; hence, Jews could not be held responsible for the Crucifixion because their country was occupied by a foreign power.[162]

By late 1927, the B'nai B'rith Anti-Defamation League led a high-profile protest against *King of Kings*, which culminated in a three-page list of demands to alter and censor the film. The list argued that the film promoted invidious Jewish stereotypes and reinforced the notion that Jews had been responsible for the death of Christ. In March 1928, *The Jewish Daily Bulletin* reported that DeMille regretted having made *King of Kings*.

Waging a two-pronged defense, the MPPDA mustered support from both Jewish and Catholic groups. First, Carl Milliken contacted Senator Alfred M. Cohen to help broker an agreement between the MPPDA and the national leadership of B'nai B'rith.[163] Subsequent showings of the film were subject to everything from accompanying benevolent ministerial statements to outright censorship. For example, in 1937 when the film was shown to churches in California, two entire reels were censored. The deleted scenes included Judas accepting the bribe, his betrayal of Jesus, mob scenes, the activities of the high priest, and the Crucifixion itself. Before the film, a minister was to make a statement "completely exonerating the Jews" from any responsibility for the Crucifixion. Even these amendments did not totally allay fears that the film might incite religious hatred. Between 1937 and 1940, the National Conference of Christians and Jews tried to discourage church exhibitions of the film.[164]

Despite reaching some level of agreement with the national B'nai B'rith, the MPPDA had to contend with the organization's renegade local chapters in Denver and Omaha, which were still leading community efforts to boycott the film.[165] When an exhibitor in Denver requested that he not show the film because of local protests, the MPPDA demonstrated just how well it had learned its lesson from *The Callahans and the Murphys*. Milliken suggested that Cohen "indicate to his Jewish friends the facts regarding the negotiations and the changes made" to the film. Shoring up its Catholic support, the MPPDA also contacted Mrs. Thomas A. McGoldrick. Representing the International Federation of Catholic Alumni, McGoldrick had spoken quite forcefully in 1926 against the Upshaw bill that would have created a national censorship board. Now Milliken "arranged the usual letter" to be sent from her to "sixteen Catholic clergymen in Denver."[166]

DeMille and the MPPDA concurrently mounted a broader public relations effort for the film and, by extension, for the industry that had produced it. Publicity for the film boasted of its unique religious advisory board, which included both Christian and Jewish clergy. The MPPDA helped place articles in various newspapers across the country, including – incredibly enough – the anti-Semitic *Dearborn Independent*, published by automobile magnate Henry Ford. In his letter to MPPDA's public relations director, Jason S. Joy, Kirk Russell noted "the value of this article to the motion picture industry because of the previous critical articles which *The Dearborn Independent* printed." The article by *King of Kings* advisor the Reverend William E. Barton pleased Russell, as the MPPDA had "tried to have them print a constructive article but failed." Russell hoped that the story would keep the *Independent*'s editor "from printing any more vicious articles" attacking Jews and Hollywood. Neither this article nor Ford's 1927 retraction of anti-Semitic statements had improved the newspaper's reputation for Jew-baiting, however. Russell, in New York, had to request that the Los Angeles office of the MPPDA send him a copy of the story, because New York newsstands were still boycotting the publication.[167] That Russell could not obtain a copy of this newspaper in New York was telling. One of the most notorious invocations of the Hollywood Question, *The Dearborn Independent* editorials and their subsequent republication in *The International Jew* were perhaps the most potent response yet to the changing face of modern America.

HENRY FORD AND THE PROTOCOLS OF THE AMERICAN MIND

Perhaps it is oddly fitting that Henry Ford, credited with pioneering technologies that would so irrevocably alter the way people moved through the physical space of modern America, also played such an integral role in the formation of the Hollywood Question. Not only did Ford make transportation affordable by implementing mass-production techniques. As America was paving its transportation routes for the successors to the Model T's and A's, Henry Ford was mapping out what he called the "community mind," using his vast resources to pave the ideological routes that led to and through the Hollywood Question.

One should note that Ford did not so much invent the Hollywood Question as bring his publication empire to bear upon translating and popularizing it for a mass audience. As previous chapters have shown, anti-Semitic accusations of Jewish control were nothing new. *Life*'s theater reviews fueled the Question. Protestant moral reformers like Wilbur Crafts and Catholic groups had already couched their agendas in terms of an insidious ethnic agency. Indeed, Ford's lasting achievement for the Hollywood Question was to break down the *Protocols of the Elders of Zion* – initially, an obscure, anti-Semitic forgery from Russia – into bite-sized chunks. Taken out of context, these fragments could then serve as powerful connectors, moving people through the ideological space of modernity. The editorials that first appeared in Ford's weekly newspaper, *The Dearborn*

FIGURE 12. Henry Ford leaving the White House after a visit
with the President, 1927. Library of Congress,
National Photo Company Collection.

Independent, later appeared worldwide in *The International Jew.* This multi-volume reprint shows how the collected editorials of the *Independent* linked older traditional and individualized stereotypes to diffuse yet powerful loci of a changing America. Looking out over the tree-lined palimpsest of Main Street, U.S.A., Ford's audience could only see the faintest outlines of a complex, modern institution. Like the lines on a map, the negative space of this vision represented a great deal. This image of Hollywood, allegedly Jewish, harbinger of popular entertainment for a mass audience, charted with dramatic and lightning speed the fears and desires of an older America.

In spring 1920, a year after industrialist Henry Ford had purchased *The Dearborn Independent* for unspecified reasons, the small newspaper began running a series of articles on so-called Jewish subversion. Boris Brasol, author of *The World at the Cross Roads*, was busily promoting the *Protocols* to Ford and others. With the *Independent*'s editorials, the *Protocols* achieved new relevance. Both *The Dearborn Independent* and subsequent volumes of *The International Jew*, which reprinted articles from *The Dearborn Independent*, selected highly edited passages from the *Protocols* out of context, never once printing the original document in its entirety. By the time these editorials had been collected and reprinted, Albert Lee estimates that ten million copies of *The International Jew* reached an audience in the United States alone.[168] Mixed with fin-de-siècle Shylock stereotypes, the passages conjured up a more protean image of conspiracy. Whether or not one agrees with David Nye's contention that this mélange had little to do with Populist anti-Semitism, these attacks clearly drew upon what Nye calls "a long tradition which previously had vilified Masons and Catholics" during the 1800s.[169]

Ford's personal activities betrayed a particular brand of conservatism, what Nye calls "the rhetoric of Manichaean imagination."[170] Although Manichaeism originally referred to a variant of Christianity during the Roman Empire, its more modern connotation characterizes that religion's dualism between good and evil forces in the world. Ford certainly maintained such a worldview. Rather than supporting workers' rights to organize, Ford vigorously countered these efforts. According to a 1939 *New Masses* article by John Spivak, Ford enlisted the aid of Father Charles Coughlin and labor spy Harry Bennett to break up the United Auto Workers' union in Dearborn, Michigan, during the 1930s.[171] Such antilabor attitudes often went hand in hand with anti-Semitism. One anecdote claims that Ford had expressed his belief in Jewish world domination at a November 1915 luncheon with peace activist Rosika Schimmer.[172] *PM Magazine* recounted how at least one Ford plant displayed a sign on the gate of its parking lot. What the sign said revealed as much about the company's toleration of anti-Semitism as its toleration of a particular political outlook:

Jews Teach Communism
Jews Teach Atheism
Jews Destroy Christianity
Jews Control the Press

Jews Produce Filthy Movies
Jews Control Money[173]

Ford's *Dearborn Independent* was more than a dalliance with the world of publishing. Henry Ford forced dealerships across the country to carry the newspaper. Enunciating conservative politics through anti-Semitism, the *Independent* made the *Protocols* relevant to modern North America in three ways. First, the automobile magnate presented the notion of an international Jewish conspiracy to a mass audience. Having built a mass-production empire, Ford went on to create his own publication empire, ostensibly to promote his notion of clean living to automobile dealers and their customers. Perhaps this empire would eventually serve Ford's political ambitions. But after publishing a series of editorials on alleged Jewish control, which excerpted choice passages from the *Protocols*, Ford's publication empire set its course to expose Jewish corruption and control.

Second, Ford brought the *Protocols* to bear upon Hollywood. Since the *Protocols* referred only to the press and "amusements, games and pastimes," one had to make the document's allegations relevant to movies as well. After all, a large number of immigrant Jews had entered this new industry. And because of their popularity, movies enjoyed access to millions of American minds. By updating the *Protocols* to address the film industry, Ford made the faked document pertinent to North America in a third way: he simply lifted the rhetoric and code of anti-Semitism appearing in *Life's* theater reviews and cartoons and applied them to Hollywood.

Third, the weekly anti-Semitic editorials of *The Dearborn Independent* enunciated the Hollywood Question within a larger set of concerns. These include: alleged Jewish control of world finances through a system of debt and control of industry; alleged Jewish control of education and schools, and alleged Jewish of what the *Independent* called "the public mind." This was accomplished through both "a most complete system of allurement" and the sowing of "the seeds of disruption" through Communism, unfettered capitalism, and anarchism.[174]

The Dearborn Independent recalls the Harvard-inspired *Life's* theater reviews – not the Time-Life photojournal of the 1930s – when decrying Jewish commercialism and debasement of high culture. "It is perfectly natural," argues one 1921 editorial, "that the complete Judaization of the theater should result in its being transformed into 'the show business,' a mere matter of trade and barter. The real producers are often not culturally equipped for anything more than the baldest business." And, like *Life*, the *Independent* consistently invoked the image of the Jewish parvenu in protesting commercialism and debasement. "With their gauge of public taste," the *Independent* declared, "with their whole ideal modeled upon the ambition to pander to depravity, instead of serving legitimate needs, it is not surprising that the standards of the Theater should now be at their lowest mark."[175]

The *Independent* rejected the rags-to-riches success myth – a keystone of the American Dream as well as the legacy of Henry Ford himself – maintaining an ideological status quo of strict class divisions. Ford, after all, epitomized Horatio Alger–like success, the positive meaning of capitalist ambition. Jews, on the other hand, represented the dark flip side of this ambition, a figure informed by Shylock and Judas stereotypes, anti-immigration sentiments, and the threat of political and cultural subversion.

The notion that Jews controlled Hollywood articulated the distinction that Ford, the "self-made man," could make between his own rise and the rise of the ethnic Other. While the *Independent* held nothing against "any successful business man" who once "sold newspapers on the streets, or peddled goods from door to door, or stood in front of a clothing store hailing passers-by to inspect his stock," it deems Jews socially unworthy to serve as arbiters for mass taste. "Men who come from such employments," the newspaper noted, have "no gradations between." They have "nothing but a commercial vision of 'the show business,' can hardly be expected to understand, or, if they understand, to be sympathetic with a view of the picture drama which includes both art and morality."[176]

Such arguments often appeared in *Life*'s theater reviews. The *Independent*, however, updated and transplanted this view to Hollywood in 1921. Yet the *Independent*'s accusation of Jewish control over the media provided what was perhaps the ultimate accusation of the Jewish blight on culture: movies made live theater obsolete. "The motion picture 'industry' – and it is rightly named an 'industry' – is entirely Jewish controlled." Hollywood was "pushing its way into the legitimate theaters and crowding out human players." Gentile theater managers, already victimized by Jewish influence over the stage, now would "bow" to Jewish movies "more and more."[177]

The *Independent* asserted that Jews lacked true talent and genius. Parasites upon the Gentile mind and culture, Jews at best merely exploited what was originally Christian. "Jews did not invent the art of motion photography," one 1921 article contended.

"They have not produced any of the great artists, either writers or actors, which have furnished the screen with its material. . . . But by the singular destiny which has made the Jews the great creamskimmers of the world, the benefit of it has gone not to the originators, but to the usurpers, the exploiters." The *Independent* attributed only sets, costumes, and props to Jews. "The Jewish producer prefers to put his faith and his money in wood, canvas, paint, cloth and tinsel of which scenery and costumes are made. Wood and paint never show contempt for his sordid ideals and his betrayal of his trust."[178]

If the *Independent* drew from traditional notions of Shylock when referring to Jewish commercialism, it also privileged the *Protocols*'s perspective on conspiracy in describing the nature and scope of so-called Jewish influence. One 1920 article blamed alleged Jewish greed for the spate of poor pictures. It asked if there were a "more sinister motive behind" films that portray a newer, different kind of America: "the 'night life' of great cities," "marriage ties that do not bind," "the jazz life of the cabarets," and overall derision of "the living of sane, ordered existences such as we all once enjoyed." Other articles, such as "Jewish Jazz Becomes Our National Music" (1921), outlined a massive Jewish conspiracy:

> Whichever way you turn to trace the harmful streams of influence that flow through society, you come upon a group of Jews. In baseball corruption – a group of Jews. In exploitative finance – a group of Jews. In theatrical degeneracy – a group of Jews. In control of National war policies – a group of Jews. Absolutely dominating the wireless communications of the world – a group of Jews. In the menace of the Movies – a group of Jews. In control of the Press through business and financial pressure – a group of Jews. War profiteers, 80 per cent of them – Jews. Organizers of active opposition to Christian laws and customs – Jews. And now, in this miasma of so-called popular music, which combines weak-mindedness with every suggestion of lewdness – again Jews.

At almost every level of society, the *Independent* found Jews "at the neck of the bottle where they can absolutely control what goes to the public."[179]

The *Independent* cultivated an air of mystery when it referred to Jewish control. "The public, of course, does not see and does not know these gods before whom they pour their millions yearly," one 1921 article claims with regard to the stage, "nor does the public know from what source theatric vileness comes." Yet the *Independent* called upon its readers to recognize the control as inherently, racially Jewish. "Protests will be entirely useless," the newspaper argues, unless people realize "that behind the movies there is another group of definite oral and racial complexion."[180]

The *Independent* exploited the growing split between urban and rural communities, characterizing the Jew as "a product of city life which is found in the ghetto." To the *Independent*, "the Jews in control of the movies have no knowledge of American rural life, and therefore no feeling for it." Like every other problem it perceived, the *Independent* found "the Jewish problem in the United States . . . essentially a city problem."[181]

The *Independent* couched its fear of Jewish control in profoundly moral terms. "Reader, beware!" warns one 1921 article. "If you so much as resent the filth of the mass of the movies, you will fall under the judgment of anti-Semitism. The movies are of Jewish production. If you fight filth, the fight carries you straight into the Jewish camp because the majority of the producers are there." Often, the publication linked two or more social vices when demonizing Jews. "As soon as the Jew gained control of American liquor, we had a liquor problem with drastic consequences. As soon as the Jew gained control of the 'movies,' we had a movie problem." To the *Independent*, "the genius of that race [was] to create problems of a moral character."[182]

The *Independent* also related its moral concerns to patriotic ones. The "*idea of drink* will be maintained by means of the Jewish stage, Jewish jazz," and Jewish comedians "until somebody comes down hard upon it as being incentive of treason to the Constitution." In other words, if "a Jewish comedian" indulged in a monologue satirizing Prohibition, along with Liberty and the Pilgrims, he "openly" praised violating the Constitution of the United States.[183]

The *Independent* linked its moral and patriotic concerns to a particular vision of white racial supremacy. Americans descended from "men of the Anglo-Saxon-Celtic race. The men who came across Europe with civilization in their blood and in their destiny; the men who crossed the Atlantic and set up civilization." For the paper, any nonwhite person had eventually to subjugate him- or herself to the "men who drove west to California and north to Alaska; the men who peopled Australia and seized the gates of the world at Suez, Gibraltar and Panama; the men who opened the tropics and subdued the arctics – Anglo-Saxon men, who have given form to every government and a livelihood to every people and an ideal to every century."

In short, Anglo-Saxons were "the Ruling People, Chosen throughout the centuries to Master the world." In characterizing the threat of Jewish control, the *Independent* thus rendered the conflict as one between Anglo-Saxons and "Orientals." Jewish "Orientalism" "served as a subtle poison to dry up the sound serum of Anglo-Saxon morality." When a 1921 *Independent* article discovers that "the American feel has gone out of the Theater," it finds that "a dark, Oriental atmosphere" and "sensuality" has taken its place.[184]

The *Independent* also expressed its unique perspective on race in discussions of white aggression against blacks. "Negro outbursts and lynching," a 1921 article argues, were the results of what it called " 'nigger gin,' the product of Jewish poisoned liquor factories." In other words, Jews were behind the reason blacks committed acts justifying white violence. The *Independent* also devoted a number of articles to the evils of what it called Jewish jazz. "Jazz is a Jewish creation," one 1921 article asserts, in marked contrast to standard musicology, which traces American jazz to African music. "The mush, the slush, the sly suggestion, the abandoned sensuousness of sliding notes, are of Jewish origin." Of course, the newspaper gives African Americans some credit, characterizing so-called Jewish jazz as "monkey talk, jungle squeals, grunts and squeaks and gasps suggestive of cave love."[185]

Hardly simplistic, the *Independent*'s definition of Jewish control extended well beyond ownership. "Ownership in the newspaper business is not always synonymous with control," a 1920 editorial argues. "If you wish to know the control of the newspaper, look to its attorney and the interests he serves; look to the social connections of its chief editors; look to the advertising agents who handle the bulk of Jewish advertising." In the end, money matters little to this definition of control. The *Independent* views mass media as "a matter of *keeping certain things out of the public mind and putting certain things into it.*"[186]

The image of "Jewish manipulators of the public mind" proved to be highly captivating. One 1921 editorial invokes a vision of mapping "the community mind of whole sections of our cities" to "trace the impressions of American people, American habits and American standards which those mind-groups hold." When discussing the "millions of people crowding through the doors of the movie houses at all hours of the day and night," the *Independent* wants to know "who draws them there, who acts upon their minds while they quiescently wait in the darkened theater, and who really controls this massive bulk of human force and ideas." While the paper fears "public distrust of the Press," the result of "minority seizure of control," it also fears the very nature of mass communication. Ironically, the *Independent* does not acknowledge its own role within mass media. Instead, the newspaper never reconciles its influence with that of the rest of the mass media, allegedly controlled by Jews:

> Every night hundreds of thousands of people give from two to three hours to the Theater, every day literal [*sic*] millions of people give up from 30 minutes to two hours to the Movies; and this simply means that millions of Americans every day place themselves voluntarily

within range of Jewish ideas of life, love and labor; within range of Jewish propaganda, sometimes cleverly, sometimes clumsily concealed. This gives the Jewish masseur of the public mind all the opportunity he desires.[187]

Of course, the passage never elaborates upon how this "massaging" maintains a particularly Jewish cast. And, of course, the passage doesn't need to explain its assumption of ethnic intentionality. The idea of a Jewish masseur plays upon the perceived cultural conflict between Jewish countersubversion and a dominant Protestant elite. Judaism simply remains antithetical to the American Way.

In fact, the *Independent* feared, not just Jewish control itself, but the way in which this control lulled the American mind with its massage of new ideas. One 1922 article compares the free flow of ideas to poison gas. "Men are thinking ideas today that poison them morally, socially and economically. These ideas are as deliberately shot into society as poison gas was shot into ranks of soldiers in France. Our mental hospitality has been grossly abused, the public mind has been made a sewer." The editorial then proposes raising a "custom barrier . . . for the examination of imported ideas. Unrestricted immigration of ideas has been as bad for the American mentality as unrestricted immigration of people has been for American society." Another 1921 article fears educational reform, characterizing the threat as a racial one. "Colleges are being constantly invaded by the Jewish Idea. The sons of the Anglo-Saxon are being attacked in their very heredity. The sons of the Builders, the Makers, are being subverted to the philosophy of the destroyers."[188]

These claims did not go unanswered. At least three people brought lawsuits against Ford because of what the *Independent* had printed about Jews. In 1921, producer Morris Gest sued the *Independent* for $5 million when the paper attacked his plays. In 1924, the *Independent* began running a series of articles attacking Aaron Sapiro, founder of the National Council of Farmers' Cooperative Marketing Associations. The group purportedly represented 700,000 farmers. The organization folded within a few short years, but not before the *Independent* had sniffed a conspiracy and published a series on Sapiro and the "Jewish Exploitation of Farmers' Organizations."[189]

Whatever his managerial shortcomings, Sapiro was a well-known, respected lawyer. In 1927, he filed suit against Ford and his publishing company for libel. Ford retained Senator James A. Reed, a Missouri Democrat who would persistently argue in court that one cannot "libel a race."

In the court case, Judge Fred S. Raymond disallowed any specific mention of *The Dearborn Independent*'s promotion of *The Protocols of the Elders of Zion* and other allegations of Jewish conspiracies. After Ford survived a mysterious car accident, and after the defense alleged that a Jewish conspiracy had tampered with the jury, Judge Raymond declared a mistrial. Faced with the prospect of starting the process all over again, Ford met with Louis Marshall (then with the American Jewish Committee and later to become a Supreme Court justice) in July 1927. Marshall drafted a public retraction for Ford; Sapiro and another plaintiff, Herman Bernstein, agreed to drop both of their suits. Ford closed the offices of the *Dearborn Independent* in December of that year.[190]

Even some of those who refuted the editorials in the *Independent* still acceded to the discursive terms of the Hollywood Question. *The Jews in America*, by Burton J. Hendricks, first appeared in the Roman Catholic monthly *World's Work*. Published in 1923 by Doubleday, the book makes no secret of its response to Henry Ford's *Dearborn Independent*, the *Protocols*, and other anti-Semitica appearing at the time. But in responding to anti-Semitism, it too invokes the Hollywood Question, frequently tying Jewish involvement "in the cloak and suit trade" to other successful endeavors. Hendricks cites "their activities in the moving picture business" as one example, "for it is a business of the crassest sort." He makes much of the fact "that the Eastern Jews dominate the 'movies' just as overwhelmingly as they dominate the clothing trades." Entertaining "the American masses is provided almost exclusively by men who a few years ago were occupied in clothing them."[191]

Even while disputing charges of a Jewish conspiracy in banking, Hendricks nonetheless promulgates negative, individual stereotypes of the Jewish mogul. Discouraged writers, Hendricks charges, "must discuss their scenarios and whose critical judgment they must appease are almost exclusively ex-buttonhole makers, basters, and pressers, whose knowledge of the English language is very limited." Although "there is much discussion to-day as to what is the matter with moving pictures," Hendricks finds the problem quite obvious: "the trouble lies in the fact that they are merely one department of the cloak and suit industry."[192]

How Hendricks could reinforce anti-Semitic stereotypes even as he was ostensibly criticizing Ford's editorials exemplifies the extraordinary influence of the Hollywood Question. By the late 1920s, the Question had managed to structure an entire way of looking at ethnic agency in the motion picture industry. Capitulation to the Hollywood Question was present even in the publicity surrounding seemingly "Jewish" texts. The souvenir program for *The Jazz Singer*, for example, notes how "the Jewish race" has had a great many accomplishments in the arts and the theater.[193] The program also notes how the Warner brothers achieved success through "brains, perseverance, and honest business dealings. These men had the will to succeed and refused to allow any little tricks of fate to retard them."[194] While the program makes no specific mention of Ford's editorials, such statements have clearly assumed the discursive precepts of race, albeit in a slightly more pro-Semitic fashion. The myth of individual success – that anyone with brains, perseverance, and integrity can rise to the top – seeks to show the more positive rather than the negative racialized characteristics of Jews.

Arguably, most people will remember *The Jazz Singer* as a harbinger for the talkie film. As a narrative, however, the film typifies a particular genre, popular at the time. *The Jazz Singer* is all about getting mixed into the melting pot. Although Jewish, young Jakie Rabinowitz wishes for nothing other than to abandon the Old World and rigid ways of his father for the license and freedom afforded by American popular culture. Just as the souvenir program praises the abilities of real-life Jews, so *The Jazz Singer* touts the accomplishments of its eponymous Jew. For both fiction as well as fact, being Jewish does not have to do with practicing the religion. Rather, being Jewish is about belonging to a race, and thus cultivating racial characteristics. While the film affirms a very different conclusion from the one espoused by the *Dearborn Independent*, the same race-talk links both the movie and the newspaper's editorials. Nor was *The Jazz Singer* particularly unique in conveying this message. Although mogul Jack Warner married a non-Jew, the story of being Jewish yet acting and especially romancing in an American way had long since served as a tried-and-true formula, dating back to Israel Zangwill's 1908 play *The Melting Pot*.

Despite both Ford's retraction and these kinds of responses – or perhaps because of them – both the *Protocols* and eventually *The International Jew* survived well beyond the 1920s, informing the assumption of Jewish control over Hollywood. The *Protocols* united the accusation of Jewish control over the press with moral outrage over Jewish commercialization and debasement of high culture appearing in charges of Jewish control over the theater. The *Protocols*, responding to the rise of the popular culture, perceived a mass consciousness easily accessible and easily misled. Central to this fear of confusing a perceived single yet public mind, the *Protocols* decried any change in the status quo or any diversity in opinion, politics, or culture.

The Dearborn Independent and its *International Jew* series delivered its highly selective exegesis of the *Protocols* to a mass audience. *The International Jew* series made the *Protocols* relevant to Hollywood, transferring *Life*'s charges of Jewish control over the theater to the movies. By combining older Shylock stereotypes with the *Protocols*'s images of conspiracy and fantasies of racial supremacy, the *Dearborn Independent* helped to lay the ideological foundation supporting the accusation of Jewish control over Hollywood. Imbuing its vision of the "public mind" with individualistic moral concerns, the *Independent* depicted mass culture as an invaded body. Jews operated as an invasive Other and movies functioned as a sinister Trojan Horse for American culture. Seeking a single yet clearly ill-defined "community mind," the *Independent* could only find a consciousness shot through with so-called poisonous, new ideas. The accusation of Jewish control over Hollywood could now draw from this will to map the "community mind," constructing a new cultural topography featuring conspiracies, Shylocks, and the malignant paths of mass-mediated debasement.

Meanwhile, this uniquely American interpretation of the *Protocols* had migrated across the Atlantic to Germany. Although what occurred in that country was very different from what transpired in the United States, both the American inflection of the Hollywood Question and its promoter profoundly influenced the rise of Nazism. In the investigation following Adolf Hitler's attempted takeover of Munich in November 1923 – known as the Beer Hall Putsch – the Bavarian Diet reported that it had "long had the information that the Hitler movement was partly financed by an American anti-Semitic chief, who is Henry Ford." The report goes on to note that Hitler, imprisoned at the time, "openly boasts of Mr. Ford's support and praises Mr. Ford as a great individualist and a great anti-Semite. A photograph of Mr. Ford hangs in Herr Hitler's quarters."[195] By 1942, the Ford Motor Company had superintended the manufacture of hundreds of thousands of trucks that its German subsidiary provided to the Nazi Wehrmacht.[196]

PART 2

The Hollywood Question for a New America, 1929–1941

3

A New Deal for the Hollywood Question

"A DEEP-TONED SYMPHONY"

On the eve of the 1929 Great Depression, Will Hays, head of the Motion Picture Producers and Distributors Association, delivered a stirring address on the place of movies in an emerging, modern, and pluralistic America:

> One stands on a high mountain and sees long lines of men, women, and children moving slowly forward. They come from everywhere. They are rosy-cheeked girls from the farms, and their paler-faced sisters from the cities whose feet ache from long hours of standing behind bargain counters. There are plow boys, and sons of millionaires, and boys with the sallow cheeks of the tenements. There are old women with hands reddened and coarsened by work, and with eyes grown listless with long waiting. There are old men who hobble on crooked sticks, and children with the flash of the sun's gold in their hair and the happy laughter of innocence in their voices. There are the schoolboy, and the savant, and the man of no learning at all. There are men and women of every race and of every tongue, moving slowly forward, seeking something, seeking, searching, yearning – asking for a place to dream. All about them is the roar of the cities, the confused jangling noises of life that is hurried, rushed, propelled forward at a breathless speed. Every minute of every hour of every day they come – millions of them. And over and above them, and in front of them, attracting them on, offering that which they desire, are billions of flickering shadows – the motion picture. Who shall estimate its importance? Who shall attempt to say what it means to the world?[197]

Unlike others who had previously used similar imagery to invoke the Hollywood Question, Hays used such rhetoric to expand the Question into an even larger discourse about America itself, redirecting the discursive power of what these images of America represented. Instead of becoming victims, refugees from the American hinterland joined the urban proletariat in a vibrant melting-pot fulfillment of the American Dream. By emphasizing the "importance" and meaning of those "billions of flickering shadows" to this semidifferentiated mass, Hays was constructing an emergent hegemony of a newer, modern, and pluralistic America. His eloquence revealed how the motion picture could help to fulfill this depression-era rendering of Manifest Destiny. The movies were, for Hays, "the epitome of civilization and the quintessence of what we mean by 'America.' "[198]

According to this panegyric for a new America, there were "special reasons" why motion pictures emerged out of melting-pot culture. "America is in a very literal sense the world-state," Hays wrote:

All races, all creeds, all the manners of men that exist on the globe, are to be found here – working, sharing and developing side by side in a reasonable degree of understanding and friendship, more friendship among greater diversities of tribes and men than all the previous history of the world discloses. America's people do not speak of themselves primarily as Germans, Englishmen, Greeks or Frenchmen; as Catholics, Hebrews, Protestants, but as Americans.[199]

Of course, few American Jews would speak of themselves as Hebrews, either. Use of this term was more the result of a Gilded Age sensibility that perceived Jews as Hebrews as opposed to a more modern depiction of American Jews eager to be assimilated.

Hays argued that one could find in this diversity "the greatest single unity among all nations, because America represents a harmony of diversified interests," much like a "deep-toned symphony. Is it not possible that this very quality of harmonized diversities enabled America to express itself to the world by the creation and the development of the world's most universal method of expression – the motion picture? The nation required a method of universal expression. The motion picture is that method."[200]

While motion pictures could fulfill – or at least appear to fulfill – a powerful universal ideal, reactions to the symphony struck some rather discordant notes. In the 1928 book *Hollywood*, Jack Richmond found "gain, sordid gain" the "driving force behind" movies.[201] "Hollywood," editorial columnist Walter Lippmann wrote in 1935, "is an artistic parasite living upon the talents evoked in the healthier open competition of the older arts."[202] Lippmann's statement, made in the throes of an economic depression, represents a deeply shared concern over the universalizing power of motion pictures. For its time, Lippmann's appraisal was neither idiosyncratic nor emblematic of a particular brand of anti-Semitism; despite his use of the resonant image of a "parasite" in referring to movies, Lippmann became a staunch anti-Nazi prior to Pearl Harbor. The same power celebrated by Hays could mobilize disparate voices, including exhibitors, Protestants, Catholics, anti-Semitic demagogues, respected newspaper columnists, even Jews. Of course, these various entities gave the Hollywood Question different inflections. Nevertheless, the Question itself had become a remarkably consistent way to look at both Hollywood and the New Deal.

A NEW DEAL FOR MOTION PICTURES

Unlike other industries of the time, the film industry was remarkably successful. In 1929, Hays estimated that Hollywood permanently employed 255,000 and pumped $125 million into the economy.[203] Throughout this period, the industry was one of the few to weather the stock market crash of 1929 so successfully. During this time, it even managed to retool its studios and theaters for sound. Hollywood endured these economic crises and technological shifts, in part because it was able to consolidate its economic control. The five major studios that emerged during this time – Metro-Goldwyn-Mayer (MGM), Paramount, Radio Keith Orpheum (RKO), Twentieth Century-Fox, and Warner Bros. – developed ownership over the production, distribution, and exhibition of motion pictures. Opponents of the industry dubbed this ownership in all three areas "vertical integration." The major studios owned virtually every aspect of the business, from the resources to produce films to the means to transport them to the theaters that showed them. As a result, independent film producers faced great odds in reaching the American public, dwarfed as they were by the resources and access that the major film studios enjoyed.

The major studios also developed several strategies to maximize profits on individual films. An elaborate system of run-zone-clearance guaranteed that first-run films would initially play in prestigious theaters in select, high-end districts charging premium ticket prices. After a particular duration, the films would then proceed to successively to more remote, poorer neighborhoods or zones, where ticket prices cost less. A high-prestige picture with recognizable stars, for example, would only appear in a subsequent zone once it had completed its run in a prior one. Meanwhile, studios perfected a set of tactics ensuring that lesser-known films and stars received maximum exposure. Rather than allowing theaters to rent individual films,

FIGURE 13. Driving out the money changers in the midst of the 1931 presidential
campaign. "Yes, Columbus Did Discover America!" San Francisco, 1931.
Estate of John Gutman. Masters of Photography. Co.

the studios forced exhibitors to rent "blocks" of films. Studios would often
force theaters to "bid" on these films, sight unseen. Theater owners complained loudly that this system of block booking and blind bidding gave
too much control to the major studios and alienated theaters from local
community interests. Block booking and blind bidding, according to some
exhibitors, served the financial interests of the studios rather than those of
the American small town.

The financial success of the studios, coupled with the business practices
of a vertically integrated industry, aroused increasing regulatory concern.
As Lippmann noted in a January 1935 editorial, "the real evils of the
movies come not from too much liberty for the giants but from the destruction of real liberty by the giants." Beginning in 1928, Congress began to
investigate block booking and blind bidding and continued to do so
through the thirties. According to Kenneth G. Crawford, the MPPDA and
Hays were always able to head off efforts at legislation.[204] Then, in late

FIGURE 14. Inauguration of President Franklin Delano Roosevelt. Photo: Theodor Horydczak,
1932. Library of Congress, Theodor Horydczak Collection.

1932, presidential and congressional elections brought sweeping changes to
the role of the federal government in domestic policy. On 6 March 1933,
shortly after his inauguration, Roosevelt closed the nation's banks. Three
days later, Congress began to enact Roosevelt's broad package of fiscal and
social reforms known as the New Deal. One of its first bills, the Currency
Act of 1933, categorically resolved the gold-silver debates of the 1890s.
The act dropped the gold standard, bringing the U.S. economy in line with
international finance while giving the president broad centralized powers
over the economy. Subsequent measures making dramatic domestic and
fiscal reforms furthered this centralization. In addition, although these reforms faced oppositional skirmishes, most notably from the Supreme Court,
later legislation reenacted central Roosevelt policies concerning organized
labor. The Roosevelt administration also established foreign-policy strategy.
Beginning in 1936, the Roosevelt administration implemented a series of

essential reforms in American diplomacy, thus altering the country's long-time isolationist stance in world affairs.

Later in 1933, Congress enacted the National Industrial Recovery Act (NIRA), which set out to stimulate economic growth while lowering unemployment. The act created the National Recovery Administration (NRA), headed by General Hugh S. Johnson. Denoted by a symbolic bold blue eagle, the NRA drew up hundreds of fair-practice codes for all industries, including motion pictures. Meanwhile, the Roosevelt administration worked to strengthen labor conditions. In 1935, Roosevelt signed the Emergency Relief Appropriation Act, creating the Works Progress Administration (WPA) and providing work for millions of unemployed Americans. Later that year, the president backed the National Labor Relations Act (sponsored by Senator Robert Wagner), which codified workers' rights to organize, unionize, and collectively bargain. With these and other reforms, Roosevelt won reelection by a landslide in 1936. Democrats won races in every state except Vermont and Maine. Southern Democrats, progressives, and extreme conservatives – opposed to some or all of the New Deal – could not overcome the popular mandate for Roosevelt's slate of economic and social reforms.

Most of the NIRA reforms foundered when the Supreme Court struck down the act in 1935. At the urging of President Roosevelt, however, Congress continued to investigate the increasing concentration of power in American business. Concern over this concentration of power implicated all industry, not just Hollywood. In his 29 April 1938 directive, Roosevelt appealed to Congress to study the problem. "The liberty of democracy," Roosevelt noted in his opening letter to Congress, "is not safe if the people tolerate the growth of private power to a point where it becomes stronger than their democratic state itself."[205] Such sentiments continued a long-standing American suspicion of powerful private interests. The Temporary National Economic Committee (TNEC) issued scores of reports on every sector of industry, including motion pictures. Yet, unlike other heavy and light industries, according to David Lynch, the TNEC never discussed the film industry, only issuing a report authored by Daniel Bertrand.[206]

Throughout the 1930s, the Hollywood Question nonetheless resonated with larger antitrust concerns. In September 1933, the NRA held public hearings in Washington, D.C., on proposed reforms for the motion picture industry. According to Daniel Bertrand, "many controversial subjects were thoroughly discussed at the hearings."[207] General Hugh Johnson chose Sol A. Rosenblatt, a high-profile New York City attorney, to investigate the practices of the motion picture industry for the National Recovery Act.

FIGURE 15. Franklin Delano Roosevelt, 1933. Library of Congress,
Prints and Photographs Division.

Rosenblatt assimilated these controversies into his report to Johnson.
While the charges against the industry – mainly excessive salaries for
executives and stars and unfair business practices – were not anti-Semitic
in and of themselves, they did resonate with older, traditional Jewish
stereotypes. In one instance, Rosenblatt even attempted to investigate
industry nepotism – a charge traditionally leveled against Jews. Although
Rosenblatt's office gathered this data, he explained that he did not attempt
to tabulate it. The data offered "an incomplete picture" that "would not
substantiate true conditions, nor serve as a basis for fair and equitable
conclusions."[208]

Later that year, Johnson tried to persuade A. Lawrence Lowell, president
of Harvard, to head the NRA's Motion Picture Code of Fair Competition.

Unlike the Roman Catholic–inspired Production Code Administration, the NRA Code of Fair Competition meant to reform the industry's business practices as opposed to screen images. In terms of the Hollywood Question, Lowell was an inspired choice. He had implemented a quota system limiting the number of Jewish students who could attend Harvard. As head of the Motion Picture Research Council, he was also a vocal critic of the motion picture industry.[209] He would have been able to draw together disparate groups such as educators, Protestant reformers, and exhibitors to work under the aegis of a political administration highly sympathetic to Hollywood. Lowell, however, declined Johnson's offer. Linking traditional antitrust rhetoric to a preoccupation with the community mind, Lowell stated that under no circumstances would he work with the film industry. According to the college president, "five large producing companies" had "by their business methods . . . obtained a controlling grip upon the business and . . . put forth upon the community any films that they please."[210]

Lowell had articulated what was to become a constant refrain in attacks upon the film industry. In testimony before the 1936 Senate hearings on block booking and blind bidding, Stephen P. Cabot, the attorney for the Motion Picture Research Council, argued that Hollywood took "away the freedom of our New England towns." Cabot cited blind bidding and block booking as a "constant threat and danger dictated by this great industry in Hollywood, in being able to dictate to and tell a community 3,000 miles away what it shall see."[211] The council, which Cabot represented, had denounced the movies before. In the early 1930s, it had conducted an influential series of studies called the Payne Fund. These studies attempted to determine the influence of movies on children. Yet children were not the exclusive concern of this council. In articulating its anxiety over the vulnerable small town, the council engaged in a discourse that resonated with the concerns of the Hollywood Question. As Garth Jowett, Ian Jarvie, and Kathryn Fuller contend in their history of the Motion Picture Research Council's Payne Fund studies on movies and children, a fear of direct effects of the media girded the studies' approach.[212]

The Hollywood Question reverberated throughout the 1938 and 1939 Senate Interstate and Foreign Commerce Committee hearings on blind bidding and block booking. Sponsored by Matthew Neely of West Virginia and Samuel B. Pettengill of Indiana, the Neely-Pettengill Hearings were the decade's most sustained legislative attack on the industry. Publicizing the studios' monopolistic activities, the hearings posed more of a threat than previous investigations into blind bidding and block booking, according to Kenneth G. Crawford, because they unified exhibitors with reform organizations.[213] Neely made no secret of his religious affiliation. According to Crawford, the West Virginia senator once compared the "Motion Picture Trust opposition lobbyists" to "locusts and lice" overrunning Washington like they "overran the land of Egypt in the days of Pharaoh the King."[214]

Helping to give these hearings added momentum, the Department of Treasury released motion picture salaries for 1937 to both the public and Congress. To a nation in the throes of an economic depression, such wealth seemed inconceivable. Of the sixty-three people earning $200,000 or more, movie personnel accounted for forty. One witness, reading from the report, testified to the committee that at $1.3 million, Louis B. Mayer was the highest-paid employee in the country, earning "more salary in 1937 than all members of the United States Senate combined."[215]

For many speaking on behalf of the Neely-Pettengill bill, Hollywood and its disproportionate wealth represented the schism between urban and rural America. Exhibitor F. J. Daugherty complained of having to run MGM films such as *Romeo and Juliet* (1936), *Conquest* (1937), *The Emperor's Candlesticks* (1937), and *Parnell* (1937) at his Palace Theater in Helena, Arkansas. "These are big-town pictures and were never made for small situations, and we lost plenty of money on them." Hollywood was trying to foist the city on the country, and getting rich in the process. With the arguable exception of *Romeo and Juliet*, none of these films did particularly well at the box office in either the city or the country. The distinction between city and country served as the vehicle to protest the practice of block booking by MGM.

Exhibitor letters in support of the bill consistently depict "the little man" struggling against a massive, wealthy, and omnipotent foe. Dan Thornburg of West Hollywood opined how "the Will Hays crowd seem to always confuse any issue which will benefit the public or the little-theater man. This crowd has the money to buy anything they want. They have always been able to influence enough legislators to get what they want. They do the same thing in the courts."[216]

The majority of these letters pointedly make reference to Hollywood's centralized control in a manner recalling earlier Populist and antitrust rhetoric. Harry Fried of the Bryn Mawr Seville Theater described the producers as a "dictatorship." Alex Schreiber, president of Associated Theatres, Inc. in Detroit, depicted the "Producers Trust" as a "monster" with "claws." Al Bang of the Brainerd Theater Co. in Brainerd, Minnesota, compared the producers to "octopuses" who would not let theater owners run business in "our own way." Bunchie Stevens of the Berger Amusement Co. in Bemidji, Minnesota, complained of "Wall Street combines."[217]

In this testimony, the Hollywood Question thinly veiled commentary upon the plight of European Jews. Some made overt comparisons between Hollywood and Nazism. F. J. Daugherty accused the studios of using tactics "to get the last dime" that "would not be tolerated by Hitler."[218] Mary Bannerman, legislative chair of the Motion Picture Research Council and the Washington, D.C.–based National Congress of Parents and Teachers, deemed "a more appropriate cloak for such trade practices" to "be the swastika."[219] Drawing parallels between Nazism and the film industry carried the veneer of a sophisticated irony given the perception of ethnic motivation behind every studio business practice. No letter writer or witness advocating federal reform ever attempted to draw a parallel between the movie moguls and the robber barons of the industrial age. The film industry simply followed the example set by the Carnegies, the Rockefellers, and the Fiskes. That Hitler served as the analogue, as opposed to the early capitalists, reveals the extent to which one can avoid recognizing monopoly capitalism and at the same time intently focus upon alleged ethnic motivation.

Others were slightly more circumspect, but the link between Hollywood and the plight of European Jews clearly remained evident in a number of statements. James C. Quinn, writing on behalf of the American Federation of Theaters, surmised that "if the legislators of the Nation could only get a clear view, a behind-the-scenes view" of Hollywood, they would see "the danger of leaving in the hands of Hollywood's Big Eight." The studios use their "compulsory block-booking power for propaganda, political, racial, religious, and so forth." The real dictator, Quinn implied, was not overseas; rather, the dictatorship resided in Hollywood and used events in Europe to sow discord. Legislators, Quinn implored, should "not rest until they had done everything in their power to remove the temptation from those who have consistently demonstrated that they place personal profit ahead of the common good." At the end of the letter, Quinn notes that "130,000,000 people are told what the Big Eight will permit them to see. Talk about dictatorships!"[220]

Fear of such overwhelming control recalled an earlier Protestant preoccupation with the savaging of the public mind. The influence of Protestant reform efforts is evident. At one point, Mary Bannerman cited scores of articles from two Protestant publications, the Episcopalian *Churchman* and *Christian Century*.[221] Unlike Catholic reform efforts bent on shaping the community morality, however, Bannerman's argument hinged on what Hollywood would do to the national character in creating "homogeneous robots with standardized tastes all guided from and by" the centralized film industry. "Waving the flag, and singing the Star-Spangled Banner while attempting to justify such monopolistic-trade practices as compulsory block booking and blind selling do not spell democracy."[222]

The thinly veiled fear of a Jewish plutocracy destroying a Protestant democracy continued into 1940 hearings on the Neely-Pettengill bill. Mary R. Carver, representing the Council of Women for Home Missions in Washington, D.C., distinguished "the Christian women of America" who "work to create the spirit of good will among the peoples of various races in our own country and between nations." Motion pictures, on the other hand, "do not encourage such a spirit but tend to create misunderstanding." For Carver, "the present system is fundamentally undemocratic," since "one group" is "able to nearly dictate the policies of the whole industry, as is true with motion pictures," thus undermining "the ideals of democracy which we still claim to cherish in the United States."[223]

Although the Neely legislation passed the Senate Interstate and Foreign Commerce Committee in 1939 on a 46 to 28 vote, it did not reach the House in time for a vote.[224] When the hearings reconvened in 1940, some legislators had begun to challenge the Protestant metonym of community as nation. Mary T. Bannerman, now speaking as chair of the National Committee for the Legislation to Abolish Compulsory Block Booking and Blind Selling of Motion Pictures, argued that "community taste throughout the Nation is above Hollywood's taste."[225] Representative Martin J. Kennedy of New York challenged Bannerman. How would one "find the community spirit in a city like New York or Chicago?" Kennedy asked.[226] Communities, Bannerman contended, built around public schools. Here was the schism between a modern, urban America and the more rural, traditional small-town confederation. "We are dealing with millions," Kennedy asserted, "and you are talking about hundreds." Bannerman was not so concerned about the "producer-controlled theaters" in the urban downtown areas. "The big cities do not need so much help. They are pretty well taken care of."[227]

The debate – really a set of competing visions to render the demographic topography of the United States – had hardly just begun. As the Neely-Pettengill bill had shown, the Hollywood Question could galvanize this competition. Moreover, while the bill's momentum ultimately petered out in Congress, its central concerns with undue media power and influence would vigorously return to public discourse. In 1941, the same Senate committee that had considered the Neely-Pettengill bill opened its hearings on motion picture propaganda in an attempt to resuscitate federal regulation and reform of the industry.

A NEW DEAL FOR ANTI-SEMITISM

While Will Hays waxed eloquent in 1929 over the role that movies played in unifying an urban, pluralistic America, United States immigration policy had finally codified scientific racism into law. In 1924, Congress passed the Johnson-Reed Immigration Act, which used 1890 data to restrict immigration by national origin to no more than 2 percent per country. It completely banned Japanese and African immigration. The act later served as the basis for turning away 937 Jewish refugees aboard the SS *St. Louis* in 1939. Nearly all of these refugees eventually perished in concentration camps.[228]

One can interpret the Johnson-Reed Act as part of an emergent reaction against New Deal America. Although Roosevelt's initial package of economic reforms passed both House and Senate quite easily, protesting them along anti-immigration and anti-Semitic lines gave voice to an older rural and agrarian America. This America remained both opposed to centralization of political power and at odds with a modern, urban, industrial America. Louis T. McFadden, a Pennsylvania Representative, served a rural Pennsylvania district from 1915 to 1935. Nominated by both the Prohibition and Republican parties in his district, McFadden had experience with finance. Seniority, plus a stint as president of a small bank in Canton, Pennsylvania, earned him the chair of the House Committee on Banking and Finance. In a 1933 address to Congress, McFadden claimed that Roosevelt's New Deal would force "Americans to pay tribute to foreign rulers and potentates." Urging Congress to "take back this country or perish in the attempt," McFadden implored his fellow members to "let this be our own country again." The Representative presented the vote as a choice between serving "God or Mammon." The decision pitted a "defense of the faith of our fathers" against "the money changers who have unlawfully taken all our gold and lawful money into their own possession."[229]

The accusation of Jewish control over finances, the press, and the presidency played an important role in McFadden's image of a besieged America. When he spoke of "the money changers" and "Mammon," he was referring to Jews. The Democratic administration had "given the gold and lawful money of the country to the international money Jews of [*sic*] whom Franklin D. Roosevelt is familiar." McFadden went on to cite a passage from *The Protocols of the Elders of Zion* reprinted in *The Dearborn Independent*. In 1933, he was the first member of Congress to do so. Asking whether the "predictions" in the *Protocols* had "come to pass," McFadden warned of the situation "in the United States today," wondering if "Gentiles" would "have the slips of paper while the Jews have the gold and lawful money." Roosevelt's New Deal was no less than "a bill specifically designed and written by the Jewish international money changers themselves in order to perpetuate their power."[230]

A few weeks later, McFadden railed against a bill that would have allowed "200,000 unwanted Communistic Jews in Germany" to immigrate to this country. "There is no real persecution of Jews in Germany," McFadden told Congress, "but there has been a pretended persecution of them." The "Warburgs, the Mendelssohns and the Rothschilds" were "on the best of terms" with Hitler. "We would be very foolish," warned McFadden, "to allow Germany to dump her unwanted Jewish population on the United States."[231]

Before the Russian Revolution, McFadden argued, Americans had "allowed" Jews "to come in here and to take the bread out of the mouths of our own American citizens." These Jews would then return to Russia, where they would claim land as American citizens. According to the Representative, "disorders occurred and were exploited in the American press." While Jews sowed discord in Russia, "a shameless campaign of lying was conducted here, and large sums of money were spent to make the general American public believe that the Jews in Russia were a simple and guileless folk." The turbulence of world politics resulted from "control of the organs of American publicity," which lulled Americans into believing "Russian Jews and 'Yankee' Jews were being persecuted in Russia." The international Jewish bankers, McFadden announced, had hoped that their propaganda would foment war between England and Russia.[232]

To McFadden, international Jewish bankers lurked behind every industrial and political change in America and the world. "The United States should remember George Washington's advice," McFadden warned as he invoked the American patriarch. The country should steel itself against "the Jewish international bankers" who were trying "to drive it into another war."[233] Jacob Schiff was "the agent of certain foreign money lenders. His mission was to get control of American railroads. This man was a Jew." Once he had "made a great deal of money here for himself and for the Jewish money lenders of London," Schiff "began to give orders to the Presidents." McFadden did not "blame him for being a Jew," however. He did "blame him for being a trouble maker." Banker Max Warburg provided Leon Trotsky with the necessary credit to "finance the seizure of the Russian revolution by the international Jewish bankers." McFadden attacked the Roosevelt administration along antilabor lines as well. Frances Perkins, secretary of labor and the first woman appointed to a cabinet-level position, had to be "an old hand with the international Jewish bankers. If she were not, she would not be here in a Jewish-controlled administration."[234]

Of course, McFadden failed to provide any evidence of a rate of recidivism among Russian Jewish immigrants. Nor did he mention the legal restrictions barring Jews from owning land in Russia. To him, a campaign of Jewish lies explained away pogroms and the anti-Semitism of the Nazi state. Such obvious fallacies and crude invectives against international Jewish banking had little appeal. Following a McFadden missive, Cyrus Adler, president of the American Jewish Congress, immediately dispatched a letter to the House debunking the *Protocols* as a forgery. Adler's letter was promptly read into the record. Samuel Dickstein, Representative for New York's Lower East Side and the initial force behind the House Un-American Activities Committee, said of McFadden that he had never seen "such stupid ignorance." No one came to the Pennsylvania Republican's defense; a year later, he lost his House seat to a New Deal Democrat.[235]

However, McFadden did articulate a nascent theme that would later emerge amid the great debate over whether the United States should enter World War II. A major feature of the Hollywood Question, this proposition, when explicit, alternately helped bring about the collapse of isolationism yet drove post–World War II anti-Communism with a tacit yet relentless precision. McFadden's view that Communism and internationalism were rooted in Judaism and at odds with a traditional American national identity did not so much characterize a monolithic American attitude toward the Jew (as predict) the paths that anti-Semitic protests would take.

If McFadden had to reckon with the popularity of the New Deal, he also had to consider a divided and shifting public response to an increasingly volatile world situation. In Germany, measures barring Jews from employment, ownership, and enrollment in universities began in 1933. By 1935, the government had enacted the Nuremberg Laws, classifying Jews as an inferior race. In 1938, these measures had gradually contributed to an anti-Jewish sentiment that reached its climax in the Reich's Kristallnacht. At the urging of the Nazi government and in reaction to the murder of a German diplomat by a Jewish émigré, German citizens vandalized and looted synagogues and businesses owned by Jews. Nazi Sturmabteiling (SA) units beat and murdered Jews in the streets. The Nazis eventually interred Jewish citizens in concentration camps, along with Communists and other so-called enemies of the Reich. Whereas proponents of Nazi legislation argued that restricting Jews from employment in banking, industry, and culture took the necessary steps to remove an undue racial monopoly on

German society, defending Nazi violence proved more difficult. Meanwhile, Hollywood opposition to General Francisco Franco's 1936 coup against Spain's democratically elected Republican government stirred renewed accusations of film-industry pro-Communism, as the group fighting Franco, the Loyalists, had been accused of having Communist sympathies. When Franco began openly to side with Hitler and Mussolini, the battle lines of American public opinion only grew murkier. Rather than swell support for the Loyalist cause, the alignment of Franco with other fascist dictators still did not alter the perception of Communist ties to Loyalists, especially among American Catholics. Franco, after all, supported both Church and Crown.

American popular opinion remained highly ambivalent toward world affairs during this time. Recent developments in polling techniques, for example, yielded some surprising results concerning American popular support of Nazi policies. When a January 1936 *Fortune* survey asked if "Germany will be better or worse off if it drives out the Jews," the response was uncertain. While nearly 54.6 percent of those polled said Germany would be worse off, 31.4 percent said they did not know. The highest numbers of incertitude came from the American West, where nearly half the people interviewed expressed ambivalence when faced with the question.[236]

Actual membership in the pro-Nazi German-American Bund remained relatively modest, ranging between twenty to twenty-five thousand throughout the 1930s.[237] Support for the Bund appeared to crest in February 1939, when twenty-two thousand attended a Bundist rally at Madison Square Garden.[238] The Bund operated a training camp. The leader of the organization, Fritz Kuhn, even called for members to boycott Jewish movie theaters and use the forty cents they would have spent on admission to contribute to the camp.[239]

Mass rallies and camps do not necessarily indicate widespread support. At the very least, however, the Hollywood Question did retain power for some. According to James Metcalfe, an investigator for the House Un-American Activities Committee, the Los Angeles German-American Bund was responsible for using front organizations to circulate anti-Semitic propaganda throughout Los Angeles during the 1930s. The American Nationalist Party distributed a "proclamation" calling upon the public to "BUY GENTILE! EMPLOY GENTILE! VOTE GENTILE!" The sheet warned that "your dime spent at the movies may endorse and support further Jewish attacks upon our Christian morality."[240] The use of the term "Gentile" – as opposed to "Christian" – brims with implicit meaning. Originating in Latin, the word refers to belonging to the same clan. Declarations of alleged Jewish

FIGURE 16. Los Angeles anti-Semitic leaflet from the 1930s. The Jewish Federation Council of Greater Los Angeles' Community Relations Committee Collection, Urban Archives Center, University Library, California State University, Northridge.

intrusion provided the necessary inspiration for strengthening the bonds of Christian clannishness. Another organization, called the "Anti-Communist Federation of America," distributed a poster imploring "Christian Vigilantes" to "ARISE! – BUY GENTILE – EMPLOY GENTILE – VOTE GENTILE." The leaflet singled out Hollywood for approbation.

> Boycott the movies! – Hollywood is the Sodom and Gomorrha [sic] where International Jewry controls Vice – Dope – Gambling – where young Gentile girls are raped by Jewish producers, directors, casting directors who go unpunished – The Jewish Hollywood Anti-Nazi League controls communism in the motion-picture industry – Stars, writers, and artists are compelled to pay for communistic activities.[241]

If the Hollywood Question served the interests of the German-American Bund, it did so only within the context of a much older, ultraconservative, and homegrown religious tradition. These fliers were less indicative of Nazism than they were of a uniquely American discourse. During the thirties, a number of charismatic figures emerged who articulated this discourse, amassing power and attracting new audiences through mass media like the newspaper and radio. Nonetheless, this did not preclude their demonizing the very mass media they used to articulate their protests. These religious ideologues had emerged from rural America, and all of them had vigorously condemned the mass media as emblematic of a larger and unwelcome modernity. For Father Charles Coughlin, Bob Shuler, Gerald B. Winrod, and William Dudley Pelley, the mass media, and especially Hollywood, best represented how America had changed. Departing from their idealized traditional image, these changes boded poorly for the future of this country.

Father Charles Coughlin gave his first radio broadcast in 1926. By the early 1930s one estimate placed his audience at over thirty million listeners. When CBS tried to censor Coughlin's address attacking the Versailles Treaty, the network received nearly 1,250,000 letters of protest.[242] At first reluctant to lend Roosevelt his support, Father Charles Coughlin had begun as an enthusiastic champion of the New Deal. After meeting Roosevelt in 1932, Coughlin began peppering his sermons with catchy phrases like "Roosevelt or Ruin!" or "The New Deal is Christ's Deal!" A Catholic priest, Coughlin was an important ally for Roosevelt during the 1932 election. As Alan Brinkley notes, the "Radio Priest" bridged both the rural Protestant and urban Catholic vote. In addition, Coughlin provided an important link to disaffected urban Catholics, who were hard-hit by the depression and could be readily mobilized through such organizations as the Catholic Legion of Decency. Another observer of the time argued that the New York working class formed the core of Coughlin's organization, the Christian Front.[243] Yet the Radio Priest also had unpredictable tendencies, which ultimately proved to limit his popularity. He championed 1936 presidential challenger William Lemke, a relatively unknown North Dakota congressman and ardent defender of the farmer.[244] Eventually, the Catholic Church stifled Coughlin's radio activities.

By 1935, President Roosevelt had alienated Coughlin over an old Populist issue: the monetary standard. Voicing the familiar refrain, Coughlin had urged Roosevelt to return the country to the silver standard. A 1939 series of exposés by John L. Spivak appeared in the leftist *New Masses*, demonstrating Coughlin's ties to extreme right-wing politics. One article in particular revealed how Coughlin had secretly worked with the Ford Motor Company to bust a union at one of the Ford plants. According to Spivak, in at least one meeting, anti-Semitism appeared to drive Coughlin's antilabor stance.[245]

As Coughlin's political power waned, he increasingly relied upon the Jewish Question to vent his frustration. By 1938, Coughlin was using the image of a Jewish conspiracy to vent his dissatisfaction with American mass media and the United States's shifting role in world affairs. He asked how Jews "can be so unkind to us with their admitted preeminence in banking, in press, in cinema and in radio, and with the law on their side?" Their "controlled press" veiled the nation's eyes "against the Christian blood which has run ankle deep" in Spain, purportedly spilled by Communists during the 1936 revolution. "Members of your race," Coughlin said, had devised ways to censor him from telling "America the truth." Movies parlayed "pitiless propaganda . . . upon the silver screens of our nation to deceive us." Coughlin spoke of his "fellow Jews" as "piercing the very heart of America; yes, driving in the lance to let the last drop of blood flow from the godless, lifeless corpse of our once glorious civilization."[246]

Coughlin had clearly taken up an anti-interventionist, anti-Communist stance. In a November 1938 broadcast sermon, he called Nazism "a defense mechanism against Communism." A week later, he warned of regrettable consequences "if Jews persist in supporting Communism. . . . By their failure to use the press, the radio and the banking house, where they stand so prominently, to fight Communism as vigorously as they fight Naziism [sic], the Jews invite the charge of being supporters of Communism." In his Christmas message of 25 December 1938, Coughlin railed against the "vicious propaganda, counter to that pronounced by the angels," that "sounds over radio and is multiplied in the press." Coughlin saw newspapers as "strewn with anti-Christian propaganda of the war-mongers who are concerned not with advancing the kingdom of Christ, not with promoting the teachings of Christ, but with the expectancy of profits resulting from their policy of 'non-serviam,' the policy of ill-will, the policy of Lucifer."[247]

Nevertheless, Coughlin's invocation of the Jewish Question remained a strictly marginal one. Although Opinion Research Corporation polls conducted in 1939 and 1940 on behalf of the American Jewish Committee found that 40 percent of those polled listened to Coughlin occasionally, only 6 percent admitted to listening to the Radio Priest on a regular basis. Coughlin enjoyed renown – over 90 percent of those surveyed in April 1940 recognized his name. However, according to the same survey, only 17 percent approved of what he was saying.[248] Only later would others espouse similar views perceived by Americans as emanating from the mainstream.

Unlike Coughlin, who had been born in a Canadian suburb outside Windsor, Bob Shuler was a product of rural America. Like Coughlin, however, Shuler also turned to radio to promote his ministry. Born in 1880 in the Blue Ridge Mountains of Virginia and raised in a log cabin in Tennessee, he became a Methodist preacher like his father. The younger Shuler held William Jennings Bryan and the Ku Klux Klan in high regard; Jews, Catholics, movies, jazz, liquor, and dancing provoked his withering opprobrium. In his last sermon before retiring, Shuler described himself as "a scrapper for God," and scrap he did – both legally and physically. Shuler first served as pastor at the University Methodist Church in Austin, Texas. Frequently agitating for Prohibition, "Fighting Bob" would often hold rallies on the lawn of the state capital. In 1920, he transferred to the Trinity Methodist Church in Los Angeles, where he became nationally renowned through his own publication, *Bob Shuler's Magazine*, and a radio station that he owned and operated. By 1930, Shuler had increased the church membership from a paltry nine hundred to forty-two thousand. When Mrs. Lizzie Glide, a wealthy oil heiress, gave Shuler $25,000 to buy KGEF, the station already had two hundred thousand listeners. Shuler increased this audience by nearly a hundred thousand people each year. A 1930 contest estimated that out of twenty Los Angeles radio stations, KGEF ranked as the city's fourth most popular station. The station also reached audiences throughout the Southwest.[249]

When Shuler was not busy attacking corrupt, or allegedly corrupt, public figures over the air, controversy kept him occupied. He eventually lost his radio station, fended off libel suits, and even got into fistfights. One of Fighting Bob's many targets included Hollywood Jews. In Shuler's view, "a few millionaire Jews [were] debauching the whole nation with suggestive and licentious films, in order to swell their gate receipts and practically own and dominate, control and dictate to one of the greatest cities in America." In a 1924 article, Shuler attributed his "trouble with the Jews" to his initiating a "fight on the vile and sex saturated movies of the land."[250]

Shuler did not just object to Jews or Jewish control; he objected to newer and largely urban forms of entertainment that he feared would rend apart American morality. "Isn't it horrible," he asked in 1924, "that the Jews appear to be so determined to corrupt the morals of our people. They virtually own the corrupt movie business. Four-fifths of the dance halls of America are in their hands. The road houses and cabarets that are a menace to every community which they infest are almost entirely Jew-owned." To Shuler, Jewish control merely enabled the threat from popular and mass culture to traditional America.[251]

Shuler, who had expressed concern over Rome's hunger "for the vitals of our government" during and after World War I, revamped his anti-Catholic crusade for an attack upon so-called Jewish Hollywood. In a 1927 "open letter" to the American mother, the Reverend had invoked the image of the victimized Christian female, destroyed by her own dreams of stardom and ethnic collusion. Unless the star-struck daughter "is a Jewess" or "carries the right kind of recommendations from her Priest," Shuler warned, the "young girl who you kiss goodby [sic] for Hollywood" can expect to "land in a restaurant" or "a cheap dance hall." Worst of all, portended Shuler, the child will "be forced to hire out to a dance hall at 5 cents per dance and anything she can make on the side."[252]

In 1931, the Federal Radio Commission (FRC, later to become the Federal Communications Commission) decided to hold hearings on Shuler's application for station license renewal. The Radio Act of 1927 required that broadcasters operate in the "public interest, convenience or necessity." Because the FRC had received a number of letters critical of Shuler, it would review whether Shuler's radio station was indeed serving "the public interest." By the end of the year, the FRC refused to renew Shuler's license – in part because of Shuler's provocations of various religious groups. The FRC's decision, subsequently upheld by the courts, legitimized the concept of both the "public interest" and the role of the FRC in making this determination. Not only did this case set an important precedent for media law; it foretold the increasing power of the federal government in dealing with the extreme religious right.[253]

During the 1920s and early 1930s, before facing sedition charges along with William Dudley Pelley in 1942, Gerald B. Winrod was a respected

Christian Fundamentalist leader. Born in 1900, he dropped out of school after the fifth grade. At fifteen, he edited a small paper called *Jesus Is Coming Soon*. Soon he began preaching, like his father, an ex-bartender whose conversion inspired the senior Winrod to found the Wichita (Kansas) Healing Tabernacle. By 1925, Gerald Winrod had formed the Defenders of the Christian Faith, whose mission was to stave off liberal elements within Protestantism and return to the basics, like the literal interpretation of the Bible. A year later, Winrod began *Defender* magazine. Meanwhile, the organization grew. In 1927 alone, 1,300 Kansans joined. By 1934, the Defenders boasted with some credibility of having 60,000 members.[254]

Winrod's fundamentalism responded to changes he perceived in culture and, in particular, the increasing importance of a mass-mediated, urban-oriented culture. "Billows of immorality are sweeping over the land like waves over the ocean," the *Defender* warned in 1928. "We view it on the stage and the screen, at magazine stands and in the press, in women's dress, and modern fashions, in slums and high society – *everywhere, animalism, animalism, animalism*." Meanwhile, as Winrod lobbied against teaching evolution in the public schools, he and others grew increasingly alienated from what they perceived to be a liberal Protestant "modernism."[255]

Although Winrod once accused Jews of "conspiring to inject immorality and radicalism into the movies," he had feared movies, more than Jewish control over them, as a mysterious, powerful by-product of modernity. In 1931, he had written of Hollywood drawing "several hundred thousand upturned faces to gaze daily at a screen which smells of filth, lust, vice, crime, and sex." Winrod's objection to movies, however, had gone beyond mere moral outrage. In *The Great American Home* (1935), he described "the silver screen" as possessing an "element of mystery," subjecting the mind of the viewer to an unprecedented degree of control:

> The semi-darkness of the theater, the music, the glamour, the quiet atmosphere, the flashes of light off and on the screen – all combine to produce the kind of psychological atmosphere in which a person literally loses himself. One naturally puts everything out of his mind. His attention is focused, one hundred per cent, upon what he is seeing flashing constantly in front of him.
>
> Then, later, these subconscious reactions are bound to come to the surface. And when they do, they produce all manner of abnormal results – results patterned according to the pictures which were photographed into the chemistry of the brain, into the recesses of the soul.[256]

In this passage, distress over the movies' influence upon the public mind is separate from Winrod's perception of Jews. Indeed, during the 1920s, Winrod and other Fundamentalists viewed Jews as both potential converts and, through Zionist emigration to Palestine, as harbingers of a Second Coming. By 1933, however, Winrod was championing *The Protocols of the Elders of Zion*. After brief opposition to Hitler, the evangelist announced his support of Nazism, based on his fears of Communism and a Jewish conspiracy. Like Shuler, who ran for the U.S. Senate in 1932 – shortly after he lost his radio station – Winrod also ran for the Senate in 1938. Vying for the Kansas vote, Winrod had built *Defender* circulation to 110,000. Despite the conspicuous absence of Jewish conspiracy rhetoric from his campaign, Winrod faced stiff opposition from the Reverend L. M. Birkhead, a Unitarian minister from nearby Kansas City, Missouri. Both Winrod and Birkhead had exchanged barbs since the 1920s. Birkhead represented everything that Winrod opposed. In Birkhead's 1929 *The Religion of Free Man*, the one-time Methodist suggested dropping "God out of consideration," minimized heaven and hell as little more than "fictions," and called the Bible a "gravely overrated book." In the 1930s, as Birkhead's political convictions against Nazism coalesced, the minister founded Friends of Democracy, an organization to fight indigenous American fascism. Birkhead chose Winrod as one of Friends of Democracy's first targets. After coming in third in the electoral race with 53,149 votes, Winrod publicly blamed "Jewish financial interests" for his loss. Despite Winrod's strong showing, anti-Nazi forces were gaining strength. A few years later, the federal government would prosecute both Winrod and William Dudley Pelley on sedition charges.[257]

Like both Shuler and Winrod, William Dudley Pelley faced an America increasingly at odds with his spiritual beliefs and his image of small-town wholesomeness. Born in 1890 in Massachusetts, Pelley spent his formative years in New England. His father alternated between pastorates and small businesses. By 1907, the family had moved near Syracuse, New York, where the elder Pelley launched a successful enterprise manufacturing toilet paper. As a sophomore in high school, Pelley was an avid reader, debater, and editor of the school literary magazine. He also attended YMCA lectures, where he heard William Jennings Bryan, Senator Henry Cabot Lodge, and Senator Robert M. LaFollette speak. That year, however, Pelley's father took him out of school to work at the toilet paper factory. Under protest, young Pelley acquiesced to his father's demands. He still maintained his literary interests, however. Two years later, he began editing a small paper called *The Philosopher*, espousing highly liberal positions. For example, the paper rejected patriotism and even flirted with socialism, calling Jesus "Comrade Christ." After buying and selling a series of small-town newspapers, as well as publishing a few short stories, Pelley left the United States to report on missionary work in the Far East in 1918. When World War I interrupted his work, he joined the American Red Cross, serving in Siberia. After the war, he returned to New England, where he continued to run newspapers, publish short stories, and write novels.[258]

After a brief stint in 1921 as a reporter for the *Bennington Evening Banner* in Vermont, Pelley left for Hollywood. There he wrote such films as *The Fog* (Metro, 1923), adapting his own novel; *The Sawdust Trail* (1924), a Western; and *Torment* (1924).[259] One of Pelley's short stories became a Lon Chaney vehicle called *The Shock*. As a screenwriter, Pelley's labor consciousness grew. In 1925 he pondered organizing a union for his fellow screenwriters. That year, Pelley also went to Washington, D.C., to pursue legal action after a film project on which he had worked had stalled. Historian Leo Ribuffo surmises that while there Pelley met a Justice Department official and a reporter. The two convinced Pelley of a Jewish Communist conspiracy. By 1928, suffering an emotional and mental collapse, Pelley retreated to the mountains of California, where he claimed to have had a near-death experience and a spiritual rebirth. In 1929, *American Magazine* published "My Seven Minutes in Eternity," Pelley's account of his spiritual awakening. The article, he claimed, prompted twenty thousand people to write to him describing similar near-death and rebirth experiences. Because of this widespread interest, Pelley founded his own magazine, *Liberation*, in 1930.[260]

During the 1930s, Pelley argued that Jewry served as the antithesis to Christianity. Between 1930 and 1933, *Liberation* exhibited a spiritual mélange of Christian Science, astrology, biblical prophesy, the occult, even Darwinism and atheism. During this time, Pelley intermittently discussed "International Shylocks," or "predatory cliques." Then, in 1933, Pelley announced the creation of the Silver Legion on the same day President Paul Von Hindenburg appointed Adolf Hitler to serve as Chancellor of Germany. From then on, Pelley openly supported Nazism and its mistreatment of the Jews. One observer estimated that by early 1934, the "Silver Shirts" could claim fifteen thousand members. Pelley frequently inflated such figures, however, which in turn served the paranoia of anti-Semitism quite well. Donald Strong argues that the legions of Silver Shirts were mostly comprised of former Klansmen and Protestant ministers disaffected by the depression. Even Strong had to admit, however, that economic disillusionment could not sustain this membership size. By January 1938, the Silver Shirts had dropped five thousand.[261] On the other hand, Pelley's organization certainly formed a substantial part of the German-American Bund, as Sander Diamond argues.[262]

A magazine cover from Pelley's *Liberation* articulated this depression-era alienation from modernity. "*Consider this!*" the 1939 cover reads. "A nation with stupendous resources in raw materials; completely equipped to turn these materials into consumable products; an abundance of workmen, able and willing to produce, manufacture, distribute – and consume.... *What is the mysterious force that interferes with this natural, workable process?*" The bottom caption of the page states, "the Answer is Not to Be found in the Jewish Brand of Planned Economy."[263]

Pelley had attributed economic failures to Jews since the early 1930s. In 1931, he had written that "demon" spirits lived in Jewish bodies. In 1935, he wrote that Jews maintained a "preponderance in all of our most cherished Christian institutions." Despite Jewish control over "the press, screen, and radio" and their "studious and premeditated anesthetizing of the public," he wrote in 1935, the "true American, and the Christian" would one day "find this out." In 1936, Pelley wrote of how *Golden Rubbish*, a novel "exploring ... mystical Christianity," inspired "every Jewish book reviewer" to descend "on the novel with hot picks and spiked boots." When he could, Pelley supposedly quoted from Jews to show just how much of a threat they posed to Christianity. "You make much noise and fury about undue influence in your theatres and movie palaces," reads one quotation in a 1940 issue of *Liberation*. "But what is that, compared to our staggering influence in your churches, your schools, your laws and your government?"[264]

Pelley's views on Jews remained part of his response to the changing face of America. In his 1936 autobiography *The Door to Revelation*, Pelley wrote of a consumerism that he saw encroaching upon America's spiritual center. *American Magazine*, the "spiritual institution" that had printed "My Seven Minutes in Eternity" in 1929, had become "just another magazine." Stories on "golf, motoring," and "money-grubbing" existed alongside "articles by incipient Communists, or the brashest of Jew propaganda." To Pelley, one could explain depression-era America in terms of "Dark and Sinister forces," plotting "to seize hold of, and strangle, America under an effluvia of evil." For him, Jews were behind the "best-sellers" that had "disparaged things American, or told some exaggerated exotic story of wholesome ideals gone introvert." The small town in particular had become the butt of a Jewish joke:

A very real conspiracy *was* afoot to disparage and discount the American small town, to make fun of everything American, to create a vast national dissatisfaction with American ideals and wholesome institutions. Get the Gentile millions disgusted with small-town life so that they could come to the cities where they could be controlled or polluted – that was the strategy. Not for several years did I commence to discern that book after book, film after film, that was voraciously heralded and promoted to the public, always had something in it, or extolled a motif, that was basically negative, that poked fun at everything constructive and inspirational, that brought to general attention the vapidity and asininity of American life in some aspect or another.[265]

One must also look at Pelley's invectives against Jews and Hollywood as a reflection of his disenfranchisement from the mass media. "Jews of the nation" controlled advertising and engineered "a constant daily censorship over the material put out by press and radio." If one could "control those two agencies," one could "control the thinking of a nation itself." An advertisement in *Liberation* placed control of the "screen, radio, press" with "money and credit." With almost all sectors of society "almost entirely in the hands of or controlled by Jews," the reader could not afford to be without the booklet *What Every Congressman Should Know*. Pelley especially feared what he called "Jewspapers." In 1936, he claimed, "Jewish newspaper reporters had penetrated" meetings of the Silver Shirts, and came away to "write the vilest fabrications." Jews made up "62 percent" of the American Press Association, Pelley claimed in 1938, and controlled "85 percent of the American dailies." When *Liberty Magazine* refused to publish Pelley's response to an article about him in 1940, the leader of the Silver Shirts commented on a picture of the editor of the magazine: "Good Lord, what a schnozzle!"[266]

Pelley's protests over the rise of modern media could also manifest a more traditional isolationism. The cover of a 1939 issue of *Liberation* sports a kinky-haired, pudgy Jewish stereotype entreating a virile representative of U.S. citizenry to "kill my enemies!!" The two stand atop a seemingly endless sea of papers labeled "War Propaganda." "Jewish War Plans" remain beneath the foot of "Citizenry," as the ethnic caricature brandishes a list of "Opponents of Jewish Control" that include the Axis powers.[267] Charging that "a few hundred people" controlled the movies, another article urged that movies be "broken wide open to free competition, so that anyone with real creative talent can try his hand at 'em without eating from the same gveltefische bowl with a clique of nepot[ist]ic Israelites."[268]

Pelley tended to depict American society in extremes. Gentiles constituted a monolithic sleeping giant, ready to rise up against the yoke of

Jewish media control. For the time being, however, Jews had "educated" a "great, dumb, propagandized public" with "nightly diatribes in the newspapers, written by Jews or agents for Jews." Jewish control over the movies had made the American citizen "a member of the new order of American peasantry." Jews, on the other hand, were dominators and usurpers. Unable even to acknowledge dissent over Hollywood within the Jewish community, Pelley interpreted such disagreements as yet another example of Jewish control. When a letter from the Anti-Defamation League boasted of its successful fight against Jewish film stereotypes, Pelley cited this document as proof of a Jewish conspiracy.[269]

Pelley used his experience as a screenwriter to add credibility to his accounts of a Jewish-controlled Hollywood. "I know all about Jews," Pelley wrote. "For six years I toiled in their galleys and got nothing but money." After receiving $7,500 for a script, the former writer watched in disgust as "a Jewish production crew" completely changed it. When he tried to protest, no one would listen. "Who was I," he wrote in his autobiography, "a mere author – the lowest form of life in Jewish movies – to utter my asinine protest." As "a man who did not approve of the manner in which Jews were everywhere succeeding to a petty racial tyranny," Pelley found that "no Jewish film company anywhere in the country" would distribute his films.[270]

Hollywood, according to Pelley, was destroying the American ideal. In particular, the leader of the Silver Shirts contested that the female body was a site of power to which both Hollywood and Jews posed a sexual threat. The "Owner Jew so dearly loves to touch," he wrote in 1938, the "living phalanx" of his stars' "Gentile flesh." When Pelley asks if the reader thinks him "unduly incensed," he replies that he has "seen too many Gentile maidens ravished and been unable to do anything about it. They have a concupiscent slogan in screendom, 'Don't hire till you see the whites of their thighs.'" Given the choice between a film about the life of Jesus and a sex story, according to Pelley, the Jew would choose the sex story any day. As an example, he recounts the following conversation between him and a Jewish producer:

"I'm telling you something," declared a particularly offensive little Jew to me. . . . "Ve ain't makin' it moom-pitchers about your bastard Christ nor his loafs and fishes. Vat ve vant it in moom-pitchers is *legs*. Understand me? . . . Legs! . . . Vimmin's legs! Ven ve get done vill you Christians, I guess you find out vy ve got it control of movies, and it ain't to preach no servoms in a church. I'm telling you! Better ve should put every goy girl in a whorehouse, and by gott you'll like it!"[271]

In creating his image of Hollywood Jews, Pelley alternately depicted them as either above or below him, but never as his equal. When Pelley supposedly tricked Irving Thalberg into offering Lon Chaney more money, Pelley observes that "Jews are like that ... so smart that it costs them money." When Chaney told Universal head Carl Laemmle that he wanted to play the Hunchback of Notre Dame, Pelley had reported Laemmle as crying: "What? You should do a football pitcher?" Of course, others had recounted such dialect jokes without overt reference to Jews. Yet, when such jokes associated Jews with stereotypical malapropisms, radical sensibilities, parvenu status, and humble origins, then Pelley and others were reinforcing the association between Jews and these stereotypes. Thus, when Pelley referred to Laemmle as an "ex-cloak-and-suiter," he helped to establish the term "cloak-and-suiter" to signify the Jewish parvenu.[272]

Pelley promoted the view that Jews were both Communists and capitalists. The "Hollywood Production Schedule for 1939" allows for "Communist screen features" during the week, leaving "patriotic films for Americanism" to show only on Saturday afternoon. On the other hand, Pelley associated Jews with the accumulation of wealth. *Liberation* frequently listed the salaries of Jewish film executives and stars. Why were Jews making money, Pelley argued, when the rest of the nation was in the throes of an economic depression? To further establish Jews' separate status, Pelley employed race science to underline the threat that Jewish Hollywood posed to Christian civilization. Jews were an inferior race, "the fleshpots of Hollywood," and "Oriental custodians of adolescent entertainment." For Pelley, there was "one short words [sic] for all of it – JEWS."[273]

Pelley also attracted others who had worked in Hollywood and articulated frustration with what they perceived to be Jewish control. Upon leaving MGM's publicity still department in 1937, Kenneth Alexander joined Pelley's Silver Shirts, heading their Los Angeles chapter. A year later, he wrote his own exposé of Hollywood. Although written by Alexander, the article reflects Pelley's perspective on Jews and Hollywood. Alexander used *The Protocols of the Elders of Zion* to establish the legitimacy of his argument. Extensively quoting from the forgery, Alexander adopted it "as a background against which we may throw the picture of the Jews who dominate the Hollywood movie scene." Jews "have penetrated all fields of entertainment to the point of saturation," but in Hollywood "their domination is the most complete of all."[274]

Alexander had depicted the Jew as the usurper of Christian ideas and inventions. Despite Jewish predominance in Hollywood, Alexander argued, Thomas A. Edison, "a Gentile ... was the inventor of motion pictures.

Again, we have the Gentiles who create and build – and in these days, as of old, it is the Jews who glean the benefits." To Alexander, Jews had taken jobs that rightfully belonged to Gentiles. They "pack the casts with Yiddish ham actors and female Yidds who thus take jobs away from Gentile per-formers – and assure the producers of results more Jewish than ever." Alexander, however, doubts the efficacy of boycotts like the one proposed in "A True Indictment" (1937) in cleaning up "Hollywood's movie colony filth." Instead, "an avalanche of Gentile wrath and intelligent determina-tion" must meet "the Jewish problem of America." Only when Gentiles "shovel the Jews out of the picture in all American fields" will "Gentiles of worth and competence" retake the film industry "and turn this great artistic medium into constructive channels."[275]

The few Gentiles who did work in Hollywood had no choice but to "play the besmutting Jewish game." Those who did not play found them-selves on "the dreaded OGPU [the Soviet Secret Police] kosher *Black List*." By linking the power of "a few cynical, venal and dictatorial Yiddishers" to the OGPU, Alexander had linked Jews to Communism. "This Hollywood is, in effect, already a 'Little Russia,'" Alexander writes, "fully prepared, manned and organized for the coming of the expected *United States of Soviet America*." Both their status as "Communistic" and their inability to "speak the language of our country correctly" made Jews "totally incompetent to be in charge of this greatest artistic medium." Alexander also showed a fascination for uncovering the secret identity of stars. In "Who's Who in Hollywood," he listed actors and actresses, their religion, whether married to a Jew, and their "real name." Alexander also used information from World Service, the Nazi news agency, to show that Charlie Chaplin was really a Jew whose name was Tonstein. After listing the names of producers in the "one hundred percent Jewish controlled" industry, Alexander im-plores the reader to "*find the Gentile!*" To Alexander, Jews also were sexual predators. Talent agencies, "100 percent Jewish controlled and operated," had "the pick of choice young Gentile womanhood." The victimized Chris-tian female "must pass the insolent inspection of these cynical agency Jews."[276]

By the late 1930s, Pelley's rhetoric of a combined spiritual and national disenchantment had assumed a more political cast. The leader of the Silver Shirts still viewed America as a fundamentally Christian nation. Yet he, like so many others, became increasingly opposed to Roosevelt, the policies of the New Deal, and what he once called "the camel of pagan sovietism." Not unlike the Federal Motion Picture Council, Pelley had once called for government control over radio and film in his manifesto *Chief Pelley's Silver*

Shirt Program. With the election of Roosevelt, Pelley could no longer trust any institution to be free from Jewish taint. Despite a barrage of literature that would essentially reinforce the religious and moral demonization of Hollywood, Pelley's nationalism now lay at odds with America's increasing role within world affairs. The power to determine and define "the American small town" and its "ideals and wholesome institutions," would pass, ironically enough, from the hands of men like Pelley and into the hands of Hollywood writers and producers.[277]

If the Hollywood Question could express Pelley's longing for an idealized version of traditional America, it could also effectively mark a vocal alienation from the liberal and progressive politics allegedly espoused by the film industry. For Shuler, Winrod, Pelley, and even Coughlin, the Question expressed alarm over Hollywood's perceived effect upon traditional America. Yet, at best the Question could only assist these powerful and charismatic figures in delivering a message that resonated with nostalgia for a bygone way of life. For the Protestant and especially the Catholic Church, the Hollywood Question generated a much greater momentum, leading to the institutionalization of moral and religious censorship in this country.

THE PRODUCTION CODE AS HOLLYWOOD QUESTION

As Danae Clark notes, the Production Code, the film industry's self-imposed system of censorship, maintained an integral connection to the New Deal. Initially implemented in 1930, the code experienced its spiritual rebirth when all of the major studios "reaffirmed" their commitment to it on 7 March 1933. On that day, Roosevelt declared a national bank holiday. In aligning an economic crisis with a moral crisis, the industry could effectively consolidate both its discursive and its economic power.[278] Yet in acquiescing to one of the essential tenets of the Hollywood Question – that movies were fundamentally in need of moral overhaul – the industry also had to relinquish control of film content to religious anti-Semitism.

To be sure, the concern for morality was not the exclusive domain of Protestantism or Catholicism. It appears in the film industry's Fair Practice Code, part of the contract the movie studios signed with Roosevelt's National Recovery Administration. The agreement pledges the industry's "combined strength to maintain right moral standards in the production of motion pictures as a form of entertainment." Both earlier and later Protestant-based attacks on the industry, however, made similar claims. The notion that films were "a form of entertainment" vigorously recurred in the

1941 Propaganda Hearings.[279] Ultimately, such compacts effectively staved off federal regulation. As Douglas Gomery notes, Will Hays had been able to fend off antimonopoly advances throughout the 1920s.[280] In the midst of the depression and the election of Roosevelt, however, the Republican political influence of Hays waned. Hays and the industry now faced antitrust litigation. Roosevelt's liberal attorney general, Thurman Arnold, and a powerful coalition of women's groups, religious organizations, and independent theater owners called for a ban on block booking and prohibiting studios from owning theaters.[281]

Hays, however, faced much more than just a loss of political power. Throughout the early 1930s, Protestant and Catholic organizations effectively channeled public protest. In her testimony before the Neely-Pettengill hearings, Mary Bannerman cited scores of articles from two liberal religious periodicals, the Episcopalian *Churchman* and the liberal Protestant *Christian Century*.[282] The Hollywood Question could and did inflect this popular discourse. As film historian Richard Maltby finds, a June 1929 *Churchman* article blamed "shrewd Hebrews" for selecting Will Hays "as a smoke screen to mask their meretricious methods . . . of playing to the tabloid mind."[283]

Throughout the 1930s, the *Christian Century* also continued to promulgate the view that Jews – *as Jews* – controlled Hollywood. In 1930, this official publication of the Chicago Theological Seminary ran a series on Hollywood.[284] The articles, by Fred Eastman, displayed a sophisticated understanding of the industry. Eastman, who by 1940 had become the magazine's associate editor, explained the complexities of block booking, where distributors force exhibitors to take undesirable films; and vertical integration, where the studios own the means of production, distribution, and exhibition. In "Who Controls the Movies?" Eastman flavored this analysis with an echo of traditional city hatred and hostility toward the Jewish parvenu. "The movies were born in the slums," Eastman writes. "The men who introduced them there were, for the most part, small Jewish cloak and suit merchants." To Eastman, one could use the words "Jew," "immigrant," and "merchant" interchangeably when referring to Hollywood. Estimating that "90 per cent of the upper strata of control is Jewish," Eastman stated this figure "simply as a matter of fact." He claimed to lack "the slightest prejudice against either Jews or immigrants." Both Jews and movies were products of the city. "You cannot understand the situation today," Eastman wrote, referring to his figure of 90 percent, "unless you know how it originated. America sowed the slums and reaped the movies!" Eastman's series prompted a Crawfordsville, Indiana, reader to exclaim that asking "Will Hays to stop the progress of an industry of Jews is asking too much!"[285]

A year later, *The Christian Century* published an "Open Letter" to Jews from one who was "ashamed." "I am a Jew," the alleged author writes, "but I am ashamed of my kinship with you Jews of Hollywood. I am ashamed of kinship with a people who have wholly forgotten their spiritual mission and are now engaged only in the feverish acquisition of wealth by pandering to the worst instincts of humanity." Of course, Jews hardly constituted the sole audience for such a letter. Instead, the "open letter" revealed a larger religious-spiritual crisis in which new values promulgated in mass culture had supplanted the morals and values once promoted by those who saw themselves attuned to small-town America.[286]

Less obvious invocations of the Hollywood Question in the *Christian Century* retained powerful connections to antitrust and Populist rhetoric. One editorial looks to P. S. Harrison, publisher of the exhibition trade journal *Harrison Reports*, to articulate its objections. Harrison claims that movies "are breaking down the home and destroying all the principles that fathers and mothers have been endeavoring to instill into their children. There is no vulgarity they do not teach them; they are insidious, wrecking whatever character home and school and church have been able to build in them." Worse than the producers, Hays has "protected the producers of such pictures until now they are so cynical that they laugh at his edicts."[287]

By 1934, however, the mostly Protestant push for federal censorship had stalled amid a series of congressional hearings, despite numerous censorship boards at the state and local level. Meanwhile, the Catholic Church and its lay members assumed an increasingly activist role in fighting to implement censorship. In the summer of 1933, Joseph I. Breen, public relations advisor to Will Hays, and motion picture trade publishing magnate Martin Quigley met with the Church hierarchy in Cincinnati.[288] The Legion of Decency resulted from this meeting, launching a campaign for a country-wide boycott against the movies. By April 1934, the Legion began flexing its muscle through a series of boycott pledges distributed throughout dioceses. The Catholic press played a crucial role in mobilizing support for the Legion of Decency. According to one observer, Fort Wayne's Archbishop Noll and Bishop Boyle of Pittsburgh were chosen to serve on the Legion of Decency committee because their ties to the Catholic press could "train the spotlight . . . on whatever program might be adopted."[289] Such orchestrated campaigns ultimately forced Hays to hire Breen as head of the Production Code Administration, the industry's self-censorship arm.

FIGURE 17. High hopes for the Legion of Decency from the
Catholic Press. *The Monitor*, 23 June 1934: 3.

That anti-Semitic hostility directed toward Hollywood in the Catholic press had anything but abated. Perhaps with the rise of Nazism, the Catholic hierarchy hoped, leaders of the film industry would prove more accommodating to Church demands. At an August 1933 dinner meeting arranged by Will Hays, Catholic layperson Joseph Scott "lashed into the Jews furiously," according to Joseph I. Breen, who would eventually head the industry's Production Code Administration. Grouping the studio heads together with Jewish Communists and anarchists, Scott accused Hollywood Jews of not showing enough gratitude and loyalty to America. Invoking the specter of Nazism, Scott implied that box-office returns would be the least of the studio heads' concerns if Christian forces within this country mobilized. With the exception of Samuel Goldwyn and Nicholas Schenck, the predominately Jewish studio heads reportedly gave Scott a standing ovation.[290] In another 1933 letter, the archbishop of Los Angeles, John J. Cantwell, glowed over the prospect that "Jews are afraid of things that may possibly happen in this country to them," while "Jewish control of the industry is alienating many of our people."[291] Cantwell later encouraged the idea of a Legion of Decency–sponsored screenplay contest, arguing that screenwriting was at present "largely in the hands of Jews and people without any faith." This, in Cantwell's eyes, explained the dearth of religious themes in pictures.[292]

In public, such callousness rarely appeared so overtly. Modulated to appear as a reasoned discourse, however, the Hollywood Question could still interrogate Jews as Jews. Who is "responsible" for Hollywood's "vileness and worse?" Archbishop Cantwell asks in his report to the Catholic hierarchy, ghostwritten by Breen.[293] Who made movies "serve as the instrument of debauchery of the youth of the land? The Jews? Yes – and no." Cantwell notes that "most of the producing-distributing-exhibiting companies are operated and managed, when they are not actually owned, by Jews." Estimating that "Jewish executives are the responsible men in ninety per cent of all the Hollywood studios," Cantwell argues that "it is these Jewish executives who have the final word on all scenarios before production is actually launched." If "Jewish executives" wanted "to keep the screen free from offensiveness," they could. As Jews, according to Cantwell, they chose not to do so. For Cantwell, however, Jews alone could not explain "all the filth of the pictures." Instead, they belonged to part of a system completely at odds with the traditional religious values of America. Just as Cantwell estimated that "ninety per cent" of Hollywood was in the hands of Jews, so too did he figure that "seventy-five per cent" of screenwriters were "pagans."[294]

Cantwell's report appeared in the February issue of *Ecclesiastical Review*, and Cincinnati Archbishop John T. McNicholas ordered a thousand copies distributed to churches nationwide.[295] While the article generated little response in the trade press, it did prompt a series of attacks from the Catholic popular press on the motion picture industry.[296] It also managed to raise some eyebrows in the Jewish community. According to Walsh, several community leaders wanted to condemn the article publicly but heeded subsequent advice. Carleton Hayes even warned Cantwell that he was sowing seeds similar to those sown in Germany. Cantwell stated to the Columbia University professor and cochair of the National Conference of Christians and Jews the unavoidable fact that "our Jewish neighbors" controlled the movies.[297]

Fear of such overt confrontations appeared to help shore up ostensible support of the Legion. As Paul Facey notes, many Protestant and Jewish groups supported this effort. According to one report, Jewish women in Denver delivered a thousand pledges on behalf of their Temple Sisterhood and Council.[298] Yet Jewish support of the Legion, at least from the Jewish Reform Central Conference of American Rabbis (CCAR), appeared to be driven by a concern for rising anti-Semitism. "The situation is a very serious one," wrote Rabbi Stephen S. Wise, the leading reform rabbi and founder of Hebrew Union College, "and something should be done."[299] A letter to CCAR president Samuel H. Goldenson expressed concern over "the Catholic religious press," which "has been publishing attacks upon the Jews for their association with the low standard of morals in the movie industry." The author notes that "important Jewish organizations have joined with other religious groups to decry, and protest against, the objectionable movies," but suggests that the CCAR adopt "a strong resolution . . . to which we could give wide and effective publicity."[300]

While the Legion of Decency pursued what appeared to be a massive bloc of public opinion, Catholic leadership began to pressure banks in turn to put pressure on the studios. Cardinal George Mundelein of Chicago enjoyed personal contact with Harold L. Stuart of Halsey, Stuart. According to historian Gregory Black, Mundelein rewarded Halsey, Stuart by facilitating a series of loans for an extremely lucrative client: the Vatican.[301]

In the face of such pressure, the Motion Picture Producers and Distributors Association finally offered to create a subsidiary called the Production Code Administration (PCA). The PCA would enforce a list of Hollywood do's and don'ts called the Production Code. Lay Catholic Martin I. Quigley, owner and publisher of the influential industry trade newspaper *The Motion Picture Herald*, and Daniel A. Lord, a Jesuit priest and St. Louis University professor, drafted the code in 1930. Hays ultimately hired Breen, a lay Catholic and a former reporter for *The Motion Picture Herald*, to head the Production Code office.[302] Every studio had to submit every script and film to the Production Code office for review. Films failing to conform to the code's standards faced a ban on exhibition, a hefty fine, or both.

As Gregory Black finds in *Hollywood Censored*, Breen's Roman Catholic involvement informed much of his lay activities. After he had served as Overseas Commissioner of the National Catholic Welfare Conference, the 1926 Eucharistic Congress appointed Breen head of their press relations. Under the pseudonym "Eugene Ware," he wrote a series of anti-Communist articles for the Roman Catholic *America*. Also head of public relations for the Peabody Coal Company, he dismissed a 1929 labor strike against the company as inherently Communist.[303] As evidenced by his ghostwritten report, Breen had a less than charitable view of Hollywood executives. Throughout the early 1930s, he railed against the Jews. As Walsh notes, none of the bishops or priests ever chastised Breen for his anti-Semitism in their written communications.[304] He blamed evil films and Hollywood's dissolute lifestyle on the "lousy Jews," claiming that "95 percent . . . are Eastern Jews, the scum of the earth." He pressed Bishop John J. Cantwell to "work on the American (not Jewish) bankers to bring pressure on the industry."[305] In a 1932 letter to Catholic theologian Wilfred Parsons, he called the studio heads "simply a rotten bunch of vile people with no respect for anything beyond the making of money." When Breen heard about a rabbi who "attacked Jewish movie producers" for bringing "disgrace upon the Jewish people," he made sure to share this information with Paramount producer Emanuel B. Cohen. Some months before the inception of the Legion of Decency in 1934, Breen suggested that the Philadelphia Archdiocese establish a censorship committee and appoint public prosecutors to it. According to Breen, the Church needed to take such measures because "Jewish boys" are "impressed and terrified by officials connected in any way with the police or the courts." In the letter, Breen called the Warner Bros. Philadelphia district manager "a kike Jew of the very lowest type."[306] Hollywood was "Paganism rampant and in its most virulent form." To the future head of the PCA, "these Jews seem to think of nothing but money making and sexual indulgence. . . . They are, probably, the scum of the scum of the earth."[307]

While Breen and others within the Catholic hierarchy rarely expressed such attitudes publicly, popular culture did. Throughout the 1930s, the Hollywood Question took root there. The stereotype of the Jewish movie mogul implicitly addressed crises representative of New Deal concerns. Hollywood could blandish a rags-to-riches myth, but, especially for nubile young Christian women, social mobility came at a price. The immoral, leering, hook-nosed, cigar-chomping executive became yet another enthymeme of the Hollywood Question – a lament for an older, traditional order and a protest against a newer, urban, diverse, and global one. For many surviving the crisis of the Great Depression, the movie mogul explained a great deal about what had happened and was happening to America.

4

The Hollywood Question in Popular Culture

WHAT PRICE, HOLLYWOOD QUESTION?

Hollywood ultimately invited – perhaps even required – interpretation and explanation of itself. The publicity departments of the movie studios generated apocryphal tales of larger-than-life stars and behind-the-scenes intrigue. Countless books shared "inside information" on how to break into movies, how to write for them, and how to become a star. The familiar tropes of the American Dream reverberated throughout this discourse of almost attainable success. Desired by many, only a lucky few could achieve, keep, and enjoy it. Indeed, such perceptions had some basis. Considering the industry's output and worth, Hollywood employed relatively few people, as Leo Rosten found in 1941. Approximately thirty thousand people were working in Hollywood in 1937, yet the industry supposedly ranked fourteenth of any U.S. industry in its volume of business, and eleventh in its total assets. Such discrepancy between industry size and economic stature was conspicuous, especially during an economic depression.[308]

Within popular culture, the interpretation and explanation of Hollywood – highlighting both its contradictions and its peccadilloes – consistently invoked the Question in a way that faithfully and obviously hailed heterosexual whites. While one could scrutinize the motion picture industry from a variety of subject positions, the Hollywood Question viewed America through the eyes of its whites. Nonfiction and fiction alike, religious literature, political protests from both the right and the left, voices from the mainstream and on the margins – even Hollywood movies themselves – ultimately acceded to a belief in Jewish agency. This belief – that Jews ultimately behaved as Jews – had nothing to do with the diversity and complexity of the American Jewish experience. Rather, it used the image of the Jew as a vehicle to protest mass culture and modernity.

Using this image, self-styled experts and pulp fiction authors helped audiences make sense of Tinseltown. Entertainer Oscar Levant purportedly implemented this actual nickname for Hollywood when, in the early 1940s, he prognosticated that if one were to "strip the phony tinsel off Hollywood ... you'll find the real tinsel underneath."[309] The sobriquet Tinseltown stuck, but such cynicism for Hollywood had begun well before Levant's quip. Throughout the twenties and thirties, the film industry begot a series of experts – many disgruntled – who carried with them the weight of their authority and experience, having encountered the industry either as one-time employees or as bemused journalists. Clearly constructing their own Hollywood status as a marginal one, their marginality in this setting ultimately garnered the necessary authority to interpret the film industry for white America. While insider nonfiction spoke to this white America authentically, popular fiction further naturalized this way of speaking by drawing upon it as if it were fact. Jewish Hollywood provided the necessary flavor and color, sufficiently contrasting the white Christian protagonist with the darker hues of the Oriental background.

In terms of the Hollywood Question, these articulations operated within a broader range of discursive positions. The somewhat doctrinaire accusation of a protean, partially visible Jewish conspiracy, so thoroughly developed by *The Dearborn Independent* in the 1920s, continued throughout the depression of the 1930s. In fiction and nonfiction alike, however, established stereotypes from the late nineteenth and early twentieth centuries reemerged. These stereotypes rendered Jewish agency in graspable terms, slapping a stereotyped face upon stereotyped facelessness. Movie moguls and producers were the new Shylocks: Hollywood operated as a kind of usury, and control over the culture meant a new form of exacting pounds of flesh.

The sharp profile of these alien interlopers – a profile emphasizing both physiognomy as well as behavior – provided much in the way of melodrama, comedy, and what at the time undoubtedly seemed like cultural insight. Ignorant, crass, lascivious, and unable to shed a thick, mittel-Europa pidgin, the mogul stereotype remained as relevant to earlier caricatures of the Shylock impresario and control over the theater. Nonetheless, the image of the movie mogul also possessed its own unique identity. By the 1930s, the stereotype came to represent, not just a parvenu, but a stubborn foreign influence unwilling to yield to an assimilated national identity. Unworthy of his salary, the Jewish movie mogul supposedly lined his pockets with the hard-earned money of millions of decent, American-born citizens. While he appeared to enjoy his high income, many others remained jobless. The stereotype tapped into deep Populist resentments; as the conquered millions scraped for pennies, the foreign potentate plundered their resources and ostentatiously displayed his ill-gotten wealth.

Perhaps the most notable distinction of the mogul stereotype was the older fear of ethnic conspiracy that inflected this reemergent Shylock. The Hollywood Question had always feared that control over the movies would give perceived Others access to the far reaches of a public mind. Not only did the movie executive appear unworthy of this responsibility, but his power had a sinister aspect. As America watched yet another world war engulfing Europe, some wondered whether similar events could plague the United States. Jews might push the country into war by spreading anti-German propaganda. Propaganda – a term popularized after World War I by Walter Lippmann, himself Jewish – reflected a fear of the covert influences of the mass media. The Hollywood Question thus addressed this fear of mass-media effects, locating it on the site of ethnic Jewish agency.

While not all references to movie moguls employed anti-Jewish stereotypes, not all anti-Jewish stereotypes announced their anti-Semitism. True, movie moguls often represented any foreign influence, not a particularly Jewish one. By 1930, however, both the image of the foreign parvenu and the image of the Hollywood movie mogul shared many similarities. Moral, religious, and polemic literature had already consistently expressed the belief in Jewish control over Hollywood. Terms like "immigrant" and "cloak-and-suiter" often existed interchangeably with "Jew." Although not everyone who berated or satirized the Hollywood movie mogul consciously meant to demonize Jews, such statements operated within the discursive frame of the Hollywood Question. Rarely, if ever, did any criticism of the film industry ever challenge the notion of Jewish control over the movies. The Question could always provide a powerful if unspoken discursive position from which to criticize, mock, or even praise the film industry.

Ubiquitous, the Hollywood Question occupied this position even in children's literature. As part of the Tom Swift series, a collection of adventure books for young boys, *Tom Swift and His Talking Pictures* (1928) is practically a compendium of anti-Jewish stereotypes. The story, written by Victor Appleton, depicts the heroic Swift warding off the machinations of Hollywood moguls and their anarchist proxy, Jacob Greenbaum. The Jews try to destroy Swift's invention: a television transmitter and receiver. At first, Greenbaum surreptitiously poses as a laboratory assistant in order to gain access to Swift's invention. Swift, however, does not trust this "clever Jewish inventor." For the rest of the book, the hero refers to Greenbaum as simply "the Jew." When Swift discovers this true identity, he arranges a meeting with the moguls on the suitably christened "Rattlesnake Island."

Snake imagery reinforces the long-standing association between Jews and treachery. "They say the rattlesnakes are all gone," Tom tells himself, but still worries. "Even if their bite isn't always deadly, it's bad enough." Meeting the moguls in an unlit abandoned house on the island, Tom demands that they turn on the lights, as he is "not used to doing business in the dark." One of the ever-thrifty moguls asks him why "spend a lot more money in having more electricity?"

The passage teaches a mannered ambivalence toward these Hollywood Jews. Familiar stereotypes are readily apparent. For example, although they all wear black masks, Tom feels himself "being sharply scrutinized." Yet to Greenbaum's bomb-throwing anarchist the moguls play Shylock. From "an entirely different class" than the anarchist Greenbaum, the moguls give "two or three little signs" revealing their status as "wealthy Jews." Tom suspects that "these were substantial business men – men of some culture and presumably position in the world – though they did stoop to desperate means to gain their ends." When the moguls remove their hoods, Swift sees that they are "all important figures in the theatrical and moving picture business." Moreover, although Shylock imagery plainly informs this picture of movie moguls, Tom ultimately surpasses their craftiness, cutting a tough deal and exacting what the book dubs as Tom's "pound of flesh."[310]

However, to understand this Hollywood Question for children only in terms of its Jewish stereotypes provides an incomplete picture. Appleton's depiction of the Jew emerges in sharp distinction to the book's other ethnic image, that of blacks. Swift's entourage includes Eradicate, a "faithful colored servant," who calls Swift "Massa." The book describes another domesticated savage, Koku, as never "able to master the English language." He nonetheless manages to learn his role as Swift's "faithful servant." These racist expectations of blacks emerge in sharp contrast to stereotypes of Jewish wealth. Captured by a band of Negroes on Rattlesnake Island, Swift notices that "the language of these Negroes was above the average," since "they did not talk like poor, old Eradicate. Rather their talk was that of the man who has seen service in wealthy families."[311] Apparently, Jews and their faithful servants had not learned their rightful place in the social hierarchy.

Within the mainstream, the Hollywood Question rarely posed its championing of whiteness so overtly. Nonetheless, even Hollywood could proffer the Hollywood Question, albeit with a different kind of inflection. Popular with audiences, behind-the-scenes views of show business often addressed ethnicity in some fashion. As the Great Depression began to break, *The Jazz Singer* (Warner Bros., 1927) and *Broadway Melody* (MGM, 1929) had earned 3.5 and 3 million dollars, respectively.[312] Throughout the 1920s, films like *Broadway Broke* (1923), Edward Sloman's *The Beautiful Cheat* (Universal, 1926), and *The Talk of Hollywood* (1929) featured Jewish film executives.[313] *In Hollywood with Potash and Perlmutter* (1924) even satirizes the film's producer, Samuel Goldwyn. Part of the phenomenally popular MGM series, the film made *The New York Times*'s ten-best list that year. Unlike the controversial Universal series *The Cohens and the Kellys*, which featured the comic, cross-cultural ethnic divide between the Irish and the Jews, *Potash and Perlmutter* focused on the antics of two Jewish fools. While assimilation dramas like *The Jazz Singer* gradually subdued their references to Judaism, Hollywood's depiction of its bosses bore the traces of ethnicity. As Patricia Erens observes, the cinematic representation of the movie mogul often featured a foreign-sounding name and accent. "Known facts about the studio bosses," Erens argues, encouraged one to read their characters as Jewish.[314]

In fact, a whole subgenre of films about Hollywood emerged in the 1930s for depression-era audiences. Films like *Manhattan Parade* (1931), *Movie Crazy* (1932), *The Tenderfoot* (1933), *Start Cheering* (1938), *Hollywood Cavalcade* (1939), and *Star Dust* (1940) all feature movie mogul parts, although the last film parodies Zanuck, who many incorrectly believed was Jewish.[315] Perhaps the best-known image of the mogul appears in RKO's 1932 film *What Price Hollywood?* which later served as the basis for the perennial vehicle *A Star Is Born*. Character actor Gregory Ratoff played the benevolent studio dictator Julius Saxe, a model subsequently reprised in other films depicting Hollywood, like *Once in a Lifetime* (1932), *Let's Fall in Love* (1934), and *Sitting Pretty* (1933).

Films about Hollywood throughout both the twenties and thirties, of course, have little to do with Jews. Rather, Jewish ethnicity became a vehicle to transport another set of ideas. In the 1920s, assimilation and ethnic identity were that ideological cargo. In the 1930s, the Jewish movie mogul embodied the possibility of achieving success, although the rise-and-fall narratives evident in these films suggest that this success is tenuous, at best. Consequently, the portrayal of the successful movie mogul reflects a certain degree of ambivalence. Early in *What Price Hollywood?*, for example, Saxe capitalizes upon the marriage of his newfound star by turning it into a publicity event. By the end of the film, however, his star, Mary Evans, has humanized the mogul. Mary gives up her career, fully devoting herself to her newborn infant. After she separates from her drunken director husband, Mary's motherhood draws out a more fatherly yet platonic side to Saxe. The white, working-class Mary thus succeeds in taming the voracious business instincts of the mogul, in part by fulfilling established expectations of gender and sexuality.

Films like *What Price Hollywood?* do not so much activate the Hollywood Question as respond to its narrow terms of Jewish agency. Whether malignant or benign, the movie mogul stereotype spoke to the assumptions and expectations of white audiences. In order to respond to these expectations and assumptions, one ultimately needed to accept the seemingly natural terms of this position and its authority. Through its ever-consistent narration, insider accounts of Hollywood had solidified the authority of whiteness in looking at the film industry.

"TAILORS TURNED CALIPHS": THE AUTHORITY OF THE INSIDER ACCOUNT

The Hollywood Question could approach its subjects from at least two related viewpoints. One position, rooted within a distinctly American experience, focused upon the social mobility of the ethnic Other to express nostalgia for an idealized bucolic past. The other position, while sharing a similar fascination with an idealized past, used the body of the racialized Hollywood Jew to interpret melting-pot culture for its audience. Both positions, complementary and closely related to one another, together constructed a powerful way to look at Hollywood through the eyes of those who had experienced it firsthand. Both vantage points generate discursive power through the construction of insider expertise. The speakers had either worked in Hollywood at one time or encountered it through journalistic reportage. In a number of instances, the expert often reports dubious or apocryphal anecdotes. Nevertheless, as the observer carries the authority of experience, the tales expressing resentment toward upward mobility of the ethnic Other appear to speak authentically.

In certain cases, one could refer to an ethnic but not necessarily Jewish Other. Perley Poore Sheehan, coauthor of the screenplay for Lon Chaney's *The Hunchback of Notre Dame* (Universal, 1923), bemoans the inadequacy of Hays's and Hollywood's need for "reform." Hollywood "has prayed for a Lincoln or a [Theodore] Roosevelt. There was so much, and is so much, that a real leader could do!" In *Hollywood as a World Center* (1924), Sheehan neither ties the need for reform to religious efforts nor indicts Jewish control. Instead, he singles out "so-called leaders of the industry" as the responsible parties "for the low moral tone" of motion pictures.

While Sheehan fails to blame Jewish control, he uses a rhetoric that resonates with anti-Jewish stereotypes. A strong leader, Sheehan argues,

"could rid the films" of what he calls a "loathsome and degraded Orientalism that has oozed into them from above."[316] He ultimately attributes this
oozing Orientalism to the untamed social mobility of the movie moguls:

> A seismic upheaval threw into their hands a newly created source of
> wealth. There has been no selective process, no preliminary training,
> no gradation of rank based on merit. If things had continued as they
> were, the future movie-profiteers would have remained inoffensively
> obscure. But in the sudden rush of riches, unexpected and unearned,
> they swelled up. They lost their heads and their souls.

Sheehan ultimately links this lack of proper breeding to a moral argument targeting white Christians. As reprehensible as the biblical "high
priests" of Moloch who demanded child sacrifice, the moguls and their
greed corrupt the nation's youth and morals. "Yesterday they were servile
and fawning," Sheehan writes of the film executives. "Today they are
arrogant and gross. They abhor Truth and worship Publicity. To them Love
means Sex. Would they make the right choice between Good and Bad,
they heed but the still small voice of the Box-Office."[317]

To underscore the danger of such rapid mobility, the expert often reported dubious or apocryphal anecdotes. In Homer Croy's *How Motion
Pictures Are Made* (1918), for example, the anecdote reinforces the movie
mogul's foreign-ness. The mogul appears as an undeserving alien, "still with
the accent of the fatherland about him," deciding "the dramatic and artistic
merits of literary creations" on the basis of his "knowledge of credit and
discount." Great literary works never make it to the screen because of the
moguls' boorishness. To prove his point, Croy obsesses over dialect. In one
anecdote, an executive turns down the rights to Pudd'nhead Wilson, asserting: "ve don't vant to knock the President." The joke succinctly draws
upon traits that would eventually signal the Jewish movie mogul: pidgin
English, lack of appreciation for high culture, and a craven disposition
toward patriotism. While these passages express a sentiment more anti-
immigrant than anti-Semitic, the image of the parvenu who speaks in
dialect and is knowledgeable in "credit and discount" reverberates with
other, more overtly anti-Jewish statements.[318]

Like others who invoked the Hollywood Question in more obvious
fashion, Croy – an established screenwriter and novelist – expressed the
tension between an older, rural America and an increasingly modern world.
While he contributed to an installment in the popular Cohens and Kellys
series, his comedies often drew upon an agrarian ideal. *Down to Earth*

(1932) starred Will Rogers, a comedian who built a whole persona around his mordant homespun humor. Other titles suggest stories far removed from the city: *Down on the Farm* (1938) and *I'm from Missouri*.[319]

Satires of Hollywood often portrayed the Jew at odds with small-town principles of community and fair play. Before Tay Garnett directed such classic Hollywood films as *Bataan* (1943) and *The Postman Always Rings Twice* (1946), he published *Tall Tales from Hollywood* (1932), a collection of fictional Hollywood anecdotes. Hollywood began, according to Garnett, when a Mr. Ginsburg "sold out his cloaks and suits at a profitable sacrifice" and formed the corporation, "Ginsburg, Ginsburg, Feinstein, Murphy, Schmaltz, Schmaltz and Ginsburg." The moguls created additional jobs when "there weren't enough jobs for all the Cousins." One day, the production supervisor (and a relative of the studio head) would find an appropriate opportunity to leap "like an outraged Semitic Tiger," firing everyone on the set and hiring "all the Relatives for weeks to come." Like the Tom Swift adventure, such humor often revealed a particular way of looking at other ethnic groups. When someone proposes that the studio film *Black Beauty*, the well-known children's book about a girl and her horse, the joke at once serves many functions. Engaging in wordplay, it both indicates mogul ignorance and uses a racist articulation to make blacks the butt of a joke. "You want that I should leave you make 'Black Beauty'!" the executive exclaims. "They ain't no market for them Nigger Operas!"[320]

Such anecdotes, while apocryphal, reinforce a particular way of understanding Hollywood. The representation of this kind of language play never occurs for its own sake. Rather, it connects the reader to deep-seated cultural assumptions and resentments. In the collection *Hollywood Shorts*, for example, actor Charles Ray uses pidgin to "catch" moguls in the act of desecrating art.[321] Spoken completely in dialect, the short story "Sans Tarte" depicts an ongoing conversation between producers Abe and Ike Stein. The Steins hire a comic director from France to produce comedies that do not include pie throwing. Upon catching a glimpse of the rushes, Ike Stein tells his brother that the film is just "hokay. Jus' about like ours." Abe winces. "Gee, as bad as dot?" Oblivious to the irony, Abe declares that "our comedies ain't to be laughed at!"[322]

In addition to desecrating language and culture, the mogul desecrates womanhood through his licentiousness and immorality. In "Tarzan Clutches," Ray emphasizes the role that producers with names like "Max Steinbalm" play in making movies that flaunt the Hays Office Code. Like the Steins, Steinbalm speaks in heavy dialect. After producing "Western pictures on a shoestring," his "financial inspiration made him go sexy" and

FIGURE 18. Illustration from Charles Ray's
Hollywood Shorts (1935).

produce "with a gee string." In another story, Ray pokes fun at the self-importance and licentiousness of the movie mogul. The main characters, a group of writers stuck without any ideas, discuss their boss, Mr. Emanuel B. Schmaltzing, whom they observe stands "like a little Napoleon." Seeing their boss with a woman prompts one of the writers to ponder "if he's showed 'er how nice and cool it is in the projectin' room."[323]

Of course, not everyone expressed such outward hostility. Yet one could maintain a more ambivalent stance toward the mogul and still do so from a position of whiteness. In *Los Angeles, City of Dreams*, *Los Angeles Times* editorial writer Harry Carr gives an insider account of the moguls. Carr helped Lillian Gish with the only film she directed, *Remodeling Her Husband* (New Art–Paramount, 1920). Later, he worked with Dorothy Arzner on the story and script for *Old Ironsides* (Paramount, 1926) and with Erich von Stroheim on *The Wedding March* (Famous Players Lasky–Paramount, 1928). At one level, Carr respects the moguls a great deal. He wonders "if any other class of men" could have welded "a group of creative arts to a factory system." He finds the producers rank "well in point of intelligence." Yet Carr also sees the moguls as suffering from "a social inferiority complex," which causes them "to snatch at new baubles" and become "suckers for Big Names." Rather than disputing the image of the parvenu, Carr incorporates it into Horatio Alger–like visions of the American Dream. After noting how the moguls are "sneered at as button-hole-makers, ex-junk men, cornet tooters, sweat-shop penny-squeezers," Carr acknowledges the validity of this perception. In discussing nepotism, he announces that "the film industry is cluttered up with nephews." Such clannishness "is an inevitable hang-over from the long centuries of Jewish persecution." However, he also celebrates the moguls' upward mobility, seeing no difference between them and rail-road presidents who have been section hands "or" a president of the United States who had been an illiterate tailor. Although applauding the success of "Jewish producers who have fought their way up from the gutters," Carr still believes that Jews are gullible and have "too much loyalty to their own."[324]

The Hollywood Question could also look more overtly upon the racialized Jewish body, locating essential truths about the nature of the American melting pot. British authors such as Jan and Cora Gordon, R. J. Minney, and J. B. Priestley seemed especially fascinated with the Jewish body. In the late 1920s, the Gordons traveled to Hollywood, where they toured a number of studios. Their book, *Star Dust in Hollywood* (1930), candidly addresses the Jewish presence in Hollywood. When they meet Jewish screenwriters, the Gordons describe them as both racial and foreign to America. The "imported authors" fall into three basic types. One is a "slender, young, intellectual Jew." Another is "short and thickset." A "blonde type" shows "how far the modern Jewish race has traveled from its Mosaic progenitors." Despite invoking race discourse, the Gordons favorably compare Jews "to the unlettered emigrant or the negro [sic]." Such reliance upon race science reveals a certain degree of ambivalence toward Jews. Distinguishing themselves from other allegedly inferior groups, Jews are "both intelligent and hardworking." Yet, they are also seen as an "imported" race.[325]

The Gordons also comment upon the upward mobility of the Jew. A clerk who behaves rudely toward them appears as a parvenu: "his hair" remains "polished, his collar and tie as near star-like perfection as could be achieved with cheap means." When he speaks, he grunts and talks in dialect ("Wadjer want?"). Although the authors do not identify him as Jewish, his appearance remains consistent with other stereotypes of the Jewish parvenu. In the book, such upward mobility appears to have a deleterious influence upon Christian culture. Noting the irony of a film about "Our Saviour . . . undertaken with Jewish money for Jewish profit," the Gordons visit the set of *King of Kings*. There, one of the film's writers walks on to the set of the Last Supper, callously suggesting that the producer "get in a coupl'a a dozen extras and make it a fine big banquet."[326]

This way of looking at the racialized Jewish body can even achieve added momentum by appearing to undercut itself. Invited by Darryl F. Zanuck to adapt his book and play *Clive of India* into a movie, author R. J. Minney later served as a film producer in postwar Britain. In Minney's *Hollywood by Starlight* (1935), the author, a British soldier and technical advisor for a "defense of the realm" epic, comments upon the pervasiveness of the mogul stereotype. When Minney meets producer Sam Goldwyn, he expects to see "a surly, vulgar, gross little Jew." Instead, Minney finds Goldwyn "most likeable." Yet Minney reinforces other stereotypes often associated with Jews. Goldwyn has "an amazing head for business." When the mogul takes them to see Max Reinhardt's production of A *Midsummer Night's Dream*, Minney quotes Goldwyn in dialect – ("Vell, I'm one of the backers. I've gotto like the show.") – noting his "marked Jewish accent."[327]

Similarly, in *Midnight on the Desert* (1937), British author J. B. Priestley undercuts some mogul stereotypes while reinforcing others. After a brief stay in Hollywood during the 1930s, Priestly suggests that we take "the funny stories about the Hollywood film magnates" with a grain of salt. Yet, the author also finds moguls "unique in their mixture of shrewdness and ignorance, bombast and humility." The mogul serves as metaphorical critique of industry at large. "Rich men in the film industry are often ignorant and stupid and have far too much power," he writes, "but then rich men in many other industries are often ignorant and stupid and have far too much power." Priestley uses stereotypes commonly associated with Jews to describe the mogul. When "little Russian-Jews" say goodbye to an executive boarding a California train "to the great beating heart of Paramount Films," Priestley feels like he is in the opulent Sergei Diaghilev ballet *Petrushka*. Later, he describes the moguls as mere "emperors of make-believe" and "tailors turned caliphs." The "humble, ill-educated aliens," Priestly wryly observes of the magnates, enjoyed movies "all the more because they were not fully inarticulate in any known language." Such partial literacy resulted from their sudden ascent "high in the air on magic beanstalks, or whirled from three back rooms in Brooklyn to a pseudo-Spanish castle in Southern California."[328]

In interpreting the film industry for a popular audience, the Hollywood Question helped cement a concept of whiteness that would carry over into popular fiction. Insider expertise lent the Question's anecdotes an air of authenticity. However apocryphal, these accounts fixated upon Jewish agency as a way to comment upon upward ethnic mobility in general. By racializing the image of the Jewish body, the insider could locate seemingly profound truths about the American experience. So flexible was the Hollywood Question that it could even gain credibility by appearing to undercut one set of stereotypes while replacing them with another. The Hollywood novel would rely heavily on these assumptions, always drawing from similar notions of ethnic agency and race science to reinforce its way of looking. Never questioned, the way in which the Hollywood novel saw Jews did more than just provide local color. Although the novels were fiction, the Hollywood Question's insider account had already established a particular way of viewing an ethnic Other that appeared to be reality.

"HEBREWS ARE ORIENTALS": THE DEPRESSION-ERA HOLLYWOOD NOVEL

Interestingly, no one of the slew of novels dealing with Hollywood was ever an all-out blockbuster before 1940. According to the *1939–1940 Motion Picture Almanac*, of the seventy-three top-selling novels of all time up to then, not one dealt with the film colony.[329] Rather, blockbusters like Margaret Mitchell's *Gone with the Wind* topped the list. Not until the phenomenally popular *What Makes Sammy Run?* (1941) did the Hollywood novel achieve any significant popularity. Yet, in its heyday during the 1920s through the 1940s, the Hollywood novel nonetheless crystallized a particular way of looking at American culture, drawing upon already extant imagery and arguments depicting the film industry. Although Jewish stereotypes existed in these stories, the novels had little to do with Jews. Often, but not always, Jews existed on the narrative periphery. Yet even at the periphery, the image of the Jewish producer or mogul pervaded the genre's commentary upon American culture at large. Hollywood novels, even later ones by respected authors such as Nathanael West, F. Scott Fitzgerald, and Budd Schulberg, all had something to say about a changing national identity. These novels did not propound the belief in a Jewish conspiracy; rather, they used the Jew as a metonym. The metonym represented both

Hollywood and, to a certain extent, various shifts taking place in America. These transformations seemingly characterized a new kind of culture: the urban had supplanted the rural. Elite, high culture had succumbed to mass, accessible culture. Cultural uniformity gave way to cultural diversity. Tradition yielded to modernity. Of course, accusations and images of conspiracy remained. Yet these allegations were substantially different from those made by old-line Protestants and Catholic pressure groups. In moral and religious literature, the Jew represented an influence at odds with American ideals; in the Hollywood novel, the Jew represented a new set of ideals. The Hollywood novel used the image of the Jew to respond to how these new ideals embodied a new kind of America.

Most of these novels follow the same basic narrative. An innocent, often from the Midwest, comes to Hollywood in search of fame and fortune. Once there, this innocent achieves some measure of success. The actions and behavior of the protagonist are in sharp contrast to the Hollywood Jew. Ultimately, the protagonist finds him- or herself to be incompatible with Jewish Hollywood and returns home. These narratives of faltering Christian morality and redemption provided a framework within which to express older fears of the Jewish threat in three ways. First, like the image of the mogul in religious and political tracts, the Jew was seen as threatening Christian culture through the sexual degradation of aspiring female starlets. Second, one could explain the meteoric rise of the movie mogul in terms of the Jew's implacable disregard for fair business ethics. Jew had displaced Gentile from the latter's rightful place at the helm of Hollywood. The Jew degraded the delicate art of the motion picture with his knowledge of credit and discount, and his prurient interests. Finally, the Jew threatened national identity through his ability to access the American mind and appeal to its lower tastes and values.

Although most early Hollywood novels focus on a Gentile hero, the mogul and other Jewish movie executives appear as integral figures, providing both Hollywood atmosphere and what Edward Said calls an "aura of apartness, definiteness, and collective self-consistency." The image of the mogul precluded the possibility of a diverse Jewish identity along class or ideological lines. Instead, the collapsing of the mogul image with traditional Jewish stereotypes helped define Hollywood against an older national identity. Several of these lesser-known novels develop a mogul stereotype that overtly articulates the most hostile forms of the Hollywood Question.[330]

In other novels, however, Jewish stereotypes express a certain older ambivalence toward immigration and assimilation. In the 1924 novel *On the Lot and Off*, for example, names like David Schusshel, Ernest Sapp, and

Jake Steinberg, serve as important markers of difference. Yet the novel links the exuberance of its protagonist, Izzy Iskovitch, to motion pictures and the possibilities of the American Dream. "Probably never, in all the history of wealth, since conscienceless Commerce trifled gaily with Art and produced as lusty bratling the Motion Picture Industry," the book explains, "has any one so radiated the joy of success as did Izzy Iskovitch."[331] Izzy's family, however, ties him to the Old World. Uncle Abraham is a "junk dealer,"[332] Uncle Moche a "pants presser."[333] His Uncle Solomon runs "the narrowest and dingiest little pawnshop" on "the narrowest and dingiest" of streets in the "Old World" slums of Los Angeles.[334] In order to convince Uncle Sol to finance a movie, Izzy explains this investment in terms of usury – a strategy Izzy knows will lure Sol into the financial scheme.[335]

If such stereotypes could ultimately celebrate the American Dream, they could also express ambivalence over this success myth. Before short-fiction and screenwriter Adela Rogers St. Johns's original story for *What Price Hollywood?* received an Academy Award nomination in 1932, the author had written another 1924 novel about Hollywood entitled *The Skyrocket.* The image of the mogul also appears there, albeit in less sympathetic fashion. *Skyrocket*'s mogul, Irving Spencer Kohl, speaks in a "guttural voice, which still had the tempo of the foreign language to which he had been born." Mogul Sam Hirtfelz shares Kohl's commercialism. However "gentle and visionary" and "handicapped in social intercourse" by his lowly origins, "Sam Hirtfelz was a rock when it came to money. A financial wizard, manipulating all sorts of profitable deals on Wall Street, controlling the fluctuations of public opinion and of the money-market to the advantage of the Hirt corporation, he felt in money the one solid thing in his universe." *The Skyrocket* includes at least two aspects of the mogul image. St. Johns includes a physiognomic description of Kohl as a "hawk-faced little man." Aaron Savage – Kohl's rival – lives up to his surname by finding Hollywood "a happy hunting-ground for pretty women."[336]

Both Sharon Kimm, heroine of *The Skyrocket,* and Mary Evans in *What Price Hollywood?* eventually abandon the industry and their careers in favor of more domestic pursuits. St. Johns draws the stakes more clearly in *The Skyrocket,* however, when Kimm realizes that she has sacrificed her virtue for Hollywood. Shooting on location in Mexico, she and a Mexican prostitute exchange glances:

Sharon saw for the first time in her life the naked look of the woman who has sold herself.

And Sharon saw, too, the vision of her own face, stamped with the look of sisterhood, forever, beyond redemption.

Sisters. She and the girl in the Plaza.

Then she knew. Like a great light the revelation came upon her, tearing the veils from eyes. False gods, false standards fell away. . . .

A harlot was a harlot, whether she sold herself for a dollar bill or for Paradise.[337]

The term "Paradise" has special meaning, since it ostensibly refers to Kimm's house, on which she owed a large sum of money. Because the actress no longer gets parts, she has to borrow money from her former director in exchange for sex. Thus, Kimm realizes that her experience in "Paradise" binds her to the experience of a Mexican prostitute. The term "Paradise" also conjures up those intangibles defining Hollywood: wealth, success, power. In short, the American Dream.

A successful novelist, photographer, and a white proponent of black culture, Carl Van Vechten satirized Hollywood in his 1928 book *Spider Boy*. Like St. Johns, Van Vechten uses animals to characterize the movie mogul. Ben Griesheimer has "a great hooked nose and bead-like eyes," making him resemble "a sinister eagle." The appearance of animals also mocks the pretensions of the parvenu – a photograph of Griesheimer's "Jewish children" sitting on the mogul's desk shows them "with a family of Norwegian elkhounds." Griesheimer comes from a humble background in the "cloak and suit business," allegedly having achieved success in movies by setting his store on fire and collecting the insurance money. An immoral influence, Griesheimer makes his motto "Purity First," even though he's not above putting in "quite a lot o' necking" if you "keep your story moral."[338]

Novels about Hollywood by respected authors like St. Johns and Van Vechten augured a series of books written by lesser-known writers. In these books, moguls play a small but integral role in establishing the mood for Hollywood. And while both St. Johns's and Van Vechten's work may be more complex stylistically, the ways in which they depict the mogul are not all that different from those in lesser-known works of fiction. Author Gladys Denny Shultz, using Anne Gardner as a nom de plume, wrote on many issues affecting women. Between 1927 and 1945, she covered child care for *Better Homes and Gardens*. After *Reputation*, her first novel, Shultz also penned such titles as *The Love Coward* (1930), *Working Wives* (1931), and *The Husband Campaign* (1932). All dealt with women's changing role in modern society. Shultz herself bucked tradition when she ran for editor

FIGURE 19. Portrait of Carl Van Vechten by Prentiss Taylor, 1932.
Library of Congress, Prints and Photographs Division.

of her college paper and won. Her *Reputation* (1929) depicts April Low, whom the book's subtitle refers to as "the Wickedest Woman in Hollywood." An ironic deployment of gender stereotyping, "wicked" in this context simply means Low's stubborn adherence to her own morality despite men like Hollywood publicist Morris Golden. Low resists Golden's crass commercialism when he tries to create a "bad" image for her. Golden, with his "jutting nose and chin . . . sharp enough to cut something," dresses "in the perfect symphony of colors" that is in just "slightly imperfect taste." The image of this parvenu defines Hollywood against Low's more home-grown femininity. While Shultz's book did not achieve best-seller status, its publisher, A. L. Burt, had become the fifth-largest publisher in the country by 1936. A major press rarely published first novels. Even if the book itself remained relatively obscure, Hollywood and the Hollywood mogul remained relatively bankable commodities for publishing.[339]

Smaller presses capitalized on Hollywood as well. In *Reckless Hollywood* (1932), published by Amour Press, author Haynes Lubou describes the city as a "little world of glorified adventuresses, black sheep [and] shrewd Jews." The blurb in the overleaf entices the reader with the image of leering moguls who "decide on a girl's sex appeal by personal experiments." Petty Love, the protagonist, manages "to escape these personal experiments on Broadway and tried to escape them in Hollywood." In *Hollywood's Bad Boy* (1932), published by a small Hollywood press, mogul Sam Loeffler appears as "cold, merciless, and cruel." Although he "had been quite human in the early days," he now sees Gentile women as his chattels. Loeffler refuses to let one of his stars marry. "We look at her as a valuable piece of property," he tells her suitor, "that must be guarded from every angle to save our investment." In Jack Hanley's *Star Lust* (1934), originally published by W. Godwin and later reprinted by Charles Grayson – author of another Hollywood novel, *Spotlight Madness* (1931) – mogul Alvin Helser preys upon Gentile women. Hanley, whose other titles include such titillations as *Tomcat in Tights* and *Violated One*, describes Helser as having "an enormous cigar smouldering in his fat fingers, bandy legs spread apart bracing his stocky little figure." He talks with "a guttural foreign sound; not so much by accent as by twisted construction and a slight thickening of final consonants." Helser is barely able to curb his sexual appetite for the Christian women whom he makes stars. Just before he succumbs to his desire and lunges for the "arched white sweep" of his protégé's throat, a convenient deus ex machina prevents their tryst. A crazed former lover, a tormented yet true artist of religious themes, crashes through the window and kills Helser before the mogul can rape his star-to-be.[340]

If the image of the mogul in minor Hollywood novels implicitly shares much with stereotypes of the lascivious, miscegenating Jew, the image of the mogul in Horace Wade's *To Hell with Hollywood* (1931) explicitly draws upon these stereotypes. Wade himself remained relatively obscure, writing only one other novel, *Great Scott* (1932). Dial Press – hardly a minor concern – published both of these. Founded by two Harvard alumni, Lincoln MacVeagh and Scofield Thayer, the press published a wide range of material, from a collection of E. E. Cummings poems (1925) to W. R. Burnett's *Little Caesar* (1929). That Dial chose to publish a relatively obscure author signifies less an indication of the work's merit than the attraction Hollywood held as literary subject matter.

The novel contains the typical mogul stereotypes. Abe Zeidstein smokes "a fat, black cigar jammed jauntily between his lips." His "jowls [reek] with smug complacency – a sort of 'Behold me, cooties, I am Abe Zeidstein, a motion picture magnate and God's gracious gift to man.' " Wade balances his protagonist, Jack Jarvis, against the Jew. Jarvis appears as the American ideal, fighting a quixotic war against an unseen, powerful enemy. By conflating art with women, Wade depicts Jews as a threat to this ideal. Jewish control simultaneously pollutes culture and race. Jarvis, for instance, gets "hot under the collar" when he thinks how the Jewish mogul both "murders art" and places Gentile maidens in jeopardy. Jarvis envisions the Jew picking "a bunch of greasers [Hispanics], bohunks [Poles], wops [Italians] and racial rats to paw over pretty girls." *To Hell with Hollywood* employs many general stereotypes of the Jew. The parvenu "hook-noses and slick-haired mollycoddles" are "unlettered as the back of a tombstone." Before Jarvis even meets a mogul, he envisions him as "a pompous squirt with tonsured dome, threading me like a needle with his slitted eyes and gesticulating like a tailor patching pants." To Jarvis, Hollywood is "a tailored business," where "gobs of gold have swollen the ego of the erst-while needle-threaders." Jews did not invent Hollywood; they conquered it. "Just beggars on horseback," Jews exploit Christian ingenuity to get to the top. "Edison's genius" had "foisted [them] into the saddle."[341]

Jarvis resents Jews for not knowing their proper place. Hollywood Jews had "exchanged the humility of ghettos for gold, goose and goulash." By controlling the movies, "a bunch of Eastside Jews, still yapping Yiddish, can say to a Gentile, 'this is our game; beat it or we'll call the bounder!' " Jarvis's objections to perceived Jewish exclusivity, however, merely mask his contempt for upward mobility among ethnic groups, whom he deems not fully American. Jarvis is "sick of Greasers [Mexicans], Bohunks [Poles], Wops [Italians] and Kikes [Jews] getting first call over 100% Americans." Jarvis uses particularly offensive racial and ethnic slurs to express his distaste. "Kike," for example, is a derogatory term that refers to Jewish foreignness. It may derive from a caricature imitating Eastern European names ending in "-ski" and "-sky."

Jarvis's love interest, a woman named Tootsie, echoes these sentiments in a speech she gives at the end of the book. Looking like "a valiant daughter of the Vikings," Tootsie once believed

there was enough Americanism in the industry to give the descendants of the men and women who built this republic at least an occasional chance. I was all wrong. It's the "inskies," "wowskies," "steins," "bergs," and other outlanders who get the cream. The public often thinks Americans are getting a break when the names of stars are Anglo-Saxon, but dig under them and a Wop, Mexican, Spaniard, and Pole, and not infrequently a German or Polish Jew, will be hiding.

Both Jarvis and Tootsie believe that the inclusion of any minority ethnic group to be at odds with Anglo-Saxonism. The latter term harks back to the turn of the century, invoking the weight of race science to signify Manifest Destiny and other traces of supposed Anglo-Saxon superiority. Tootsie singles out Jews as especially unworthy to participate in the film industry, as "Hebrews are orientals, and orientals are moles burrowing underground." Jarvis can only perceive Jewish success in terms of Christian displacement. "The tailor's goose has pushed the eagle off his perch," Jarvis says. He invokes the image of both the commercial and the ignorant Jew, who doesn't "have to speak English. Dollars talk!"[342]

The image of the victimized Christian female recurs throughout *To Hell with Hollywood*. The hero, Jack Jarvis, comes to Hollywood to produce a project called The Minotaur. Referring to the Greek myth, Jarvis wishes to show how sacrificing our "loveliest daughters" to the movies is analogous to "the higher-ups of the motion picture industry." *To Hell with Hollywood* also borrows from Christian anti-Semitic imagery. When Jarvis discovers his own blacklisting, he vows to put up a fight. "Christ was persecuted by the Jews," he tells Tootsie, to which she responds, "And crucified." When Jarvis discovers that a Christian has been working for the moguls, he accuses him of Judas-like behavior, protecting "Jew gold . . . at the expense of Gentile virtue." When Jarvis learns that his former secretary, Vera Popinksi, wishes to come out to Hollywood and become a star, he tries to dissuade her. Hardly concerned about her womanhood, he begrudges the fact that "the greasy little Slav has a name that would sound musical as a Strad to studio magnates." A letter Jarvis sends to Popinski vents his frustration through gratuitous anti-Semitic imagery. "The Jew boys who spin the top out here are pretty clanish [sic]," he writes her. Hollywood's "inner circle" consists of Jews who "wash their hands with invisible soap, shrug their shoulders and inspect buttonholes."[343]

Other novels on Hollywood, like Shepard Traube's *Glory Road* (1935), try to emphasize positive aspects of Hollywood and Jewish executives. Traube wrote and directed a series of B-films during the 1940s. *Beasts of Berlin* (1939) remains notable as one of the first American films before World War II to depict Nazi Germany. Written by Traube and based on a published short story, *Beasts of Berlin* even includes scenes in a concentration camp.[344] Traube's *Glory Road* gives an extremely sympathetic portrayal of mogul Karl Lustig, whom his wife describes as someone who "would never be content, never satisfied with what he had. Always there was the restless urge in him to make things bigger." Lustig sees himself as a "plainsman, setting out into the unknown to break through the wilderness." Like the pioneers of the 1800s, westward expansion offers him "promise and hope" in building a motion picture industry. As for others who preceded him, the West would "shape . . . his own destiny." *Glory Road* shows these traits as admirable. The book compliments "this little man, the immigrant to a new world," who "could become a colossus." The novel also obliquely attacks the Gentile establishment as manifest in the motion picture patents trust. While Lustig manages to keep his studio open, he loses "faith in the power of the courts ever to do him and his brethren justice."[345]

Despite *Glory Road*'s sympathy for Lustig, Traube still uses traditional stereotypes of moguls. The director Bamberger appears "oily, fat, vulgar." He is the quintessential parvenu, oozing "conceit" yet a complete "ignoramus." Fortunately, he is a "good commercial director," not unlike the stereotype of the commercial Jew. Lustig's financial backer, Anton Brewer, appears as an international banker. Brewer's armaments "interests" cause him to push Lustig to make "as many anti-German pictures as possible" during World War I. Even within a relatively sympathetic account of the movie mogul, stereotypes of the financially motivated warmonger appear. "Within the next few months public sentiment will have reached a pitch of enthusiasm that will greet such films eagerly," Brewer tells Lustig. "We stand to make enormous profits, if you act quickly."[346]

Hollywood's literary draw extended beyond novels about Hollywood. Many murder mysteries are also set in Hollywood and have something to do with the film industry. Often, the movie mogul appears as a minor character. In Cromwell Gibbons's *Murder in Hollywood* (1936), for example, mogul Abe Goldsmith appears as "flashy, corpulent and partly bald," a man who "fought his way to the top" from New York's garment trade. While Gibbons never says that Goldsmith is Jewish, the name of the character, his physiognomy and New York garment industry origins all remain consistent with Jewish stereotypes.[347]

Both *Murder in Hollywood* and *Tom Swift and His Talking Machine* refer to stereotypes commonly associated with Jews. These stereotypes appear, not just in Hollywood novels, but in a large body of popular literature interpreting Hollywood for a general audience. The former book uses the familiar character of the movie mogul to set the ambiance for a Hollywood murder mystery, while the latter inculcates young boys with Manichaean notions of Jews battling Gentiles over their rightful "pound of flesh." Even *Glory Road*, which objects to the overt anti-Semitism of the Hollywood novel, ultimately accepts the terms of the Hollywood Question. In generating sympathy for its protagonist, Karl Lustig, *Glory Road* lapses into its own stereotypes of the crass parvenu and the international banker.

The Shylock Jew, present in accusations of Jewish control over the theater, shares many of the same characteristics of the Hollywood movie mogul. Physically and racially repulsive, the mogul must prey upon aspiring Christian actresses to satisfy his lustful urges. Ignorant and unlettered, he is incapable of completely shedding his pidgin tongue, which thereby marks him as alien. Knowledgeable about acts of commerce, the mogul debases, not just high art, but the Christian sense of fair play. Self-interest and an ability to cheat the system vault the mogul to his parvenu status. Moreover, as a racial inferior in a position of power, the mogul threatens North American culture by excluding whites yet allowing other racial inferiors to enter Hollywood.

Despite or because of such fears of the racial diversity and social mobility of a perceived ethnic inferior, Hollywood held a certain fascination for the public. It demanded explanation by both insiders and outsiders, critics and boosters. Images of Jewish control and echoes of Jewish stereotypes ultimately helped to define the image of Hollywood. As the blatant demonization of Jews and their alleged conspiracies waned, the image of the foreign, parvenu mogul prevailed. Not always overtly Jewish, characterizations of the mogul nonetheless shared many of the same stereotypes that had earlier depicted Jews.

By the mid-1930s, however, these attitudes toward Hollywood began to shift as a result of other political and social changes. Following President Roosevelt's package of social and economic reforms, America began to emerge from its economic depression. After a landslide reelection of the Roosevelt administration, the country began a debate on entry into World War II. Meanwhile, Hollywood achieved unprecedented success as a mass medium, rallying American audiences to a new patriotism emphasizing democracy and plurality. All of these factors contributed to a change in attitudes toward Hollywood and putative Jewish control. These shifts in mainstream national identity would inevitably lead to a showdown between older America and an increasingly modern, globally aware America. Within the parameters of this showdown, the demonization of Jewish control over Hollywood would retain a special significance, marking a major transition from isolationist, agrarian America to modern, global, security-state America. The Hollywood Question, in its uniquely versatile fashion, continued to address this and other shifts. Notions of racialized Jewish agency now began to speak to a variety of domestic and international political concerns facing America on the eve of its entry into World War II.

5

The Politics of the Hollywood Question

"INTELLIGENT GENTILES"

The Hollywood Question indexes powerful shifts within deep structures of perception. In particular, the Question helped to shape a whole way of thinking about a variety of issues concerning American life. As this chapter discusses, the Hollywood Question ultimately asserted an older version of American politics, one better suited to an unwired, premodern, agrarian America and the nostalgia that attends this myth. Throughout the 1930s, the Question espoused a vision of American foreign and domestic policy at odds with its nemeses: the Roosevelt administration, a cohesive cultural diversity, and a burgeoning sense of internationalism. At best, the Hollywood Question responded apathetically to Nazism: instead of articulating opposition to the Nazi treatment of the Jews, it explained German anti-Semitism as a natural response to Communism, and anti-Nazism as an overreaction that would bring even more hardship upon Jews. During this period, the Hollywood Question also found new ways to implicate Jews as Communists, seeing evidence of ethnic culpability in the world political climate and shifts in the country's domestic agenda. Communism had purportedly duped American Jews, playing upon their "natural" fears of domestic Nazism and fascism. And the Question explained that Jewish-Communist labor had strong-armed Jewish-controlled Hollywood into supporting the New Deal.

Because the Hollywood Question served as a uniquely flexible response to modernity, it could address a diverse range of political configurations. Channeling traditional anti-Semitic stereotypes, the political incarnation of the Hollywood Question covered a spectrum of liberal and conservative interests. It addressed the older, inherently Populist ideals of both Progressivism and isolationism. At the same time, the Question connected these ideals to an emergent anti-Communist paranoia over the unseen global enemy.

Of course, the Hollywood Question did not cause this change in ideals. Rather, it expressed a myriad of depression-era fears, resentments, and shifting alliances. Before schisms within the Democratic Party developed, Most Progressives had supported Roosevelt and the New Deal. In 1925, Robert M. La Follette, Jr., succeeded his father in the Senate as a progressive Republican. An early ally of Roosevelt, La Follette endorsed elements of the New Deal throughout the president's first term. A series of key events – most notably, a plan by Roosevelt to pack the Supreme Court with sympathetic judges – alienated La Follette and other liberals. Disenchanted with the Republican Party, Roosevelt, and the New Deal, La Follette helped organize the Progressive Party in 1934. In 1936, he convened the Senate Committee to Investigate Violations of Free Speech and Rights of Labor. Compared to the House Un-American Activities Committee (HUAC) headed by Texas Democrat Martin Dies, however, the La Follette committee received relatively scant attention. According to 1938 polls, only 24 percent of Americans had heard of the La Follette hearings, whereas 66 percent had heard of the Dies hearings. The brainchild of Representative Samuel Dickstein, HUAC initially sought to investigate Nazi activity in the United States. The House voted Dickstein's measure down. Several members questioned the necessity for such an investigation and wondered aloud whether Jews in this country might bring "racial bias" upon themselves.[348] Eventually, parliamentary maneuvering edged Dickstein out and replaced him with Representative Dies. Dies swore to investigate both Communists and Nazis.[349]

Meanwhile, by 1941, a new internationalism had emerged out of both the New Deal and the vicissitudes of an impending world war. The Roosevelt administration's heightened sense of international responsibility – widely supported – conflicted with an older, Populist and more traditional isolationism. Although the Hollywood Question did not induce these defining political moments, it certainly used Jews and Hollywood to aggrandize both isolationism and anti-Communism, propelling isolationist traditionalism through familiar discursive routes. Ultimately, however, the Question's allegations also helped undo the movement. In America, the Question's overt stereotypes, once so popular between the 1880s and the 1930s, had fallen into disfavor; they resonated too closely with the antidemocratic ideals of Nazism. Of course, the resonance was hardly accidental: Henry Ford's *The International Jew* had achieved what Ford's biographer Keith Sward calls a "world-wide" market by 1927, when Ford had issued a statement renouncing anti-Semitism. As Sward notes, the volume achieved its greatest impact in Germany, where one publisher there printed twelve different translations of the work throughout the 1920s. In the American edition of *Mein Kampf*, editors note entire passages from *The International Jew*, lifted word for word.[350]

Inflected by a complementary set of fears, the anti-Communist question had its own set of repercussions. Its paranoid assumptions concerning agency helped structure investigations into the motion picture industry by the House Un-American Activities Committee after World War II. Building upon earlier fears of a protean Jewish conspiracy, the anti-Communist question seemingly deethnicized its accusation of conspiracy, even though others had already firmly established the association. In 1931, a congressional committee study alleged that 70 percent of the U.S. Communist Party were aliens, and that most of these aliens were Jews.[351]

The way in which one made this association, however, had changed. One could still associate Communism with Jews, yet never make the association explicit. Thus anti-Communism claimed the lives of Ethel and Julius Rosenberg while rarely naming them as Jewish. This phenomenon paralleled the rise of a "code" to refer to Hollywood Jews. In *An American's History of Hollywood* (1940), G. Allison Phelps – Los Angeles radio commentator, president of the American Enterprise Foundation, and founder of the Indoor Sports Club, Incorporated – never once mentions the word "Jew." Instead, he connects "the Hollywood Joy Boys" to typical stereotypes of aggressiveness and pushiness. When the House stepped up its campaign to rid the country of a perceived Communist menace in 1948, it targeted Hollywood and named the Jewish-sounding names of screenwriters and producers. Charged with new energy, the Hollywood Question now spoke of ostensive Communist agency and conspiracies, just as Bob Shuler had once replaced the threat of a Catholic conspiracy with the threat of a Jewish one.

One can trace this covert postwar hostility to prewar Nazi sympathies. For example, letters to the *Christian Century* reflect public favor for the 1935 Nuremberg Laws. A professor in the New Testament Department at the University of Dubuque in Iowa rationalized these measures, designed to ensure Aryan purity. Anyone familiar with Germany after World War I, he argued, "knows that Jewish leadership propagated socialism and later communism, that Jews dominated law, literature, the theater, the press, the financial world, the clothing industry, and seemed to semitize the entire German culture." [352]

By the mid-1930s, however, such overt allegations of a Jewish conspiracy began to appear less acceptable. While still invoking the Hollywood Question, the *Christian Century* soft-pedaled the more openly anti-Semitic aspect of allegations of Jewish control. In debunking various justifications for "the unwholesome tendency in commercial films," Fred Eastman and Edward Ouellette referred to the common belief that "the producers have low ideals" while acknowledging that "certain reformers" single out "certain producers of a particular racial group" in this judgment. In the 1930 *Christian Century* series "Who Controls the Movies," Eastman himself had charged that, within the film industry, "90 per cent of the upper strata of control is Jewish." By 1936, however, Eastman and Ouellette were warning that one must "examine and puncture" this assumption, emphasizing that producers must not be made "the goat."[353]

Within the film industry itself, charges of Jewish control took place behind closed doors. In 1937, Joe Breen, head of the Production Code, worried over efforts "*to capture the screen of the United States for Communistic propaganda purposes*," noting that "most of the agitators are Jews."[354] In 1939, publisher Martin Quigley privately conferred with Breen on the threat of Jewish control. "Amongst our Semitic brethren," Quigley writes, "there seems to be growing an acceptance of the idea of radical propaganda on the screen." Yet, publicly, Quigley maintained that Hollywood's lapses in moral standards were not due to the "producers as a group," as "glib and superficial observation so frequently asserted." Rather, Quigley attributed the poor moral tone of films to a combination of "subversive elements" unwittingly serving "some of the more obvious phases of the public's amusement taste," since they lacked an appropriate "sensitiveness to moral issues."[355]

Privately overt and publicly covert, the Hollywood Question shored up Production Code censorship. In his proposed screen treatment of the Warner Bros. film *Black Legion* (1936), producer Robert Lord depicts a KKK-like group recruiting a disgruntled factory worker after he loses a promotion to a Jewish coworker. In censoring this treatment, Breen cited Code policy as forbidding "stories which raise and deal with the provocative and inflammatory subjects of racial and religious prejudice." Should Jack Warner express a willingness to revise the story "with careful treatment," Breen would find the film "basically satisfactory."[356] According to a 19 June 1936 Production Code memo to Breen, representatives of that office met with Lord and screenwriter Abem Finkel, informing them that the story "was basically satisfactory, except for the introduction of the element of religious prejudice." When "Lord seemed disposed to object on the ground that this was truth," Code representatives Geoffrey Shurlock and I. Auster rejoined that "this was primarily a policy matter." After the Hays Office and the Code forced Lord to alter his initial treatment, the coworker became a Pole named Dombrowski, although the June memo omits reference to this solution, making note only of the conference ending "with an understanding that a treatment would be made in which Mr. Lord would treat the subject as broadly and strongly as he wished." Lord thus could "test out the limit of the acceptability of the treatment of such subjects as religious and racial prejudices."[357] And test the film did. According to Production Code reports, a number of countries and territories rejected the film outright, including Cyprus, Trinidad, the Philippines, Alberta, Finland, Austria, and parts of Switzerland (the "picture would hurt the moral sense of the . . . population").[358]

The PCA also used the Hollywood Question to justify censorship of anti-Nazi films. Breen and the PCA prevailed upon MGM to rewrite the original F. Scott Fitzgerald–Edward E. Paramore script for *Three Comrades* (1938), eliminating all references to Nazism. The PCA even suggested making "the communists the 'heavies,'" so that several of the original impassioned speeches, originally indicting Nazism, "could stand as they are."[359] Similarly, one trade paper noted the "inevitable deletion of the Jewish question" in *Confessions of a Nazi Spy* (Warner Bros., 1939) – something the paper deemed a sacrifice of "realism." That Warner Bros. could make the film at all remained something of a miracle, however. In a memo to Jack Warner, Breen warned that *Confessions of a Nazi Spy* was "*technically* within the provisions of the Production Code," but nonetheless "*questionable*," since the Code states that "the history, institutions, prominent people and citizenry of other nations shall be represented fairly." Only the fact that "sworn testimony," given at a recent and highly publicized trial in Federal District Court and forming the basis of the film's narrative, spared it from further censorship.[360]

After the PCA tentatively approved the film, staff member Karl Lischka wrote a vehement four-page dissent. Lischka based his protest on the grounds that the film "unfairly represented" Hitler and Nazism "in violation of the Code," and ignored what Lischka called Hitler's "unchallenged political and social achievements," instead portraying him as "a screaming madman and a bloodthirsty persecutor."[361] Paramount censorship expert Luigi Luraschi relayed to Breen an excerpt of a confidential report from the studio's Foreign Department in New York. In response to Warner Bros.' announcement that it would make *Confessions of a Nazi Spy*, the Paramount office warned that, if the film were released, Jews still in Germany might experience "horrible repercussions" and Warner Bros. would "have on their hands the blood of a great many Jews in Germany."[362] Paramount used the Code's precept of refraining from making "any picture that will be obviously uncomplimentary to any nation abroad" as a way to reiterate its own policy. The studio was by no means sympathetic to Nazism; rather, it hewed closely to the Code. If the film were "in any way uncomplimentary to Germany, as it must be if it is to be sincerely produced," then it would be in violation.[363]

Ultimately, though, *Confessions* provides the exception that proved the rule. Claiming to producer Sol Lesser that there was a "consensus" not to make a picture like the proposed *Mad Dog of Europe*, Breen argued:

> This general and unofficial opinion is based pretty generally upon the thought that such a picture is an out-and-out propaganda picture and, while it might serve a good purpose from a propaganda angle, it might likewise establish a bad precedent. The purpose of the screen, primarily, *is to entertain* and *not* to *propagandize*. To launch such a picture might result in a kind of two-edged sword, with the screen being used for propaganda purposes not so worthy, possibly as that suggested by THE MAD DOG OF EUROPE idea.

Of course, the invocation of the entertainment/propaganda dichotomy addresses the Production Code more directly than it promotes anti-Semitism. As Ruth Inglis notes, "the basic premise of the code is that the movies as entertainment and as art affect the moral life of a people."[364] As the Code was meant to allay fears of direct media influence, unsubtle attempts to persuade fell outside the purview of "entertainment." Nonetheless, the distinction between entertainment and propaganda did not stop Breen and others from using the occasion to put Jewish executives in their cultural place. In his memo to Lesser, Breen intimated that a propaganda picture like this one could have a backlash against Jews. "There is a strong pro-German and anti-Semetic [sic] feeling in this country," he warned, "and, while those who are likely to approve of an anti-Hitler picture may think well of such an enterprise, they should keep in mind that millions of Americans might think otherwise." With the "large number of Jews active in the motion picture industry in this country," producers like Lesser needed to take caution. "The charge is certain to be made that the Jews, as a class, are behind an anti-Hitler picture and using the entertainment screen for their own personal propaganda purposes. The entire industry, because of this, is likely to be indicted for the action of a mere handful."[365]

Joseph Kennedy, the U.S. Ambassador to Britain and a onetime film producer himself, issued a similar warning to the movie moguls at dinner banquets. In a November 1941 letter to President Roosevelt, Douglas Fairbanks, Jr., claimed that "the less than admirable" Kennedy "apparently threw the fear of God into many of our producers and executives." Kennedy reportedly warned "that the Jews were on the spot, and that they should stop making anti-Nazi pictures or using the film medium to promote or show sympathy to the cause of the 'democracies' versus the 'dictators.' He said that anti-Semitism was growing in Britain and that the Jews were being blamed for the war."[366] In his autobiography, Fairbanks recognized the dilemma that Jews faced with the Hollywood Question. Although upset over Kennedy's remarks at the time, "an inner voice reminded me of the spot most American Jews were in. If they supported anti-Nazi movments, they would, of course, risk being attacked as warmongers anxious for America to go to war on their behalf. If they did nothing, they were criticized for turning their backs on Jews in Europe."[367]

The entertainment/propaganda dichotomy furthered the Hollywood Question and its attendant discussion of Jews' cultural place, but at the same time popular discourse hardly offered a clear consensus on the issue. In its praise of the British film *Convoy* (1940), released through RKO, *The Hollywood Reporter* effused "if this be propaganda, let's have a lot more of it."[368] *Variety* called *Confessions of a Nazi Spy* "profound entertainment," but noted "that doesn't preclude propaganda." Any "espousal of a cause . . . partakes of the nature of bias." Thus "all patriotism, indeed, is a prejudice."[369]

If the Hollywood Question could inspire such debates and charges of radical and "racial" propaganda, it was also flexible enough to serve the Progressive politics of Upton Sinclair. For Sinclair and his End Poverty in California (EPIC) campaign, the Question served to explain the political conservatism rather than the radicalism of the film industry. Sinclair had first received attention for *The Jungle* (1906), a fictional account that unmasked abuses in the meat-packing industry and led to a number of health and safety reforms, most notably the United States Food and Drug Act. In 1934, the writer and socialist received the California State Democratic Party nomination for governor and almost won. Sinclair's opponent, Republican Frank Merriam, waged a campaign that invoked xenophobic fears and enjoyed the backing of the Hollywood establishment. Ironically, the premise of a movie mogul cabal scheming to defeat a political candidate confirmed the worst fears of the Question. Yet in defeating EPIC's radical program to redistribute the wealth, the conservative alliance could also invoked its own brand of anti-Semitism.

As a writer, Sinclair had purveyed a less than charitable view of the moguls. His *Money Writes* (1927) included a story, allegedly told to him by Charlie Chaplin, of how Chaplin had sold *The Kid* to Associated First National in 1921:

The traders come, great hulks of flesh rolling out of their limousines, and they sit slouched in their chairs, and the reels are unrolled before them, and the sensitive artist sits quivering. . . . "What do you think of it? Is it good?" But the traders do not speak, they understand how to wring the artist soul. How Charlie loathes them – his form swells to greater bulk as he enacts them, his face becomes a grim mask; there comes a grunt from under the chest, and one great hog looks at the next great hog, and at last a verdict: "Vun million is enough, huh?" And the other grunts, "Vun is too much."[370]

Sinclair uses Chaplin's anecdote to characterize commercialism in the arts. The depiction of porcine merchants lording it over the sensitive artist in *Money Writes* recalls religious and moral notions that the commercial Jew posed a threat to culture. Not only do these merchants callously put a price on Chaplin's art; they conduct business like barnyard animals, grunting in dialect as they cut the deal. By establishing Chaplin as the narrator, Sinclair – muckraker and socialist – safely distances himself from the anti-immigrant undercurrent of the passage. Since many believed that Chaplin was half-Jewish (he was not, although the Nazi World Service would perpetrate this myth in the 1940s), the prospect of a perceived Jew criticizing Jewish moguls could further spare Sinclair from criticism.

One could characterize Sinclair's relationship with Hollywood as less than cordial. Approached in 1932 by a recently deposed mogul, William Fox, to write a book about the takeover of his studio, Sinclair deliberated on whether to tell this consummate capitalist's story. He ultimately accepted the offer. Describing the mogul as the owner of "a good Jewish nose," Sinclair nonetheless bonded with Fox over the view that other moguls had conspired to push the founder of the Fox Film Corporation out of his own company. MGM had also adapted Sinclair's Prohibition novel *The Wet Parade* into a movie in 1932, but only after infuriated production head Irving Thalberg had called the author "that Bolshevik," barred him from the lot, and deleted a provision from his contract guaranteeing that the production would maintain the spirit of Sinclair's book. In his next foray into motion pictures, Sinclair financed Russian director Sergei Eisenstein's unfinished prorevolution Mexican epic, *Que Viva Mexico*, long after industry executives had quietly turned down every one of Eisenstein's proposed Hollywood projects.[371]

Of course, the film industry could use the image of the language-fracturing foreigner to benefit its own interests. In 1934, the mirror image of the stereotype Chaplin had relayed to Sinclair returned to haunt the writer during his 1934 Democratic gubernatorial bid. According to Sin-

clair's campaign manager, Irving Thalberg purportedly masterminded a series of faked newsreel interviews attacking Sinclair.[372] The campaign, to
which both Louis B. Mayer and publisher William Randolph Hearst contributed as well, played upon mainstay fears of the electorate. One of these
interviews included a radical foreigner,

> a shaggy man with bristling Russian whiskers and a menacing look in
> his eye.
>   "For whom are you voting?" asked the interviewer.
>   "Vy, I am foting for Seenclair."
>   "Why are you voting for Mr. Sinclair?"
>   "Vell, his system vorked vell in Russia, vy cant it vork here?"[373]

At least one reader of EPIC's newsletter, a prominent Los Angeles
attorney, deconstructed the associations manifest within the newsreel image
of the foreigner. Reprinted in *EPIC News*, H. L. Sacks's open letter to Louis
B. Mayer noted the message that "intelligent gentiles" would support the
Republican candidate, Frank Merriam. Meanwhile, Jews with "Hebrew accents" would support Sinclair because, "as they are made to say, 'we won't
have to work.' " Sacks writes that, as a result of such newsreels, he "and
many others of the Jewish race fear that we in America are but one step
nearer to cruel and barbarous Hitlerism."[374]

Sinclair's EPIC, however, was no bulwark against anti-Semitism. While
its official newsletter published Sacks's letter, one could view such statements less in terms of the organization's righteousness than in terms of its
opportunism. In other settings, EPIC readily brokered any opposition to the
movie moguls, complete with anti-Semitic stereotypes. In *Sodom and Gomorrah* (1935), author Max Knepper crossed the muckraking style of Sinclair's *The Jungle* with a steamy Hollywood potboiler. Sinclair, never one to
err on the side of caution, wrote the laudatory preface to the book. Knepper, a writer for the EPIC newsletter, tried to defuse the charge of anti-
Semitism, accusing producers of issuing "their dismal wail of 'intolerance'
. . . to every type of criticism." The book includes a fictional account, based
on composite characters, of a victimized Christian woman and two film-
industry executives. One of the executives, an associate producer, thinks
he is the "Divinity on Earth." In fact, he is "a fat, short, perspiring gentleman of the Hebrew race, whose appearance did not coincide with his
executive ability, if he had any." He can only speak in pidgin. So physically
repulsive, the "little Hebrew executive" can "get nothing but prostitutes."[375]

The producer sits in judgment on Ireena Delmar, winner of a midwestern
beauty pageant who wishes to become a star. "You got a pretty face," he

tells her, "yah, but ve get tousands of dem. But can you act? Ve vant vot you call personality and dramatic ability. Ve got enuff beauty." When such callousness nearly brings Ireena to tears, the "Jew" looks at her "shrewdly." He eventually sends her, after business hours, to the apartment of his boss, a movie mogul unambiguously named Mr. Lechstein. "If you could love me, I would stop at nothing to make you a great star," Mr. Lechstein tells her. When the mogul tries to "maul" her, Ireena frees herself. "I hate you all, the whole tribe of you," she tells him. "You're all the same, every last one of you. You buy us with promises of fame and money, but you never mean a word you say." Knepper bolsters the charge of Jewish lechery with a quotation from a "famous red-headed star, now in eclipse, who got her start in the East Coast studios." The star told Knepper "she was 'nice to every Jew on Broadway,' her indiscriminate choice of words making a verbatim quotation impossible."[376]

Knepper connects the image of the Oriental parvenu with the theme of the ravished Gentile maiden. Comparing the moguls to Napoleon and Mussolini (and disparagingly noting that "they do not like Hitler"), Knepper describes how "inside their Moorish castles on the top of some Beverly Hills cliff, they can look down on those in the valley and imagine themselves feudal lords. Or, if their fancy dictates, by establishing a few beautiful women in luxurious apartments about town, they can convince themselves that they are Turkish sultans."

Sodom and Gomorrah uses the Hollywood Question to blur fact and fiction, much like the pseudo-real newsreels Hollywood had produced in opposition to Sinclair. Knepper casts the Jewish mogul and producer as egocentric, ignorant, and undeserving parvenus. Their "delusions of grandeur are always most tragic" in their ignorance. They "have no foundation whatever on which to base their mad pretense of greatness." The "uncouth tailors" who became "rulers of the canned-drama" simply happened to be in the right place at the right time. From "flimsy props" they "erected glorious thrones on which they sit and imagine they are gods."[377] Neither these stereotypes nor their appeal to the Hollywood Question were the exclusive domain of fringe conservative politics. Rather, they would come to define two of the most important political movements of the mid-twentieth century.

"NOT AND NEVER HAVE BEEN MEMBERS OF THE COMMUNIST PARTY"

Hollywood's heightened political consciousness, along with its high-profile personnel, set film community activism apart from similar efforts in other fields. A relatively new industry, Hollywood underwent bitter labor struggles during the 1930s and 1940s – much later than the watershed organizing efforts of railroads and the mining industry of the late nineteenth century. Labor organizing within the film industry inspired a high degree of political activism, particularly among Hollywood's creative community. Hollywood writers and actors, along with many American authors and artists, overwhelmingly sided with the Spanish Loyalists against General Franco's Nationalists during the 1936 Spanish Civil War. Hollywood personnel also remained acutely aware of the situation in Nazi Germany. By the end of the 1930s, mainstream journalism hailed Hollywood both for its militant stance against Nazism and for its efforts to shelter European Jews. In 1933, a few days after Hitler came to power, the Nazis barred Jews from the German film industry. Samuel Goldwyn announced that he would "welcome to our motion picture ranks" refugees "who, because of their Jewish heritage, are being deprived of a means of livelihood and an outlet for their talent." While Goldwyn may have had a personal interest in welcoming German Jews to Hollywood, the film industry had already whisked away countless professionals from foreign countries, including Germany. From an employment standpoint, Nazism presented an occasion for Hollywood to justify what it was already doing. As David Welch argues, "racial purification" served as a primary reason for nationalizing the German film industry. Although many left the film industry, Welch argues that many were still willing to stay.[378]

Overall, Goldwyn's offer remained the exception that proved the rule, as United States immigration policy continued to be anything but welcoming. Carl Laemmle assiduously worked around immigration law to obtain visas for German-Jewish émigrés. In a 1938 letter imploring David Selznick to sponsor refugees, Carl Laemmle confesses that he had "issued so many personal affidavits that the United States won't accept any more from me."[379] A 1935 letter asks Leon Lewis, head of the Jewish Community Council, to help get an affidavit for the German director Max Ludwig Berges. "I have issued quite a number of affidavits in the past few years to relatives, near-relatives and close friends," Laemmle writes. "These affidavits naturally put me in a very responsible position so far as the government is concerned and I cannot conscientiously obligate myself to others."[380]

Luminaries like Eddie Cantor and Oscar Hammerstein joined officials from the American Federation of Labor and the American Legion in speaking against fascism at rallies kicking off the Hollywood Anti-Nazi League.[381] In addition to rallies, the five thousand-member league published their own newspaper, sponsored a weekly radio show, canvassed Southern California for a boycott of German products, and blockaded meetings of the pro-Nazi Los Angeles German-American Bund. Hollywood personnel often remained active in such activities. Fred S. Meyer of Universal alerted Leon Lewis to area businesses selling German products. Newberry stores "handle any amount of product made in Germany," while the "Lamaze Café, probably our foremost restaurant which is patronized about ninety per cent by Jews, is featuring German wine."[382]

Observer Leo Rosten would later claim that the figure of five thousand was "probably an overstatement," but the Hollywood Anti-Nazi League did attract a good deal of attention. The organization publicized the visit of Vittorio Mussolini, the son of the Italian fascist dictator, causing much embarrassment. Similarly, when German director Leni Riefenstahl visited Hollywood at the behest of Walt Disney, the league brought her presence to public light as well.[383] Not everyone remembers Riefenstahl's self-professed impartiality toward Nazism. Herbert Luft recalls Riefenstahl telling a group of producers that reports of the atrocities coming out of Germany before the outbreak of World War II were the "gruesome propaganda of irresponsible journalists."[384] The League did not always succeed in rallying support for such actions, even among the Jewish community. By 1937, the B'nai B'rith issued a statement refusing official backing for the anti-Nazi boycott, instead leaving that decision up to individual members. "The B'nai B'rith has many lodges in Germany," writes B'nai B'rith district secretary Leonard H. Freiberg, "who [sic] number among their members the most able and influential Jews in that country. For the B'nai B'rith to endorse the boycott would mean not merely a decision as to the wisdom of the course, but would expose the members of the Order in Germany to more violent persecution than that to which they are now subjected."[385]

The Hollywood community played an important role in both the La Follette and Dies Committees. Extremely popular with the film community, the La Follette Committee investigated violations of civil liberties and free speech – something that appealed to those for whom such freedoms affected their livelihood. When La Follette began investigating California agricultural interests and the miserable employment conditions of the state's migrant farm workers, Hollywood writers, directors, and other personnel enthusiastically supported the committee, finding a kindred political and social agenda outside their own labor and union struggles. Meanwhile, Hollywood personnel lobbied for projects that maintained increasingly overt stances against fascism. Films like *Blockade* (United Artists, 1938), *Confessions of a Nazi Spy* (Warner Bros., 1939), and *The Mortal Storm*

(MGM, 1940) would later provoke the ire of political conservatives and isolationists. As one correspondent lobbied Will Hays:

> It is hoped you will see fit to ban *all* the present crop of hate foment-
> ing war propaganda films such as *The Mortal Storm* and others now
> being rushed to completion.
>
> At a time like this we need all of our reasoning faculties to retain
> an even mental keel. These rabid rabble rousing pictures will only stir
> up emotions against one side of the European conflict, and you know
> we must do all in our power to remain neutral.[386]

Indeed, Hollywood's high-profile political engagement had its hazards. The charge of "propaganda" in particular proved an attractive vehicle to discredit these films and their makers. Producer Walter Wanger's *Blockade* (United Artists, 1938) encountered tremendous opposition from the Vati-can and Roman Catholic Church, staunch supporters of Generalissimo Francisco Franco and his military coup against a democratically elected republic. The Knights of Columbus Hollywood Council 1938 *Bulletin* de-cries the making of *Blockade*, linking it to an insidious propaganda. On the film's release, the Supreme Board of Directors sent a telegram to Will Hays, noting resentment over "this excursion of the motion picture industry into the field of Leftist propaganda." Raising the specter of a boycott, the board – "representing 500,000 members in 2,500 councils throughout America" – demanded "prompt and positive assurance" from Hays that their members could "continue to patronize motion picture theaters without being exposed to films that offer, under the pretense of entertainment, nothing more than special pleading in behalf of forces inimical to the ideals of American democracy and the Christianity which they profess."[387]

Such hazards extended beyond attacks on the films themselves. By the late 1930s, George E. Browne and Willie Bioff's corrupt leadership and their ties to organized crime nearly ruined the International Alliance of Theatrical Stage Employees (IATSE), one of Hollywood's most important unions. Political activism held perils as well. In the tumultuous events leading up to World War II, allegiances often shifted radically. As August Raymond Ogden notes, prior to the German–Soviet Pact of 5 September 1939, virtually every Communist opposed Nazism. The 1933 Moscow Third International gave rise to the Popular Front, a vow to fight Fascism by uniting with Socialism. However, the 1939 pact proved to be one of the most traumatic events in the history of Communism. When Stalin signed this short-lived treaty with Germany, Communists either had to repudiate the Soviet government or risk appearing as its tool. Demonstrating the central and arbitrary power of Moscow, the pact alienated party membership, spurring many to leave the organization over this issue. Inside Russia, Stalin "purged" his opponents, sending them to death camps and ordering widespread executions. Though not new, such actions taking place under Soviet-style Communism received increased scrutiny.[388]

Meanwhile, the anti-Communist, antilabor and anti–New Deal Dies Committee launched a series of offensives against both the La Follette Committee and Hollywood. Dies accused the La Follette Committee of harboring Communists. As Hollywood supported the La Follette hearings, Dies assumed that Hollywood was Communist too. Traveling to Hollywood twice, Dies conducted his investigation out of his hotel room. On his second trip, after two weeks of personal interviews, Dies concluded that the movie moguls and stars were sufficiently opposed to Communism. While Hollywood earned a short-term reprieve, Dies's "investigation" set a disturbing and sinister precedent.

The manner in which Dies conducted his investigation of Hollywood "propaganda" marked a turning point in congressional advocacy. As Ogden explains, the Dies Committee belonged to a long tradition of government by congressional hearing.[389] Congressional hearings had publicized the Teapot Dome scandal of President Harding's administration – in which Will Hays had served as postmaster general. Senator Gerald Nye had exposed the power and influence of the World War I munitions industry in a much lauded series of congressional hearings. In most cases, these investigations went after abuses of power.

The Dies Committee maintained the same morally righteous stance that had defined earlier investigations against unscrupulous trusts, presidential cronyism, and abuses of public confidence. But the Dies Committee applied this stance to something much less circumscribed. Approved by the House in 1938, Dies's measure proposed to investigate "the extent, character, and objects of un-American propaganda activities in the United States" and "the diffusion within the United States of subversive and un-American propaganda that is instigated from foreign countries or of a domestic origin and attacks the principle of the form of government as guaranteed by the Constitution."[390]

The allegation of "propaganda" and "subversive activities" lacked the focus of previous congressional hearings, thus making such charges the ideal conveyance with which to mount a broad range of protest. During the HUAC hearings, Dies attacked the Works Progress Administration, the Federal Theatre and Writers' Project, the National Labor Relations Board, the Department of Labor, the Workers' Alliance, and the American Youth Congress.[391] In the committee, whatever one did not like one called Communist "propaganda." J. Parnell Thomas, who would figure prominently in the House Committee when he continued his membership after World War II, claimed that the Federal Theatre and Writers' Project was a "vast and unparalleled New Deal propaganda machine."[392] Alleging that Communists had infiltrated "a majority of the activities on the West Coast," Harper Knowles, head of the California American Legion's radical research committee, testified that the American Civil Liberties Union (ACLU) was Communist.[393] Objecting to a section of the ACLU platform calling for the abolition of state motion picture censorship boards, Knowles asserted that the allegedly Communist ACLU "would soon have the producers catering to the perverted minds in our country through suggestive, lewd, and licentious pictures."[394] In fact, the ACLU would prove to be anything but Communist. As Victor Navasky has shown, the organization publicly opposed Communism throughout the 1950s while privately encouraging those accused of Communist leanings to name names.

Yet another disenchanted New Dealer like La Follette, Martin Dies found in the allegation of "propaganda" and "subversive activities" a way to articulate his own conservative political agenda. Anti-immigrant, anti-union, anti-Communist, and ultimately anti-FDR, Dies – like others who articulated the Hollywood Question – reacted out of what John R. Poe describes as a fear of increasing "centralization."[395] Born in Colorado, Texas, in 1901, Dies Jr. had followed in his father's footsteps. Also a Democrat, Dies Sr. had served as a congressman for ten years, opposing the United States's entry into World War I and breaking with President Woodrow Wilson over the League of Nations. Elected at age thirty to serve in the U.S. House, Dies Jr. initially supported New Deal measures through Roosevelt's first term before opposing the president over the 1937 court-packing plan. Dies, however, had already established his ultraconservative agenda. In order to make jobs for "native-born" citizens, Dies once proposed that America deport six million aliens, and in 1936 he sided with General Motors during the United Auto Workers sit-down strikes.[396]

Dies and the committee did investigate homegrown Nazism. After six months, investigator James Metcalfe listed forty-six Nazi and Fascist groups operating primarily in the eastern, midwestern, and southern regions of the United States.[397] Most notably, the committee exposed an anti-Semitic plot to take over the United States, implicating high-profile figures like the retired and near-senile General George Van Horn Moseley.[398] Though Moseley's means may have been off-putting, his message resonated with a long-standing perception associating Jews with Communism. Reading a 1938 excerpted speech into the record, committee counsel Rhea Whitley noted how Moseley called upon Jews to renounce all ties to Communism:

"It is the greatest opportunity that has been offered the Jewish people in all their history. If they will accomplish that, there will be an applause go up from ocean to ocean.

"How can they do it? They can stop communism in the United States in just 30 days by doing what? By using what power? The power that they now have so completely over the radio; the power that they have over the public press; the control they have over the 'movies'; and, finally, the power they have now at home and internationally, in the money markets of the world."[399]

Throughout its hearings, the committee persistently demonstrated how overt anti-Semitism like that of Moseley was no longer fashionable. But Dies's anti-Nazism appeared at best half-hearted. According to Dennis Kay McDaniel, Dies accepted inflated speaking honoraria from various Jewish groups that hoped to influence the HUAC to pursue its investigation of anti-Semitic organizations in the country.[400] According to Crawford, Dies had kept his chief investigator, Edward F. Sullivan, even after some unsavory facts had emerged. In addition to having a police record, Sullivan, who had once spied on labor for the "malodorous" Railway Audit and Inspection Company, Inc., allegedly had ties to the rabidly anti-Semitic James True. Crawford ultimately described Sullivan "as a professional baiter of Jews and Catholics," and noted how, once part of Dies's office, Sullivan was now loudly complaining that Hollywood was rife with Communists.[401]

Even if these claims appear somewhat overstated, the committee's investigation into Nazism consistently referred back to Communism. The following exchange between Dies and Bernhard Hofmann, president of the Wisconsin Federation of German-American Societies, reveals not so much a sympathy for Jews as a passion for anti-Communism:

DIES: "Do you feel that any effort to arouse racial or religious hatred is distinctly un-American."
HOFMANN: "I do."
DIES: "Do you feel the same way about any effort to arouse and promote class hatred?"
HOFMANN: "I do; definitely so."
DIES: "Do you not classify class hatred with racial and religious

hatred? In other words, those who promote class hatred, are they not inviting race and religious hatred?"

HOFMANN: "Yes; they are."

DIES: "Has not that been the story in Europe, that the first movement started as a movement of class hatred and then came the religious and racial hatred?"

HOFMANN: "You are entirely correct."

DIES: "And many of those who claim to be the champions of racial and religious tolerance are themselves promoting class hatred; is not that a fact?"

HOFMANN: "That is correct."

DIES: "And they are bringing upon their own heads a boomerang in the form of racial or religious hatred; is not that a fact?"

HOFMANN: "That is correct."

DIES: "So as Americans, we must not only fight racial or religious intolerance, but class intolerance as well?"

HOFMANN: "I believe you are correct, Mr. Chairman."[402]

The notion that Communism had somehow brought about the rise of Nazism powerfully resonated with the Hollywood Question. A letter to the committee from Jack Peyton, secretary of the National Protective Order of Gentiles, argues that "there are tremendous problems to be solved in our own country, which leave us little or no time" to fight for what he calls "a grudge a racial minority has against a nation in which their power and activities have been somewhat restricted."[403] The Legion of Decency's executive secretary, John T. McClafferty, found *Confessions of a Nazi Spy* more pro-Communist than anti-Nazi and complained that German director Leni Riefenstahl had not been treated with proper deference when she visited Hollywood, shortly after Kristallnacht.[404]

Dies's invocation of the Hollywood Question reveals how the HUAC implicitly associated Jews with Communism. In a series of articles written for *Liberty* magazine in 1940, he accused Hollywood of having been "completely duped by the Communists" along with "every professional liberal" and "racketeer." Dies contended that Hollywood producers were

naturally and properly opposed to Nazi activities and fearful of the growth of any anti-Semitic feeling throughout the country. Being sensitive on this point, they naturally sympathize with any group or organization which professes strong opposition to Nazi or Fascist ideologies. . . . They are therefore anxious to do everything within their power to prevent the spread of Nazism and Fascism in America.[405]

In Dies's view, Jews functioned as little more than dupes of a larger, insidious Communist plot. "Most of the producers are Jews," he writes, "who have made a remarkable success in building the film industry." While Dies expressed sympathy for the plight of the Jews, he believed that Jews were more susceptible to Communist influence than any other ethnic group. In the Hollywood Question, Dies found an explanation for Jewish Communism that could reconcile harsh, conspiracy-laced accusations articulated by opponents to the New Deal with growing public sympathy for Jews, the latter consisting of both opposition to Nazism and a celebration of the Horatio Alger–like success of movie moguls. Amid this support, Jewish moguls and stars had to prove that they had not been duped by Communism but were patriotic Americans. Once the Dies Committee achieved notoriety after World War II, assuming the moniker of the House Un-American Activities Committee, film industry executives were more than eager to disassociate their studios from the Communist bogey. For anti-Communist opposition to the New Deal, the Hollywood Question was never more than a means to an end. But it was an effective means that attracted public attention and eventually cost hundreds of careers, and even some lives.

Dies's eventual visits to Hollywood during the summer of 1940 eerily prefigured the postwar actions of HUAC. In the first, relatively unpublicized visit, Dies got former Communist John L. Leech to name names in a closed executive session. According to Leo Rosten, Dean James Landis of the Harvard Law School "had all but called Leech a pathological liar."[406] Disclosing the names of forty-two celebrities, Leech had a proven past as a friendly witness who had testified at the deportation trial of Australian labor organizer Harry Bridges. Dies handed this list of names to Los Angeles District Attorney Buron Fitts, who promptly subpoenaed fourteen members of the Screen Writers Guild.[407]

If Dies's investigation of Hollywood prefigured later HUAC investigations and closed-door accusations, it also impelled the film industry to rehearse an emboldened, organized stance that would later emerge in the face of isolationist attacks. When Fitts began proceedings against the Screen Actors Guild, the guild promptly published a laudatory letter it had solicited from the district attorney weeks earlier.[408] Former HUAC secretary Robert Stripling, who accompanied Dies on both of his trips out to California, claims that the Representative appeared decidedly less interested in ferreting out Communists after meeting with the head of Paramount Studios, Y. Frank Freeman.[409] In a prepared statement to the press outside Dies's hotel room, Freeman agreed to cooperate with "a complete and impartial investigation," yet he made it clear that the industry's thirty-two thousand employees were "not willing to yield to anyone in their true Americanism."[410] Dies's investigation fizzled, and his second trip served more as a conciliatory gesture. Meeting with James Cagney, Humphrey Bogart, Fredric March, and Phillip Dunne, Dies later pronounced that they were "not, and never have been, members of the Communist Party."[411]

THE HOLLYWOOD QUESTION AND ISOLATIONISM

While the Dies Committee – informed by the Hollywood Question – helped lay the discursive roadbed over which both later investigations of the film industry and responses to such investigations would travel, its immediate impact remained relatively minor. Although polling data show high public recognition of the Dies Committee, similar data suggest strong support for the committee to take a different focus in its investigation. Throughout the 1930s, many opposed U.S. entry into yet another world war. According to a November 1936 American Institute Opinion Poll, 95 percent of the American people opposed American participation in the war.[412] The debate over this entry had less to do with foreign policy, however, than it had to do with a fear of the mass media. A 1939 Gallup Poll found 42 percent of the public believed that investigating war propaganda was more important than investigating Nazism, Fascism, or Communism in America.[413]

This fear reflected a larger set of concerns over the increasing centralization of presidential power. Many who either enthusiastically or grudgingly supported the New Deal eventually grew disenchanted with its program, believing that its measures had stopped short of radical financial and social reform. Roosevelt further alienated both liberal and conservative supporters in 1937, when he introduced his "court-packing plan" to consolidate presidential power. The Supreme Court had consistently ruled against the constitutionality of New Deal reforms; born out of Roosevelt's frustrations over these rulings, the plan would have given the president broad authority. For every Supreme Court justice who failed to either resign or retire before his seventy-first birthday, Roosevelt proposed to appoint an additional justice of his own choosing. As Wayne Cole notes, Congress had called for ways to obviate Supreme Court decisions since the early 1900s; but both Republicans and Democrats viewed Roosevelt's proposal as a dangerous threat to the traditional balance between executive and judicial branches of government. And, of course, politicians across the liberal-conservative spectrum eyed Roosevelt's willingness to involve the United States in World War II with suspicion, wondering if the country had learned anything from its participation in World War I.[414] Ultimately, however, battles over Roosevelt's court-packing plan and U.S. intervention reflected heightened usage of public opinion polls. As Cole notes, both Roosevelt and isolationists used polling data extensively throughout this era. Although this data supported some United States involvement in World War II, the public overwhelmingly opposed an outright declaration of war. Isolationists paid little heed to this distinction, even though they consistently referred to one finding that showed 80 percent of the public opposed a formal announcement of war.[415]

Well before Pearl Harbor in December 1941, President Roosevelt was using his presidential power to escalate U.S. involvement in World War II. In September 1940, he unilaterally traded fifty American destroyers in exchange for leases to British bases. A few weeks later, he signed the Selective Training and Service Act, which called for the first peacetime draft in U.S. history. Throughout 1941, the Roosevelt administration pushed the Lend-Lease Act through Congress. Providing Great Britain with $7 billion in weapons to defend itself in exchange for U.S. leases on strategically located British military bases, the legislation merely codified what Roosevelt had already been doing for years. The Lend-Lease Act only formalized the president's ability to provide massive foreign-aid packages, allowing him to "authorize . . . any department or agency of the Government" to sell, transfer, exchange, lease, lend, or engage in any other disposal of U.S. weapons and aid, first to Great Britain and then to the Soviet Union.[416]

Concern over these efforts to assist Britain also focused on the president's ties to the film industry. The federal government, of course, had worked closely with Hollywood throughout the New Deal era. But Roosevelt ostensibly had other means of influence as well. Samuel Goldwyn hired his son, James Roosevelt, as a studio vice president. Roosevelt's son-in-law, John Boettiger, had worked for the Hays Office. As editor of the *Seattle Post-Intelligencer*, Boettiger publicly opposed block-booking legislation.[417] To isolationist eyes, such nepotism reflected a larger pattern of centralized influence and control.

Concern over increased centralization, or even the appearance of such, connected isolationism to older, more traditional themes. Isolationism itself had historical roots in a long-standing American policy that steadfastly refused to engage in "foreign entanglements." Yet despite its traditionalism, as Wayne Cole notes, isolationism shared more in common with liberal progressivism than it did with conservatism.[418] Isolationist motifs resonated with the themes of international banking, trust-busting, and wartime propaganda that had appeared in Populist and Progressive discourse since the late nineteenth century. Coupled with a folksy, commonsense appeal to grass-roots activism and a straight-talking radicalism without apologies, isolationism could draw upon these themes in a highly persuasive manner.

Key figures of the isolationist movement – John Rankin, Burton K. Wheeler, and Gerald P. Nye – had all come from Populist and Progressive backgrounds. Mississippi Representative John Rankin, who would succeed in making the HUAC a standing committee after World War II, had promoted rural electrification, increased federal aid for farmers, and advocated a progressive tax and increased regulation of big business during the 1930s. Trust-busting rhetoric informed Rankin's attitudes toward Jews. When Rankin, like Louis McFadden, passionately spoke of "international" Jews, his zealotry expressed – among other things – opposition to big business and monopolies. Rankin saw Nazi persecution as the logical reaction to Jewish international banking. Jews had brought their plight upon themselves and would incur a similar wrath in the United States if they were given the chance. Jewish bankers "first crucified the German Republic," Rankin told Congress in 1941, "and in doing so they created Hitler. He is their baby. Hitler never would have been heard of if it had not been for these elements swarming into Germany and undermining the German Republic."[419] Yet Rankin, while not exactly known for his philo-Semitism, would not have considered himself anti-Semitic. Rather, isolationist discourse helped him draw the distinction between "the international Jew, whether he is an international banker or an international Communist, and the American Jew who makes this his home, who is trying to build up and defend his country, and who must now suffer for the misconduct of these international Jews who are always stirring up trouble for them." In Rankin's estimable opinion, the "international" Jews rallying for U.S. intervention were "making the greatest blunder since the Crucifixion," thus giving all of Jewry a bad name.[420]

However insensitive, such rhetoric marked a significant departure from the racial stereotypes and obsession with moral turpitude so prevalent in the literature and imagery depicting the theater and Hollywood. Racialized images of Jews were secondary role to the rhetoric condemning Communist banking conspiracies, inspired by *The Protocols of the Elders of Zion.* Yet isolationist anti-Semitism was hardly just the spawn of European anti-

Semitism. More recent images of Jewish "conspiracies" remained a distinctly American phenomenon, cutting across political and cultural boundaries. Heavily influenced by Populist and Progressive opposition to international finance and war, the nationalist demonization of Jewish control over the media simply articulated a belief that Jews lurked behind a creeping centralization in everyday American life. In the heyday of Progressivism, Robert M. La Follette, Sr., had argued that international banking had caused World War I and enslaved farmers. With the help of the *Protocols* and a crisis within capitalism, one could easily shift Progressive rhetoric from an emphasis upon ban*king* to ban*kers*.[421]

Like Rankin, Senator Burton K. Wheeler had emerged from a strong Populist and antitrust tradition. Born in Hudson, Massachusetts, in 1882, Wheeler recalls in his autobiography the 1896 presidential debates between William Jennings Bryan and William F. McKinley. "I took the side of William Jennings Bryan," Wheeler writes. Not only did Bryan "convert" him to the Democratic Party; Wheeler "had been for the remonetization of silver ever since."[422] In 1906, Wheeler began his career as a personal injury attorney for miners in Butte, Montana. There, he encountered large, powerful companies like the Anaconda Copper Mining Co. and the Montana Power Company. Elected to the Montana legislature in 1910, he served as U.S. district attorney from 1913 to 1918.[423] As district attorney, Wheeler began to notice a number of cases where mining interests tried to discredit labor organizers by claiming that, under the Espionage Act of 1917, they were disloyal. Himself opposed to U.S. entry into World War I, Wheeler noted with alarm how large corporations would then publicize these charges in company-owned newspapers.[424]

Wheeler's political tactics prefigured McCarthyism by more than twenty years. After losing a state gubernatorial bid in 1920, he won a seat in the United States Senate two years later. In a story later immortalized by Frank Capra's *Mr. Smith Goes to Washington* (Columbia, 1939), the freshman senator headed an investigation into Harry Daugherty and his "Ohio Gang." Wheeler accused the attorney general for the Coolidge administration of being soft on crime, taking bribes, and ignoring the Teapot Dome scandal when he had served, along with Will H. Hays, under the Harding administration. In conducting his investigation, as Donald Cameron notes, Wheeler, like McCarthy, smeared his opponent with as yet unproven allegations. In an interview with Cameron, Wheeler even admitted that "he didn't have one piece of conclusive evidence" when he launched the Senate hearings, instead going on a "hunch."[425]

Handpicked by Robert La Follette in 1924 as the Progressive Party's vice-presidential candidate, Wheeler reiterated familiar Populist refrains throughout the campaign. According to Cameron, Wheeler repeatedly gave the same basic speech, blaming Wall Street; accusing a small group of people of controlling resources and government while exploiting everyone else; and preferring "a dictatorship of the common people of America to a dictatorship of the House of Morgan."[426] Once ensconced in the Progressive Party, Wheeler later helped Roosevelt gain the 1932 Democratic nomination, even coaxing Louisiana Governor Huey Long into endorsing the presidential candidate.

An early advocate of New Deal programs, Wheeler parted company with Roosevelt over Populist mainstays. In addition to objecting to Roosevelt's court-packing scheme, Wheeler vocally supported the remonetization of silver, even meeting with Father Coughlin in 1933 to press for his support of the issue.[427] Despite differences over this and other issues, the Roosevelt administration nonetheless courted Wheeler – albeit unsuccessfully – for a 1940 vice-presidential bid.[428]

Wheeler's traditional Populist politics included a particular interest in the regulation of mass communications. Appointed in 1934 to serve as chair of the Interstate Commerce Committee, Wheeler vigorously opposed " 'soap operas' and too much jazz music." Fighting against communication monopolies, he forced an FCC investigation that ultimately lowered AT&T long-distance rates. He ardently supported the creation of the CBS radio network, fearing that NBC's ownership of two networks – the Red and the Blue – threatened democracy by putting "such powerful opinion-forming organizations in the hands of a single company."[429] His opposition to a 1939 plan by FCC commissioner and their James Fly to implement radio superstations reveals how Populist ideals helped Wheeler to define the public interest in terms of the American small town. "I pointed out," Wheeler writes, "that the super-power stations would have all the best programs and thus get all the business. A little station serving a community could not compete. I also told Fly that only a rich political candidate could afford to buy time on a super-power station." Wheeler later proposed a Senate resolution placing a ceiling of 50,000 watts for all radio stations. Although it never had the force of law or FCC policy behind it, the FCC nonetheless tacitly enforced this ceiling for years to come.[430] Firmly committed to the principle of "public interest, convenience and necessity," Wheeler argued that "the air space was owned by the public" and that "those who used it had responsibilities to the public and should not look upon it as a private preserve to be exploited solely for profit."[431]

Although Wheeler's concern for the public interest emerged out of a deeply felt Populist tradition, he shared neither the sympathy for Nazism nor the suspicion of Hollywood evinced by isolationist and anti–New Deal counterparts like Rankin. Wheeler had publicly condemned anti-Semitism and Hitler, and supported the creation of a Jewish homeland. In 1938, he addressed the Brooklyn Chapter of the United Palestine Appeal, urging the United States to "exert its influence in favor of allowing maximum Jewish immigration to Palestine."[432] And although Wheeler assembled the Senate subcommittee that would investigate war propaganda, Kenneth Crawford argues that the senator remained relatively sympathetic to Hollywood. The film industry had offered his son a job, which the latter declined, but Wheeler had attended a Hollywood junket in the late 1930s. And although Wheeler's appointments to the Senate subcommittee were overwhelmingly isolationist, many of its members had also opposed the Neely bill outlawing block booking and blind bidding.[433]

North Dakota Senator Gerald P. Nye also sprang from the same Populist tradition shared by Wheeler and Rankin. Wheeler even campaigned for the Progressive Republican's unsuccessful 1926 senatorial bid.[434] Born in 1892 in Hortonville, Wisconsin, Nye served as editor of a series of small-town newspapers in Wisconsin and Iowa before moving to North Dakota in 1911. Editing a newspaper there, he ardently supported La Follette in his 1924 presidential campaign. Appointed to the Senate in 1925 by the state governor, Nye later won a full term in 1932.[435] A 1926 *Gaelic American* article lauded Nye for his opposition to Calvin Coolidge over the World Court, a precursor to the United Nations.[436] As chair of the Public Lands Committee he investigated millionaires Harry F. Sinclair and Andrew Mellon. Nye's greatest exposure came in 1934, when he chaired a well-publicized investigation into the munitions industry. Its revelations proved particularly embarrassing to financier J. P. Morgan and made the arms industry appear to be a threat to world peace. Ultimately, the munitions investigations brought about the 1935 Neutrality Act. Drafted by Nye, the act proved a worthy obstacle to Roosevelt's interventionist efforts, facilitating 1937 legislation that further strengthened American neutrality. When Roosevelt tried to repeal the act's embargo on arms sales in 1939, Nye remained at the forefront of the opposition.[437]

During these investigations, Nye hired John T. Flynn, a respected journalist for a variety of magazines, including *The New Republic*. Flynn, like Nye, had started his career as a newspaper editor. Flynn had also served as economic advisor to the 1933–34 U.S. Senate Committee on Banking and Currency investigation into the stock exchange before Nye tapped him for the munitions investigation.[438] As editor of *Collier's*, Flynn would later lend

insight into the murky world of economics. A 1937 article authored by
him, for example, purports to examine deficit financing by looking "at our
dear old Uncle Samuel Shylock, money-lender, in action."[439] A year after
leaving his post at *The New Republic* over the magazine's interventionist
stance, Flynn would join Nye in shepherding the 1941 Motion Picture
Propaganda Hearings.[440]

As Wayne Cole observes, the Populist-inflected isolationism of both
Nye and Flynn resonated with Nye's political constituency. Predominately
white, Christian, and hailing from German, Scandinavian, English, Scot-
tish, and Irish backgrounds, this constituency occupied the margins of an
increasingly urban, industrialized, culturally and ethnically diverse America
moving toward ever-growing importance within world affairs.[441] Perceiving
themselves as in conflict with railroads, bankers, financiers, cities, big business, big government, big military, and the urban East Coast elite,[442] Nye's
voters, according to Cole, resided in the "rural, agricultural, small town,
small business" of American life. "The America that Senator Nye identified
with and spoke for (and that most other western progressive isolationists
spoke for)," Cole writes, "was overwhelmingly rural and small town. It was
an America consisting largely of farmers on the soil and of small businessmen buying and selling to those farmers in countless small towns scattered
across the prairies and Great Plains."[443]

Hardly dead after Pearl Harbor, this Populist-inflected isolationism
would thrive in the politics of the Old Right. In postwar years, John Flynn
championed its arch-conservatism, calling for a limited, decentralized federal government, a radically deregulated market economy, and an end to
welfare, militarism, the United Nations, and income tax. Owing much to
the liberalism of Wheeler, Wagner, and LaFollette, Flynn's Populist sensibilities developed into a rabid anti-Communism that could both defended
Senator Joe McCarthy and attacked the New Deal as part of a Soviet-
inspired plot.[444]

Before World War II, Populist isolationism sustained Nye's opposition
to Roosevelt and the Democratic Party. The senator battled Roosevelt over
neutrality laws. Replacing fellow Progressive William E. Borah on the
Senate Foreign Relations Committee in 1940, Nye opposed aid to the
Soviet Union, Roosevelt's peacetime draft, and his lend-lease efforts. No
friend of organized labor, he nonetheless criticized the Democratic Party for
abandoning the principles of the New Deal in favor of banking, big business, and a bloated military and governmental bureaucracy.[445] When the
isolationist America First movement coalesced in the summer of 1940, Nye

– a powerful and eloquent foe of the Roosevelt administration – agreed to serve as its unofficial spokesman.

America First emerged as the foremost dissenting voice against the United States's entry into World War II. Initially called the Emergency Committee to Defend America First, the association complemented the efforts of other antiwar groups like the Committee to Defend America by Aiding the Allies, which had already started to organize war protests. The son of a Quaker Oats executive, Robert Douglas Stuart, Jr., got his father's company to subsidize office space in Chicago. After unsuccessfully approaching Burton K. Wheeler, Stuart then convinced U.S. Army General Robert E. Wood to head the organization.[446] Wood brought prestige to America First. A war hero, he had put down the Philippine rebellion and helped build the Panama Canal. As well as serving as vice president for Sears Roebuck and Company, Wood served on a number of boards of directors, including the conservative, pro-business National Association of Manufacturers.[447]

The New Republic writer and Nye ally John Flynn took an increasingly active role in America First, eventually becoming the chair of its New York City chapter. A small but high-profile contingent of liberals that included Oswald Garrison Villard, former editor of *The New Republic*, Amos Pinchot, and Samuel Hopkins Adams joined him.

Articulating mainstream opposition to Roosevelt, isolationist groups like America First faced an influx of extreme right-wing marginal voices. Well-financed and supported, America First issued its first press release on 4 September 1940. A few months later, it began coordinating a barrage of radio speeches, meetings, and paid political statements in newspapers across the country. The difference between the views issued by this well-funded political organization and those of the Roosevelt administration characterized what many called "The Great Debate."[448] According to Anne Lindbergh, people attending a 1941 Madison Square Garden rally for America First booed John Flynn when he warned of possible support from fascists, bundists, and members of the Christian Front. Both Flynn and Wheeler feared that the German-American Bund, Coughlin's Christian Front, the American Destiny Party, Pelley's Silver Shirts, and the Ku Klux Klan were trying to infiltrate America First.[449]

The views and influence of these groups, however, remained extremely unpopular. In particular, Flynn constantly remained on guard against their penetration of America First. Rankin's views soon proved unpopular as well. In a 1941 address before the House, Rankin accused "Wall Street and a little group of our international Jewish brethren" of both "plunging us into the European war unprepared; and at the same time . . . fomenting strikes by harassing industry and slowing down our defense program." New York Democrat E. Michael Edelstein delivered an eloquent denunciation of this accusation, noting how Hitler had referred to the Jews in similar fashion and calling such thinking "unfair" and "un-American." So agitated was he by Rankin's diatribe, however, Edelstein suffered a fatal heart attack just minutes after he had addressed the House.[450]

Edelstein's sudden death marked a turning point in toleration for such anti-Semitic rhetoric. The New York Representative became a martyr. Newspapers across the nation denounced Rankin and such views. As Edward Shapiro notes, Southern newspapers – overwhelmingly interventionist – began to question Rankin's views on blacks and Jews for the first time. Even Rankin's hometown paper, *The Tupelo Journal*, stated that now they were "heartily ashamed" of his "Jew-baiting."[451]

Although Edelstein's death on the House floor had provoked an unequivocal, widespread condemnation of public Jew-baiting, this response also coincided with the increasing unpopularity of Nazi anti-Semitism. Yet if the country's sentiment had swung in favor of intervention and away from the views of men like Rankin, the future, constituency, and principles of Progressive politics became increasingly cloudy. Beginning with the fall 1936 elections, a conservative Democratic coalition consistently voted against the president. Roosevelt had enjoyed the support of his own party in the predominately urban, liberal Northeast corridor. But when the president targeted conservative senators within his own party for defeat, most ended up winning their elections – and carrying renewed antagonism toward Roosevelt. Meanwhile, America First, whose founding members had envisioned a democratic pacifist organization, soon had to grapple with members sympathetic to Nazism and Fascism.

Clouded by more than just anti-Semitism, Progressive politics faced a shifting national identity and a new set of attendant myths. Hardly stable since the end of World War I, this identity underwent significant changes in the period leading up to World War II. The struggle between rural-agrarian and urban-industrial America yielded to an emergent, third identity: America as global superpower and national security state. Amid these discursive shifts and struggles, the ever flexible Hollywood Question could help to define the meaning of this new national identity, who would partake of it, and who would reap its benefits.

Members of Congress opposed to Roosevelt's New Deal and foreign policy tried to resist the changing national identity. Such resistance often entailed associating Jews with Communism or attacking alleged Hollywood-Jewish propaganda. The usefulness of these arguments, however, required a presentation compatible with the nationalism of the day. After what Senator Nye would refer to as the "inborn hatreds and prejudices" of Hollywood, the isolationist Senate Subcommittee to Investigate Motion Picture Propaganda lasted less than three weeks before collapsing amid widespread allegations of anti-Semitism. On the other hand, the House of Representatives had recently renewed funding for the Dies Committee. Initially envisioned as a congressional weapon against Nazi activities in the United States, this committee successfully reshaped the accusation of Jewish control over Hollywood to fit within a prevailing anti-Communist rhetoric.

With the United States's entry into World War II, a new national identity emphasized conformity, patriotism, and a nascent anti-Communism in ways that relegated the traditional, more overtly anti-Semitic charge of Jewish control to the margins of public discourse. In Hollywood, Jewish movie executives followed public opinion, ostensibly embracing calls for "national unity" issued by the Roosevelt administration and interventionists. As Cole notes, anything short of such an embrace risked accusations of Fascism, Nazism, and Fifth Column sympathies.[452] Of course, embracing "national unity" could also lead to motion picture personnel being hauled before various congressional subcommittees investigating Hollywood. For the time being, however, the embrace proved an effective public-relations strategy, in line with both the president and opinion polls. Meanwhile, American writers living and working in Hollywood used their real-life environs as a fictional backdrop to capture and comment upon the social implications of this national identity. To varying degrees, these books emerged out of a larger response, implicating Hollywood Jews within a shifting nationalism and the failure of the traditional American Dream myth. Using the racialized image of the Jew to comment upon these upheavals, the Hollywood Question even helped drive a response to anti-Semitism. Largely pro-Semitic, this response nonetheless subsumed Jewish ethnicity under the rubric of a hypernationalized identity.

6

Answering the Hollywood Question

THE ANTI-SEMITISM OF "A VERY SICK DONKEY"

Because of its unique flexibility, the Hollywood Question was able to address a number of shifts taking place in America during the late 1930s. One of these was an emergent discourse on national identity and the changing role of America in foreign affairs. Capable of deferring internal conflicts over rapid urbanization, industrialization, and ethnic diversity, the anti-Communism of the Question connected older Populist sentiments with newer concerns for the national security state. The altered Question talked about Jews and anti-Semitism in a way that complemented this newer national identity. Hostile to anti-Semitism at home as well as increasingly sympathetic to the plight of Jews abroad, the more modern incarnation of the Question nonetheless still articulated mainstay precepts. Hollywood movies themselves, for example, responded to the Question by subsuming ethnic agency into a rubric of idealized, deethnicized narratives of "Great Men" in history. Meanwhile, various authors responded to the Hollywood Question by inverting its stereotype of racialized Jewish agency. These authors – Nathanael West, F. Scott Fitzgerald, and Budd Schulberg – rehabilitated the Shylock Jew as part of a larger critique of the American Dream, locating this stereotype not in some Other but within the very fabric of everyday American life. Finally, Leo Rosten's "sociological" study of Hollywood – the first of its kind – implicitly responded to the Question by asserting a set of principles emphasizing a cohesive national identity. Rosten's "social science" response, as well as the literary ones of West, Fitzgerald, and Schulberg, ultimately resonated with the Question. While these responses helped set the stage for the isolationist 1941 propaganda hearings, they also acceded to basic tenets of the Question. In suggesting that the Jewish movie mogul represented, not Jews, but some universal American experience, the Question could turn itself inside out, ultimately propelling a complementary set of assumptions and stereotypes into postwar discourse.

This rearticulation of the Hollywood Question did mark a decided shift in the way one talked about Jews and anti-Semitism. Outright anti-Semitism could prove a political liability rather than galvanizing rhetoric. When Senator Burton Wheeler attacked international banking, Protestant theologian and social activist Reinhold Niebuhr denounced appeals that demonized the once acceptable bugaboo of world finance. As chair of the anti-Fascist, anti-Communist, and interventionist Union for Democratic America, Niebuhr accused the senator of having "stooped to indications of anti-semitism."[453] And anti-Semitism could also be downright un-American, along with organized crime and Communism. In his 1938 testimony before the Dies Committee, investigator John C. Metcalfe warned of "a rising tide of anti-Semitism" in America sparked by both pamphlets and world events.[454] Often duplicitous, Metcalfe claimed, anti-Semitic organizations in the United States were "rackets" or "simply letterhead organizations" that "have practically no members." Anti-Semitic racketeers operated "not so much in the countryside," but "in various large cities," disrupting economic security by engaging in "whispering campaigns against legitimate merchants."[455]

Although anti-Semitism met with increasing antagonism, the image of the Jew could still articulate deep-seated beliefs and desires. Instead of appearing as Shylock or Judas, the Jew might epitomize fulfillment of the American Dream. In Catholics, Jews and Protestants (1934), for example, authors Charles Edwin Silcox and Galen M. Fisher hail the "irrepressible" Jew who "succeeds in spite of handicaps" and "thrives despite persecution."[456] According to the authors, Gentiles fear the "superior brains" of Jews. Instead of recognizing "superior ability," Gentiles explain Jewish success in terms of a "plot." Hardly anti-Semitic, such statements nonetheless essentialized ethnic Jewish agency. Portraying Jews as racially capable, the Hollywood Question can even double back on itself, reproaching those who do not perceive Jewish agency in the proper light. "Seeing Jews so prominent in the management of the theatre, the motion picture, the book publishing business, etc.," Silcox and Fisher explain, "the Gentile feels that the Jew is seeking to control him by controlling the organs of public opinion."

The authors explain discrimination against Jews in terms of fear. Emblematic of success, "the Jew seems irrepressible; he succeeds in spite of handicaps; he thrives despite persecution." Gentiles explain Jewish success, not in terms of their "superior brains or superior ability," but as a conspiratorial "plot" along the lines of the *Protocols of the Elders of Zion*.[457] As the authors observe, the Hollywood Question directly descended from this fear. "The predominant control of the motion-picture by a limited number of Jews is resented by many Gentiles," Silcox and Fisher observe, "and made the occasion for casting aspersion on the character of all Jews. The cinema is an institution of unique power in the formation of character and interests, and many Gentiles feel that it has fallen into the hands of a group who are racially inhibited from properly appreciating the real tastes and ideals of the vast body of the population."[458]

This discussion of anti-Semitism allows Silcox and Fisher to uphold a much more pluralistic vision of America in which Jews and Gentiles work together for the greater good of the industry. The authors note how a local group representing Protestants, Catholics, and Jews investigated whether Jews controlled Hollywood. The group "discovered that Gentile producers were as prominent as Jews, some of whom have been second to none in standing for high moral standards."[459] In this idealized vision, Jews possess "superior brains and superior ability," but with positive rather than negative effects.

This celebration of racialized Jewish intent accompanied a growing distaste for anti-Semitism. Throughout the 1930s, ever-growing attention sought to explain or even discount an alleged rise in anti-Semitism in terms of national well-being. An important series of *Fortune* polls charted public opinion toward Jews and Nazism. Commissioned by publisher Henry Luce in 1935, pollster Elmo Roper achieved national attention when he predicted Roosevelt's 1936 election within three points.[460] Roper's statistical snapshot of sympathy, antipathy, and apathy paralleled the rise in increasingly sophisticated methods of measuring of opinion, first begun in the midst of World War I to mobilize public support for entry into that war. Like George H. Gallup's American Institute of Public Opinion data, the *Fortune* polls were a kind of propaganda for modern statistics, touting the scientific methods used to randomly sample three thousand people across the country. What the *Fortune* polls discovered – that a majority of Americans were either indifferent or opposed to anti-Semitism – assured the business magazine's readership that Fascism's bark was worse than its bite. Rather than simply providing statistical snapshots of public opinion, as Gallup's first polls tried to create, *Fortune* used Roper's statistics to locate fundamental American norms. A 1936 poll, for example, showed that the majority of Americans (54.6 percent) believed that Germany would be "worse off if it drives out the Jews." Based on these figures, *Fortune* declared that anti-Semitism was not politically viable in the United States. Some of the figures suggested, however, that certain areas of the country offered potentially more fertile ground for anti-Jewish sentiments than others. The poll, for example, found that 49.2 percent of those polled in the American West "didn't know" whether Germany would be better or worse off for driving out the Jews. And in a conclusion that surely bolstered later claims of Populist anti-Semitism, 20.9 percent of farmhands harbored unfavorable attitudes toward Jews.[461]

When popular magazines like Luce's *Time* reported on anti-Semitism to a general readership, these news stories also purveyed similar dismissals of anti-Semitism. In a story commenting on a *New Masses* exposé of Washington journalist James True, *Time* deems him a "little-known pamphleteer" who runs "two obscure enterprises" furnishing information that appeals to a certain "ignorance about Washington." Yet the brief news item is really a condemnation of *New Masses* and its portrayal of the anti-Semite. *Time* chided the "Leftist" *New Masses* for not treating True as "a clown" and "an industrious, leather-conscienced [sic] hack," instead telegraphing its findings to President Roosevelt.[462]

Polling could thus serve as a kind of social science–inflected response that reinforced the dismissal of both anti-Semitism and the seriousness of its threat. As the preface to the 1966 *Jews in the Mind of America* observes, the rise of Nazism prompted the utilization of "the tools of social science in both gauging and combatting the spread of anti-Semitism" – particularly "public-opinion polling."[463] This social scientific approach offered much more than simply a barometer of public opinion. It conveyed a powerful vision of national identity. Though it could acknowledge the existence of anti-Semitism, this approach suggested that such attitudes occupied the margins of American experience. While these attitudes could flare up at any moment, much like Nazism did in Germany, opinion polling reassured American Jews, locating prejudice at an individual psychological level. It ignored and could not explain the culture and subtext of anti-Semitism and the Hollywood Question. Rather than revealing any particularly regional truths, the *Fortune* articles capture a certain ambivalence and even confusion regarding American Jews and anti-Semitism. In 1935, *Fortune* assigned editor Archibald MacLeish to draft a report on American Jews after accounts of a wave of Nazi atrocities had surfaced. Poet and future Librarian of Congress, MacLeish played a key role in the Roosevelt administration's Office of War Information. As MacLeish's biographer Scott Donaldson notes, MacLeish may have garnered the *Fortune* assignment as a result of his mother's participation in the National Conference on Christians and

Jews.[464] Donaldson finds that MacLeish himself remained somewhat less predisposed toward Jews, revealing "traces" of anti-Semitism in his correspondence and poetry well into the thirties.[465] After the series first appeared in 1936, Random House later published it as a small book. *The Jews in America* lists "The Editors of *Fortune*" as its author, but Donaldson claims that MacLeish actually wrote it, and in the process overcame his own anti-Semitism.[466] Indeed, MacLeish remained so confident of the work's integrity that he sent out advance copies to Justice Felix Frankfurter, banker Felix Warburg, and other high-profile figures, all of whom MacLeish claimed believed the article was "valuable and should give offense to no one."[467]

The article disparages both anti-Semitism as well as concern over it. Significantly, MacLeish's "preliminary memorandum" defines anti-Semitism as a belief that Jews were "becoming too powerful in politics, in finance, in business, in the professions."[468] As Donaldson notes, MacLeish therefore "took care to dismiss" both this preconception and the robustness of anti-Semitism itself.[469] "Misgivings and uneasiness have colored the thinking of American Jews," the article contends.[470] "There is no reason for anxiety," as "anti-Semitism in America, judged by its exponents, is a very sick donkey."[471] If anti-Semitism warrants such little attention, as the article argues, then the excessive attention devoted to it greatly concerns MacLeish. One can read this concern as representative of a shifting discourse on Jews. Denouncing anti-Semitism becomes yet another way to further the Hollywood Question.

Indeed, the *Fortune* article argues that Jewish sensitivity to anti-Semitism is more of a problem than anti-Semitism itself. Little if any effort needs to be exerted to address this antipathy in the first place. "The virus has not been acclimated on this continent," MacLeish claims, and "the efforts of the doctors to inoculate the American mind have failed for that reason."[472] The article consistently compares anti-Semitism to other forms of prejudice, arguing that Jews were never subjected to the institutionalized discrimination and prejudice in the United States that Quakers, Baptists, Irish Catholics, and blacks experienced. Even when discussing Henry Ford's *Dearborn Independent*, MacLeish contends that Jews had only begun to experience what Catholics had faced all along.[473] Critical of "certain Jews," MacLeish likens how they "carry their race" to "an Irishman's fighting shillelagh." Jews allegedly react to "any reference to their blood" as if "it were a deliberate insult," thus "avoiding friends who speak of it, boycotting publications which publish it in print."[474]

Even when MacLeish criticizes anti-Semitism, his reproaches ultimately resonate with the Hollywood Question's assumptions. While denying that

Jews are "a racial unit," he nonetheless attributes physical and emotional features to a "cross between a long-headed, tallish, dark Mediterranean race (the Bedouins) and a short-headed, shortish, dark Alpine race."[475] Unlike other "immigrant peoples" who "accept the culture of the country into which they come," Jews allegedly give people an "underlying feeling of foreignness."[476] While claiming that "there is no basis whatever for the suggestion that Jews monopolize U.S. business and industry,"[477] MacLeish notes that Jews have made "fair progress toward monopolizing . . . subdivisions of industry."[478] In addressing the charge of ethnic intent, MacLeish ultimately accepts its most basic assumption that Jews will act as Jews. "What difference does it make," he asks, "even if Jews do run away with the system? Why shouldn't they monopolize any profession or branch of industry they are intelligent enough to capture?"[479] In addition to its Fascist ties, anti-Semitism also poses undesirable consequences. These consequences, however, result from what hostility toward a minority provokes in the minority. "Any nation which permits a minority to live in fear of persecution," MacLeish contends, "is a nation which invites disaster. Fearful minorities become suspicious minorities and suspicious minorities, their defensive reactions set on the hair trigger of anxiety, create the animosities they dread. The consequence is a condition dangerous to the State at any time and doubly dangerous at a time like the present when the primitive emotions of men have been deliberately exploited in the interest of Fascism."[480]

Rather than focus on anti-Semitism or even the attention that Jews give it, however, MacLeish spends most of his time determining which industries are Jewish-controlled and which are not. He methodically goes through finance, heavy industry, light industry, retail, and the media. A special appendix discusses the motion picture industry. His findings do dispute common wisdom concerning alleged Jewish control. For example, of 420 listed directors serving on the boards of nineteen financial institutions, the article identifies only 30 of them as Jewish.[481] Yet even to go about disproving Jewish control over certain industries (and "proving" control in other industries like scrap metal),[482] MacLeish activates a certain set of assumptions. In his view, Jews are capable of acting as Jews, although not in the way that anti-Semites expect them to act:

> Jews do not dominate the American scene. They do not even dominate major sectors of the American scene. They do, however, monopolize certain minor provinces. What is remarkable about the Jews in America, in other words, is not their industrial power but their

curious industrial distribution, their tendency to crowd together in particular squares of the checkerboard. The reason for their crowding must be found in their most pronounced psychological trait – their clannishness, their tribal inclination. The reason for their choice of particular squares into which to crowd must be found in historical accident. Jews are in scrap iron because they were once in the junk business and they were once in the junk business because a penniless immigrant could make a start there on a shoestring. Jews are in movies because they were in movie theatres and because a few successful cloak-and-suit manufacturers invested their cloak-and-suit profits usefully in the amusement business. (The connection between the movies and the cloak-and-suit business is still esthetically betrayed from time to time.) Were the four and a half millions of American Jews scattered more or less evenly over the whole industrial acreage, and were they as fond of rural communities and small towns as they are of great cities, their presence as Jews would hardly be noticed by other Americans. The whole point of the whole inquiry is that wherever the Jews may be, industrially or culturally or professionally or merely geographically, they are always present in numbers and they are almost always present as Jews.[483]

The motion picture industry becomes central to this argument of essential Jewish agency. Movies "are the chief point of anti-Semitic reliance. And there a persuasive case may be made." The "case," in its sympathetic incarnation, rehearses what after World War II became a powerful and influential invocation of the Hollywood Question, stressing a rags-to-riches story of the moguls. "Jews were the first exhibitors of movies because the early movie theatres could be operated with little capital: they were commonly empty stores with folding chairs for seats and a derelict piano. Large returns in such ventures tempted them into production." According to MacLeish, even "the cultivated Jew" must admit that "the influence upon the popular taste" of certain "Jewish producers" was "unfortunate."[484] Propelling the basic tenets of the Hollywood Question into modern public discourse, MacLeish simply lists which studios operate under Jewish control and which do not. While only "three of the eight principal companies are owned and controlled by Jews," MacLeish contends that Jews have a far more pervasive influence. "Though Jews do not monopolize the industry moneywise," he writes, "they do nevertheless exert pretty complete control over the production of pictures."[485] The "great influence of Jews in the movies," he concludes, gives them access to "the great power of the movies in the influencing of modern society."[486]

By powerfully reshaping the familiar stereotypes of clannishness, urbanity, agency, and control, MacLeish ultimately reasserts what he calls the "Jewish problem." In making this reassertion, he demonstrates remarkable familiarity with the story of the Wandering Jew. Although Jews and fascism do not pose any real threat to the country,

> the future of the Jew in America is puzzling. Can this universal stranger be absorbed in the country which has absorbed every other European stock? Does he wish to be absorbed? Can he live happily and in peace if he is not absorbed? The answers must be guesses. Upper-class Spanish and German Jews *have* been pretty well absorbed. There are, however, numerous Jews who look upon the loss of Jewish identity as a kind of social suicide. If those groups, Jewish and non-Jewish, who wish the identity and distinction of the Jews preserved are able to carry their point, then the only hope for the Jews in America is mutual toleration and respect. Since, however, toleration and mutual respect are also the only hope of all who wish to preserve or re-establish democratic institutions in this country the Jews in America will have numerous allies. The first condition of their success will be the quieting of Jewish apprehensiveness and the consequent elimination of the aggressive and occasionally provocative Jewish defensive measures which the country has recently and anxiously observed.[487]

Hardly unique, this kinder, gentler activation of the Jewish Question shares much in common with leftist film criticism of Hollywood. A radical Marxist, screenwriter, and critic for the *New York Times*, *The New Republic*, and *Close Up*, Seymour Stern also edited the influential journal *Experimental Cinema*. In "The Bankruptcy of Cinema Art" (1936), he echoes many of the same claims that MacLeish makes. Hollywood populated its "studios, from executive office to 'prop' department, with their own kind."[488] The movie moguls were "the original crowd of cloak-and-suit manufacturers who gained possession of the industry" and were "solidly in the saddle of power." Such a situation was worse "than ever before" because "the cloak-and-suit" crowd had teamed up with banking interests "who lend financial and strategic support."[489]

Fellow *Close Up* writer and founder Harry Alan Potamkin interrogates the Question more directly, but ultimately accedes to its implicit doctrine. Coming out of a tradition of depression-era Communism, Potamkin advocated a leftist intellectual stance against American mass culture and its attendant commercialism. The mass-culture critique could thus deploy the Hollywood Question as a way to locate ethnic elites foisting false consciousness upon the masses. "Much has been said and written," he writes in 1930, "upon the dominance of the Jew in the commerce, industry and creation of the film." Potamkin does not deny that the movie industry "is replete with Jews," but he does characterize their views as ranging from "the film-as-merchandise up to the film-as-art." Entitled "The Jew as Film Subject," the article written for *The Jewish Tribune* critiques the way in which Hollywood represents Jews. "If the Jew has been important in the industrial and commercial development of the cinema," Potamkin writes, "he has been strangely inactive and inept in presenting himself as film-subject."⁴⁹⁰ Potamkin shows that if Jewish control over Hollywood exists, it certainly does not benefit Jews. By presenting the Jew as responsible for ethnic images, Potamkin, himself Jewish, accepts a basic assumption that Jews *could* wield control over these images as Jews. He finds a certain hypocrisy inherent in Jewish protests against these images. In Hollywood films, the Jew appears as either "a clown or a sentimentalized scarecrow," Potamkin writes in 1934.⁴⁹¹ No one protested against these images, but when *King of Kings* (DeMille-Pathé, 1927) appeared, "Jewish upper-class dignity is offended by the portrayal of historic (biblical) characters, and what a lamentation is heard! To these silk-hat Jews Cecil B. DeMille, the director replies, beating his breast, 'Would I insult the Jews? I'm half-Jew myself.' And so we get the Negro on the half-shell, the Jew on the half-shell, the worker on the half-shell, as an appetizer for middle class attitudes."⁴⁹²

In some ways, such statements reinforce typical stereotypes of the movie mogul. Film, according to Potamkin, is "in the hands of high finance." The producer is usually "a small merchant, or manufacturer, a gambler or the like, under financial hegemony." In other ways, however, Potamkin distinguishes between Jewish control and social power. Movie owners only act "in behalf of the ruling class," which is not necessarily Jewish. And some early films before 1920 had "revolutionary suggestions" because Jews were "not yet in established social positions." Thus, Jews did not pose a threat to the social order but acted in accordance with it. In fact, Potamkin argues, Hollywood Jews often work against Jewish interests. Universal, "Jewish owned and Jewish managed," released the 1932 German film *Der Rebell* in the United States and according to Potamkin later made its own pro-Nazi film in this country. Nazi propaganda minister Joseph Goebbels cited the film as making "an indelible impression," and one that could "overwhelm even a non-National Socialist." Belonging to the German "mountain film" genre, one could read this costume epic as paralleling the ascendancy of National Socialism in its depiction of an 1809 Tyrolean peasant revolt.[493]

One needs to remain circumspect with regard to such accusations of Jewish complicity, however. Potamkin does not mention the name of the supposed pro-Nazi film, although it may have been the 1932 antiwar film *The Doomed Battalion* (Universal) in which *Der Rebell*'s actor-director Luis Trenker appears. As for *Der Rebell*, historian William K. Everson notes that "the mountain film was to Germany what the Western was to America." Like the Western, the mountain film was also flexible enough to convey different kinds of allegories. Thus, while *Der Rebell* found favor with National Socialists, Goebbels later blacklisted Trenker from working in Germany. Trenker's *The Firedevils* (1940) also treats the Tyrolean uprising against Napoleon, but according to a *Baseline* biography, Goebbels interpreted this film as an unflattering parallel to Nazi forces invading smaller European countries.[494]

Potamkin's pointed observations ultimately link his statements to more mainstream discourses targeting Jewish ethnic agency as a craven sellout. The *New York Times*'s Douglas Churchill surmised that Hollywood had not produced Sinclair Lewis's *It Can't Happen Here* because studios feared Germany would see the film as Jewish revenge against Nazi policies and thus justify worse anti-Semitism.[495] In one of the more amazing invocations of the Hollywood Question, *Hollywood Spectator* editor Welford Beaton published an open letter on Thanksgiving 1938 calling upon the motion picture industry to take a more courageous stand against Nazism. Addressing the letter "To the Jews Who Control the Films," Beaton noted that only Hollywood Jews could use the "one mighty voice in America" to help save "your persecuted blood-brothers. You control that voice. It is the voice of the screen! You have controlled it from its inception. You have used it only as something to make money for you. You have your money. Will you now use it, if not to express your own feelings, at least to give expression to the feelings of Gentiles?"

Here, Beaton invokes the basic tenets of the Hollywood Question as a way to justify what others were calling propaganda. Yet he employs the same underlying assumptions of Jewish control so influential in Nazi doctrine: "During all the years you have owned the film industry you have used it for your personal gain. You have not permitted it to take a definite stand on anything that would promote or defend civilization. You have practiced business methods that have made you vulnerable."

Thus flexible, the Hollywood Question could propose that Jews make a "Hebrew" movie, because the Question remained coherent in how it represented and addressed Jews:

> Make your picture a Hebrew undertaking. Cast it with Jews until it itself is a demonstration of the heights to which members of your race have risen in the screen art.
> But make it! Make it a Hollywood effort to protect the members of your race, and devote the big profits it would earn to the relief of those Jews who need it so badly.
> At present the situation is: Civilization versus Barbarism.
> On which side do you stand, Gentlemen?

Yet even when Beaton learned that Warner Bros. planned to film a story called *Concentration Camp*, the editor made the disparaging suggestion that the studio produce the movie as a Dead End Kids movie, urging "the Jews who control the films" not to "offer for sale the agonies of German Jews."[496]

A wide variety of voices used the Hollywood Question to denounce anti-Semitism. Yet aspects of their critique ultimately accepted the Question's discursive parameters. For instance, reference to the movie moguls as "cloak-and-suiters" commonly appeared in overtly anti-Semitic tracts. Jewish control over Hollywood often pointed to a Jewish banking conspiracy. And the belief that Jews did in fact have a responsibility to represent themselves appropriately was based on the presumption that Jews could control these images, as Jews – the same presumption of ethnic agency that had operated for the Hollywood Question. Aware of the Question, the film industry challenged such deep-seated assumptions privately – and sometimes passionately – while publicly addressing them in a circumspect, highly elliptical manner.

"WORKING FOR GENTILES": THE HOLLYWOOD QUESTION IN HOLLYWOOD

To many, Hollywood's support for intervention and the Roosevelt administration reinforced belief in the Hollywood Question. Rallying both to the Loyalist cause and against Nazism, Hollywood personnel frequently engaged in fund-raising efforts throughout the 1920s and 1930s. Producers like Jack Warner and David O. Selznick actively participated in Jewish causes, heading United Jewish Welfare Fund committees throughout these decades.[497] Selznick passionately advocated support for organizations combating anti-Semitism. In a 1936 letter to George Backer of the Jewish Telegraphic Agency, Selznick noted that he had "repeatedly pointed out" to Jews in the motion picture industry "that their contributions were in large measure, in self-defense."[498] Given the pro-Zionist stance of this New York–based news service, Palestine certainly had its appeal as a form of self-defense against Nazism. Yet rarely if ever did the studios produce a film espousing Zionism before 1948. Hollywood did produce a small but visible number of films making impassioned pleas against Nazism. The same year MGM released *Ninotchka* (1939), a comedy that took its jabs at Communism, and Warner Bros. introduced *Confessions of a Nazi Spy* (1939). Based on the firsthand experience of an FBI agent who infiltrated a Nazi spy ring in the United States, the film aligned Nazism with antidemocratic (and therefore anti-American) forces.

Films like *Confessions of a Nazi Spy* fueled the belief – especially among more extreme elements – that Hollywood would push the country into war by manipulating public opinion. A Father Coughlin radio address made note of star Edward G. Robinson's "off-stage name," and warned that "there is propaganda at work while you pay to be propagandized."[499] Fritz Kuhn's pro-Nazi *Deutscher Weckruf und Beobachter and The Free American*, a single newspaper published by the German American Bund, included a list of the film's credits in which nearly everyone's name was preceded by the word "Jew." Warning that "only the tremendous resources required to combat the Jewish Hollywood combine can stop this basest of fighting methods," the newspaper implored its readers to "marshal the resources of public indignation at a *raw deal! Go see this film* and see a classic example of how 'public opinion,' made to order by those who have reason to fear our arguments, is being whipped up against us! Then help us reach the confused, unenlightened stranger! *Help by telling the nation the truth about it! Help fight,* so that these mind-poisoners may be made powerless before Americanism is destroyed."[500]

Confessions of a Nazi Spy also occasioned criticism of Hollywood for failing to take a stronger stance against Nazism. In 1938, *Boxoffice* columnist Ivan Spears praised Warner Bros. for "their disregard of the cloak of hypocritical indifference which has been the too popular garment of Hollywood's prominent Jews in their open reactions to the issues of Nazism."[501] More recent scholarship has argued that studios responded to Nazism through censorship. Patricia Erens has pointed out that studios reduced on-screen Jewish roles as a response to the anti-Semitism of the 1930s both in the United States and abroad.[502] Michael Rogin has observed that "Jewish moguls evaded anti-Semitism by simply eliminating Jews from the screen."[503] On closer examination, however, one can see the film community's response to the rise of Nazism as having been marked, not by indifference or cowardice, but by the constraints of the Hollywood Question.

Far from being indifferent, Hollywood personnel remained acutely sensitive to anti-Semitism. Researcher Christine Colgan found that Harry Warner kept personal files on various American anti-Semitic groups and individuals.[504] In response to a series of anti-Semitic pamphlets amid controversy over *Confessions of a Nazi Spy*, union, craft, and guild representatives sought to refute the charge that industry was predominately Jewish. Their investigation found few Jews among union ranks.[505] Hollywood executives privately responded to the threat of anti-Semitism quite expediently. On 13 March 1934, Mendell Silberberg, a lawyer and power broker in the Los Angeles Jewish community, called a meeting of studio heads, producers, writers, directors and community leaders at the Hillcrest Country Club. The subject of the meeting was the recent "attack on the movie industry." Copies of William Dudley Pelley's *Liberation* and *Silver Ranger* accompanied each place setting. Amid "considerable discussion," Louis B. Mayer vowed that "he for one was not going to take it lying down" and professed "that he believed it was the duty of the men present to" provide both "money and intelligent direction" in combatting such attacks.[506] Silberberg then appointed a committee consisting of high-ranking executives from each major studio: Irving Thalberg of MGM, Harry Cohen of Columbia, H. Henningson of Universal, Nick Schenck of 20th Century, Jack Warner of Warner Bros., Emanuel Cohen of Paramount, Sol Wurtzel of Fox, and Pandro Berman of RKO. The committee would then fund-raise at least $15,000 from the studios to help finance the proposed endeavor. According to a financial audit of the committee, the "Motion Picture Group" had raised $21,701.21 between 30 March 1934 and 31 October 1935 – by far the lion's share of the Community Committee's $31,434.40 income during that period.[507]

While Hollywood personnel remained highly vigilant about anti-Semitism, they located their efforts under the aegis of the Jewish community. In a June 1934 letter, Cyrus Adler of the American Jewish Committee urged "that local anti-Jewish activity be dealt with effectively by one central authority," preferably "a small committee to represent the various groups in your community, interested in combating such activity."[508] The tens of thousands of dollars raised presumably went toward the creation of an extensive espionage network brokered by the Los Angeles area Jewish Community Council (JCC). Throughout the 1930s, the JCC infiltrated numerous anti-Semitic and Nazi organizations in southern California. The

March 1934 meeting established a contact between JCC officer Leon Lewis and Paramount executive Henry Herzbrun, in which Herzbrun "would work in direct cooperation with [Lewis] at all times." Among other things, the JCC provided copies of spy reports to executives like Herzbrun detailing studio anti-Semitic activity.[509] But those affiliated with the JCC's espionage network also did much more. Lewis's notes show that Louis Greenbaum, a well-connected Los Angeles attorney, prevailed upon Mrs. Carl Sheldon, chairman of the Motion Picture Committee of the Federation of the Women's Christian Temperance Union, to table a series of motions that "were very unfair to the Motion Picture Industry and our Jewish citizens." One motion "severely condemn[ed] the motion picture industry," listing "only Jewish names . . . as being members of the companies." A compromise motion praised "Catholic and Protestant Groups for their fine efforts in assisting to obtain better and cleaner pictures." Greenbaum notes how he failed "to include the Jewish Groups in the resolution as commending them, because all of our fight was centered on preventing them from being con-demned."[510]

Such behind-the-scenes maneuvers resonate with obsessive attempts to gauge public opinion. Not indifferent to anti-Nazi causes, Harry Warner purportedly told guests at a 1937 fund-raiser that, as a Jew, he was "helpless" to do anything because "people misconstrue the purpose if we do certain things."[511] Warner's statement reflects a concern for public perception. Often, film industry executives used opinion polls to gauge public percep-tion of their ethnicity and their industry. After an Alvah Bessie profile of Selznick appeared in the *New Yorker* magazine in 1942, Selznick commis-sioned George Gallup to conduct his own personal poll. One of the things he wanted to know was whether the article would have "unfortunate anti-Semitic repercussions."[512] At the very least, a 1939 *Motion Picture Almanac* advertisement suggests the economic potential of this concern. Above a throng of people, a headline asks, "Do you know what they think of you?" Knowing "the thoughts, preferences and tastes of the masses" has always been important, but "it is even more necessary right now to the motion picture industry." The ad promises to "put down a blanket survey for you in every state in the nation; within a week you can know what your customers think of you and your work."[513]

Although top-level executives wielded a certain level of power and control in monitoring and combating anti-Semitic activity, mid- and lower-level management could use their power and control to engage in anti-Semitism. One report to Leon Lewis, for example, describes Silver Shirt canvassing on the MGM lot.[514] Lewis regularly tried to intervene on behalf of Jews who had experienced sudden layoffs with little or no explanation. In attempting to intercede on behalf of onetime MGM employee Harry Zutto, Lewis wrote to Fred Pelton noting "other instances where injustices have resulted to Jews who have been charged with being this, that, or the other thing, in order to keep certain departments one hundred percent Aryan." Reports like this one were clearly an ongoing concern. In his letter to Pelton, Lewis notes an earlier "conversation which I had with you a couple of years ago on this subject matter."[515] Similarly, Lewis provided Paramount attorney and vice president Henry Herzbrun with a copy of a letter he had received from Mrs. Leo Strauss, a carpenter's spouse. According to her, foreman Julius Sodoski had dismissed her husband from working on the set of a Cecil B. DeMille picture after asking "if he were a Jew." The letter indicated that another Jewish carpenter had met with the same fate. Repeated attempts by the union to intercede failed. When Herzbrun asked a subordinate to investigate the matter, Sadoski claimed "very definitely that the man is not a good carpenter." Herzbrun's emissary found that he was "not able to prove or disprove that [the carpenter] was asked regarding his religion."[516]

Specific films – especially controversial ones – often provided a litmus test for public perception of the industry. While Harry Warner would later claim that *Confessions of a Nazi Spy* received 550 letters, telegrams, and postcards from 110 cities praising the film,[517] the film also elicited a number of adverse letters decrying Jewish influence and propaganda in films. Warner Bros. saved these letters in a "Crank" file. Stereotypical associations with Communism, foreignness, and clannishness frequently implicated Hollywood Jews. Signed only "AN AMERICAN BORN," one letter suggested that Warner Bros. follow *Confessions* with " 'I am a Communist' starring Eddie Cantor and a few other Communist Jews in order to let the public know what progress the Communists are making in this country, and who the people are who support these Reds." The author then warned Jack Warner that Americans were not "as dumb as you think they are." T. Haesle of Riverside, California, asked that Jack Warner present his letter to all of the moguls "at one of your Executives' meetings." Haesle accused motion picture heads of favoring "only the 'reds,' " asking if such behavior resulted from being Jewish and hating Hitler or from being "in favor of atheism." Other people complained that studios like Warner Bros. were pushing the country into war. Ruth Herriman of Brooklyn, New York, claimed that "Aryans, Americans, are not fooled by the jewish [sic] propaganda today. We know they want to bring war with Germany and want us to fight for them. If they want to fight let them go ahead, but not include us."

Other letters interpreted *Confessions* as purely an expression of Jewish self-interest. "It does seem so passingly strange," wrote J. J. Bone of St. Louis, Missouri, "that both your patriotism and passion for revealing espionage remained so passive until a certain minority was unfortunately dispossessed." J. P. Thompson, also of St. Louis, tried to shame the moguls for making "a picture like the [Confessions of a] Natizi [sic] Spy." A "true American citizen for three generations" whose "grandfather fought in the Civil War," Thompson called *Confessions* "gross Jewish propaganda." The writer went on to protest the film by invoking a virulent nationalism and stereotypes of clannishness. "I bet somewhere in your large Jewish family," Thompson writes, "there are some with German blood who resent to have their race so degraded. You did not hurt any one but you will have more people hating the Jew because a Jew produced it to show his hatred."[518]

For the most part, the Roosevelt administration's war effort would vindicate films like *Confessions of a Nazi Spy*. But these films of the 1930s and early 1940s belonged to a larger, paradoxical relationship between the film industry and the state. Some federal initiatives – like Roosevelt's National Recovery Act – favorably served studio moguls rather than workers; but other legislation and judicial rulings created adverse conditions for the studio leadership. Labor unions in Hollywood, for instance, successfully used the Wagner Act to fight studio efforts to break union organizing. Before Pearl Harbor, as Hollywood helped rally the country toward intervention – in line with the Roosevelt administration's foreign policy stopping just short of war – the Justice Department began to pursue legal action against the monopoly that studios held over the production, distribution, and exhibition of motion pictures. When studio personnel did actively campaign for the relief of European Jews, they did not do so independently, but under the aegis of the United Jewish Welfare Fund. The use of film industry apparatus, not to mention films themselves, to guide public policy or opinion on the plight of Jews remained completely taboo. When Jewish film executives opposed anti-Semitism, they placed themselves within a broader discourse of patriotic national identity.

A scene from Charlie Chaplin's *The Great Dictator* (United Artists, 1940) epitomizes the dilemma in which many film industry executives found themselves. In the film, Adolf Hynkel's assistant, Garbitch, tells the Hitlerian leader that the country will subsidize its war effort with a loan from the Jewish banker Epstein, as "all the board of Directors are Aryans."[519] The gag pokes fun at the notion of a Jewish conspiracy, kind of an in-joke for an industry widely perceived by those both inside and out of Hollywood as quintessentially ethnic. Producer David O. Selznick, for example, frequently referred to working for Gentiles. Starting at RKO in the early 1930s, he soon moved to MGM, where he produced a number of prestigious pictures. By the end of the decade, he started his own independent studio, Selznick International Pictures (SIP). Zealous in fighting anti-Semitism, Selznick nonetheless remained ambivalent toward using his own position as an SIP executive officer to support Jewish causes publicly. When asked to donate studio money to an American Jewish Congress benefit, Selznick did not think, "as a company largely owned by Gentiles, we are privileged to donate . . . money to Jewish organizations." He instead offered to personally donate fifty dollars. His memoranda joke that, as a Jew he lacks control over the studio, ultimately working for Christians. During a United Jewish Welfare Fund drive, Selznick asked his vice president and general manager, Henry Ginsburg, if he could get director Josef Von Sternberg to pay his pledge, "so I can forget about the Jews and go back to work for the Gentiles."[520]

Even if these observations constitute no more than self-referential office humor, the humor reveals a more nuanced view of ethnic agency within the structure of business hierarchy. Industry executives passionately worked behind the scenes to keep material they deemed anti-Semitic from public view. John Hay "Jock" Whitney, chair of Selznick International Pictures' board of directors, asked Selznick to preview Golgotha, a 1936 French film directed by Jules Duvivier depicting the crucifixion of Christ. Selznick found the film grossly anti-Semitic, but instead of contacting Whitney, his superior, he immediately contacted the Hays Office to have it banned. When Whitney reprimanded him for taking this measure, Selznick justified his action in terms of ethnicity. "It is my duty as a Jew," Selznick wrote Whitney in 1936, "to do everything in my power to keep the picture from being distributed or exhibited in this country, and I will stop at nothing to achieve this end."[521] On the same day Selznick sent his missive to Whitney, the motion picture executive also contacted journalist Herbert Bayard Swope to start a propaganda committee "of our own . . . manned by the most prominent Jews in the publishing and entertainment fields." Selznick feared that "we Jews are sitting back and doing nothing in self-defense." Fund-raising "for the relief of the persecuted" was all well and good, but "if anti-semitism [sic] grows, there will not be enough money in the world for relief."[522]

Harry Warner took a similar activist stance with publishing magnate

Henry R. Luce. In 1938, Warner banned *Inside Nazi Germany*, a March of Time newsreel documentary, from showing in Warner Bros.–owned theaters. Despite endorsements from both Rabbi Stephen T. Wise, spokesperson for Reform Judaism and key White House contact, and New York Anti-Nazi League president Samuel Untermeyer, Warner argued that the film's visual origins as pro-Nazi propaganda overrode its critical narration. Luce responded by issuing a statement expressing relief that "Mr. Warner does not control the entire motion picture industry."[523] Later that year, Warner took Luce to task for the way *Time* magazine referred to Jews. *Time* had frequently referred to "prominent citizens as 'Jew Morgenthau' or 'Jew Lehman.'" But a reference to Hollywood producers' "misconduct with 'Aryan' women" prompted a reply from Warner. "This is the first time that I have seen an American publication of national importance apply the Nazi 'Aryan' race theory to American citizens. Certainly, when TIME begins to segregate American citizens into Aryan and, inferentially, non-Aryans, are you not embarking upon a course of intolerance and 'pressure-group emotionalism'?"[524]

Of course, neither Warner nor Selznick spoke for all movie moguls or Jews in these actions. But their efforts do suggest a certain rationale for combating anti-Semitism. Privately, they used their power and influence to persuade other decision makers and help monitor marginalized Nazi and anti-Semitic groups. Acutely aware of how such tactics might appear in public, however, both Warner and Selznick acted within the constraints of the Hollywood Question. Often such activities entailed positioning oneself within a hypernationalist discourse. This discourse, which flattened ethnic differences, could also justify countersubversive measures. In a 1940 address to Warner Bros. employees, Warner encouraged them to comply with an FBI investigation attempting to ferret out studio subversives. He also implored them to "unite and quit listening to anybody discussing whether you or I am a Jew or a Catholic or a Protestant or of any other faith – and not allow anyone to say anything against anybody's faith – or we will fall just the same as they did over there."[525]

Efforts to combat anti-Semitism often worked to subsume ethnic difference rather than highlight it. Even when he asked Eddie Cantor to consider "the possibility at some time of injecting material" into the singer's program, the material Leon Lewis, head of the Los Angeles Jewish Community Committee, suggested was a relatively benign message preaching "brotherhood" and "goodwill."[526] Using the screen to promote what many believed were "Jewish causes" remained taboo. Yet organizations like the JCC and the American Jewish Committee (AJC) consistently courted Hollywood executives. A memo from JCC head Lewis notes a special advisory council meeting held at Irving Thalberg's office. "The time and place are not very convenient for any of us," Lewis commiserates, "but as one of the principal purposes in holding the conference is to enlist Thalberg's cooperation in getting other executives at MGM to do their part, I feel sure that you, as well as other members, will put up with the inconvenience."[527] More often than not, however, executives like Selznick exerted caution in using ties between the Jewish community and the motion picture industry to promote a positive vision of the Jew. Both Selznick and Thalberg had attended a 1936 AJC meeting where they had received story outlines for films that would "more definitely" utilize the medium to promote "a healthy public sentiment in the United States." Selznick had indicated that the outlines "might do good work as propaganda," but "their presentation is not a simple one and requires careful thought." During the period leading up to American involvement in World War II, Selznick became more entrenched in his belief that Jews should be depicted with caution. Less than a year after the country's entry into the war, he suggested that Emeric Pressburger, the Hungarian writer-director who teamed with Michael Powell to make a series of feature films highly sympathetic to Great Britain, direct a war film featuring one hero from a representative ethnic group. "I don't think we ought to do anything other than just present one Jew," Selznick wrote. Under no circumstances should Pressburger "attempt any Jewish propaganda."[528]

Selznick was not alone in his belief that cooperation between Hollywood and Jewish groups needed to proceed with the utmost care. The AJC itself shared this fear. It consistently turned down requests for funding from Jewish news services like the New York-based Jewish Telegraphic Agency (JTA). "It has been the traditional and consistent policy of the American Jewish Committee," wrote Morris Waldman, a representative of the AJC, in 1941, "to make no contribution to the Jewish Telegraphic Agency because on the one hand the Committee is opposed to the idea of controlling news services, or newspapers, and on the other hand, we believe that news service should be free from the control of any and all Jewish organizations."[529]

Selznick himself sought out funding on behalf of the JTA but adamantly criticized its name. Any article from the news agency "will automatically be discounted by non-Jewish readers as prejudiced," Selznick wrote in a 1937 letter. "It might actually boomerang through being construed as Jewish propaganda." Even the head of the agency concedes that the name "is a decided handicap," and that in the past Adolph Ochs and Arthur Sulzberger of the *New York Times* had both urged the elimination of the word "Jewish" from the Jewish Telegraphic Agency's name.[530]

By 1942, Selznick expressed some ambivalence about dodging "the word 'Jewish' " in the name of a motion picture organization designed to combat anti-Semitism and giving "color to untruths that have been spread about the control of Hollywood." However others, like top Hollywood agent Phil Berg, remained acutely aware of the implications that a name might hold for Jews:

> There is no reason to wave two red flags – even in the name of our organization: "Motion Picture" and "Jewish." This immediately apprises everyone that we are a pressure, political, and propaganda group, and you know that the effect of propaganda is completely nullified if it is known that its source emanates from an organized body.[531]

Conscious of these potential repercussions, Selznick believed that the way to combat them was to maintain complete honesty about the nature of the proposed organization:

> It must be made crystal-clear that this is no Jewish cabal, meeting in cellars to devise ways and means of slaughtering Gentiles; and that [the organization] is not designed to pressure alleged Jewish control of the motion picture business. In fact it ought to be made clear that we expect to continue to be at each other's throats in the same disgraceful fashion as we have been in the past![532]

For Berg, however, the solution to anti-Semitism lay not in confronting it but in assimilating into American culture: "Today we are looked upon as 'those Motion Picture Jews' on the other side of the fence. It is only through meeting with the Gentiles as members of a community that we have any hope of dispelling their prejudices."

When someone suggested that Berg "could join the fire-brigade," the agent bristled at the snobbery of the comment: "There is no glory, and certainly very little fun in participating in picayune endeavors, yet such participation, drudgery as it may be, must be engaged in by as many of us as possible in order to be accepted as part of the civic life of the community and as Americans."[533]

A little over a week after the Selznick–Berg exchange, Mendell Silberberg, the informal liaison between Hollywood and the AJC, weighed in on this unnamed organization that would defend democracy, attack anti-Semitism, and raise funds for various Jewish charities. Founded in 1936 by Rabbi Stephen Wise, the organization remained both pro-Zionist and vehemently anti-Nazi. Silberberg specifically cited "anti-Semitic activity" that made Hollywood "a primary target" and "the necessity that the truth regarding the Jew and the motion picture industry be presented to the people of the United States" as "reasons for the necessity of this organization." Silberberg suggested that the relationship between this group and the AJC remain loose. Nonetheless, it would work in tandem with AJC's goals of "militantly" meeting "attacks on Jews or upon the motion picture industry" by using "the talents and abilities" of Hollywood.[534]

The initiative foundered, however, perhaps because of internal dissension over how "Jewish" or "propagandistic" such an organization should appear. In a 1944 letter to Selznick, Norman Salit notes the "tragic" inaction of Hollywood producers: "Accused of controlling the industry," the Jewish producer may have "done so little to nullify the growth and effects of the movement that has reveled in that accusation."[535] But such inaction did not result from a lack of concern. If anything, concern over this accusation spurred Hollywood studios to respond with a particular genre of film.

Throughout the 1930s, Hollywood produced a series of biographies detailing the lives of great men in history. These films often proved to be immensely popular. According to *Motion Picture Almanac*, for example, Warner Bros.'s *The Life of Emile Zola* (1937) grossed over $1.5 million.[536] As overt references to Jews on the screen appeared to wane, prestigious pictures depicting great men who happened to be Jewish flourished. This generic strategy – highlighting the universal aspects of individual identity while downplaying the particulars of ethnicity – was consistent with assimilationist culture. The narrative of Jewish achievement against Gentile odds but in the service of universal cultural values proved so compelling that, as Colgan finds, Warner Bros. re-released its 1929 biography of the British statesman, *Disraeli*, to capitalize on Twentieth Century–Fox's success with another film featuring actor George Arliss, *The House of Rothschild* (1934).[537]

Few could have predicted the success of the latter film, however, and discussions by Hollywood personnel regarding *Rothschild* indicate a high sensitivity to the Hollywood Question. Furthermore, these discussions reveal the economic and industrial function of Production Code censorship. Not only did the PCA operate as a kind of audience research mechanism for predicting how and where films such as this one might encounter problems with local and foreign censorship boards; in many cases, Breen's office actively worked with studio publicity departments, facilitating testimonials from religious and civic organizations. Even before rehearsals on *Rothschild* began, Zanuck solicited suggestions on the final script from both Breen's office and various high-profile figures, including Arliss himself, Rabbi Edgar Magnin, banking magnate A. H. Giannini, and studio executives Louis B. Mayer, Joseph Schenck, and Samuel Goldwyn.[538] After obtaining an endorsement from Joseph Jonah Cummins, editor of the *B'nai B'rith Messenger*, Zanuck shared a photostat of Cummins's letter with the PCA. "Since you have already received the favorable reaction of the Editor of the *B'nai B'rith Messenger*," James Wingate suggested, "in view of the very delicate relations existing between Jews and Germans," Zanuck should "secure the reaction of some representative of the German Government."[539]

In his monthly report to Will Hays, Joe Breen reiterated the PCA's role in anticipating potential censorship problems and offering solutions.

> We found nothing questionable in [the script] from the standpoint of either Code or censorship, though there might be some possibility of difficulty from the German angle, inasmuch as it gives a historical portrayal of the treatment of the Jews in Germany at the beginning of the Nineteenth century. We took occasion to suggest to Mr. Zanuck that it might be well for him to protect himself on this angle, particularly as he indicated that he had already got some advice on the Jewish angle.[540]

To "protect" oneself, in this context, meant to contact the German consul. Rather than illustrating mogul avarice, correspondence regarding *The House of Rothschild* reveals a set of diffuse institutional forces exerting pressure to cooperate with the Nazis. In his letter to James Wingate, Frederick L. Herron, foreign manager of the Motion Picture Producers and Distributors Association, suggests that his New York office handle any complaints on behalf of the Nazi government. While Herron accuses Los Angeles German consul Georg Gyssling, of "looking for trouble" and "narrow minded," the MPPDA foreign manager finds the New York consul "a very fair minded individual and very pleasant to deal with."

> I am working with him now on Warner Brothers' *Captured* and Columbia's *Below the Sea*, both of which have very bad scenes in them from the German standpoint, but I know we are going to work them out, while the German Consul in Los Angeles wanted to ban

the whole picture in both cases. This is just an example of what can be done if you deal with intelligent people, rather than with obstructionists of the type of Dr. Gyssling.[541]

Breen's response to Herron reiterates the role of the PCA in anticipating potential controversy and the institutional practice of regularly consulting representatives of foreign governments:

We have noted no effort on the part of the German Consul in recent days to nose into the business of script reading. The observation contained in Dr. Wingate's letter to Zanuck dated Dec. 2nd was merely a precautionary move against the possibility that there might be some serious German criticism of the picture if it were to go out as it now is. I am reasonably certain that no effort has been made by any of the local German officials to intrude themselves into this particular enterprise.

You may count upon us to refer to you any attempt made by the Germans or any other foreign group who get hot and bothered about the picture.[542]

The suggestion that Twentieth Century–Fox consult the German consul prompted a strong response from Zanuck, who not only indicates an awareness of the Hollywood Question but positions himself in relation to it. After thanking Wingate and noting that "it was a tough job to keep from offending anyone and yet stay to historical facts," Zanuck demurs to Wingate's suggestion: "I do not think it would be a good idea to send it to a representative of the German government at this time. In the first place, I am told that the present government of Germany does not look with favor upon American moving pictures, especially Hollywood producers whom they have classed as Jews."

Zanuck feels compelled to clarify his own ethnic stake in the Hollywood Question. "It just so happens that I am of German-Swiss de[s]cent and not a Jew," he writes, "but I still think that anyone at the present time who is pro-Hitler, such as any representative of the German government must be, might take a radical viewpoint of the story." Zanuck's response to the Hollywood Question is ostensibly industrially based. Even though he had shared the script with Wingate and Cummins, he claims to "shy away from submitting a printed manuscript," believing that it would "only be unnecessarily inviting a possible dispute if we called in the local German Con-sul."[543]

In response, the PCA and its parent organization, the MPPDA, asserted their industrial role in censoring ethnic content. After Breen telegramed Hays, noting Zanuck's disagreement with the suggestion that Twentieth Century–Fox consult any representative of the German government, Hays contacted Zanuck in an attempt to bring him into line.[544] In his response, Hays demonstrates an awareness of the Hollywood Question. Although he uses this awareness to invoke a set of ostensibly universal positions against "race prejudice," the invocation has consequences for film content:

> As you know, the Rothschild picture has been causing some con-cern.
>
> I am certain that you have in mind the element in such a picture which should be carefully dealt with if it is not to prove highly prejudicial at the present time. I know you are interested, just as we are, in avoiding anything in any picture that would create a race prejudice. That is true as to any race, and particularly it is important that nothing be done now that might possibly feed the unreasoning prejudice against the Jews which is in some places. A widespread factor in this unfair and prejudiced attack is the false allegation that all Jews acquire money for power, with the inference that such power may be used.
>
> The historical prominence of the House of Rothschild is such that hostile propagandists have tried to make the very name a synonym for sinister, world-wide political power, growing out of accumulated riches. The fact that in the case of the Rothschilds the power of money was rightly used may be overshadowed by the greater impres-sion of the Rothschilds as an example of Jewish power through dom-ination by money.
>
> I know you have all this in mind and are worrying, too, about it and I know the desire of yourself and Mr. Schenck to exercise the greatest care. It is really a cause of worry. There will be a difference of opinion on this matter probably, but thinking Jews themselves might interpret the picture as provocative of further propaganda against the race. The danger is, of course, that the ordinary treatment of the theme might emphasize in its effect a basic element of anti-Jewish propaganda; that an audience may not distinguish between the right use of power, as the Rothschilds did use it, as against a bad

use of power which they might have exerted if they had not been influenced by the wisdom of the oldest brother to use it rightly. It is very important, as I know you realize, that you leave the right impression of the sympathetic characteristics of the principal people.[545]

In ensuing discussions over the film, *The House of Rothschild* emerged as an important site of struggle, the outcome of which would determine both how motion pictures would represent Jews and how biographies of great men would function as an important ideological vehicle for this representation. In his response to Hays's letter, Zanuck dismisses Rabbi Magnin's objections to the project:

Without exception, I received a completely clean bill of health from everyone else and, in fact, several of them cautioned me that the story might be too pro-Jewish and suggested that perhaps I had painted the lily too white. Now, of course, our only interest is to make an entertaining box-office picture that will please millions of theatre-goers, we are not interested in boosting or knocking anyone.

Just as others would subsequently justify their biographies of great Jewish men, so Zanuck justifies *Rothschild* by maintaining a centrist position that refers back both to the project's authenticity and to high-culture legitimacy:

Our story is based on historical facts as well as the famous stage play *Rothschild*, which has been produced innumerable time[s] all over Europe with great success. That Dr. Magnin could find any objection to it and should write other individuals in an effort to stir up propaganda against the picture is honestly inconceivable. I don't know whether you have read the scenario or not. I hope you have, because if there was ever written a greater tribute to any race for production on the screen, I have never seen it or read it.[546]

Not only does the high cultural capital of George Arliss remain crucial to countering the "radically obsessed" protests of Magnin and others to the project; the star persona also plays a key role in speaking for race and ethnicity:

Mr. Arliss made probably the greatest individual success [of] any person in the world, on the stage and screen, playing *Disraeli* and yet he has received several hundreds of letters from Jews denouncing him for one reason or another for playing this character. Their reasons for this denouncement were as peculiar and varied as is the opinion of Dr. Magnin against that of the other prominent Jews who read the scenario. Mr. Arliss having played Voltaire, Alexander Hamilton, Disraeli, Richelieu, Robespierre over a period of thirty years, tells me that the criticisms he has received on these portrayals has invariably come from the race or nationality that he glorified the most in his portrayal and he warned me against sending the script to anyone, but stupidly I did not take his warning.[547]

Negotiations over content, contestations over the significance of the Hollywood Question, and assertions of institutional censorship all resulted in a genre that spoke to the Hollywood Question even as it omitted overt references to ethnicity. After a preview screening of the film "in a town that is considered to be a German community and a Nazi hotbed," Zanuck gleefully reported to Breen that the 125 preview cards received

are the most remarkable endorsements of a picture that it has ever been my pleasure to read. Their unqualified praise for the picture as a picture, the subject as a subject, were absolutely unanimous, which indicates to us that the audiences of America will view the production strictly in the light of enjoyable entertainment, and not at all concerned about what might be interpreted by a very meagre minority as the politics involved.

I am enclosing the opinions of the critics, which are in themselves obvious indications of the public's viewpoint. They were not at all impressed by the picture because it was a religious or political document, but were impressed by its merits from the standpoint of entertainment.[548]

Breen echoes this amazement to Hays, noting that "there is only one out of the entire number which even hints at the Jewish flavor of the picture. Really, these cards are astonishing."[549]

The resultant genre of the "biopic" targets Jews even as it seeks to delete overt reference. In a letter to Breen, for example, Zanuck included a photostated letter from Cummins, who invokes his ethnicity as a vantage point from which to praise the film:

As a Jew, I sat with mixed emotions of doubt and apprehension as the film unrolled. I did not want to behold Jewish propaganda in this film, and I certainly did not expect to find anti-Jewish propaganda. The very production of such a picture at this time found subconscious opposition within me. Yet [the film] left me with nothing but praise for everyone who had a hand in its making.[550]

In his letter to Breen, however, Zanuck notes that "we are not seeking publicity of this sort."[551] The souvenir book accompanying the film offers further evidence of this omission, not once mentioning any trace of Jewishness, either in the plot synopsis or in the scores of critical accolades it reprints.[552]

Key figures at both Twentieth Century–Fox and the PCA no doubt experienced a degree of relief at such responses. "Mr. Zanuck seems to be a bit disturbed," Breen wrote Will Hays, "because of what he tells me is an attempt on the part of some Jews, even now, to find fault with this picture."[553] Breen ultimately issued a favorable report of the film, admitting that, while "it may be true that some Jews may, themselves, interpret the picture as potentially provocative of further propaganda against the Jews," other "Jew haters may write into the story an attempt at Jewish heroics." In his report, Breen stresses that "a fair estimate is to accept the picture as a fine dramatic presentation of an important phase of modern European history."[554]

Hollywood personnel clearly saw at least some of these biographical films as thinly veiled commentaries upon contemporary events. For example, *The Life of Emile Zola* focuses on the renowned author's involvement in the 1898 Dreyfus affair, a French incident pillorying army captain Alfred Dreyfus. The topic had already served as the basis for many films versions, including an 1899 French silent, a 1931 British film with Sir Cedric Hardwicke playing Dreyfus, and a German version from 1930 directed by Richard Ornstein, who changed his last name to Oswald before fleeing Nazi Germany. Although the 1937 Warner Bros. movie makes only one unspoken reference to anti-Semitism – a vivid close-up of a traveling finger, pointing to the word "Jew" on a list of names – PCA head Joe Breen privately complained of the film's "propaganda" in a personal memo to its producer Jack Warner. A scene in which a mob burns Zola's books is too suggestive of "recent activities in Germany, as regards the books authored, or published by Jews. The inclusion of these scenes in your picture may leave your picture open to the accusation that it is propaganda and, as such, unworthy of serious notice. We suggest that, throughout the script, where there is danger that this suggestion of propaganda be drawn, you eliminate the scenes or dialogue responsible for such suggestion."[555]

In pointing out such instances of possible "propaganda," Breen and the PCA helped the film industry achieve a financial interest. As its own censorship entity, the PCA monitored other censorship boards in the United States and around the world. Having to prepare scores of different edited versions for a crazy-quilt patchwork of local audiences and varying tastes could prove costly. In order to justify its existence, the PCA thus had to assert its role in censoring a version that appealed to one common denominator. The financial benefits of censorship ultimately served moral purposes, but not in terms of the individual morality so often painted as mogul cravenness or, less often, as Catholic anti-Semitism. Rather, the PCA demonstrates how financial interests implicitly upheld and complemented the morality of the Hollywood Question, ultimately concealing the inner workings of a set of beliefs that lay behind an outward concern for maximizing profit.

In a 1938 letter to Walter Wanger, for example, PCA head Joe Breen warns the producer of *Blockade* (1938) "not to identify, at any time, the uniforms of the soldiers" that appear in this story set against the backdrop of the Spanish Civil War. "You will have in mind that your picture is certain to run into considerable difficulty in Europe and South America, if there is any indication in the telling of your story, that you are 'taking sides' in the present unfortunate Spanish Civil War. It is imperative that you do not, at any time, identify any of the warring factions." A number of letters from Breen to Wanger repeatedly emphasized the economic pitfalls of "taking sides."[556] To assist Robert Lord in the making of MGM's *Underground* (1940), Breen shared a copy of a report authored by Paramount's British censorship expert Derek B. Mayne explaining why the British censor had passed *Confessions of a Nazi Spy* (Warner Bros., 1939) but not the Soviet film *Professor Mamlock* (1938), which depicted the fate of a Jewish doctor in Germany. *Confessions* was "based on a *record of facts* established during" a trial, while *Mamlock* was "just some author's *personal idea or prejudice*." According to this report, any studio planning to release an anti-Nazi film in England "will have to walk very carefully."[557]

Fear of an anti-Jewish backlash often set the limits within which the Hollywood biography could respond to anti-Semitism. Warner Bros. had originally intended to produce the story of Revolutionary War financier Haym Salomon as an A-feature starring Paul Muni, John Garfield, or the popular George Arliss, the Gentile actor who had played lead roles in *Disraeli* and *House of Rothschild*. The studio, however, ultimately made the film part of a series of Warner Bros. patriotic short subjects.[558] Even in its truncated form, Warner Bros.'s general sales manager, Gradwell Sears, expressed concern that the film would be perceived as "out and out jewish [sic] propaganda" unless certain steps were taken to remove "any curse of propaganda."[559] *Boxoffice* columnist Ivan Spear summed up the paradox of the film's projected success, noting that "it must place Salomon in a favorable light," yet the public might perceive such a light to be "pro-Jewish propaganda," thus making the film "an unwise boxoffice experiment."[560]

Fear of this backlash, however, could also propel this genre as a response to the Hollywood Question. In his 1938 pitch for *Dr. Ehrlich's Magic Bullet* (1940) to Warner Bros. producer Henry Blanke, Norman Burnside made it clear that the subtext for this project about the scientist who discovered a cure for syphilis would counter Nazi anti-Semitism. "Continued unemployment, continued unrest, continued Nazi propaganda, continued Ford-financed Father Coughlin propaganda are nudging the American masses toward the pit of fascism and anti-semitism in its sadistic stages," Burnside wrote, warning of what might happen if Hollywood ignored this situation. "I call to mind the Jewish producers in pre-Hitler Germany. Nazi hooligans in the streets were slugging rabbis and women and children. And the Jewish movie producers for the most part hid their heads like ostriches."

Burnside accused Hollywood producers of actively fomenting anti-Semitism:

> If producers in Hollywood merely ignored the Jews, it would be better than what they have been doing. But ninety-five out of a hundred portrayals of Jews on the screen show pawn brokers, corner delicatessen dealers, low comics like Eddie Cantor, Willie Howard, Sammy Cohen. Why can't we have pictures in which more representative Jews are shown – people of distinction and charm, physicians, chemists, engineers, artists, writers, musicians, etc., instead of buffoons who appeal to the lowest prejudices?

The life of Ehrlich, he argued, would address the shortcomings both of Jewish characters in film and of Blanke's own *Life of Emile Zola*:

> In Zola you made a great picture but the Jewish question was handled pianissimo.
>   You told me you wanted a story for Paul Muni. Why not the life of Ehrlich – and in the picture instead of minimizing Ehrlich's Jewish traits, put them in boldly and honestly – the ugliness, the doggedness, the combination of humility and pride, the eccentricity which led to

the conquest of syphilis. And I would hit hard the anti-Semitism that hampered Ehrlich.

Such honesty – warts and all – would prompt "even the most rabid anti-semite" to admit that, while " 'all the Jews are as bad as I think they are, they must be saved if they can give us a guy like Ehrlich once in a while.' " And while "this is no easy job," Burnside believes that "there isn't a man or woman alive who isn't afraid of syphilis." The film would "let them know that a little kike named Ehrlich tamed the scourge – and maybe they can persuade their hoodlum friends to keep their fists off Ehrlich's co-religionists – in spite of the political Spanish fly spat out by Coughlin, Winrod, Ford and others."[561] Less than alluding to either Spanish fascism or sexual arousal, the reference to Spanish fly invokes images of irritation and irresponsibility. Made from the crushed bodies of beetles, the substance irritates the bladder and the urethra when ingested. French authorities imprisoned the Marquis de Sade, ostensibly for the writer's so-called depravity but technically for his use of the substance.[562] The responsible Ehrlich, on the other hand, had produced a cure for a disease resulting from licentiousness. The image of Ehrlich could also serve as the pro-Semitic antidote to the irritation of anti-Semitism as expressed in the irresponsible rhetoric of Coughlin, Winrod, and Ford.

Judging from most contemporary trade reviews, *Dr. Ehrlich's Magic Bullet* hardly appears to "hit hard" on either anti-Semitism or Ehrlich's Jewishness, although these reviews do commend the sensitive way in which the film treats the subject of syphilis. In a March 1940 letter to Joe Breen, Paris correspondent Harold Smith sent a copy of an article by Arthur Duff-Cooper, former minister of war for Great Britain. The article, which appears in the French-language *Paris Soir*, criticizes the American "terror of propaganda." In "The United States Risk Losing Freedom of Speech Because of Fear of Propaganda," Duff-Cooper discloses his "great surprise" that "during the entire film, the fact that Ehrlich was a Jew was not mentioned." He also notes how the film makes no mention of how the Nazis attempted to "suppress memory" of Ehrlich, or how "some of the pseudo-scientists of the Nazi regime have even tried to cast doubt on the value of his discoveries" – all "for this reason" of Ehrlich's Jewish origins.[563]

Behind the scenes, however, Ehrlich's Jewishness did receive conspicuous notice, even after producer Henry Blanke took a less prominent role in production than producer Hal Wallis. A United Press wire story on the upcoming release of the movie surmised that Warner Bros. might end it by showing the "Nazis destroying the statue of Dr. Ehrlich, changing the title of his hospital and erasing his name from the signs on the Berlin boulevard."[564] When the PCA report and certificate for the release print identified Ehrlich as a "sympathetic" lead character, the report made note of his being "Jewish" in parentheses. The report again refers to Ehrlich as Jewish when listing the "Races or Nationals" represented in the film. And, under additional remarks, the PCA report notes the "excellent characterization of the great Jewish bacteriologist, Dr. Paul Ehrlich, whose contributions to medical science have saved thousands of lives."[565] In response to Smith's letter from Paris, Breen bristles at Duff-Cooper's remarks. He "ought not to be taken too seriously, chiefly because the gentleman seems not to know just what it is he is talking about." That the film makes no mention of Ehrlich's Jewishness "is a mis-statement of fact. It is clearly indicated in the picture that Dr. Ehrlich was a Jew." That Warner Bros. would "deem it undesirable to cite facts which might be interpreted as propaganda is very wise. It was not necessary, in the telling of the story, to launch any attack upon the Nazi government, and to do so would expose Warner Brothers to the charge of using the motion picture screen to propagandize."[566]

When Detroit censors rejected PCA-approved films *Strange Cargo* (MGM, 1940) and *The Primrose Path* (MGM, 1940), Breen complained to Will Hays. Noting that Duff-Cooper "was entertained extensively" in Hollywood, Breen compared his recent article to the reaction of the Detroit police commissioner and the Legion of Decency condemnation of *Strange Cargo*. "He condemns Warner Brothers for neglecting to attack the Nazi government in their picture, *Dr. Ehrlich*. This gentleman makes the statement that the picture makes no reference whatever to the fact that Ehrlich was a Jew, despite the fact that this is clearly established by dialogue early in the picture."[567]

The tension between ethnicity and the erasure of ethnicity abounds throughout the discussion of the film. Denying that this is a film about syphilis also becomes a way to downplay the specificity of Ehrlich's Jewishness. After "making quite a number of changes" in the script, producer Hal Wallis stressed to Joe Breen "that this is considerably more a story of a great scientist and his contribution to humanity than it is a story about syphilis."[568] Although Edward G. Robinson ultimately starred in the lead, that the producers initially had Paul Muni in mind only reinforces how a quasi-ethnic Jewish actor could be an ideal vehicle for addressing anti-Semitism by ultimately not really addressing anti-Semitism. Robinson first achieved stardom by playing an Italian gangster in *Little Caesar* (Warner Bros.–First National, 1930). Originally having performed in the New York

Yiddish Theater under his given name, Muni Weisenfreund, the actor achieved even wider prominence with an Anglicized name and his role in the 1932 Warner Bros. feature *I Was a Fugitive from a Chain Gang*. Significantly, in that film Muni does not overtly appear as a Jew. Instead, the injustice of his persecution at the hands of a brutal Southern criminal system had a more universal appeal. Like his name, Muni appears exotic enough to warrant attention, yet such difference ultimately harks back to the consensus of assimilation. He may have been a Jew, but not until the 1940s did he play one in the movies, and an assimilated one at that.

PART 3

The Hollywood Question, 1941 and Beyond

7

Popular Culture Answers the Hollywood Question

"THE IDEA OF RIVINGTON STREET": THE HOLLYWOOD NOVEL AND NATIONAL IDENTITY

By the end of the 1930s, the Hollywood Question became a way to the New Deal, foreign policy, even anti-Semitism. It had shaped film content and censorship. Yet the Question was not simply an activation of anti-Semitism, nor was it only a response to perceived hostility toward Jews. Rather, the Hollywood Question allowed for a series of responses that subsumed ethnic Jewish identity under national identity. If the Question could provide "a little kike" to speak against anti-Semitism, that "little kike" could also point to the failure of the American Dream. Three classics of American literature responded to the Question by inverting its assumptions. Using familiar Jewish characters and stereotypes, these works suggest that Hollywood "kikes" are the product rather than the cause of a failed success myth.

By the beginning of the forties, *Day of the Locust* (1939), *The Last Tycoon* (1941), and *What Makes Sammy Run?* (1941) had mirrored a significant shift in the Hollywood Question. Rather than offering a positive stereotype of the movie mogul, these books marginalize overt, hostile versions of the Question while using certain of its elements as metonymic commentary upon post–New Deal America. Like other Hollywood novels, these books by Nathanael West, F. Scott Fitzgerald, and Budd Schulberg comment upon the failure of the American Dream. Critics have accused all three novelists of promoting anti-Semitic stereotypes. Yet the way in which these novels invoke anti-Semitism differs markedly from the tenor of other Hollywood novels. In each of these three novels, references to American anti-Semitism, as well as to a Hollywood Question–driven image of the Jew, comprise a larger commentary on the failure of essential traditional values.

Both Nathanael West and F. Scott Fitzgerald existed on the periphery of Hollywood and both met similar fates. The day before West died in an

FIGURE 20. Nathanael West in Hollywood. Los
Angeles Public Library, *Herald-Examiner* Collection.

automobile accident, Fitzgerald suffered a fatal heart attack. Fitzgerald, once
the epitome of the Jazz Age, passed away in relative obscurity, leaving a
handful of short stories, a few screenplay credits, and an unfinished novel –
The Last Tycoon – to bolster a sagging, latter-day reputation. Hollywood
had lured both Fitzgerald and West from the East Coast, and both had
found screenwriting more lucrative – even when scraping for assignments –
than writing novels. Publishing fiction, which had caused Hollywood to
take notice of West and Fitzgerald in the first place, proved costly and
disheartening. Unlike West, whose obituaries could not even get the names
of his novels right – *The Day of Locusts* and *Miss Lovely Hearts* are cases in
point – Fitzgerald did receive some posthumous acclaim. Once a literary
phenomenon and a symbol of the Jazz Age, Fitzgerald died doing rewrites
for studio scripts, lapsed into alcoholism, and was barely capable of getting
Esquire magazine to publish his short stories.[569]

In its own way, West's *Day of the Locust* (1939) serves as a kind of anti-
Hollywood novel. In keeping with the literary genre, it attacks the city's
glamour and pretension. Moreover, consistent with this genre, *Locust* contains its share of anti-Semitic imagery. Yet West's novel is less about
Hollywood than it is about pathetic, marginal souls. The book offers a
glimpse of how their lives connect, before a climactic mob lynching claims
Homer Simpson, one of the book's main characters, at a Hollywood premiere.

Like West's other works, *Miss Lonelyhearts* (1930) and *A Cool Million*

(1934), *Day of the Locust* is a satire, albeit a bleak one. The novel satirizes Hollywood, showing it through the eyes of various failures. In the book, studio underling Tod Hackett encounters a variety of characters: Faye Greener, a nymphomaniac unattainable to Tod, and her washed-up vaudevillian father, Harry. Homer Simpson, the gullible Midwestern victim, falls prey to Faye's charm. In addition, there are sundry lesser characters – a vicious dwarf, a washed-up cowboy extra, his Mexican friend, and the like. Scenes at the movie studio, like the disastrous movie-set re-creation of the Battle of Waterloo, reveal a certain cynicism: the grandiose attempts at historical accuracy result in actual casualties due to shoddy construction. Yet, such depictions do not convey overt anti-Semitism.

West wrote *Day of the Locust* during a difficult stint as a Hollywood screenwriter. One of many Jewish writers lured from the East Coast, West enjoyed only moderate success. He received a few screen credits, most notably as cowriter for John Farrow's *Five Came Back* (1939). After Random House published *Day of the Locust*, in May 1939, the book sold 1,486 copies – an abysmal number. However, before he and his wife died in a 1940 car wreck, West's screenwriting career had begun to show more promise. His weekly RKO salary was six hundred dollars, nearly twice the royalties he had received for *Day of the Locust*.[570]

Unlike earlier Hollywood novels, *Day of the Locust* undercuts the genre's usual penchant for implying Jewish predominance in the film industry. The book makes fleeting references to such beliefs, but West depicts them as part of Hollywood itself. Early in the book, protagonist Tod Hackett attends a Hollywood party. At one point, he overhears someone asking how "to get rid of the illiterate mockies that run the movie industry?" In addition to using the pejorative "mockie" – possibly an alliterative form of the Yiddish verb for "to make" – the passage cites typically anti-Semitic stereotypes. For example, Jews have "got a strangle hold on the industry" and "they're intellectual stumblebums, but they're damn good businessmen." As the anonymous partygoer envisions it, Jews "know how to go into receivership and come up with a gold watch in their teeth."[571]

West evokes a sense of ambivalence toward the perception of Jewish control in Hollywood. He mocks both Hollywood and those who create its myths. At the same party where Tod overhears the reference to "illiterate mockies" he also listens to someone rue the men who work in Hollywood. They "grouse all the time about the place, flop on their assignments, then go back East and tell dialect stories about producers they've never met." Though anti-Semitic stereotypes appear in *Day of the Locust*, their appearance occasions mockery. Only at a Hollywood party could one overhear resentment expressed toward both "illiterate mockies" and men who parlay "dialect stories." Yet West's own descriptions reinforce the Hollywood Question in a way that parallels it's cruder invocation in earlier novels. The book includes the absurd character of Chief Kiss-My-Towkus, an American Indian sporting a Yiddish accent. This ethnic collision recalls less ironic attempts to align Jews with alleged racial inferiors. The electric sign of a studio – MR. KAHN A PLEASURE DOME DECREED – looms over the mob as they lynch Homer Simpson at the movie premiere turned riot. A romanticized image of the Arab and the image of the parvenu are conflated on this sign. A play upon Kubla Khan of Samuel Taylor Coleridge's poem, the banner of the sign ties the Jewish mogul Kahn to the Oriental – in this instance, Chinese ruler Khan. Its convoluted English mocks the pretentious display of "culture."[572]

West both satirizes and poses the Hollywood Question, but only to depict the failure of the American Dream. Reduced to selling door-to-door, Harry Greener can only relive his vaudeville days through yellowed press clippings. Once her father dies, Faye must abandon her dreams of stardom. She turns to Homer Simpson for shelter. His own dreams dashed by Faye's infidelity, Homer tramples an obnoxious, taunting child actor. Upon witnessing this act, the crowd at a Hollywood premiere chases Homer through the streets before pummeling him, presumably to death. West's depiction of the climactic mob scene itself appears to be an outburst of frustration. The mob, no longer believing in the Dream, can derive pleasure only from viewing movie royalty from afar and fighting one another just to get a glimpse of someone else's success. Scenes like these put *Day of the Locust's* images of anti-Semitism in perspective. The flip remark made at a party of movie executives, a Yiddish Amerindian, and an electric sign are part of West's larger critique of false hopes in depression-era America.

Fitzgerald's opus features a larger body of unfavorable Jewish depictions. *The Great Gatsby* (1925) features a Jewish gangster, Meyer Wolfsheim, who had fixed the 1919 World Series. Fitzgerald's series of short stories, published in the men's magazine *Esquire* during the 1930s, details the exploits of Pat Hobby, a washed-up writer in Hollywood who takes an occasional jab at Hollywood Jews. In *The Last Tycoon*, however, Fitzgerald wanted to avoid touching "the racial angle," and instead depicted a man who had climbed "out of a thousand years of Jewry into the late the [sic] eighteenth century."[573]

In the Pat Hobby series, Fitzgerald alludes to Jews and Jewish stereotypes, but the person who garners the most attention and pity is Hobby himself.

FIGURE 21. Portrait of F. Scott Fitzgerald by Carl Van Vechten,
1937. Library of Congress, Prints and Photographs Division.

The difference between the Hobby series and most other Hollywood por-
traits is that Hobby himself is mocked. He is a sympathetic hero, but a
pitiable one as well. This kind of deprecation blunts any satire of Hollywood where Hollywood is the focus of the attack.

In "A Man in the Way," Hobby begs production head Jack Berners to
hire him to develop a story idea. Berners casually dismisses Hobby, suggesting that he try to get one of the contract writers interested in it. Hobby
protests, fearing that someone will steal his idea. As Berners walks away, he
says to Hobby, "we're not in Poland." In a bitter retort, Hobby mumbles,
"good you're not. . . . They'd slit your gizzard."[574]

In marked contrast to *The Last Tycoon* and its praise for the upward
mobility of Monroe Stahr, this passage does evince certain resentment

toward the parvenu Jew. Berners, who so cavalierly dismisses Hobby's fear of plagiarism, offers only token solace by trivializing European pogroms. Moreover, Hobby dislikes this treatment from someone who himself might have been the victim of these pogroms. The passage captures the essence of his resentment: Hobby, an unfortunate, expects the parvenu to lend a more sympathetic hand.

Although one could argue that the remark represents a gratuitous anti-Semitic utterance on Fitzgerald's part, one should also remember that he portrays Hobby as a pathetic figure. Far more sophisticated than most hostile Hollywood fiction, the Hobby series reveals the amorality of its eponymous character. Hobby's utterance discloses as much about anti-Semitism as it does about Hobby's frustration and disenchantment. Thus, perceptions of Jewish control, like those voiced in the party scene in *Day of the Locust*, characterize a particular kind of anti-Semitism rather than simply espousing it.

More telling of Fitzgerald's attitudes toward Jews, "Boil Some Water – Lots of It" reveals an outsider's ambivalence. Here, Hobby unwittingly intervenes in an elaborate practical joke involving a writer dressed up as a Cossack. Pretending to be an extra, the writer behaves rudely to a group of executives. When the extra draws his sword on one of them, Hobby, not getting the joke, cracks a cafeteria tray over his head. The short story indicates Hobby's status as an outsider. He misses the inside joke; he can never be a part of this group with a collective memory of oppression. Yet the story also underlines the Jewish status as parvenu. As in "A Man in the Way," Fitzgerald reminds the reader that Jews really experienced oppression and really did fear Cossacks. Now they run studios and use their former status to play practical jokes upon one another. Hobby takes the joke seriously and then feels humiliated when he realizes his overreaction. The parvenu draws Hobby into this humiliation through an inside joke, compounding the insult.[575]

The depiction of anti-Semitism helps to explain pathetic Hobby's character. *The Last Tycoon*, however, challenges the genre's usual perception of Jews by attempting a relatively complex, sympathetic portrait of them. Although the novel has one or two passages that resonate with the overt anti-Semitism of the Hollywood novel, Monroe Stahr is no Meyer Wolfsheim. Whereas the Hobby series depicts the parvenu peripherally, *The Last Tycoon* offers a highly sympathetic portrait of the parvenu written from the perspective of the parvenu himself. Minimally narrated, or rather introduced, by Cecilia Brady, daughter of a Gentile movie mogul, *The Last Tycoon* opens by presenting two different kinds of Jews. When Fitzgerald first introduces Monroe Stahr through Cecilia's admiring eyes, his image recalls the melding of pioneer and artist celebrated in Glory Road. Stahr is one of "the capitalist men of action," a "pioneer." A creator as well as a ruler, Stahr is not just the last tycoon but "the last of the 'merchant princes.' "[576]

Cecilia Brady contrasts her adoration for Stahr with another kind of parvenu, Manny Schwartz. Compared to Stahr, Schwartz appears vulgar and crass. As he finds himself edged out of the company he helped to build, he commits suicide upon the altar of Andrew Jackson's Hermitage. Cecilia imagines him as coming "a long way from some ghetto to present himself at [the Hermitage's] raw shrine. Manny Schwartz and Andrew Jackson – it was hard to say them in the same sentence. It was doubtful if he knew who Andrew Jackson was as he wandered around." While Brady, and perhaps Fitzgerald himself, might be loath to mention Schwartz and Jackson in the same breath, a far more telling association occurs between Stahr and Schwartz. Schwartz epitomizes a kind of crassness both indigenous to the film industry and at odds with North American culture. The movie industry is itself foreign. Stahr works for an Englishman, and another mogul is Greek. The other eight moguls in the book are Jewish. Even with Schwartz's death, Stahr still appears as the parvenu, albeit a desirable one. As Jonas Spatz observes, Fitzgerald's notes depict Stahr as a "scrapper, one of the boys, a boy destined to succeed."[577]

In The Last Tycoon, Fitzgerald uses a variety of characters to rework many of the invidious stereotypes of Jewish movie moguls. A director "had worked with Jews too long to believe legends that they were small with money." Cecilia discovers a naked woman in her father's office, displacing the common stereotype of lasciviousness from a Jewish mogul to a Gentile one. Ironically, the woman who flirtatiously tells Stahr that "you people are supposed to be such horrors" turns out to be a call girl.[578]

Ultimately, however, sympathetically reworking common stereotypes does not fully escape the ambivalence toward Stahr, and by extension the parvenu Jew. Although Fitzgerald's urbane Stahr prevails over the partially assimilated Schwartz, this image of upward ethnic mobility occupies a larger theme within the novel. The Last Tycoon is about the death of the American Dream – Stahr, a fitting sacrifice to it. Modeled after legendary MGM production executive Irving Thalberg, Stahr is dying a slow death as he desperately battles the industry labor organizing so frequently associated with Jewish radicalism.

As parvenu insider, Stahr epitomizes both Jewish success and Gentile ambivalence about this success. Fitzgerald never fully deals with Stahr's ascent: does his success displace others' opportunities or does it simply mark the failure of a system that never fully worked? Because Fitzgerald leaves this question unanswered, some of his observations, put in the mouth of Stahr, reveal an embittered undercurrent. At a party, for instance, Stahr wonders at how horseracing had captured the imagination of Jews. "For years it had been the Cossacks mounted and the Jews on foot," Stahr mused. "Now the Jews had horses, and it gave them a sense of extraordinary well-being and power." Although Fitzgerald discounts the myth that most Jewish moguls were "wizards or even experts" with money, he nonetheless writes that their "different and incompatible qualities" result from clannishness that "carries along the less adept."[579]

The eulogies for Fitzgerald that came with reviews of *The Last Tycoon* evidence how the novel's largely sympathetic portrayals offered critics the chance to clarify their own stand on the accusation of Jewish control over the movies. John Dos Passos lauded Fitzgerald for his characterization of movie executive Monroe Stahr. Dos Passos, whose own novel *The Big Money* (1936) includes a rather unflattering portrait of the mogul Margolies, praised Fitzgerald for avoiding a familiar trap. In developing Stahr, Fitzgerald wrote "not as a poor man writing about someone rich and powerful," nor does he make "the impotent last upthrust of some established American stock sneering at a parvenu Jew."[580]

Both West and Fitzgerald wrote about Jews in Hollywood from their perspective as East Coast natives. Budd Schulberg, on the other hand, grew up in Hollywood and had already worked on such movies as *A Star Is Born* (Selznick, 1936) – the movie about movies.[581] His father, B. P. Schulberg, was one of the first Jewish movie moguls. Being the son of a Paramount executive, Schulberg was able to hobnob with celebrities like Fitzgerald. In 1939, producer Walter Wanger teamed Fitzgerald and Schulberg. The two would do research for the film *Winter Carnival* (1939) by attending the annual festivity at Wanger and Schulberg's alma mater, Dartmouth College. The two writers ended up on a disastrous drinking spree. Wanger fired Fitzgerald, and after this incident, the author could barely find work in Hollywood. Schulberg, on the other hand, kept his coscreenwriter credit. That same year he wrote *What Makes Sammy Run?*[582]

Schulberg expanded *What Makes Sammy Run?* (1941) from an earlier short story. His protagonist, Sammy Glick, is a ruthless hustler whose relentless drive to succeed finds fertile ground within the vicissitudes of Hollywood. Another Sammy had appeared in a 1932 synopsis Schulberg sold to RKO at the age of eighteen. "In Your Own Backyard" recounts how

Sammy, "a little colored boy in poverty row," befriends Steven, who comes from a rich white family. At the melodramatic climax, black Sammy drowns while rescuing Steven from the ocean. Arriving too late, Sammy's mother "sings tearfully the song she had told him so often 'stay in your own back yard.'" A precursor of sorts to the later Sammy Glick, selfless Sammy commits an act of social transgression that ends in disaster. Ironically, so does Sammy Glick.[583]

What Makes Sammy Run? owes much to Jewish-oriented fiction, as Patricia Erens rightly points out. The work of Anzia Yezierska, Samuel Ornitz's *Haunch, Paunch and Jowl,* Henry Roth's *Call It Sleep,* and Jerome Weidman's *I Can Get It for You Wholesale* all remain highly critical of the Jewish urban ghetto. As Erens observes, this literature viewed the ghetto as the place that produced unscrupulous Jews like Sammy Glick.[584] Rather than staying in his own backyard, Sammy should have never even been there in the first place. As an emerging national identity placed the interests of a security state above ethnic diversity, American Jews had to depart the immigrant, urban ghettos. The ghetto could explain Jewish agency, but, according to this argument, collective indifference and intolerance had created the Sammy Golem.

For years after *What Makes Sammy Run?* appeared, popular critics and academics found the Glick character to embody some fundamental social truism. As Sander Gilman notes, Erik Homburger Erikson turned to the fictional Glick in 1950 when describing the "bad" Jew, "the Luftmensch, the wheeler-dealer, rootless, without morals or goals," who lived by his wits and "luft," or hot air. Others found that Sammy Glick captured "the brutally aggressive drive our society can produce." Virgil Lokke notes how Leo Gurko, Marshall McLuhan, C. Wright Mills, and David Riesman all used Glick to reveal some essence of popular culture. In his 1941 review of the book, Fred T. Marsh simply called Glick an "all-American heel."[585]

Arguably, the history behind *What Makes Sammy Run?* is as fascinating as the novel itself. According to testimony Budd Schulberg gave before the House Un-American Activities Committee in 1951, the author battled with the Communist Party (CP) between 1937 and 1939 in an effort to retain creative control over his short stories. Schulberg broke with the CP after its leadership tried to discourage him from turning his *Liberty* magazine short story "What Makes Sammy Run?" into a book.[586]

Charles Glenn of the *Daily Worker* reviewed the book twice, first praising it as "the Hollywood novel," according to Schulberg. But others in the CP told Schulberg that his first novel "was much too individualistic," in spite of it being "the first book to speak positively of the strike at the [Writers

Guild]." The CP later forced Glenn to recant his review at a public meeting. Glenn subsequently wrote a second review critical of the book.[587]

Despite this controversy, contemporary discussions of the book provide little mention of the Jewishness of the characters. In addition, if, as Erens argues, the book belongs to a tradition of Jewish-oriented fiction, the strictures of the Hollywood novel inform this tradition. Sammy Glick fulfills the classic stereotype. He chomps on a cigar, possesses a material instinct, engages in parvenu behavior, and flaunts his lascivious behavior. He rises to success by claiming credit for a script his friend and fellow Jew Julian Blumberg wrote. Later, he plagiarizes Hecht/MacArthur's *The Front Page* and Somerset Maugham's *Rain*. Glick completely lacks creativity; he is, according to Al Mannheim, "prouder of the method with which he had triumphed than if he had thought of the original suggestion himself."[588]

Schulberg modulates the caricature of Glick with sympathetic Jewish characters. The narrator and moral center of the story, Mannheim, barely conceals his contempt for Glick. Julian Blumberg, the shy, sensitive Jew, falls prey to Glick's immoral behavior. In addition, Sidney Fineman, the kindly, intellectual studio head, eventually loses his job because the blue-blood stockholders of his studio control the company, fire him, and hire Glick to take his place.

Schulberg uses Glick to demonize any kind of parvenu, Jewish or otherwise. Glick becomes a universal symbol. People as diverse as "a titled Englishman and a famous poet and an aesthetic nance and a tough, drunken ex-reporter . . . all really had the same idea Sammy had. They were all running. Sammy was just a little bit faster, that's all." To Kit Carson, Glick's white Anglo-Saxon lover, Glick represents "the id of our whole society. . . . the core of your basic appetites which the super-ego dresses in the clothes of respectability to present to the outside world." Glick doesn't get "dressed up" like the others, with "all their sammyglickness covered up in Oxford manners or have-one-on-me sociability or Christian morals that they pay their respects every Sunday morning when they don't have too big a hangover. I think that's what first hit me about Sammy. He wasn't trying to be something else. He was the thing itself, the id, out in the open."

What Makes Sammy Run? indicts, not Glick, but an entire way of life that has turned sour. When Glick connives to seize Fineman's job, he tells Mannheim it makes him feel "patriotic." Moreover, at the close of the novel, narrator Mannheim calls "the record of where Sammy ran . . . a blueprint of a way of life that was paying dividends in America in the first half of the twentieth century."[589]

Schulberg uses the character of Mannheim to back away from any accusation of anti-Semitism. Mannheim sees "too many Jewish nebs and poets and starving tailors and everyday little guys to consider the fascist answer to *What Makes Sammy Run?*" When Mannheim visits the impoverished Lower East Side to crack the eponymous riddle, he quickly dismisses "the fascist charge that Jews have cornered the wealth of America." Yet Mannheim believes there is something in Glick's heritage that provides "the breeding ground for the predatory germ that thrived in Sammy's blood, leaving him one of the most severe cases of the epidemic."[590]

What Makes Sammy Run? does not demonize Glick for the sake of demonizing Jews as much as it demonizes the Jewish Glick to criticize the American Dream. Mannheim is particularly hostile to Glick's immigrant background. He thinks of

> Sammy Glick rocking in his cradle of hate, malnutrition, prejudice, suspicions, amorality, the anarchy of the poor; I thought of him as a mangy little puppy in a dog-eat-dog world. I was modulating my hate for Sammy Glick from the personal to the societal. I no longer even hated Rivington Street but the idea of Rivington Street, all Rivington Streets of all nationalities allowed to pile up in cities like gigantic dung heaps smelling up the world, ambitions growing out of filth and crawling away like worms.[591]

At a time when many Jews placed nationality above ethnicity, the highest form of assimilation would be to renounce one's ethnic roots. Schulberg's vision of this renunciation, seen through Mannheim, overdetermines the assimilation process. Not only does Mannheim denounce ethnic identity as incompatible with Americanism; Schulberg appropriates anti-Semitic imagery to show how ethnic identity provides the breeding ground for all that is at odds with the American Dream. Mannheim refutes what he calls the fascist answer to the riddle of the novel. While he refers to the charge of a Jewish banking conspiracy, however, not once does he ever mention the accusation that Jews control Hollywood.

The book received most of its praise for its unflinching indictment of an American way of life gone sour. Robert van Gelder, in a 1941 *New York Times Book Review* article, calls the novel "brilliantly effective because it is completely of this time, expressing the beliefs and hopes that begin to stand out in this period." Most of the criticism, however, centered upon the unflattering portrait of Glick. Columnist Dorothy Thompson, an ardent interventionist, called the book anti-Semitic. Philip Hartung, writing for the liberal Catholic magazine *Commonweal* in 1941, saw Schulberg's "sam-myglickia" verging on an "embarrassing anti-Semitism." According to Er-ens, Jewish groups successfully pressured Hollywood to keep Sammy Glick off the screen, although studios had optioned the book many times. When Glick did finally appear on the screen, it was when Budd Schulberg adapted his own novel for live television in the late 1950s.[592]

While Glick epitomized the negative stereotype of the Jew, however, both his character and criticism of it emerged amid a larger debate over Jewish influence in Hollywood. Simply accusing *What Makes Sammy Run?* of being anti-Semitic is to miss a crucial development in the Hollywood Question. Sammy Glick is a Jewish stereotype that comments on American acquisitiveness rather than Jewish acquisitiveness, and on American amo-rality rather than Jewish amorality. Sammy Glick is a Jewish Other repre-senting an American id; he is certainly not a Jewish id representing an American Other, as presented in so many previous Hollywood novels. What Schulberg does with Sammy is no different from the way in which Fitzgerald presents Monroe Stahr, or the way in which West includes gratuitous comments in *Day of the Locust*. In all three of these novels, the Hollywood Question no longer demonizes Jews or Hollywood. These novels really have little if anything to say about control, power, or conspiracy. Rather, their articulation of the Hollywood Question began to shape a commentary critical of American ideals and beliefs. The Hollywood Ques-tion had doubled back on itself; searching for a conspiracy of Others, it found the breakdown of the American Dream instead. What Schulberg, Fitzgerald, and West left implicit – that Hollywood existed as an essentially Jewish place – would ultimately explode onto the national scene amid the dramatic congressional hearings investigating Hollywood propaganda.[593]

"AN X-RAY INSTEAD OF A SPOTLIGHT": LEO ROSTEN'S *HOLLYWOOD* UNDER THE "MICROSCOPE OF SOCIAL SCIENCE"

Published in 1941, Leo Rosten's *Hollywood: The Movie Colony, The Movie Makers* shares a crucial similarity with its fictional literary coun-terparts. The result of a comprehensive, year-long study of the film com-munity and three years of preparation, the book never mentions the belief in Jewish control over Hollywood.[594] Yet its arguments and observations implicitly, consistently respond to the Hollywood Question. As Rosten perceptively discerns, he is examining a watershed moment in film history. Its foreign markets gone because of World War II, its domestic market under threat of an antitrust investigation, its labor unions more powerful than before the New Deal, Hollywood had undergone tremendous change by 1941.[595] Dating his preface on 2 August 1941, the eve of the Senate Propaganda hearings, Rosten's study as much responds to the hearings as it takes an inside look at a highly lucrative period for the industry between 1938 and 1941.[596]

A public intellectual, Rosten moved in many circles before his death in 1997. He achieved his greatest renown for popularizing Yiddish, most notably with *The Joys of Yiddish*. According to a *National Review* eulogy, Rosten helped found the Roundtable, a New York supper club for Jewish intellectuals disillusioned with liberalism.[597] Under the pseudonym Leonard Q. Ross, he had written a series of short stories. Based on his experience teaching English to recent immigrants, these stories appeared in *The Education of H*Y*M*A*N K*A*P*L*A*N* (1937) and *The Return of Hyman Kaplan* (1939). The humor in these stories relies upon dialect to poke fun at immigrants.[598] Though not hostile toward Jews, the dialect in these stories nonetheless creates a dynamic tension between the unversed immigrant Other and the assimilated American. Under the same pseudonym, Rosten also successfully sold the original story (along with Leonard Spigelgass) for the anti-Nazi comedy *All Through the Night* to Warner Bros. in March 1941.[599] As Colgan notes, Warner Bros. found the property especially attractive, because Rosten also served on the Defense Commission, an organization charged with encouraging "painless, unobtrusive propaganda for National Defense."[600] During the war, Rosten became Deputy Director of War Information. After the war ended, he took an assignment with the RAND Corporation before joining *Look* magazine in 1949 as an editor.

A landmark work, *Hollywood* is neither a trade promotion nor a Trojan Horse interloper investigating industry misdeeds. Readable yet scholarly in approach, the book offers the definitive picture of behind-the-scenes Hollywood. Although *Hollywood* received mixed reviews upon its initial publication in 1941, it has remained a seminal historical text for understanding the motion picture industry before World War II. One of the more ambivalent reviews even reinforced Rosten's observations about the popular perception of Hollywood. In a review for *New Yorker* magazine, Clifton Fadiman accused Rosten of succumbing to a "higher Goldwynism" that had "what he would call a 'penchant' for the 'nouveau riche' in prose."[601] Other reviews were much more favorable, perceiving the book's muted defense of the industry. Rosten "dissipates the illusion that the celluloid artists are political imbeciles," wrote John Gassner for *Atlantic Monthly*. "The film capital has traveled far since the early days when, according to Dorothy Parker, the only 'ism' in which it believed was plagiarism."[602] Anthony Bower of *The Nation* praised Rosten's role as "anything but a just critic. He has no axes to grind or vitriol to throw, and the industry as a whole is bound to find a great deal of useful information."[603] When Garth Jowett assessed the legacy of Rosten's book in his 1969 *Film: The Democratic Art*, he noted the import of its perspective. Analyzing "why the mythology which surrounded the film capital played such an important role in popular culture," this anthropological gaze had a profound impact. "Rosten, in fact, completely destroyed many of these same myths."[604]

Funded by grants from the Carnegie Corporation and the Rockefeller Foundation, "The Motion Picture Research Project" served as the first serious, substantial study of the film industry.[605] Emphasizing the importance of firsthand observation, Rosten sent out 4,200 questionnaires to employees at virtually every level of studio hierarchy. Over more than two years, he worked closely with Hollywood personnel – Joe Breen, Will Hays, Jason Joy, and Harry Warner, and Donald Gledhill, secretary of the Academy for Motion Picture Arts and Sciences – to interview hundreds of employees.[606] Walter Wanger, the Gentile, intellectually refined president of the Academy, read drafts for Rosten. The book's preface emphasizes the academic respectability of all involved in the project, which included two sociologists, an economist, and a statistician.[607] Indeed, the names of those assisting the project read like a Who's Who of American social science: Margaret Mead, Gregory Bateson, and Payne Fund scholars Herbert Blumer, Louis Wirth, Harold D. Lasswell, and Robert S. Lynd. A number of *Hollywood* scholars would complete seminal studies of their own on the film industry. Mae D. Huttig and Ruth A. Inglis each published scholarship on the industry after their participation in Rosten's project.[608]

The participation of Margaret Mead and Gregory Bateson is particularly intriguing, given the anthropological slant of the book. Tellingly subtitled *The Movie Colony*, the book even quotes Margaret Mead's study of Manus culture, suggesting that her observations could apply equally well to Hollywood.[609] More than just a scholarly gimmick, this authorial positioning as a learned participant-observer crucially advances a particular kind of response to the Hollywood Question. Entitled "The Hollywood Legend," the first chapter contends that "there are two Hollywoods: the Hollywood where people live and work, and the Hollywood which lives in the mind of the public like a fabulous legend."[610] Rosten seeks to refute what he calls a "miasma of myths and misconceptions" surrounding Hollywood.[611] "Hollywood can be placed under the microscope of social science," he claims, "like a slide on which we see, in sharper and isolated detail, the organic process of the larger social body." If its "pathology illuminates the normal,"[612] then "let us search for evidence and analyze this evidence without undue prejudice or preference. Let us place Hollywood under an X-ray instead of a spotlight. That has never before been done."[613]

Rosten's social scientific microscope refutes the Hollywood Question subtly but effectively. The method remains consistent with other social science methods addressing anti-Semitism. As a later memorandum by Floyd Ruch argues, one best confronts anti-Semitism through "less obvious technique." Posing "questions which exceed the ability of the respondent to answer" reveals "unconscious bias and repressed mental conflict." In addressing prejudice, "obviously anti-Semitism could never be studied by asking people" a question comparing Jews to Gentiles, for example.[614]

Rosten makes little outright reference to anti-Semitic attacks on the industry. He instead creates a vision of a coherent national identity open to Jews but under attack from marginal extremists. The approach resonates with emergent discursive currents minimizing both the threat of anti-Semitism and too much concern for it. In a footnote, Rosten notes how rural "traditional and familiar hostilities" drive rural opposition to "cosmopolitan" Hollywood.[615] It is only natural that "a community populated entirely by entertainers" would be the "ready-made target for hostility. The theatrical profession has always aroused suspicion in the breasts of the moral; acting is the Devil's game, and actors are children of evil." Anti-Semitism is only a minor part of this hostility. "Movie leaders who are Jewish are easy prey for the manipulators of anti-Semitism," but so are Catholics "easy targets for the purveyors of anti-Catholicism," and those Protestants opposed to "the mounting demands of anti-movieism."[616] Noting the "widespread assumption that the movie men are 'foreigners,'" Rosten dismisses any potential anti-Semitic associations. Jokes about the illiterate immigrant mogul merely update "hoary stories of the unlettered country bumpkin."

When faced more directly with anti-Semitism, Rosten gingerly frames the issue as one of an unjust and arbitrary distinction. Instead of discussing how Jews might experience anti-Semitism as Jews, he turns to "those of old native stock" who "are believed to have 'Jewish' names." This rhetorical turn reveals a great deal about conventional attitudes toward Jews – at least in Hollywood. Being Jewish comes down to no more than a name. Just as *The Life of Emile Zola* (Warner Bros., 1938) depicted Alfred Dreyfus as wrongfully singled out for both his name and his naming as Jewish, so Rosten renders the Hollywood Question as no more than a misperceived coding issue. Rosten further downplays the distinction between Jew and Christian through a bit of his own deft coding. "Some of the most important people in the movie hierarchy" according to Rosten – Paramount production head Y. Frank Freeman, Twentieth Century–Fox executives Sidney Kent and Darryl F. Zanuck, RKO head George Schaefer, Louis B. Mayer's confidant and MGM executive Eddie Mannix, the PCA's Joseph I. Breen, Paramount executive William Le Baron, and independents Hal Roach and Cecil B. DeMille – were "erroneously believed by many to be the same faith as the mother of Christ."[617] The men Rosten names are upper-level executives who maintain power and influence near but not at the top of the motion picture hierarchy, yet nonetheless within its structure.

In a neat rhetorical ploy, Rosten responds to the Hollywood Question, not by addressing its anti-Semitism, but by addressing its ill-informed, gullible, and ultimately foreign-influenced xenophobia. Instead of addressing ethnicity or religion, Rosten discusses which producers come from Russia and Poland: of 132 executives interviewed, not even 5 percent.[618] As to the charge that producers are generally foreign, Rosten responds that, of those 132 executives, 82.6 percent were born in the United States. Far from speaking pidgin English, nearly all – save eleven – were born in English-speaking countries.[619] Far from illiterate, more than half of those interviewed had attained a college degree. Those who attacked Hollywood, in fact, unwittingly abetted what Rosten calls "European propaganda." In an explanation that ultimately suits the Hollywood's business perspective, Rosten claims that "Hollywood was the target of allegations initiated in European countries by European manufacturers, film producers, and government agencies. The motion picture interests of Europe were eager to rebuild their own industry after the First World War, during which their production all but shut down, and they had to break the near-monopoly of American films on their own and the world market." The "ingenious campaign against Hollywood morals" proved particularly effective in countries with large Catholic or Lutheran populations.[620]

Rather than addressing Jewish ethnicity in Hollywood or elsewhere, Rosten depicts Jews as part of a cohesive American fabric. They are just as much a part of opposition to movies as they are a part of the movie colony itself. He notes how the Central Conference of American Rabbis joined an "astonishing variety of protests" pouring "into Hollywood week after week." Their "expostulations against movies" joined a "cosmic" number of complaints coming from "governments, foreign offices, business groups, religious orders, trade associations, fraternal societies, or professional bodies."[621]

Rosten maintains that anxiety over business and profit in foreign markets rather than ethnic self-interest motivated Hollywood's concern for the Holocaust. When he intimates a more personal aspect to this concern, he renders the European connections reflective of its "cosmopolitan" flair. "Movies are an international commodity," Rosten notes, and "the paroxysms of power politics flung the impending chaos of the world into Hollywood's lap" before the chaos hit the rest of America:

> The movie people have friends, relatives, and memories which make Europe near and real. To Hollywood's British, French, German, or Hungarian colonies, the cold news of political events means mothers, fathers, sisters, friends. It is one thing to read about the cremation of Rotterdam; it is another to telephone your uncle in Holland and get no reply. It is one thing to hear of blood terror in Rumania; it is another to receive no answer to the frantic cables you send to the staff you met there last year. A substantial percentage of Hollywood had traveled and had known the life of a Vienna which was conquered, a Paris which was overrun, a London which was bombed. And even had the network of their personal lives been less wide, the malevolence of the new Caesars constituted a *personal* threat to the movie makers; after the Nazis smashed Warsaw they arrested the movie theater owners who had ever shown films distasteful to the Third Reich, hanged them, and rolled them through the streets on portable gallows.[622]

Rosten systematically refutes each major tenet of the Hollywood Question. Hollywood does not create "its *own* values," invent "stereotypes with singlehanded omnipotence," or cause "public acceptance of banal homilies." Instead, "the movie makers are in many ways compelled to feed a popular diet to a public which is in firm possession of deplorable tastes – tastes derived from sources far older, deeper, and more potent than Hollywood. The very success of Hollywood lies in the skill with which it *reflects* the assumptions, the fallacies, and the aspirations of an entire culture. The movie producers, the movie directors, the movie writers, and the movie actors work with the stereotypes which are current in our society." Like Sammy Glick and Monroe Stahr, "they, too, are children of that society; they, too, have inherited and absorbed the values of our world."[623]

Rosten defuses the charge that Hollywood engages in political propaganda, anti-Nazi or otherwise. "Hollywood's leaders probably stand to the right of Mr. [Martin] Dies," he claims, "and make even less distinction between a liberal and a Bolshevik. The representative from Texas has never denounced the New Deal with as much animus as some of the movie leaders have done in the presence of this writer."[624] It is "utter political innocuousness" rather than propaganda that distinguishes "Hollywood output." Shunning "the political (and the realistic)," Hollywood "must appeal to the widest of mass markets, and it dare not risk offending any substantial part of that market. Patriotic stories have always been at a premium in the motion picture industry."[625]

When Rosten addresses Hollywood's organized opposition to Nazism, he finds its Communist sympathies out of step with the film community, the nation, and even the majority of those opposing Nazism. "The Anti-Nazi League could have broadened its scope and heightened its efficiency," he claims, "by taking formal steps to allay the mounting suspicion that the leaders and spokesmen of the league were in cahoots with the Communist party or the Communist party line." In "refusing to meet the issue" and "mollifying the Communists," the league's "ruling cabal" – now Communist rather than Jewish – undermined "the unity and conviction of the non-Communist majority. They were more determined to hold to the Communist party line than to further the purpose – anti-Nazi – for which they were organized."[626]

Rosten repeatedly emphasizes that Hollywood is a legitimate if successful business. Unlike the propertied wealthy, "the oligarchs of America," Hollywood's "elite" are no different from salaried employees.[627] The motion picture industry, in fact, has "startling and conclusive parallels" with the "*nouveaux riches* of banking, railroads, or real estate," with the "mores" of Oyster Bay and with "the mansions of Newport."[628] If Hollywood elites are "madmen," then how can they "operate a business which spends almost $187,000,000 a year in making pictures? How can erratic and undisciplined personalities turn out the 350–400 movies a year upon which a two-billion-dollar enterprise depends? How can supposedly illiterate egomaniacs make films which take in half a billion dollars a year at the box-offices of the United States alone?"[629]

Rosten clearly chafes over the disproportionate attention devoted to the film industry:

> If four hundred columnists and feature writers were assigned to Detroit or Pittsburgh and were charged with the sole responsibility of writing daily stories about the foibles, diet, and libidinal acrobatics of automobile magnates or steel monarchs, the public would have a different set of stereotypes about these men, and about the circles in

which they move. But industrialists are not "glamorous," manufacturers make poor news copy, and the employees of Remington Rand can never rival those of MGM for sex-appeal. The reported malapropisms of a Goldwyn have hit the front pages for a decade; the name of Andrew W. Mellon was not even printed in the New York *Times* until he was sixty-six years old. Zanuck and Warner are names familiar to the public, but the men who bestrode American industry not so long ago – Frick, Reid, Yerkes, Ryan, Schwab – were "astonishingly little known to the nation at large."[630]

Every aspect of Hollywood – "its salaries, profits, skullduggeries, and mistakes – are recorded for all the world to see. No other community in America is reported upon each day so intensely, so insistently, and with such a deplorable premium on triviality. There are, of course, other industries in the public eye – automobiles, steel, oil. But which of them is so familiar to the public? Which of them is bathed in such romanticism?"[631] Unlike "the business giants," who are "symbols of rectitude and prestige" and whose "professional acts" take place "behind oak-paneled doors," Hollywood's affairs take place "in a fish bowl with four hundred pairs of eyes glued to the sides. The struggle for financial power is framed in hieroglyphics so abstract and intricate that none but the experts understand them; the working processes of Hollywood are written in names and acts which a high-school girl can comprehend."[632]

As Rosten notes, the mogul faces a particular double standard. "In politics, business, or trade, the leading personalities are believed to have come up 'the hard way.'" Unlike these men, "assumed to have labored in their field, served long apprenticeships, climbed the high ladder rung by rung," the mogul appears "to have jumped from a loft in Manhattan" as a "tailor," "button-hole maker," or "pants-presser" to a Brentwood lodge in "one fell swoop." With a name like " 'Knudsen,' the images that appear encompass the total career-line: immigrant boy, factory hand, machinist, foreman, and so on. If you say 'Producer' the mind jumps from a humble beginning to a dazzling end – and all that took place in between is left blank."[633] While the public praises "uneducated captains of industry" as "self-made men," it dismisses "uneducated movie executives" as "illiterates." While "hard-bargaining businessmen are admired for being shrewd, their counterparts in Hollywood are denounced for being 'mercenary.' "[634]

While Rosten's analysis emphatically redirects many of the assumptions embedded within the Hollywood Question, his response also ultimately helps to propel a variant of the Question into postwar discourse. In keeping with MacLeish's admonition that Jews not create further trouble through oversensitivity to anti-Semitism, Rosten suggests that Hollywood take pride in its humble beginnings. To make a rather telling point, he uses the publisher of *The Dearborn Independent* and *The International Jew*. "When you say Henry Ford was a garage mechanic you are paying him a compliment," but when a *New Yorker* article refers to Samuel Goldwyn as "a glove salesman you are hurling an insult. In no other industry is humble origin interpreted as a skeleton in the closet rather than a proof of admirable success."[635]

Rosten's response to the Hollywood Question, then, celebrates the upward mobility of immigrants as a singularly American phenomenon. Compatible with both anti-Communism and assimilationism, the response upholds a homogenized, melting-pot experience. Symbolic of how anyone can fulfill the American Dream, the moguls attain their success with the right combination of persistence, hard work, and guile. "These men were artisans as well as businessmen, craftsmen as well as promoters," Rosten writes. "They had to be. They combined the talents of bankers and circus barkers. They possessed immense drive, resourcefulness, and an almost maniacal capacity for work."[636] When "respectable businessmen and respectable financiers shunned the movie infant for fifteen years" as "vulgar knickknacks" and no "more than a passing fad," the moguls snapped up this lucrative opportunity.

"Patronized only by the poor and the immigrant, the illiterate and the unwashed," the movies and their founders represented what was best about the industry and America. "The men who built the motion picture industry (Fox, Laemmle, Zukor, Selig, Loew, Goldwyn, Lasky, Warner, Mayer) were not drawn from the supposedly farsighted ranks of American business. They came, instead, from the marginal and shabby zones of enterprise, from vaudeville, nickelodeon parlors, theatrical agencies, flea circuses, petty trade."[637] Combining "the talents of craftsmen, impresarios, and circus barkers," these men "did not cater to small, cultivated circles." Rather, they catered "to mass desires, for they were of the masses themselves." Vulgar and unrefined, the moguls "had the virtues and failings of pioneers."

This powerful response was to shape American film history for years to come. Celebrating "the promoters and showmen" rather than "the graduates of proud preparatory schools," this proud answer to the Hollywood Question valorized Jewish agency. The early moguls "sensed and satisfied the entertainment demands of a nation into which Europe's millions were pouring – millions who could not understand English but were enchanted by pictures – a nation in which an immense laboring class found no arts within its cultural span and few diversions cheap enough for its pocket-book."[638] As this patriotic response explains, film was a truly American art founded by unlettered immigrants, assimilating millions of other immigrants and laborers into the cherished virtues of democratic citizenship. When the Senate Propaganda Hearings posed the Hollywood Question in August 1941, Rosten's answer resonated triumphantly throughout popular dis-course. It also safely complied with the anti-Communist inflection of the Hollywood Question posed by the House Un-American Activities Com-mittee after World War II.

8

The Hollywood Question in Crisis, 1941

"A MATCH LIT NEAR EXCELSIOR": GERALD P. NYE AND CHARLES LINDBERGH, 1941

According to a series of polls commissioned by the American Jewish Committee (AJC) and conducted by the Opinion Research Corporation between 1938 and 1946, approximately one-third to one-half of all U.S. citizens believed that Jews held too much power. By April 1940, more Americans expressed this belief than those who did not. By July 1945, the number of people who responded yes to the question "Do you think the Jews have too much power and influence in this country?" had peaked to 67 percent. This figure was nearly thrice the number of those who had answered no. It was not until June 1962 that a Gallup Poll showed that 17 percent of Americans would answer yes to this same question.[639]

Despite such opinion data, wartime reports of Nazi atrocities in Europe generated widespread sympathy for the plight of European Jews and aroused opposition to Germany's policy of genocide. Yet, a majority of Americans adhered to the belief that had served both Nazism and the publication empire of Ford so well: namely, that alleged Jewish power posed a threat to culture, politics, and nationhood. By 1941, this older fear would crash headlong into a newfound sympathy vaunting Jewish assimilation as the patriotic epitome of why the United States needed to fight the good fight.[640] While activating the Hollywood Question might appear as a political blunder in hindsight, before 1941 the charge had been little more than an ill-advised observation. Schulberg's "idea of Rivington Street" rendered the anti-Semitism of the Hollywood Question less potent, using a Jewish foil to show Gentiles as capable of the same peccadilloes. Nevertheless, the Rivington Street idea also sustained underlying assumptions of anti-Semitism, upgrading the Question's deep-seated stereotypes as a way of commenting on the entire culture and society. As the Hollywood Question ultimately promoted the parvenu lascivious Jew as a metonym for undesirable aspects of American society, cruder manifestations of this same image showed the Jew at odds with American culture. In the shifting rules of American popular discourse, one could use the image of Sammy Glick with relative impunity to assert a singular American experience. With even less impunity, one could slightly alter the Hollywood Question, calling someone a godless Communist instead of a Jew. Well before Senator Gerald P. Nye had made a distinction between "entertainment" and "propaganda" films, the Knights of Columbus had objected to Walter Wanger's *Blockade* (United Artists, 1938) on the same grounds, noting the production personnel's "Pink Pedigree."[641] However, in the debate over entry into World War II, a modern, articulate patriotism triumphed over an artless, excessively obvious accusation that Jews were pushing the country into war.

Wartime politics rather than the Hollywood Question fired this conflict. Those advocating U.S. intervention in Europe, however, capitalized on isolationism's coarse invocation of the Hollywood Question. Charges of isolationist anti-Semitism effectively discredited the movement. Certainly, the movement offered a mainstream haven for marginal voices. Even the accusation of propaganda resonated with an older, cruder version of the Hollywood Question. The Question, however, did not solely reside in isolationism. Sammy Glick, Monroe Stahr, and the politics of anti-Communism ultimately redirected it into a new postwar currency. Nevertheless, isolationism posed the more traditional Question in an attempt to undo the Roosevelt administration's efforts to build up both defense and popular support for Great Britain.

As Roosevelt's war policies increasingly alienated erstwhile liberals and New Dealers, his onetime allies found the film industry and its special relationship with the administration an easy mark. Roosevelt had tried to enlist the support of Hollywood – with varied success – in promoting his New Deal program of reforms. Isolationists believed that World War II simply extended this relationship. They eventually charged that seventeen feature films and countless newsreels made between 1938 and 1941 represented an unparalleled abuse of presidential power in promoting an interventionist agenda.

Hollywood remained especially vulnerable to such charges. Religious, moral, literary, and journalistic renderings of Hollywood had already alleged, with various degrees of transparency, that Jewish agency somehow thrived within the film industry. The American press had publicized Nazi policies toward Jews. However, sympathy for the plight of European Jews was one thing; allowing American Jews to use American movie screens to gain sympathy for intervention was another. At the same time, Hollywood had faced threats from a variety of nemeses. These included religious institutions, the popular press, independent theater owners who objected to the movie studios' business practices, the Justice Department's antitrust litigation, and a nascent House Un-American Activities Committee investigating Communists in Hollywood. For one brief moment in 1941, the charge of Jewish control – or at least the charge of undue Jewish influence – seemed to coalesce into a potent political and rhetorical force. That force could potentially cripple the president's war efforts and topple the multimillion dollar film industry.

Hollywood did not remain idle in the face of such attacks. Addressing the charge of propaganda, Walter Wanger – independent producer, president of the Motion Picture Producers and Distributors Association, and a WASP-ish front for Hollywood support for interventionism – defended the MGM film *Escape*. In a 1941 radio *Town Meeting of the Air*, Wanger noted:

> Hollywood made 350 pictures last year. Fewer than ten of these pictures departed from the usual Westerns, romances, and boy-meets-girl story. . . . I say the motion pictures can aid in national defense by giving us more, many more than ten out of 350 pictures which deal with democracy in the world crisis. . . . Where does Hollywood get its material? From popular books, plays, and magazine stories. Note the word "popular." Yet when we make a story which has already appeared in a national magazine, when we film a book which has already become a best seller, there are those who cry, "the motion pictures are beginning to propagandize." . . . The *Saturday Evening Post* . . . published a serial, *Escape*. Nobody accuses the *Saturday Evening Post* of warmongering. But when Hollywood put this story on the screen . . . the cry went up, "Hollywood is going in for propaganda."[642]

Key isolationist addresses by both Republican Senator Gerald P. Nye (North Dakota) and Charles Lindbergh, however, charged the Hollywood Question with an added energy resonating with overt anti-Semitism. Although Nye never referenced *Jewish* control over Hollywood quite as blatantly as Lindbergh did, *Variety* accused the senator of raising anti-Semitism to "a new form" in his August 1941 radio address at an America First rally.[643] Launching a major isolationist counterattack against the Roosevelt administration from St. Louis, Nye announced that a Senate investigation would soon begin. The body would study whether "the Government here, like the governments in Hitler's Germany and Mussolini's Italy, is using the films to poison the minds of the American people . . . in order to plunge us into the bloodiest war in history."[644] Recalling Populist rhetoric, isolationist sentiment during World War I, and his own 1934 investigations into the First World War's armaments manufacturers, Nye accused "the great American and European bankers and the powerful international munitions makers" of committing "that crime against the American people."[645] Nye associated Hollywood with money, power, and a conspiracy. "To carry on propaganda," Nye intoned, "you must have money. But you must also have the instruments of propaganda." Hollywood was no better than the propaganda ministries of Germany, Italy, and Russia. "It so happens," Nye argued, "that these movie companies have been operating as war propaganda machines . . . being directed from a single central bureau."[646]

The danger of this propaganda, according to Nye, was that "we all go to the movies. We know how, for too long now, the silver screen has been flooded with picture after picture designed to rouse us to a state of war hysteria." These movies glorified war and told of "the grandeur and the heavenly justice of the British Empire." Films like *The Charge of the Light Brigade* (Warner Bros., 1936) and others appeared to support Nye's assertion. Indeed, the Secretary of the Home Department in Calcutta, India, had complained to the American consulate general in that country about its depiction of the 1857 British Cawnpore Massacre of Indians.[647] Others, like Alexander Korda's British semidocumentary *The Lion Has Wings* (United Artists, 1939), contained stronger, more obvious propaganda, attempting to instill public confidence in Britain's air power. Indeed, as K. R. M. Short has documented, the film represented a close collaboration between key creative personnel of the British film industry – including Korda, co-producer Ian Dalrymple, and director Michael Powell – and the British wartime government. Before England officially entered the war, film-industry personnel worked closely with the Royal Air Force (RAF), the British Air Ministry, and the Ministry of Information (MoI). In numerous cases, the RAF, the Air Ministry and the MoI dictated film content.[648]

In advance of its U.S. exhibition, *The Lion Has Wings* had also bypassed the film industry's normal censorship apparatus. Instead of assigning the film to Joseph Breen's Production Code Administration for approval, Will Hays, president of the Motion Picture Producers and Distributors of America, delegated responsibility to his assistant, Frances S. Harmon. According to Short, Harmon prepared a prologue to the film informing viewers that "the management of this theatre trust that after seeing this film its patrons will be better able to contrast life in neutral America with life in the belligerent countries of Europe." Meanwhile, Harmon told Breen that United Artists, rather than the MPPDA, had persuaded Korda to accept this prologue.[649]

In his 1939 postcard to the Hays Office, S. Person Crump articulated a similar view to the one espoused later by Nye:

> While there is war in Europe, motion pictures should be made that will aid in keeping America neutral. *The Lion Has Wings*, a new British propaganda film, should not be shown in America, because it induces racial hatred and endangers American neutrality. I, like many others, think that this film should be removed from circulation. If it is impossible to do this, German films should be admitted. Producers should be encourage[d] to make anti-war films, and to make no anti-German films, because they only arouse hate and endanger our democracy.[650]

According to Nye, films like *Sergeant York* (Warner Bros., 1941), in which Gary Cooper captures Germans single-handedly during World War I, were "all designed to drug the reason of the American people, set aflame their emotions, turn their hatred into a blaze, fill them with fear that Hitler will come over here and capture them, that he will steal their trade, that America must go into this war – to rouse them to a war hysteria."[651]

To a certain extent, Nye invoked the Hollywood Question in obvious fashion, naming both names and films. "Who has brought us to the verge of war?" he demanded. "Who is pushing and hauling at America to plunge us into this war? Who are the men? Who is putting up the money for all this propaganda?" Who had made "America punch drunk with propaganda and push[ed] her into war?" The evidence included some notable films. *That Hamilton Woman* (1941), a Vivien Leigh and Laurence Olivier historical costumer set in Great Britain, offers an unsubtle message on the importance of stopping dictators.[652] *Man Hunt* (1941) tells a tense story, directed by Fritz Lang, about an attempt to assassinate Hitler. *Sergeant York* (1941), a patriotic Gary Cooper vehicle, depicts a pacifist drafted during World War I. Chaplin's satiric farce about dictators, *The Great Dictator* (1940), shows Chaplin playing the dual role of a Jewish barber and a Hitler-like dictator – Adenoid Hynkel.

Nye's accusations represented the worst nightmares of Hollywood personnel, who had privately fretted over the reception the films Nye named might receive in both the United States as well as abroad. In a memo to Will H. Hays, for example, Breen worried that *The Great Dictator* might be perceived as "a 'hate picture' " and thus provoke a "serious question of industry policy."[653]

After reading aloud the names of the movie moguls – Cohn, Mayer, Balaban, Zukor, Schenck, Zanuck, Warner, Goldwyn – Nye noted their origins in "Russia, Hungary, Germany and the Balkan countries"; they were all foreigners and all had an agenda to topple Nazism. "Go to Hollywood," he implored. "It is a raging volcano of war fever" that "swarms with refugees."[654] As he named names, all heads of studios, the crowd reportedly chanted, "the Jews." The film industry, a "mighty engine of propaganda," lay "in the hands of men who are naturally susceptible" to "national and racial emotions." While isolationists Burton K. Wheeler and Charles Lindbergh found themselves barred from lecture halls, the moguls "cunningly and persistently" inoculated the country "with the virus of war."[655] Nye connected his charge of propaganda to the long-standing Hollywood Question concern for morality, reminding his audience that the movie moguls who now appeared to be such patriots had at one time "filled their pictures with so much immorality and filth." He even recalled the religious crusades of the 1920s and 1930s. "The great Christian churches had to rise up in protest against it," Nye rallied, "and organize the Legion of Decency."[656]

Activating the belief that Jewish reactions to anti-Semitism proved more of a threat than anti-Semitism itself, Nye ultimately used the Hollywood Question to attack the presidency. Denouncing the close relationship between the president and the film industry, Nye criticized the White House showing of *Sergeant York*, where Roosevelt happily noted the film would "do much to rouse our people."[657] Nye recalled a speech Roosevelt gave before the Academy of Motion Picture Arts and Sciences, thanking Hollywood for helping to explain the Lend Lease bill to the American public. Although the moguls did not dictate foreign policy, the president was capitalizing upon their fears. "Government influence" rather than the "national and racial emotions" of the moguls ultimately prevailed. "Are the movie moguls" making propaganda "because they like to do it," Nye asked, "or has the government of the United States forced them to become the same kind of propaganda agencies that the German, Italian, and Russian film industries have become?"[658]

Public outcry accused Nye of harboring anti-Semitic attitudes. Dr. Frank Kingdon, former president of the University of Newark (formerly Dana College and subsequently a part of Rutgers) and head of the New York interventionist Fight for Freedom to Defend America, attacked Nye in a radio broadcast as "unfit for office in the United States Senate" because his reading "a list of names" of the moguls was "deliberately aimed at creating anti-Semitism."[659] A press release authored by John H. Sherman, president of Florida's Webber College, angrily denounced Nye as "a disgrace to the Senate." The "principal effort of the evening," Sherman wrote, "was a Hitleresque attack upon American Jews. Deliberately, adroitly, with every trick of timing and inflection of voice, Nye accused the motion-picture industry of fostering pro-British sentiment, and then called a list of Jewish names associated with the motion-picture industry, drolly exaggerating their most Hebraic-sounding syllables, with pauses to encourage his inflamed hearers to shout and hiss." This was "not truly an attack on the motion-picture industry as such, and not an attack on war advocates within the industry, but merely an attack upon Jews because they were Jews, in typical Nazi style."[660] Linking Nye and America First to Nazism and un-Americanism, Sherman assailed isolationist credibility by tying it to anti-Semitism. Nye's speech exemplified "the place and part" America First played "in the Hitler campaign to disrupt America." An "un-American appeal to anti-Semitic prejudice," Nye had patterned the address after "Goebbels" in a way that was "shrewdly calculated to do maximum damage."[661]

Meanwhile, Roosevelt continued to escalate American involvement in World War II. On 4 September 1941, a German U-boat fired upon the U.S.S. Greer. The next week, in a national radio address, Roosevelt used the incident to announce orders for the U.S. Navy to shoot on sight any Axis vessel in defense waters. American ships would now convoy British ships, and as American ships were involved, the convoy would constitute defense waters. The president characterized the German act as one of "piracy" upon the noncombative Greer. Senator Nye, on the other hand, accused the Roosevelt administration of actively assisting the British Royal Air Force in having the Greer trail the German submarine for hours as a way to help track it.[662]

Infuriated, isolationists struck back at what they saw as a deceptive ploy by the Roosevelt administration. Days after the U.S.S. Greer incident, John T. Flynn drafted a Senate resolution, along with Senators Wheeler and Nye, calling for hearings to investigate motion picture propaganda. Burton K. Wheeler, chairman of the Interstate Commerce Committee, would appoint members to the Senate subcommittee. Nye hired Flynn to do research, serve as economic advisor for the investigation, and later testify before the subcommittee, nominally on his own behalf.[663] Nye would deliver the stirring keynote address, elaborating on many of the same themes he addressed in his St. Louis speech. He would demonstrate how one could

FIGURE 22. Lindbergh with his mother and President and Mrs. Coolidge, 1927. Library
of Congress, National Photo Company Collection.

investigate Hollywood just like he and Flynn had investigated the World
War I armaments industry.[664]

America First tapped Charles Lindbergh to speak after President Roosevelt's Sunday address, in which the president would formally announce his
"shoot-on-sight" orders because of the *Greer* incident. As spokesperson for
the isolationist movement, Lindbergh was following in his father's footsteps: elected official Charles, Sr., had opposed U.S. entry into World
War I.[665] Senator Nye had even proposed Lindbergh's candidacy for Congress. An undeniable celebrity, Charles Lindbergh, Jr., had achieved immense popularity in 1927 when he made the first transatlantic flight. In
1931, he again encountered the media spotlight, along with his family,
when someone kidnapped his baby. Throughout the 1930s, however, Lindbergh's image was beginning to show some tarnish. A *Reader's Digest* article
written by him discussed the inherent superiority of the white race. He

FIGURE 23. Lindbergh Day, Springfield, Vermont, 1927.
Library of Congress, Panoramic Photos.

consistently reminded Roosevelt, in public, of the inherent superiority of Nazi air power.

Lindbergh had also accepted a medal from Field Marshal Hermann Goering on behalf of the Nazi government in 1938, although the United States Embassy in Germany had sponsored the dinner in an effort to maintain diplomatic ties.[666] In addition to his acceptance of the medal, Lindbergh's rhetoric edged ever closer toward conspiracy discourse. He frequently referred to a "small minority" controlling vast media resources, and to media itself as an instrument of propaganda. In a 19 May 1940 radio address on air defense, Lindbergh warned of our "danger" in entering a war because of "powerful elements in America who desire us to take part. They represent a small minority of the American people, but they control much of the machinery of influence and propaganda. They seize every opportunity to push us closer to the edge." Nearly a month later, Lindbergh spoke of "an organized minority . . . flooding our Congress and our press with propaganda for war." When Lindbergh called upon "the underlying character of this country to rise and assert itself" against the dangers of "personal profit" and "foreign interest," such warnings resonate with the Shylock stereotype.[667]

Finally, in September 1941, months before Pearl Harbor, Lindbergh spoke before a Des Moines, Iowa, crowd. In the midst of this speech, he had warned of "war agitators [who] comprise only a small minority of our people, but . . . control a tremendous influence." These agitators consisted of three "important groups who have been pressing this country toward war[:] the British, the Jewish [sic] and the Roosevelt administration."

Of the Jews, Lindbergh admitted:

It is not difficult to understand why Jewish people desire the over-throw of Nazi Germany. The persecution they suffered in Germany would be sufficient to make bitter enemies of any race. . . . But no person of honesty can look on their pro-war policy here today without seeing the dangers involved in such a policy, both for us and for them.

Instead of agitating for war, the Jewish groups of this country should be opposing it in every possible way, for they will be among the first to feel its consequences. Tolerance is a virtue that depends on peace and strength.

The greatest danger to this country lies in their large ownership and influence in our motion pictures, our press, our radio and our government.[668]

From his vantage point – white, Protestant, hailing from Middle America – Lindbergh was right about the sentiments of organized Jewry. Most Jewish groups did support President Roosevelt's attempts to intervene in the war in Europe, and even tried to press him further. Though Roosevelt's New Deal policies of reform arguably may not have given Jews greater direct access to government posts, these policies did contribute to an over-all mood emphasizing democratic principles of equal access for all. Jews had achieved a visible level of success in the mass media – including Hollywood, where five of the eight major studio heads were Jewish.

Yet Lindbergh's remarks, only a small section of the speech, caused a firestorm of controversy. Newspapers branded him as anti-Semitic. W. W. Waymack, editor of the *Des Moines Register and Tribune*, called Lindbergh's speech "ominously close to the proscriptive policies" of Nazism. Members of the board of directors for America First, the isolationist group Lindbergh represented, quickly resigned. L. M. Birkhead, National Director of the anti-Nazi Friends of Democracy, declared Lindbergh "the great American tragedy" and little more than "a fallen idol."[669] A pamphlet put out by B'nai B'rith claimed that the organization had been responding to Lindbergh's charges long before the infamous Des Moines, Iowa, speech.[670]

In countering the Des Moines speech, organizations like the B'nai B'rith did more than simply dispute the Hollywood Question. "Jews are NOT war mongers," the pamphlet asserts. Everyone knows "that the Jew HATES war, and that this war is NOT the making of the Jews." However, this denial of Jewish agency in war ultimately asserts the link between Jewish instrumentality and patriotism:

> Yes, it is true we are in sympathy with Britain and with all other Nations fighting Hitlerism. Why shouldn't we be? Our existence depends upon the perpetuation of liberty and freedom, for which these nations are fighting. Therefore, in common with all other liberty-loving people, our sympathies are naturally with the Democracies of the World. The support of our Government is our first and only concern, and we should give it cheerfully.[671]

The speech marked a turning point in American attitudes toward anti-Semitism. Before 1941, as a number of polls conducted on behalf of the American Jewish Committee found, most Americans viewed anti-Semitism as an alien and specifically Germanic influence. Yet after the Lindbergh speech, of the 19 percent answering yes to the question "Have you heard of any organizations or men who are trying to stir up feeling against the Jews in this country?" over half named either America First or Lindbergh. Twice as many named Lindbergh and America First as those who had named the much more marginal German-American Bund.[672] Meanwhile, an October 1941 Opinion Research Corporation poll found that more people could name Jews than any of the three groups Lindbergh mentioned in his speech, and forty percent could name at least one of them. Yet a Gallup poll conducted the same month found that only six percent believed that Jews were the most "active" group pushing the country into war.[673]

Arguably, one could explain both Lindbergh's remarks and the subsequent controversy over them as a brief flurry of wartime hysteria. Few went on to analyze why Lindbergh's remarks were anti-Semitic. If anything, the prevailing response to the Hollywood Question simply evaded its underlying assumptions, instead asserting a hypernationalist vision of assimilated Jewish patriotism. Crude Nazi propaganda and the marginal voices of a disaffected Populism provided the contemporary yardstick against which one measured Lindbergh's remarks. Yet the image of the Jew promoted by Nazi propaganda drew from the same source that could also inspire a uniquely American iteration. *The International Jew* had collected articles originally appearing in *The Dearborn Independent*, automobile mogul Henry Ford's American newspaper.

Lindbergh did not invent his articulation of Jewish control over the media, however nuanced by his expression of sympathy for the Jewish perspective. Nor did he simply appropriate Nazi rhetoric. He espoused a view that had appeared countless times in print with remarkable persistence. Between 1880 and 1940, Jewish control had supposedly poisoned the nation's presses, polluted American theater, and bewitched the public mind. Jewish Hollywood, in particular, had allegedly corrupted the country's morals and youth, and undermined Christianity. Jewish Hollywood presumably kept qualified Christians out while keeping Communism, organized labor, and other ideological agendas in. Jewish Hollywood evidently humiliated American Christian culture through the rape and degradation of its women. Had it not been for Lindbergh's celebrity status and the contemporary impassioned debate between isolation and intervention, the remarks made in Des Moines simply would have been a more muted instance of alleging Jewish control over the media.

For Lindbergh and America First, attacking ethnic Hollywood agency had become a political albatross. In his 1941 Iowa address, Lindbergh primarily criticized the Roosevelt administration's war effort. However, Anne Lindbergh, his wife, feared that even the briefest reference to Jews as a group, along with the Roosevelt administration and the British, pushing the country into war would cause an avalanche of negative publicity. Despite their differences in opinion, Anne Lindbergh had worked at revising and softening the "Jewish" passage for her spouse. In her journal, she tried to rationalize her husband's views; the mere mention of Jews was "not intolerant or inciting or bitter." Her husband would say "just what he says in private, while the other soft-spoken cautious people who say terrible things in private would never dare be as frank in public as he."[674]

The contrast between Roosevelt and Lindbergh's rhetoric was striking. While Roosevelt warned of the dangers to U.S. interests abroad, Lindbergh warned of Jewish "ownership and influence in our motion pictures, our press, our radio and our Government" at home. While some – like *The Christian Century* – still criticized Roosevelt, the momentum of the Great Debate swung decisively in favor of the Roosevelt administration. The credibility of America First, a respectable bipartisan effort to oppose U.S.

entry into the war, collapsed within a matter of days. Editorial after editorial accused both Lindbergh and the organization of promoting anti-Semitism and Nazism. The isolationist movement was dead, and its onetime hero accused of treason.

A few days after Charles Lindbergh's speech, Anne Lindbergh reflected upon its impact and articulation of anti-Semitism. Likening her husband's remarks to excelsior, the highly flammable packing material that preceded Styrofoam, she mused how "no one minds his naming the British or the Administration."

> But to name "Jew" is un-American – even if it is done without hate or bitterness or even criticism. Why?
> Because it is segregating them as a group, setting the ground for anti-Semitism.
> Because it is at best unconsciously a bid for anti-Semitism. It is a match lit near a pile of excelsior.[675]

"WITH LIGHTS AND COLOR AND SOUND": THE MOTION PICTURE PROPAGANDA HEARINGS, 1941

The Propaganda Hearings of 1941 comprise a turning point in the history of the Hollywood Question. Both Gerald P. Nye and Charles Lindbergh tried to tap the belief that Jews controlled the media in an effort to oppose World War II. Yet the invocation of this charge eventually backfired, aligning isolationism with incipient, Nazi-like persecution of Jews. The effort to link Hollywood to Jewish control, however, was not simply a matter of Nazi propaganda washing up on the shores of America. The charge, as articulated by both Nye and Lindbergh, reasserted an older, Populist, Progressive Hollywood Question. The hearings were, in fact, a showdown between a traditional, isolationist America and a modern, New Deal, interventionist America.

The Propaganda Hearings also marked a decisive shift in the popular perception of Hollywood. Long considered pure entertainment, the motion picture industry had acquired a great deal of legitimacy since the Supreme Court deemed it "a business, pure and simple" in 1915. That the hearings addressed film propaganda rather than moral entertainment demonstrated a sea change in the way one talked about Hollywood. On the eve of the hearings, for example, *The Motion Picture Almanac* publisher Martin Quigley believed "that the motion picture, having achieved a maturity," now "shares most directly in all that concerns the nation. Despite its dedication to the entertainment of the millions" the film industry needed to "react to all conceivable forces, political, economic and social."[676]

Of all conceivable forces there were many. Wartime politics and internal dissent powerfully marked the formation of the Senate Hearings investigating Motion Picture Propaganda. As New York City mayor and U.S. Office of Civilian Defense Chief Fiorello LaGuardia noted in a letter to one of the subcommittee members, "the focal point of the hearings seems to be the attempt of various isolationists to attack the administration's foreign policy."[677] The subcommittee included an equal proportion of Republicans and Democrats. All of them came from largely agrarian states, and all but one supported a policy of nonintervention. In making the appointments, Senator Burton K. Wheeler chose Bennett Champ Clark, with whom Wheeler had lobbied against Roosevelt's court-packing plan, and D. Worth Clark, who wanted to nominate Wheeler for president at the 1940 Democratic convention.[678] Other members of the subcommittee included Washington Democrat Homer T. Bone, Illinois Republican C. Wayland Brooks, and New Hampshire Republican Charles W. Tobey. Tobey had also served on the subcommittee for S. 280, the Neely hearings on block booking and blind bidding. Only Ernest W. McFarland, an Arizona Democrat, supported intervention and constantly harangued the other committee members for their isolationist views.

On 1 August, the same day Senator Nye delivered his America First address in St. Louis, committee chair Senator D. Worth Clark announced Senate Resolution 152. The resolution authorized the Senate Committee on Interstate Commerce to conduct "a thorough and complete investigation of any propaganda disseminated by motion pictures and radio or any other activity of the motion-picture industry to influence public sentiment in the direction of participation by the United States in the present European war."[679] Although judicial procedural law did not bind the investigation, the committee could subpoena witnesses, books, papers, and other documents.[680] Inflecting the resolution with an antitrust sensibility, Senator Nye later attached an amendment calling for the investigation to disclose "any monopoly, real or potential, partial or whole" with regard to "the production, distribution, and exhibition of motion pictures," as well as the effect such monopoly had upon "any individual in any field – economic, political, or social."[681]

The hearings were the result of Senate maneuvering. Instead of facing a full vote by the Senate, the Interstate Commerce Committee approved the investigation. Isolationists argued that they had already exhausted normal channels. In his testimony before the subcommittee, Senator Bennett

Champ Clark recounted how he had been trying to get a similar resolution passed as early as 1938. When President Roosevelt called a special session of Congress in September of that year, revising the 1935 Neutrality Act to repeal the arms embargo to so-called belligerents, Clark introduced a Senate resolution to investigate "propaganda on behalf of any foreign government" attempting to influence United States neutrality. Due to the session's short length, the resolution never reached the floor. At the 1940 Congress, the Foreign Relations Committee approved the resolution, but it then "slumbered the sleep of death" in the Committee on Audit and Control before it could reach the Senate floor. Clark then reintroduced his resolution at the 1941 Congress, which, according to him, referred the measure to a "hostile subcommittee" of a prointervention Foreign Relations committee. Clark then approached the Committee on Interstate Commerce. Along with Nye, Clark redrafted the resolution to focus on radio and film, so that it would fall within the purview of this committee. Senate Resolution 9, passed earlier in the session, allowed the Committee on Interstate Commerce to hold hearings without prior approval from the Senate. Thus, by focusing upon what Clark called "the two most deadly and insidious of all propaganda agencies," and through legislative maneuver, the hearings began as a "preliminary investigation" without Senate authorization.[682]

Such political maneuvering ultimately tainted the credibility of the proceedings, if not the entire isolationist movement. Other developments ensued. As Colgan notes, the trade press made much of a survey conducted by University of Southern California professor Floyd Ruch, which found that 77 percent of those polled were not at all "annoyed by any propaganda in feature pictures" and 66 percent held the same view with regard to newsreels.[683] A later memorandum by Ruch reveals the unpopularity of the Senate Hearings, with only 32 percent expressing agreement with Senators Wheeler and Nye.[684] As John Thomas Anderson argues, the Lindbergh speech had already "sealed the doom" of the hearings.[685] Between 1 August 1941, when the Senate passed Resolution 152 authorizing the investigation, and a month later when the subcommittee convened, the hearings came under a barrage of attacks from the press. Anderson argues that the popular press saw the impending investigation as a threat to freedom of expression.[686] By the time subcommittee chair Senator D. Worth Clark opened the hearings on 9 September 1941, he noted the "considerable comment in the press concerning this committee," and the "misapprehension as to what these hearings are all about, both as to their legality and other characteristics."

The appearance of vindictiveness and anti-Semitism only intensified the committee's negative publicity. In the midst of the hearings, Senator D. Worth Clark read a description of the Twentieth Century-Fox film *Four Sons* from the trade journal *Harrison's Reports*. Announcing the name of actress Eugenie Leontovitch, Clark asked studio head Darryl F. Zanuck if that was "a German name," given that the film took place in Sudetenland. "That is one of the great Russian actresses," Zanuck replied. "Is that a German family?" Clark continued. "No," Zanuck retorted. "That is her real name. Eugenie Leontovitch is one of the great actresses of all time."[687] When Nye read aloud Sherman's press release condemning the proceedings, Senator Tobey suggested that the subcommittee subpoena the university president "in order that we may find out the secure [sic] and the motivation of this comment of his."[688] Hardly known for his love of Jews, Tobey had referred to Representative Sol Bloom as "a Jew with all it implies; very able and always makes everything play for his own aggrandizement."[689] At the hearings, Tobey barely concealed his contempt for Jewish film executives. At one point, he imagined aloud how Nicholas Schenck was ensconced in his "magnificent offices." Schenck asserted: "I have no magnificent offices. I have a small office."[690]

Nonetheless, the essence of the charge that Hollywood films conveyed interventionist propaganda could carry the hearings' momentum. Coauthor of the resolution, Gerald Nye had named eight films as examples of Hollywood propaganda: Chaplin's *The Great Dictator* (United Artists, 1940); *Sergeant York* (Warner Bros., 1941); British films *Convoy* (MGM) and *That Hamilton Woman* (United Artists), released by American studios in 1940; 20th Century-Fox films *I Married a Nazi* (1940) and *Man Hunt* (1941); and MGM's 1940 films *Flight Command* and *Escape*. Nye's charges soon appeared haphazard. If two of the films named were British, did this constitute American propaganda? Subcommittee chair Bennett Champ Clark of Missouri had not even seen any of the movies, complaining that the "propaganda campaign" had "so disgusted" him that he "very seldom attend[ed] a motion picture show" anyway.[691] Comparing the hearings to a grand jury, Senator D. Worth Clark of Idaho argued that "you do not have to see a murder in order to" conduct an investigation. "As a matter of fact, I think my mind is clearer on this matter, not having seen the pictures."[692]

Nye could recall having seen only *The Great Dictator*, which Charlie Chaplin wrote, directed, starred in, and produced through United Artists. The film did remain steeped in controversy. In 1937, British movie producer Alexander Korda had approached his United Artists associate Chaplin about doing the satire. According to K. R. M. Short, United Artists received warning from the Hays Office in 1939 that the film – now midway through production – would encounter some form of censorship.[693] In addition to the protestations of the Los Angeles German Consul Georg Gyssling, the British Board of Film Censors warned United Artists' London bureau of another overseas pitfall.[694] In a telegram to his close friend Joe Breen, British censor J. Brooke Wilkinson tried to prevail upon the PCA to obtain a copy of the film's story and treatment. One must have "regard to the delicate situation that might arise in this country if personal attacks were made on any living European statesman. You are aware of our stringent rule that the representation of any living personage without their written consent is disallowed on the screen. Feel confident you will realise the delicacy of situation."[695]

Others, like Walter W. McKenna, displayed less circumspection. Writing to Senator Robert R. Reynolds and copying Joe Breen, McKenna noted that Chaplin was "an alien resident of the State of California" who intended to "ridicule and antagonize certain totalitarian governments of Europe." Citing Chaplin's eligibility to serve in World War I, McKenna observed that "there is no record of Chaplin's offering his services to the armed forces of either Great Britain or to the United States in the hours of that great emergency." Chaplin lived in the United States as "his special privilege" to enjoy "the generous bounty and protection of a complacent Government." The purpose behind McKenna's implicit references to Chaplin's alien status and war record become a bit clearer when he acknowledges the plight of Jews in Germany but notes that

> regardless of how much we deplore the inhuman persecution of a minority race in foreign lands, this man should not be permitted to use the United States as a background and sounding board in the proposed manner with the avowed purpose of stirring up further strife and recrimination between Germany and the United States Government.
>
> Any resident alien seizing an opportunity to embroil this Country into controversy with another Government constitutes a menace against the peace and dignity of the people of the United States and it follows that such an alien should be deported for the abuse of this Nation's hospitality.[696]

To complicate matters, *I Married a Nazi* was the foreign release title of *The Man I Married* (20th Century-Fox, 1940) and the original title of a *Liberty Magazine* series on which the movie was based.[697] Nye appears to have confused the title with *Confessions of a Nazi Spy* (1939). Although he could not remember whether he had seen *Confessions of a Nazi Spy*, a 1939 letter in which he endorsed the film later surfaced amid the proceedings.[698] Not having seen the other films accused of propaganda, Nye gleaned his impressions from the popular press and word-of-mouth. Behind the scenes, however, Joseph Breen expressed his concern to Jason S. Joy of 20th Century-Fox over films like *The Man I Married*, urging the studio to

> Take some counsel as to its general acceptability and, more especially, to its likely reception at the hands of the thinking people of the United States. You know, I think, of the lik[e]lihood that three, or four, pictures, dealing with present-day conditions in Germany, will have reached the screens of the United States before your picture is released, and that the element of quantity may influence public judgment regarding a picture of this type. There seems to us to be an almost unanimous disposition among American people, at the present time, not to look with favor upon anything that tends to promote public discussion, or encourage ill-feeling, against any of the belligerents in the present-day European tragedy. There is a possibility, in our judgment, that some of these avowedly anti-German pictures may serve as the spark to ignite a nation-wide conflagration of protest against the screen as an institution, which may cause the industry, as a whole, very serious worry.[699]

Evidence outside the movies proved decidedly weak as well. When later pressed for examples of how the Roosevelt administration had forced compliant media executives to engage in propaganda, Nye cited examples like studio-sponsored petition drives. Harry Warner had circulated a petition throughout the studio calling for the United States to give Britain our naval destroyers before President Roosevelt passed the Lend-Lease Act. One person wrote to Nye complaining of a government-sponsored public service announcement in which Archibald MacLeish impersonated various voices of oppressed people in Europe. Darryl Zanuck had distributed a memo imploring employees to attend a Wendell Willkie rally. Obviously, Wendell Willkie – Roosevelt's unsuccessful Republican challenger, who abandoned isolationism for interventionism after the 1940 campaign – remained a major figure in American politics and foreign affairs. As evidence of Hollywood propaganda, however, Zanuck's memo was weak.[700]

From the inception of the Propaganda Hearings, prointervention groups consulted with industry personnel, urging Hollywood to fight the investigation. Ulric Bell, head of the interventionist Fight for Freedom committee, recommended that Hollywood combat the hearings "with bare knuckles."[701] By 8 September, Fight for Freedom began circulating an open letter to Congress signed by a various notables, calling the hearings "the most barefaced attempt at censorship and racial persecution ever tried in this country" and accusing the senators of trying to silence interventionists through "racial and religious attacks."[702]

Although the MPPDA, the industry's trade organization, waited nearly a month before publicly responding to the Nye–Clark resolution, industry personnel moved swiftly behind the scenes.[703] At the insistence of the studio heads, the MPPDA met in Hollywood on 4 August 1941. Executives weighed a range of options concerning how to respond to the Senate's Propaganda Question. Harry Warner wanted to underwrite a nation-wide radio broadcast explaining Hollywood's side.[704] Others considered having Hays testify at the hearings. As Stephen Vaughn argues, however, the moguls expressed dissatisfaction with Hays's weak defense of the industry before the hearings.[705] Nye would later aver that Hays had warned producers "against substituting propaganda for entertainment" – hardly a rousing defense from a man hired to be the public relations emissary of the motion picture industry.[706] Concerned that Hays would ultimately undermine Fight for Freedom's aggressive strategy, moguls and major Fight for Freedom donors Walter Wanger and Darryl F. Zanuck consulted with Roosevelt aide Lowell Mellett. Mellett in turn warned Roosevelt not to see Hays until after the hearings were over. Hays, according to Mellett, wanted "to act as the sole or principal spokesman, and his idea is to prove that pictures are not being used for defense." Others, like Wanger, Zanuck, and Frank Y. Freeman, wanted to emphasize the role of Hollywood in national defense. If Roosevelt saw Hays, "he may then convince some weak members" of the MPPDA "that he is expressing your views and persuade" these executives "to pull their punches."[707]

In a brilliant tactical maneuver, Hollywood studios bypassed Hays in favor of Wendell Willkie, making the surprise announcement on 1 September 1941.[708] Ultimately, an advisory committee rather than the MPPDA hired Willkie, explaining that Hays had already volunteered to serve as a witness and could therefore not serve as counsel.[709] The trade press relished the move. "No more Hays appeasements," *The Hollywood Reporter* trumpeted. Willkie was "a hated man by Wheeler, Nye and Clark." Retaining him as defense counsel served as "a definite tip-off of a change of front on the part of our industry leaders."[710]

A onetime Democrat who opposed the New Deal, the Tennessee Valley Authority Project, and Wheeler's Utility Holding Company Act of 1935,

FIGURE 24. The Republican Party notifies Wendell L. Willkie of his nomination, Elwood, Indiana, 1940. Library of Congress, Panoramic Photographs.

Willkie was indeed a masterful and inspired choice.[711] He garnered respect from both progressives and conservatives disenchanted with Roosevelt's domestic and international policies. Before the MPPDA retained him as defense counsel, the Republican Party had drafted Willkie as its 1940 presidential nominee. Willkie had even carried Gerald Nye's home state of North Dakota after the senator had campaigned for him.[712] Throughout the election, Willkie and Roosevelt sparred over the issue of World War II. At first, Willkie accused Roosevelt of not supporting U.S. military preparedness. Only in a final effort to salvage his campaign did Willkie accuse the president of being a militarist and hawkish.

Coming out in favor of intervention a scant ten months before the hearings, Willkie mounted a vigilant defense for the motion picture industry.[713] When the subcommittee denied him the opportunity to testify, Willkie sent a letter to the committee's nominal head, Senator D. Worth Clark of Idaho, and sent copies to all major newspapers. Willkie called Nye's line of reasoning in his St. Louis speech "so contrary to the American way of thinking" that it directly opposed the "Bill of Rights and our Constitution." Although Willkie's defense inside Senate chambers hardly consisted of more than one or two protesting sentences, he actively worked behind the scenes. Bennett Champ Clark accused Willkie of passing notes to Senator McFarland, inspiring Senator Wheeler to dub McFarland Willkie's prebriefed mouthpiece.[714] Persistently badgering committee members inside and outside the hearings, Willkie publicly offered to screen the propaganda movies in question for committee members. He thus keenly reminded the public that those who were protesting so loudly against Hollywood propaganda had never even seen more than one or two of the films under scrutiny. Furthermore, Willkie added that of the fourteen films accused of pushing the country into war, only twelve came from Hollywood. As Willkie would later state, "of the more than 1,100 feature pictures produced since the outbreak of the present war, only some 50 have had anything to do with the issues involved in the war or with the ideological beliefs of the participants."

Stung by attacks from both the press and Willkie, Senators Nye and Clark insisted upon having their testimony before the subcommittee sworn in. The pageantry of having an already elected official place his hand on the Bible appeared – at best – gratuitous.[715] In his opening remarks, Nye defended himself and the committee against charges of bigotry, a characteristic the popular press now confidently deemed un-American. Veiled though it was, the mention of Jews working in Hollywood had made Nye particularly vulnerable to these charges. In a lengthy rebuttal against charges of anti-Semitism, he boasted of his "splendid Jewish friends in and out of the moving-picture business"[716] and that news reports of his earlier statements "had no foundation in fact."[717] Sensitive to the imputation of "furthering bigotry, race and religious prejudice" by pursuing "this request for an investigation of propaganda in the movies and on the radio," Nye later told the subcommittee that he "bitterly" resented "this effort to misrepresent our purpose and to prejudice the public mind . . . by dragging this racial issue to the front. I will not consent to its being used to cover the tracks of those who have been pushing our country on the way to war."[718]

In Nye's view, Hollywood was generating what he called "hate propaganda" against the Nazis. Hollywood was "in the hands" of men "born abroad in lands that have been saturated with hate, with fear, with prejudice, and with persecution." These "four or five" individuals "control well over 50 percent" of American theaters. "The power is theirs if they want to exercise it, to make the great majority of theatergoers in the United States feed upon propaganda" predicated upon their "individual likes and dislikes." Nye was even more explicit about the origins of those calling for war in other media. "Jewish radio commentators, columnists, and publications have afforded in so many instances a consistent opposition to those who have fought what they believed were steps of intervention, steps to involvement in war, that many people seem to assume that our Jewish citizenry would willingly have our country and its sons taken into this foreign war."[719]

In his opening defense, Nye himself set a tone that would powerfully evoke earlier accusations of Jewish control. The overtness of these accusations induced charges of anti-Semitism that would continue to dog the investigation. "I have spoken of the prejudicial influence by certain producers," Nye told the subcommittee, "such as Warner, Balaban, and Schenck might quite naturally bring into production of pictures in these days. It is only fair in this connection to make note that many more in the industry come from foreign lands; that they, too, bring and entertain hatreds toward things in the old country much deeper than are ours as Americans."[720]

Nye invoked the specter of race when referring to Jews, repeatedly referring to the "inborn hatreds" of foreign Hollywood personnel: "those who may have some or only a little influence in shaping the trend of pictures – these people often come with inborn hatreds and prejudices, well founded, no doubt, which can readily occasion interests which are quite foreign to America and her best interests and the lessons of memory and experience." He repeatedly warned the subcommittee that those "born abroad" had come "to our land and took citizenship here entertaining violent animosities toward certain causes abroad." These men harbored "vengeful spirits, born in the pain being visited upon their own people abroad." Nye was willing to "excuse" Jews for their "natural . . . feeling and desire to aid those who are at war against the causes which so naturally antagonize them." However, he also warned, somewhat ominously, against "closing our eyes to these interests and refraining from any undertaking to correct their error." It was "only fair," he asserted, "to make note that many more in the industry come from foreign lands; that they, too, bring and entertain hatreds toward things in the old country much deeper than are ours as Americans, who can look back over generations of history and find Europe everlastingly involved in her old hates, her new wars or continued wars, and in her power politics."[721]

By portraying the Jewish movie moguls as foreigners, Nye could align his cause with that of the Revolutionary War heroes who fought against the tyranny of a foreign conspiratorial power:

It was freedom from all this that Washington, Jefferson, and their copatriots so proudly presented the United States. It was freedom from this about which the same great patriots warned us against ever surrendering. But those who come to us from abroad – motion-picture directors, motion-picture actors and actresses, stage artists, stage property experts, and some executives – those who may have some or only a little influence in shaping the trend of pictures – these people often come with inborn hatreds and prejudices, well founded, no doubt, which can readily occasion interests which are quite foreign to America and her best interests and the lessons of memory and experience.

Right out of pre–World War I "100% Americanism," this charge asserted that the foreign movie mogul held his allegiance elsewhere. "Some of this talent" and some executives had "failed to become citizens of our country, though they have been here for years engaged in their professions. Some are still citizens of distressed lands today, with hearts bleeding for their one and only homeland."[722]

If Jews faced anti-Semitism, Nye reasoned, they brought it upon themselves. "I wish those who would be its victims," he told the subcommittee, "would sense the possibilities and afford a conduct that would not lend itself to fanning later on." Nye confessed that "the faith as would invite an anti-Semitic mind" tried even his own "patience." Blaming "those of the Jewish faith" for raising "the anti-Semitic issue," Nye traced the "growing spirit" of anti-Semitism in this country "to the quite natural Jewish sympathy for and support of" interventionism. Not only did published reports of anti-Semitism "feed" Jewish "persecution complexes," they planted "deeper the hates toward causes foreign to the United States." By "causes foreign," Nye meant Jewish ones. "It is but natural to expect," Nye predicted, "that a perplexed, angry, burdened, unemployed people will be ready to respond to the agitators who will want to help them find the scapegoat responsible for it all, someone upon whom to place the blame for every misery that grows out of this present world madness. Organized forces and their leaders will find a goat. Who that goat will most likely be we have good reason to recognize from what we are hearing and seeing every day."[723]

For Nye, Jews were not the object of prejudice, but were themselves attempting to "prejudice the issue" of the hearings. Anti-Semitism was a "selfish cause" that could "confuse the facts by dragging" what he called a " 'red herring' into the scene." Upon quoting the Fight for Freedom press release accusing the hearings of being "the most barefaced attempt at censorship and racial persecution which has ever been tried in this country," Nye accused the organization of trying "to blind the public" to "war propaganda." "Knowing the source of so large a part of the Fight for Freedom backing," Nye told the subcommittee, "I'm driven again to observe an intent to smear this study with the anti-Semitic rag." Rather than allow "would-be victims of anti-Semitism" to "feed the minds of their own people with . . . folderol as can only breed new distrust," Nye argued that Jewish minds should instead "be purged of some of the persecution complex that so oppresses."[724]

At best, the implication of Jews within this rhetorical equation was an ambivalent one; at worst, it appeared contradictory and even disingenuous. "Many Jewish and other writers" took their "cue" from the moguls named in his St. Louis address in condemning Nye.[725] "If I had it to do over," Nye told the subcommittee in reference to his St. Louis speech, "and were I determined to name those primarily responsible for propaganda in the moving-picture field, I would, in light of what I have since learned, confine myself to four names, each that of one of the Jewish faith." Had he "continued with the names of those in the motion-picture industry . . . the proportion of Jewish names would, if anything, have increased."[726] Yet Nye claimed not to single out Jews because they were Jewish. His approach would have been no different had "those primarily responsible for propaganda in the movies been in the main Methodists, Episcopalians, Catholics, or Mohammedans." Although he was denouncing Jews in the motion picture industry, he claimed to do so "without any spirit of prejudice" or "any cause as foreign" as anti-Semitism.[727]

Nye's argument that Jews were dupes of a foreign influence like British propaganda and warmongers like the Roosevelt administration was hardly flattering. In fact, he still relied upon at least a partial acknowledgment of Jewish power. Working within the motion picture industry, Jews had the power to fan "our natural hates" in the service of the Roosevelt administration's interventionist efforts. Moreover, for Nye, some Jews were even engaging consciously in warmongering. "Those primarily responsible for the propaganda pictures have a peculiar though natural interest prompting them in their work. They themselves may not be mindful of what they are doing, but this is not true of all of them."

If Nye's argument was insulting to Jews, it was equally insulting to audiences in assuming that movies had explicit effects, shooting "magic bullets" into the unsuspecting, uncritical minds of viewers. Only the flimsiest of anecdotal evidence supported isolationist claims, which had neither theoretical nor research basis. Instead, Nye appealed to World War I era pacifism. The senator wanted "to avoid a repetition" of what had happened "25 years ago, when we thought we were protecting great and important causes, and yet afterward we found we had lost everything we said we had been fighting for." Nye also appealed to the gruesome legacies left by this war. Movies that glorify war, he argued, do not show its true costs. He drew his graphic images from veterans of the First World War: audiences do not see "the sons of mothers writhing in agony in trench, in mud, on barbed wire, amid scenes of battle, or sons of mothers living legless or lungless or brainless or sightless; sons in hospitals. These alleged propaganda picture [sic] are not showing us the disemboweled sons of fathers and mothers, lying upon fields of battle."[728]

The image of greedy studios willing to parlay war propaganda into quick cash resonated with the stereotype of an unscrupulous Shylock. At the same time, this image camouflaged alternatives to the direct-effects argument that in turn might reveal greater audience autonomy. Nye argued that, unless Britain won its war with Germany, Hollywood studios would lose and were losing millions of dollars in revenues. Some studios might even go into receivership. "This selfish interest in dollars," Nye claimed, was "playing a considerable part in prompting some of the picture producers in visiting film propaganda upon" the American people. "This," Nye even acknowledged, was "a terribly cold" but inescapable conclusion.[729]

When a pacifist film failed to do well, Nye did not hold the audience accountable, but rather the business practices of the industry. To underscore this point, the senator read a letter from James K. Friedrich, president of Cathedral Pictures. Friedrich complained that Twentieth Century-Fox was burying his company's film *The Great Commandment* (1939) after the studio had purchased it for $200,000. The film is a biblical allegory of a young revolutionary Jew who tries to enlist Jesus in fighting the oppression of the Romans. Avenging the death of his brother at the hands of a Roman soldier, the Jewish revolutionary John discovers Christ's homilies of "peace on earth to men of good will" and "they that take up the sword shall perish by the sword." Wounded while killing John's brother, the Roman soldier falls under the care of John, who, inspired by Christ's teachings, "helps nurse the wounded soldier to health even though his people want to kill the soldier."[730] The message was clear: though the Nazis were indeed killing Jewish brethren, Jews should follow Christ's example in loving their persecutors anyway.

Discussion of the picture repeatedly held the movie moguls accountable for *The Great Commandment*'s lack of success. The PCA report for the film indicates that the film featured prominent "sympathetic" roles for both Jews and Romans – listed under "Races and Nationals." One trade review opined that "when a Christian minister, the Rev. James K. Friedrich, takes it upon himself to spend a huge sum of his own money to dispel the mistaken version of the Crucifixion and to sensibly present the facts of His death (due to His becoming too strong and powerful for the Roman dictator Pontius), the least the industry can do is to support it."[731] Friedrich later wrote to Nye that he had "no doubt that the men who control the motion picture industry today are working hand-in-glove with the warmongers in their attempt to persuade public opinion to fall in line with their policies."[732] That a cabal of movie moguls and warmongers actively worked against the success of the film rendered a much more expedient explanation of why *The Great Commandment* failed at the box office. The vagaries of film distribution proved relatively more complex. For example, the film featured no name stars. Cathedral Films, the Culver City–based production company funded by Friedrich's own money, planned to work with religious groups in offering special road-show engagements. As a *Variety* review indicates, however, the film never reached New York City, one of the biggest audiences in the country. And while *The Great Commandment* received some favorable reviews, *Variety* predicted that its "boxoffice potentialities are very slender," given that "as entertainment it measures up poorly."[733]

Senators and witnesses frequently and vociferously aligned isolationism with antitrust sentiments. Senator D. Worth Clark of Idaho distinguished between government censorship and "a censorship if a sufficiently small number of men controls the medium of expression. . . . It has been suggested that the screen has been made unfree by virtue of monopolistic control; and one type of censorship might be just as vicious as another."[734] Senator Tobey bemoaned that "a small group of men with tremendous financial powers" should "have a monopoly control of the moving-picture industry and a large part of the seating capacity and the eyes and ears of the public" so that they could foist "on the American people certain pictures to excite hatred and suggest going into the war."[735] John T. Flynn approached film as "a monopoly affecting opinions and ideas, [a] cultural monopoly." He distinguished this hearing from the "feeble and halting investigations of monopoly in the moving-picture industry" that had taken place previously. "The moving picture is a cultural instrument," he claimed, "an instrument capable of disseminating ideas and opinions, of shaping the public mind and public opinion." Thus, "the monopoly of the moving-picture industry is so much more serious than any other kind of monopoly."[736] Flynn linked this monopoly to "foreign" control. "When I am talking in a hall to two or three thousand people," he testified, "there is some fellow who practically has just arrived here from Europe a few months ago who is talking to 5,000,000 over the radio. What good is it to talk to two or three thousand people while the other side is addressing millions and millions of people every hour of the day in the moving-picture houses? Anybody who can get possession of those two weapons has got the other side licked almost before they start."[737]

Little if any new evidence of a motion picture trust, however, emerged from these hearings. Senator Clark of Idaho made the somewhat circular observation that motion picture propaganda was particularly "vicious because a monopoly exists to disseminate that propaganda."[738] Nye read into the record excerpts of the Justice Department suit against the Big Five

(Paramount, Loew's, RKO, Warner Bros., Twentieth Century-Fox) and the Little Three (Columbia, Universal and United Artists) that had been filed in June 1938. Similarly, however, earlier anti-trust investigations had set this precedent of a "preliminary investigation" to ferret out the necessary evidence. Thus, most of the senators had not even seen the movies in question. In the past, the strategy of acting on hunches, accusing first and finding evidence later, could pressure institutions to submit. Isolationists hoped that by activating the Hollywood Question, they would induce the American public to rise up in indignation.

However, unlike other hearings, where the Senate had investigated corruption, the Propaganda Hearings focused on something as ephemeral as "the effect upon the minds of people who see pictures" that D. Worth Clark of Idaho feared.[739] Concern for this "public mind" played a central role throughout the hearings. In justifying the study of motion picture propaganda, Nye reasoned that, although propaganda certainly appeared in the press, it was not harmful because "we know our newspapers." Motion pictures, on the other hand, contained "dangerous propaganda" that was "unloosed upon all the way from sixty to eighty million people a week who go into the moving-picture theaters of this country to be entertained. Getting there, Mr. or Mrs. or Miss America sits, with guard completely down, mind open, ready and eager for entertainment." Expecting to be entertained, Americans instead get "a speech or declaration" that is "planted" with an interventionist message.[740]

The hearings assumed that this public mind operated in pristine purity to Hollywood's inflammatory messages. According to Senator Clark of Missouri, Hollywood made films to "infect the minds of their audiences with hatred, to inflame them, to arouse their emotions, and make them clamor for war." To Nye, the purpose of "propaganda" was to "inflame the American mind with hatred for one foreign cause and magnified respect and glorification for another foreign cause." The "Propaganda pictures" had caused Americans "to change if not warp a lot of clear thinking." Nye worried "what perhaps was going on to destroy straight thinking, honest thinking, American thinking?" While the senator acknowledged "the tenseness with which some people feel the pain of brothers abroad" was motivating their attacks upon the subcommittee, for others "the cause is pure desire to deliberately mislead the people" with charges of anti-Semitism.[741]

The isolationist senators valorized older communication media with a reverent nostalgia. Responding to the charge of undue influence over the public mind as he testified before the subcommittee, executive Harry M. Warner asked whether politicians did not tend "to mold public opinion, possibly more than our pictures." Senator Clark responded that motion pictures went to work on audiences "with lights and color and sound. That is quite different from reading in cold type a statement by me."[742] In the U.S. Constitution, Senator Clark lectured, "freedom of speech meant pretty much a man's right to say what he wanted to his neighbor, or to express himself in his little newspaper, or to publish a pamphlet, or to hire a hall somewhere, or get out in a cow pasture, or up on a stile or a soap box." For Clark, the "instruments of speech were a man's tongue and lips and larynx, invented and constructed by Almighty God." Clark complained that whereas such renowned orators as Lincoln and Populist William Jennings Bryan worked tirelessly to reach thousands of listeners, any "unknown politician or newspaper columnist" could reach millions. In the old days, he argued, only oppressive laws could interfere with speech. An economic "oligarchy" of more recent times fulfilled the same basic functions that these earlier laws would have performed.[743]

A lack of faith in the intellectual discernment of the American audience remains implicit, however, in this concern for the morality of the public mind. D. Worth Clark feared that war propaganda would influence "the mind of the average American citizen," so that it would "incite him further to take this country, insofar as it lies within his power, into war."[744] When McFarland stressed that he had "the utmost confidence in the American people and in their ability to judge propaganda and that which is not propaganda," Nye cited the hysteria over Orson Welles's *War of the Worlds* 1938 radio broadcast. "When one goes into a theater" with "his guard down," Nye pondered, "why are we so sure that these propaganda motion pictures are not going to take hold and have a very lasting effect?"[745]

This lack of faith in audience discernment justified isolationist support of censorship. When asked by Senator McFarland if Nye would "suppress any opinion whether expressed in the case of the moving-picture industry or otherwise," Nye responded that he "would suppress it if it were within my own power to do it." In defending himself against charges of censorship, Nye referred to the 1915 Supreme Court decision of another era ruling movie exhibition "a business pure and simple." As movies did not enjoy First Amendment protection, Nye reasoned that legislating content in this medium did not amount to censorship.[746]

Isolationist testimony often aligned the hearings with religious censorship campaigns of the twenties and thirties concerning the moral influence of the movies. Senator Bennett Champ Clark reminded the subcommittee that "only a few years ago" Hollywood was "so fully into the practice of putting filth and immorality and ideas subversive to decency and the decent

way of life upon the screen" before "the public rose up in great indignation."
He cited the "legions of morality" and the "legions of decency" that formed.
The industry then began to "purge itself in the eyes of the people as to this
filth and immorality which were being foisted on the people of the United
States. That is the way Mr. Will Hays got his job."[747]

America First similarly hoped that the committee would galvanize a
Legion of Decency–like protest against Hollywood. Through its *Bulletin*,
the isolationist organization urged its members "to become assistants to the
Senate sub-committee":

> Write to the members of the committee. Inform them of every in-
> stance of "war propaganda" observed in the motion pictures. Give the
> name of the picture, the producer, the theater at which it was shown,
> and a brief outline of the propaganda incident. . . . Urge your mem-
> bers also to send copies of their letters to the theater managers. When
> it becomes evident that it is unprofitable to book war-propaganda
> pictures the practice will quickly be discontinued.[748]

Never clear on what they hoped to accomplish, the Propaganda Hearings used the Hollywood Question to threaten censorship, much like the
Legion of Decency had used the Hollywood Question to threaten a boycott.
Prodded to explain the purpose of the investigation, Nye cited "a degree of
legislation that will give the American people a defense against what I
consider to be the most vicious propaganda that has ever been unloosed
upon a civilized people." Rather than outlining what this legislation might
entail, however, Nye appeared to be more interested in *threatening* to pass
legislation. This strategy, of course, had and has since been an effective
means to prod industry into more stringent self-regulation. This was particularly true for the motion pictures. Similarly, however, potential legislation
constituted an actual effort to censor, and therefore remained antithetical
to the politically popular protections afforded by the First Amendment.
Thus, Nye made sure to mention his "hope . . . that we may free ourselves
of that influence without the necessity of resort to legislation," or "anything
resembling censorship." Neither Nye nor any other committee member ever
clearly articulated exactly what this freedom might entail.[749]

While this fishing-expedition strategy might have worked in the past as
a way to bring issues of influence and power into public discussion, it did
not work for propaganda. Nye's hearings on the munitions industry served
as a model, ultimately bringing about the Neutrality Act. This time, however, the vision of America driving this strategy lacked coherence, solid

data, and a compelling argument. Appearing petty and vindictive, the senators' articulation of the Hollywood Question clung to its nostalgic vision of America. As articulated by Wendell Willkie and others, on the other hand, the Hollywood Question was able to help redefine a national identity increasingly at odds with past tradition.

"WE ARE NOT NEWCOMERS": THE HOLLYWOOD QUESTION FOR A NEW AMERICA

Few foes of the Propaganda Hearings would deny the immense power of Hollywood to influence public opinion. But rather than attacking ethnic agency, many like Ruch later shuddered "to think of what might have happened had the picture business been dominated by enemies of democracy."[750] The Jewish movie moguls represented a new kind of ethnic agency, ardently defending the principles of America's founding fathers.

The hearings found few defenders outside the Senate chambers, and most of those who did advocate the investigation already occupied the margins. Hollywood Question stalwarts tried to defend the hearings, arguing that the backlash constituted industry hypersensitivity much along the lines of what MacLeish had warned. Confessing her difficulty in understanding "the wild denials" of propaganda and "cries of persecution" coming from both Hollywood and "the interventionist press," Margaret Frakas of *The Christian Century* found disingenuousness in such a stance. Instead of confronting the issue of propaganda, the industry was overexaggerating "hatred for big business and the racial prejudice of certain congressmen from the 'hinterlands.' "[751]

One could hardly ignore, however, the strenuous opposition to the film industry as well as the attention paid to these voices. As Colgan notes, *Variety* devoted much coverage to a vandalized Pittsburgh theater in mid-October 1941. Throughout the theater the word "Jew" appeared, painted in red, white, and blue, courtesy of "a true American."[752] Recalling its depiction in *Confession of a Nazi Spy*, the German-American Bund used the hearings to lament the "racially alien" elements controlling Hollywood as "our national disaster." Claiming that the "so-called persecution of Jews" was "just punishment by God" and the "unavoidable results of their own behavior," the Bund consistently referred to Jews as "Orientals."[753]

However, mainstream response to the hearings almost universally condemned them. One could hardly ignore the attacks of committee member Ernest W. McFarland. Recently elected to his Senate seat, McFarland seemed a natural for the committee. Having defeated incumbent Senator

Henry Fountain Ashurst, a candidate supported by both Wheeler and Sheridan Downey,[754] McFarland made much of his opponent's ties to East Coast bankers like the renowned Jewish financier Bernard Baruch.[755] By no means an ardent Roosevelt supporter, McFarland had voted to override an FDR veto halting road construction in the interest of national defense. The senator voted to extend Lend-Lease aid to Russia in 1941 only after he overcame his strenuous anti-Communist objections.[756] In his autobiography, McFarland claimed that Senator Wheeler served as his mentor, often appointing him to important subcommittees related to mass communication policy.[757] Once appointed to the subcommittee, however, McFarland lost no opportunity to skew the intent of the hearings. At a Cleveland speech in September, McFarland asked "isolationist leaders [to] consider the tragic" manifestation of "race prejudice" within their movement "as a means of imposing their will on the American people."[758] Noting the hypocrisy of Senate Resolution 152 calling for a "thorough and complete investigation" yet having Wendell Willkie barred from speaking, McFarland repeatedly pressed subcommittee chair D. Worth Clark to reconsider his decision.[759] McFarland also emphasized the subcommittee's lack of focus. When Senator Nye professed that he had "no specific legislation in mind" for the culmination of the hearings, McFarland asked if the purpose of the investigation was for "publicity."

Newspaper columnists like Dorothy Thompson and Arthur Crock roundly criticized the intent of Nye and the investigating committee as anti-Semitic.[760] The photojournal *Life* – unrelated to the racist and anti-immigrant humor magazine of the turn of the century – made isolationists look like buffoons. Started in 1936 as one of the first large-size photo magazines, it had achieved a circulation of approximately eight million by spring of 1940. To its advertisers, *Life* claimed a circulation of around twenty million, arguing that each magazine published had an average of ten readers. The magazine published a large picture of Gerald P. Nye showing him with a bandage over his chin. The caption explained that he had cut himself shaving. Disdainful of the proceedings, the article noted that the hearings "had never been voted by the Senate, but had been politically maneuvered by Senator Wheeler and a small coterie of isolationist politicians as a kangaroo court." The hearings were, *Life* noted, "Washington's funniest political circus of the year."[761]

Only after the first day of hearings, President Roosevelt ably mocked the investigation. When asked at a press conference if he had "noticed the danger of war propaganda" in Hollywood, the president held up a copy of a cartoon on the front page of the *Washington Star*, suggesting that newspapers widely print it. The cartoon showed Charlie Chaplin with a subpoena to appear before the Senate committee. The caption read: "Now what could I possibly tell those past-masters about comedy?"[762] Roosevelt then read aloud a telegram, obtained by his press secretary, Stephen D. Early, that someone had sent to the investigating committee. "Have just been reading book called Holy Bible," Roosevelt read to the press. "Has large circulation in this country. Written entirely by foreign-born, mostly Jews. First part full of war-mongering propaganda. Second part condemns isolationism, with faked story about Samaritan. Dangerous. Should be added to your list and suppressed."[763]

Even those who had opposed Hollywood spoke out against the hearings. Acknowledging the danger of leaving Hollywood's "huge opinion-forming machinery in the hands of a small group of men," *The Nation* nonetheless argued that the hearings belonged to no less than "a widespread campaign to 'soften up' the American people." The campaign ultimately would "make them believe that Nazism – despite all Hitler's statements to the contrary – holds no danger for this country." The article then cited Lindbergh's Des Moines speech: "The purpose of the Interstate Commerce Committee inquiry is to spread the impression that the reason we have anti-Nazi movies is because many of the big motion-picture companies are owned by Jews." To underscore the wrong-headedness of this investigation into anti-Nazi propaganda, the magazine cited the Hays Office censorship of Sinclair Lewis's antifascist novel *It Can't Happen Here* as an example of control working in Nazi rather than Jewish favor. "Far from being too vigorously anti-Nazi," *The Nation* argues, the film industry "as long as they could, avoided making any films that might endanger their markets in Germany and Italy. Business was their first consideration."[764]

Sheridan Downey, a California Democrat who had served as Upton Sinclair's running mate in the abortive 1934 EPIC campaign, testified on *behalf* of the industry, challenging both the concept of propaganda and the notion of Jewish control. In defending the free speech of the movie moguls, Downey staked out his credibility by also claiming to have isolationist sympathies. Despite his having voted for the Lend-Lease bill, he professed belief that "we have neither the power not [sic] the will to impose our kind of peace upon the world by force of arms."[765] Once part of a campaign that fell prey to a coordinated Hollywood effort, Downey now attacked the committee that was investigating motion picture propaganda. He maintained that "truth can hold its own" against Lindbergh and "certain distinguished Senators" receiving "the freest publicity in their attacks." He wondered how Lindbergh, the hearings, and isolationism could receive so much

FIGURE 25. (*Left to right*) Senator-elect D. Worth Clark (Idaho), Senator-elect James M. Mead (New York), Vice-President John N. Garner, and Senator-elect Sheridan Downey (California), 1939. Courtesy *Selections from The Bancroft Library Portrait Collection*, The Bancroft Library, University of California, Berkeley.

attention if Jews indeed controlled the media. Downey vehemently defended "untrammeled freedom of expression for all our citizens, wherever born . . . if we yield to the fear that our democratic heritage can be wiped out of our minds and hearts by a flickering propaganda, then the foundations of the Republic are weak indeed."[766]

Others echoed Downey's view asserting the universal interests at stake in the hearings. Harry M. Warner's testimony proved to be a significant high point of the hearings, during which he forcefully spoke in favor of Roosevelt's foreign policy and against Nazism because the latter harmed both Christians and Jews.[767] In his testimony before the committee, Twentieth Century-Fox executive Darryl F. Zanuck recalled how "picture after picture, pictures so strong and powerful" had "sold the American way of life, not only to America but to the entire world."[768] Arguing that "this industry had stood for a lot," Zanuck explained that Hollywood represented a distinct aspect of "the American way of life." Americans "patronize us when they wish to and . . . stay away when they do not wish to see the pictures; and we have grown only because the people have let us."[769]

Wendell Willkie had emphatically established this brand of patriotism within the opening days of the hearings. The subcommittee, rather than Hollywood, remained decidedly out of step with American ideals emphasizing individual freedom, particularly freedom of speech, and democracy. Undemocratic in procedure, the formation of the hearings did "not establish the impression of impartiality," since the Senate never actually voted upon the resolution authorizing the investigation. Censoring the radio and motion-picture industry "is just a small step" from censoring the press. And censoring the press "is just a small step" from abridging "the freedom of the individual to say what he believes."[770]

As Willkie maintained, concern for Nazism reflected an American destiny to assume an integral role in world affairs. In a letter addressed to Senator Clark of Idaho and distributed to the press the night before the hearings were to begin, Willkie argues that, if the subcommittee "intends to inquire whether or not the motion-picture industry, as a whole, and its leading executives, as individuals, are opposed to the Nazi dictatorship in Germany," that "there need be no investigation":

> The motion-picture industry and its executives are opposed to the Hitler regime in Germany; they have watched with horror the destruction of a free life within Germany and the ruthless invasions of other countries by Nazis. On behalf of the motion-picture industry and its personnel, I wish to put on the record this simple truth: We make no pretense of friendliness to Nazi Germany nor to the objectives and goals of this ruthless dictatorship. We abhor everything which Hitler represents.[771]

This kind of defense enabled Willkie to put forth a newer version of Americanism – one in which the concerns of the Hollywood Jew could serve the interests of the national security state equally well. "The United States," Willkie wrote the subcommittee, "stands for the right of an individual to lead a decent life. Hitler and his Nazis stand for the opposite." If the motion picture industry was cooperating with the Roosevelt administration, it was because of "sincere patriotic citizens" who worked there. Hollywood was "proud" to "have done everything possible to inform the public of the progress of the national defense program." The Roosevelt administration, as Nye had charged, was not forcing Hollywood to enlist in the "patriotic cause." Hollywood "would be ashamed if it were not doing voluntarily what it is now doing."[772]

Willkie countered Nye's call for freedom from foreigners by celebrating the homogeneous will of ethnic pluralism. None of the moguls Nye named in his St. Louis speech, Willkie noted, maintained alien status or held "allegiance to any country except the United States." Indeed, Willkie celebrated the plurality of Hollywood's ethnicities as representative of a larger American society. Yet, he did appeal to a vague sense of WASPish superiority by using such terms as "Nordic" and "non-Nordic":

> If the committee feels that the racial and geographic background of American citizens is a condition to be investigated, there is no need for the investigation. We frankly state that in the motion-picture industry there are in positions both prominent and inconspicuous, both Nordics and non-Nordics, Jews and gentiles, Protestants and Catholics, native and foreign-born. This industry, with many others of our country, demonstrates that neither race, creed, nor geographical origin is an essential qualification to participate in American business. This fact illustrates a basic principle of American life, as we have known it for over 150 years. The motion-picture industry, composed like other industries of loyal and patriotic Americans, despises the racial discrimination of nazi-ism and is devoted to the cause of human freedom both in this country and abroad.[773]

Unlike Nye, who argued that the motion picture industry dictated public tastes, Willkie maintained that Hollywood responded to these tastes. Reusing the Walter Wanger example of *Escape*, Willkie traced the literary origins of the movie's source. If "the picture is inimical to the safety and security of our Nation," Willkie warned, "is it not logical to examine, in chronological order, the author who wrote the book, the editors of the *Saturday Evening Post* who first printed it, the owners of Little, Brown & Co. who published it in book form, the editors of the Book-of-the-Month Club who recommended it for public reading, and the newspapers and other periodicals which reviewed it favorably in their columns?" The argument brilliantly served a double purpose, at once showing a responsive rather than dictatorial Hollywood and implying how perilously close Nye and the subcommittee were moving toward something so un-American as censorship.

"The motion-picture industry is not guided by subversive motives," Willkie asserted. It is "guided by nothing more subversive than the hope to satisfy the prevailing taste of the American people." The industry was nothing more than a business enterprise needing to gauge these tastes in order to remain successful. "The success or failure of individual motion-picture companies," Willkie wrote, "depends only on the ability to produce motion pictures that will satisfy the public. It is as simple an American business principle as that."[774]

Many of those who testified before the hearings argued against the presumption of ethnic agency. Downey chided the committee for attempting "to secure data on the foreign markets of movie companies" and "on the birthplaces of movie leaders." This "cannot be justified before the bar of American public opinion."[775] "At the outset" of his testimony, Zanuck found it "necessary to state my personal background." Born in Wahoo, Nebraska, to parents both "born in the United States of America," Zanuck noted his affiliation to the Methodist Church and service in World War I. "Senator Nye, I am sure," he opined, "will find no cause for suspicion or alarm in that background."[776] When one of the senators tried to show nepotism in Hollywood, executive Nicholas Schenck used the model of the small town to counter this claim. "When you live in a society, after all, with a small group of people," he mused, "it is the natural thing for boys to be thrown with girls, and for girls to be thrown with boys, and they will get married. But that does not say they will get married in order to tie in the business. It just does not work that way."[777]

Harry Warner issued a particularly vehement denunciation of the notion that Jews behaved as Jews. When asked if he would "use this vast engine of the moving pictures to destroy nazi-ism," Warner distinguished between "myself personally" and "the company. I started by saying you have got to divide me from my company. Our company is being handled as a business."[778] Nor did Jews conspire with one another. Professing that he had seen more of Nicholas Schenck "in this room" than he had "seen of him in 3 years," Warner objected to the notion "that we sit around and decide what to do."[779] He bristled at the suggestion that Hollywood Jews held a parvenu status. "We are not newcomers in the business," he maintained. "We helped pioneer the motion-picture industry. We are not interlopers who seized control of a large company by some trick device."[780]

Those testifying also countered claims of undue influence. "I usually find that when someone produces something that you do not like," quipped Zanuck, "you call it propaganda."[781] Unlike the isolationist senators, who saw movies as intimately connected to an American public mind, Sheridan Downey put forth an image of America in which there were separate but equal areas of discourse. "The procedures of these pictures share the same privilege with editors, soap-box orators, radio commentators, clergymen, yes, even Senators, the privilege of airing their own views in their own way on problems of public concern," Downey testified before the committee. "No Senator can control the kind of publicity that the movies may produce, nor can movie moguls find a national sounding board on the floor of the United States Senate."[782]

Rather than dictating public tastes, pro-industry voices claimed, Hollywood responded to them. Schenck's testimony revealed a very different conception of the audience than that of the senators. "We don't make pictures and give our opinion in them," Schenck told Senator Clark of Idaho. "Pictures do not mold the public. The public molds us. They are intelligent, and I assure you that they want a certain subject or do not."[783] If a film like *The Great Commandment* did not do well at its Kansas City premiere, Zanuck averred, it was not the studios that killed it. At least judging from its gross – the film earned less in its entire run than most films earn in one day – the public was not interested. Warner attacked the notion that

> I, Harry Warner, head of a motion-picture company, hating nazi-ism, will do everything in the world to incite the people against nazi-ism. You as a Senator and the chairman of this subcommittee are highly respected in this country and as such tend to mold public opinion, possibly more than our pictures, and you say that you hate nazi-ism. Now, isn't that a molding of the minds of the American people to incite them to war?

In countering the charge of undue influence, Warner also celebrated the patriotic function of catering to the public taste. If Hollywood assisted in national defense, it did so without urging but voluntarily.[784] "I have the idea that our accusers believe," Warner told the committee, "that I, together with one or two others, sit down in secret conference and plot the kind of pictures which we propose to make. Nothing could be further from the fact. Our success does not depend upon my personal opinions; it depends upon millions of Americans who find entertainment and enjoyment in pictures."[785] Unlike the few politicians who criticized movies they had not seen, "millions of average citizens have paid to see these pictures" and have enjoyed them.[786]

To exemplify that popularity of Warner Bros. pictures, Warner cited *Confessions of a Nazi Spy*. In addition to pointing out the 550 letters the studio had received praising the film, Warner read into the record a statement made by Senator Nye. Nye, who had earlier criticized Warner Bros. and propaganda, had praised the film on its initial release:

> The picture is exceedingly good. The cast is exceptionally fine. The plot may or may not be exaggerated but is one that ought to be with every patriotic American. As for myself, I hope there may be more pictures of a kind dealing with propaganda emanating from all foreign lands. Anyone who truly appreciates the one great democracy upon this earth will appreciate this picture and feel a new allegiance to the democratic cause.[787]

By the afternoon of 25 September, after Harry M. Warner's strong testimony to the committee, the isolationists had clearly changed their strategy. Senator Tobey harangued Warner, not about monopoly control or about propaganda, but about using military personnel and resources in Warner Bros. films at taxpayer expense. Tobey maintained that Hollywood was destroying planes and tying up service personnel for entertainment value.[788] When the committee adjourned on 26 September, the hearings were in disarray. Tobey tried to divert the focus of the committee to the discriminatory hiring practices of the British Purchasing Commission. What was interesting was that in an effort to disprove charges of anti-Semitism leveled against the subcommittee, the isolationists had seized upon an opportunity to publicize an older style of anti-Semitism: employment discrimination. The subcommittee appeared to be grasping at straws. The star witnesses to testify against this prejudice were one of Tobey's staff members, Robert D. L'Heureux; L'Heureux's next-door neighbor, an employee at a secretarial placement agency; the neighbor's supervisor; and Tobey's own son, Charles Tobey, Jr.

The hearings ended abruptly, recessing by the end of September, postponed indefinitely by mid-October, and ultimately canceled in December, after Pearl Harbor.[789] The subcommittee never even issued a report. As Stephen Vaughn argues, the Propaganda Hearings closed once the isolationists had lost the fight, well before Pearl Harbor.[790] The central image of the hearings – ethnic Jewish agency accessing the American mind through "lights, color and sound" – had failed. Hobbled by accusations of anti-Semitism, the hearings abortively shifted focus to the British Purchasing Commission, an agency charged with buying arms from the United States, and an alleged memo authored by British foreign secretary Anthony Eden. In the memo, Eden supposedly wrote that Britain was an oligarchy rather than a democracy. One of the senator's sons, Charles W. Tobey, Jr., accused the British Purchasing Commission of engaging in discriminatory hiring practices against Jews, southern Irish, and Germans. So incensed was he over the reckless nature of these charges, McFarland walked out of the hearings in protest.[791]

Yet the subcommittee ultimately foreshadowed the anti-Communist witch-hunts of the late 1940s and early 1950s, in which the foreigner reappeared as a threat to national security. As Senator Clark of Idaho urged the subcommittee to study Nazi as well as Communist propaganda, he noted that "we have information that a great many Communist propaganda pictures have been or are about to be circulated in the United States." Nye claimed that "unending prayers" issued forth from Americans wanting "something to be done to destroy this most vicious effort to make the people pay for propaganda." He hoped the subcommittee would call directors Victor Saville and Frank Borzage to testify on their "propaganda" films. "The producers and all studio heads," Nye implored the committee, should "be asked to reveal how many of these alleged propaganda films were the work in full or in part of refugee or alien authors, how many refugee or alien actors were cast in these pictures, how many alien writers have been financed by Hollywood and imported to Hollywood by the motion-picture industry, how many immigration visas have been arranged for motion-picture executives and by them." "I warn the President of the United States and I warn those who are so pleased with the help the movies have given them," Senator Clark of Missouri told the subcommittee, that these people may one day "find the moving pictures on the other side of some grave national or international issue in which they are interested. They will not like it then. They may ultimately find this powerful medium of propaganda used to destroy them and to destroy the very things they hold most dear."[792]

Obviously, the outcome of the Propaganda Hearings remains very different from the outcome of the later Communist witch-hunts of the late 1940s and early 1950s. Yet, the twin demonizations of propaganda and Communism do exhibit some striking parallels. As the end of a letter from Willkie to Senator Clark of Idaho predicted, anyone called before a Senate subcommittee of this kind would be compelled to testify only after "reckless and unwarranted charges [have been] repeated and widely publicized throughout the country." In an eerily prescient moment, Willkie saw the impossible Hobson's choice offered by the subcommittee's hearings. "If we are to protect our rights as citizens," then those who stand accused should "refuse to testify and then run the risk of being prosecuted or cited for contempt by the United States Senate." Taking that path, as the Hollywood Ten essentially did seven years later, proved just as dangerous as Willkie had predicted. "By that time the unfounded charges will be on the record; the damage will be done; the inference will be then drawn that he who refuses to testify has something to hide, something of which he is ashamed." In the discursive skirmish through which the Hollywood Question reinvented its political inflection, Willkie's clients gave the Question added impetus – albeit in more positive fashion – even as they protested it vehemently. The decision to cooperate with the subcommittee was really a choiceless choice. "We shall appear at your proposed hearings. We shall do so under protest. We are realists and we know that to protect the good name and prestige of the motion-picture industry, we have little choice."

The protests notwithstanding, however, the precedent had been set. Seven years later, the studios again acquiesced to the terms of the Hollywood Question, sacrificing some of their best writers and directors before a "legally" convened House committee. This time, however, the political climate was different. This time, the Hollywood Question became the Communist Question. The rampant hysteria of a Red Scare became an acceptable substitute for anti-Semitism, and the precepts of New Deal liberalism were eschewed for the interests of the national security state.[793] Although isolationism did not succeed in capitalizing upon the Hollywood Question, the Question withstood the shift to an anti-Communist America. Before the decade ended, Hollywood had reintroduced the Jew as American, the HUAC conducted its investigation of Hollywood Communists, and the Justice Department issued its consent decrees forcing the studios to divest of their theater holdings. Although ultimately redirected to an anti-Communist discourse and camouflaged by subsequent film histories, the Hollywood Question had finally generated a set of regulatory and political answers. In one way or another posed so frequently – at least since the late 1880s – the Hollywood Question had survived the transition to a modern America.

9

The New Hollywood Question

Two years after the so-called Republican Revolution of 1994, the ultra-conservative Ludwig von Mises Institute prominently featured an article entitled "How Antitrust Ruined the Movies" in *The Free Market*, its official newsletter. In it, the author, who had recently publicly beseeched the South to secede from the Union, argued that Big Government regulation was responsible for the decline in Hollywood since its golden age of the thirties and forties.[794] Hardly an aberration, the article reflects a change in cultural climate. Gone are the insinuations of Jewish control and fears of a vulnerable public mind. Resentment had shifted from overtly blaming racial and ethnic groups to blaming the more nebulous but sufficiently malignant "Big Government." Although the focus of resentment had changed, the net effect worked all the more artfully to keep certain Others at the margins. In a general climate that was hostile to notions of public interest and collective social responsibility, Congress could dismantle the last vestiges of New Deal socialism. One could redeem the poor and disenfranchised through a form of socially engineered "tough love."

Given this new cultural climate in America, the Hollywood Question had taken a truly bizarre historical twist. Movies of the thirties and forties were apparently no longer at odds with down-home Americana. The conservative idyll of the American past now harbored both vertically integrated Hollywood and the small town in which movie palaces had screened products from motion picture's golden age. Such are the vicissitudes of the Hollywood Question.

Although it is tempting to dismiss *The Free Market* as representative of a crackpot fringe, its version of film history indicates mainstream shifts in American culture. In a general sense, its charges against Big Government obliquely but profoundly resonated with previous allegations of a Jewish conspiracy, even if the more recent charges only hinted at a surrogate East Coast intellectual liberalism. In a more specific sense, the Ludwig von Mises newsletter echoes with long-standing popular resentments of the film industry, even if it conveniently overlooks an era when various organized efforts were targeting both the film industry and all of those movies from Hollywood's golden age. This resentment in the thirties and forties – along similar lines articulated in the von Mises newsletter – was used to justify government antitrust action against Hollywood.

As this newsletter exemplifies, the recounting of film history remains a highly politicized endeavor. Resentment of today's film industry can seize upon the 1947 Paramount Consent Decree to advocate less government. An awareness of the Hollywood Question can, in turn reveal the politics – paradoxical as they are – of this stance. Yet this awareness can also reveal the less overt politics of film history. Mainstream film history has for the most part favored a consensus view of the Consent Decree, abstracting the Justice Department action from popular resentments of the day. An awareness of the Hollywood Question suggests, not an isolated federal action, but the culmination of decades-long hostility toward the industry. Similarly, awareness of the Question suggests new ways in which to view other familiar sites of post–World War II film history.

In this chapter, I shall argue that awareness of the Hollywood Question offers new insight into commonly held beliefs about film history. In addition to casting new light upon the 1947 Paramount Consent Decrees, this awareness suggests a different way of looking at both the Hollywood blacklist and the postwar representation of Jews in Hollywood films. In the case of the blacklist, some scholars have already connected postwar anti-Communism to prewar anti-Semitism. Awareness of the Hollywood Question offers further delineation of this link: in its own way, industry Red-baiting continued to reiterate many of the same themes espoused in the moral crusades of the twenties, thirties, and forties. In the case of postwar representation, common wisdom has maintained that the absence of overtly Jewish characters signified the cautious and fearful climate of the day. In this chapter, I contend that this absence represented a calculated response to reactionary politics. Assertions of social cohesion and a celebration of subjugated pluralism characterized this response.

Not only has the Hollywood Question intersected these key aspects of film history; it has helped to shape the telling of film history itself. The Question privileges a particular perspective from which to view these events. In postwar film history, mention of the movie moguls' ethnic origins appears natural and normal. Yet the very naturalizing and normalizing appearance of such references remains just as politicized as an account of the 1947 Consent Decree that advocates vertical integration. Of course, any history – including one that traces the Hollywood Question – remains rooted within a set of political assumptions that help justify what to include as well as what to exclude. But such justification requires maintaining one perspective at the expense of another. Ultimately, the perspective selected in this book works alongside that found in other film histories. Nevertheless, the perspective that emerges from focusing on the Hollywood Question also departs from traditional approaches to film history. In particular, what one assumes to be "normal" or "natural" in film history represents a powerful convergence of cultural forces.

ETHNIC ABSENCE: SELLING THE IDEAL OF AMERICA

By the late 1930s, the overt representations of the Jew in mainstream American film had all but evaporated from the Hollywood screen. As previous chapters have demonstrated, moguls and producers certainly remained aware of the charge of Jewish control. Yet whether this concern drove depictions Jewish life from the screen, and the extent to which this concern might have manifested itself in executive decisions, remains an open question. Jewish fear is a powerful feature of the Question's assumption that Jews act as a result of being Jewish. The Hollywood Question did alter the image of the Jew, but through a much more subtle and complex exchange of powerful institutional forces.

The Production Code Administration (PCA) remains one factor in the disappearance of Jewish images. At first glance, one might point to the Code's prohibition against the ridicule of any religion or nationality. According to this explanation, Hollywood producers shied away from obvious references to Jews for the same reason that the code censored films depicting Nazism. As the Hays Office had discovered quite early, films could arouse different audiences in strikingly different ways. Certainly, as *King of Kings* (Paramount, 1927) had demonstrated, even Jews could exert pressure and protest. Yet though it is true that pressure groups indeed caused Hollywood concern, one should not make too much of the tension between the PCA's Catholic constituency and the studios. The Production Code made perfect economic sense for the rapidly expanding motion picture business. From an economic standpoint, the audience demographic had changed as a result of the film industry's economic success. Whereas highly specific references to Jewish ethnicity had once targeted predominantly urban audiences, stories tapping the wells of nineteenth-century theatrical melodrama could maximize profits in the rural heartland.

If a change in imagery constituted a response to the Hollywood Question, that response derived less from the inclusion or exclusion of specific characters than from a particular vision of America. Hardly unique to Hollywood, the vision powerfully configured disparate ethnic groups into an idealized vision of melting-pot assimilation. As mogul correspondence demonstrates, Hollywood kept its business ties to Axis powers for so long, not out of greed, but out of a professed concern to influence foreign audiences toward democratic virtues. In the burgeoning global marketplace, the specificity of the Jewish stereotype dissolved into the selling of abstract American ideals. Rather than representing a venal "selling out" of Jews in order to retain global markets, as some authors have suggested, the absence of identifiable Jewish screen characters indicates a "selling of" American pluralism. In this assimilationist fantasy, ethnic differences mattered little. Rather than defining ethnicity either for laughs or sympathy, the new image of America emphasized the American that the ethnic could become. One can thus view the disappearance of the Jew from the screen, not as acquiescence to the Hollywood Question, but as an ideologically charged assertion challenging an older set of assumptions.

Films that treat the representation of Jews, both during and immediately after World War II, aptly demonstrate this attempt to sell a pluralistic American ideal. As David Selznick had advised Emeric Pressburger, the war film needed no more than one Jewish soldier to depict the well-oiled efficiency and camaraderie of an ethnically diverse American military platoon. Post–World War II films directly addressing anti-Semitism took this argument even further. Part of the social-problem genre, both *Crossfire* (RKO, 1946) and *Gentleman's Agreement* (Twentieth Century-Fox, 1947) condemned anti-Semitism, not because of its prevalence, but because of its aberration. As both films suggest, anti-Semitism operated distinctly at odds with democratic ideals. In *Crossfire*, a Roman Catholic detective tracks down the seemingly senseless murder of a Jew. The trail ultimately leads to a mentally unbalanced soldier. Anti-Semitism thrives, not because of its systemic nature, but because of the aberrant psychopathology of a lone, crazed individual. In *Gentleman's Agreement*, a Gentile journalist pretends to be Jewish in order to experience anti-Semitism. Though he finds the problem widespread, even with his closest relations and among Jews themselves, the film ultimately focuses on the disparity between prejudice and democratic ideals. According to the movie, anti-Semitism is more akin to nasty personal habit. That even a Gentile can don and appropriate ethnic identity speaks at least as powerfully to the assimilationist ideal, thus discounting the cultural specificity of ethnicity, as it does to the injustice of anti-Semitism.

A more pronounced articulation of this ideal emerges in films having no

Jewish characters. In *The Best Years of Our Lives* (MGM, 1946) a former bomber pilot played by Dana Andrews loses his job at a drugstore soda counter after physically attacking a customer. In decoding one of the most dramatically charged moments in the movie, awareness of the Hollywood Question helps to explain the scene's deeply felt emotions. The scene starkly juxtaposes the two characters. Andrews's character, a war veteran, has come home to a society whose employment opportunities consist of menial jobs like that of a soda jerk. To add insult to injury, he must cater to customers who question the legitimacy of having served in World War II. As a minor character in the movie, the customer neatly inverts the charge that Jews supported U.S. intervention so long as they did not have to serve in the military. The customer provokes the fight with Andrews by claiming that "a bunch of radicals in Washington" had suckered the country into fighting against the Axis. He never mentions the word "Jew," but his insinuation is clear. The scene suggests that this character himself never served in the war. Out of this paradox, the narrative leads to an even greater clarity: the "plain, old-fashioned Americanism" with which the customer aligns himself is, of course, anything but patriotic.[795]

Until *The Diary of Anne Frank* (20th Century-Fox, 1959), no postwar Hollywood film treated the Holocaust by focusing on anti-Semitism. Yet American motion pictures before 1959 do address this cultural trauma through abstraction, omission, and allegory. Rather than focusing on the specificity of Nazi anti-Semitism, these films assert American ideals of justice and democracy. In this way, one can read these films as part of a larger commentary upon the Hollywood Question. This response conflates assimilation with Americanism, ethnic identity with nationalism, and prejudice with totalitarianism. Fred Zinneman's *The Search* (MGM, 1948), for example, poses two alternatives for concentration camp survivors. While one Jewish orphan emigrates to Israel, American soldier Montgomery Clift hopes both to adopt a child of unspecified ethnicity and to bring him to the United States. Even in George Stevens's *The Diary of Anne Frank*, the narrative emphasizes the seemingly universal – in fact, highly Americanized – aspects of Anne's adolescence: her rebelliousness, her courtship with Petr, and her gradual conformity to the ideals of womanhood. The film generates its pathos, not for distinctly Jewish Jews hiding in an attic, but for the assimilated Jews who seem to share so much in common with the American experience.

Films in which the Holocaust plays a less pronounced role also operate as part of a larger response to the Hollywood Question. In *Goodbye, My Fancy* (Warner Bros., 1950), Congresswoman Joan Crawford returns to her alma mater intending to show a documentary she has compiled on undisclosed Nazi atrocities. Although audiences never see the film-within-a-film, debate over whether the school should show the controversial film to its students drives the movie's narrative. Those opposed to screening the film appear to have more in common with the totalitarian forces depicted in the fictional documentary, while those in support of its screening exhort core American values of freedom and liberty.

The absence of overt references to the Holocaust in postwar Hollywood films is itself a kind of response to the Hollywood Question. Genre films like the Western and the biblical epic retain allegorical references to cultural traumata. As a distinctly American form, the Western appears a somewhat unlikely vehicle to address the Holocaust. But as Walter Metz has argued, Fritz Lang's Western *Rancho Notorious* (RKO, 1952) resonates with the cultural traumata of the Holocaust, addressing themes of atrocity, revenge, conspiracy, and justice. Metz's reading suggests that, rather than an aberration, the generic conventions of the Western – when applied to the Holocaust – relocate concern for this trauma away from ethnic specificity and toward distinctly American concerns. Similarly, Cecil B. DeMille's *Ten Commandments* (Paramount, 1956) encourages an interpretation that parallels the plight of the Jews in Egypt with the plight of the Jews in Europe. By using the biblical story, the film constructs a universal – as opposed to exclusively Jewish – concern for the Holocaust. The seemingly universal, of course, remains sited within an ideological set of distinctly American concerns.

Rather than keeping images of Jews and the Holocaust off the screen, the Hollywood Question generated a powerful if implicit response in postwar American films. These films consistently emphasize how prejudice and intolerance – rather than Jewishness – remain outside the core American experience. Emerging from New Deal patriotism, this response affirmed assimilation as an inherently American ideal. However, these assertions hardly represented a consensus on the answer to the Hollywood Question. Rather, older but better camouflaged invocations of the Question roiled through two other momentous events in film history: the breakup of the studio system and the implementation of a blacklist.

THE HOLLYWOOD QUESTION AND PARAMOUNT ET AL., 1948

Beginning in 1939 and proceeding sporadically throughout the 1940s, the Justice Department vigorously pursued antitrust action against the major film studios. In its 1948 *Paramount et al.* decision, the United States Supreme Court ruled that the vertically integrated motion picture industry – in other words, ownership of key production, distribution, and exhibition holdings – constituted an illegal oligopoly. The Court ruled that the industry and the U.S. Justice Department work out a settlement. In this consent decree, the Big Five studios – Paramount, MGM, RKO, Twentieth Century-Fox, and Warner Bros. – agreed to sell their theatrical holdings.

Just as the dissipation of identifiable Jewish characters did not result directly from Jewish fear of the Hollywood Question, so the consent decrees did not directly manifest anti-Semitic hostility. The elaborate system of controls developed by studios was meant to retain dominance and exclude competitors. These controls included block booking – forcing theaters to take blocks of films rather than offering individual titles – and a system of run-zone-clearance. In the latter exhibition strategy, first-run films would play in select theaters at premium prices before moving to a series of cheaper, subsequent-run houses as these films neared the end of their useful life. Thus one must view the consent decrees as having some basis in the monopolistic practices of the film industry, and not as a vindictive federal attempt to go after the Jews.

Nonetheless, the Hollywood Question can provide some insight into the culmination of the consent decrees. The Justice Department had begun its prosecution in 1941, at the height of isolationist concern over motion picture influence. The Roosevelt administration postponed prosecution for the duration of the war, using the resources of the film industry to promote national unity. As Tom Schatz has noted, industry insiders knew that this reprieve would end, although few had anticipated the extremity of the eventual changes. Divorcing the studios from their theatrical holdings attacked the practices of block booking, blind selling, and run-zone-clearance – practices that theater owners had decried since the 1930s. In past government hearings, the Hollywood Question had driven implicit assumptions behind the protests. Trying to wrest control away from studio distribution exchanges, for example, independent theater owners complained that Hollywood's urban decision making was at odds with the values of the American small town.

In examining the relationship between the consent decrees and the Hollywood Question, one must consider how these protests played into the consent decrees of 1948. By the early 1940s, Congress had authorized the creation of the Temporary National Economic Committee (TNEC) to investigate the concentration of power in American industry. Part of the National Recovery Act, the TNEC eventually issued a series of forty-four monographs. When the committee proposed a list of monographs to be published in 1940, the subject of the film industry was not on this list.[796] By 1941, however, the forty-third monograph in the series was devoted entirely to the motion picture industry, the forty-fourth being a summary of the series.

As the National Association of Manufacturers (NAM) observed in 1942, few TNEC pamphlets focused exclusively on an entire industry. Unlike other industries in which only one segment was treated, however, this pamphlet addressed the entire motion picture industry. The NAM also noted that, unlike the case with the other industries, the TNEC never conducted any hearings related to the motion picture industry.[797] Instead, the highly critical NAM review tied the forty-third pamphlet to the "ignominious and abortive" Propaganda Hearings, observing that the sudden appearance of this title remained "something of a mystery."[798]

For the pro-business NAM, the attack on the motion picture industry served as the exception that proved the rule. For this business cartel, the TNEC represented unwanted federal intrusion into the free market. The NAM reasoned that what had happened in the Propaganda Hearings could easily have happened to other American industries. In one way, it had a point. The author of the TNEC report argued that Hollywood provided a representative glimpse of American industry. Yet the consent decrees were unique, not because they regulated the film industry, but because no other agreement regulated other, similarly integrated postwar industries. In fact, since 1948 the federal government has never taken as extensive or as vigorous an action with any other industry.

Here the NAM missed another, more crucial point. Deregulatory paranoia aside, the issue is not that the federal regulation of motion pictures might have served as a model for other forms of regulation, but that something about the motion picture industry made it a model industry for regulation. The authors of the TNEC investigation point out that the movie industry "exhibits symptoms which are common to many of our great enterprises," and that "its problems are part of the larger problem of the development and direction of American industry."[799] Just as the Jewish Sammy Glick could serve as a mirror for American society, so the "Jewish" motion picture industry could ultimately stand for the workings of American business as a whole. The Hollywood Question motivated not federal intervention – warranted considering the industry's business practices – but selection for regulation. At the very least, a letter prefacing the report to the TNEC chair expresses an awareness of the controversy surrounding the industry. "The authors have been careful to present a factual description of the motion picture industry," writes Theodore J. Kreps, that does not "moralize, nor make judgments concerning the events, good and bad."[800] Of course, mere selection of the motion picture industry of which "to present a factual description" was itself a moral judgment. The Hollywood Question allowed perceptions of Jews to serve as commentary upon the broadest aspects of American life. If vertical integration of the motion picture industry resonated with the image of Jew as supercapitalist, before the end of the decade the Hollywood Question would also link the industry to this stereotype's other twin. Of those who refused to testify about their Communist affiliations before the House Un-American Activities Committee in 1947, six of the Hollywood Ten were Jewish.

ANTI-COMMUNISM AND THE NEW HOLLYWOOD QUESTION

The Jewish and Hollywood Questions have always been a function of other specific social and cultural discourses such as countersubversion, lamentation for an older America, and the dangers of mass-mediated culture. Following revelations of Nazi atrocities, anti-Communism conveniently reanimated these desires and fears. A record number of people – nearly 60 percent of the population, according to public opinion polls conducted during the 1940s – believed that Jews held too much power. Yet in postwar America the Hollywood Question had lost its political viability on an institutional or organizational agenda. Its anti-Semitism appeared less systematically and more covertly. When it did appear, this articulation occurred on more of an ad hoc basis, and its speakers were more often individuals rather than spokespeople, leaders, or elected representatives. Overt anti-Semitism surfaced less often in public and more often at the political fringes of American conservatism.[801] Organizations like the B'nai B'rith Anti-Defamation League began to keep records of fringe anti-Semites, mirroring the efforts of countersubversives who tracked alleged Communists and "fellow travelers." For example, its background file on Representative Upshaw, the same Upshaw who had railed against the movies in the 1920s, shows that he eventually moved to Los Angeles, and later became involved with Gerald L. K. Smith and the Christian Nationalist Crusade.[802]

Postwar anti-Communism both changed the Hollywood Question and revitalized it in public discourse. When the House Un-American Activities Committee reopened after a wartime hiatus, its investigation of Hollywood Communists seemed to echo the Propaganda Hearings of 1941. The committee summoned defiant, "unfriendly" witnesses to testify on Communist activity in Hollywood. Yet two weeks into these hearings, HUAC chair J. Parnell Thomas shifted the investigation to New Deal advocates in government. The Hollywood Question was an optimal publicity move to garner attention for the committee but, at this early stage, was certainly not the focus of an attack in the way the Propaganda Hearings had focused on Hollywood in 1941.

The connection between the isolationists and the anti-Communists ran deep, rooted in the Populist tradition. John Thomas Anderson notes that the isolationists, their views marginalized after the bombing of Pearl Harbor, looked upon the HUAC "with vindictive approval." In 1953, Senator Burton K. Wheeler told the Helena, Montana, *Independent-Record* that he approved of Senator Joseph R. McCarthy's methods and that he himself had used similar methods when exposing the corruption of the Harding administration.[803]

Some elements of the Hollywood Question were easily adapted to suit the political paranoia of the times. The threat of subversion continued to crop up in anti-Communist discourse. There was also renewed concern over propaganda, particularly in light of new information about a sophisticated Nazi propaganda machine. As the Nuremberg trials of Nazi war criminals took place, many people in the United States wondered how so many people in a nation could have allowed Hitler to seize power and accepted Nazism and the dehumanization of the Jews. Propaganda was indeed a crucial part of the Nazi program, with Joseph Goebbels heading up a branch of government solely devoted to that purpose.

Part of what made anti-Communism a powerful discourse was its ability to appropriate and adapt elements of anti-Nazism and the Hollywood Question. Nazism represented a dictatorship, a massive human tragedy, and an aggressive military machine. The Hollywood Question provided a psychological model of a country whose public mind could be corrupted with undesirable ideas that would make people behave in ways and believe in things that they would otherwise not consider. Anti-Communism attracted many people who had articulated a belief in Jewish conspiracy and who could now quite vehemently claim that they opposed both Nazism and Communism, often conflating the two. With Churchill's warning that an "Iron Curtain" was descending across Europe, the Soviet Union was framed as the new enemy, and a protracted Cold War was about to define national identity as the preservation of a state of mind.

There were many similarities between anti-Communism and the Hollywood Question. Both presumed an unseen, omnipresent, and protean conspiracy. To both, the enemy was foreign and represented foreign ideals that were perceived to be inimical to the national integrity of the United States. Moreover, both cast their enemies as a threat to the public mind, assuming that the entire nation thought, spoke, and believed in exactly the same way. It was an assumption at once obsolete in its willful disregard for the diversity of both media and culture yet also powerful and seductive enough to justify denying civil liberties and to drive Cold War foreign policy to illogical and irrational extremes.

From a historical standpoint, then, awareness of the Hollywood Question can facilitate a deeper understanding of the cultural context within which anti-Communism, antitrust efforts, and ethnic representation all operated. The Question's own origins emanated from a shifting set of general responses to modernizing America. Anti-Semitism, xenophobia, and hypernationalism all helped to constitute this set of responses. Yet hardly stable in themselves, these articulations were undergoing profound shifts. Beginning as a focus upon individual ethnic deviancy, anti-Semitism after World War I embraced the notion of a collective ethnic will. Such views complemented an increasing hostility toward immigration, manifesting itself as an assertion of 100 percent Americanism. With the rise of mass media at around the same time, the Hollywood Question could flourish through its appropriation of earlier allegations of Jewish cultural influence. While theater reviews in *Life* magazine gave such alleged influence its stereotypical countenance, the imported *Protocols of the Elders of Zion* located such stereotypes within a more sinister, protean conspiracy.

Reinforcing fears of an inimical Jewish influence over culture, the idea that movies existed "as a business pure and simple" resonated with stereotypical assumptions of an ethnic Jewish aptitude for commerce. Such views prompted two major responses from religious organizations. Protestants mobilized to form pressure groups exhorting federal censorship and intervention. The Catholic Church and community, on the other hand, articulated a more localized strategy independent of federal intervention. At the same time, the publication empire of Henry Ford rendered the *Protocols* in a set of distinctly American terms. These terms resonated profoundly with the desires and laments expressed by both Protestant and Roman Catholic groups. Ford's *Dearborn Independent* and the subsequent *International Jew* asserted their vision of America as a maplike grid of smaller, distinct communities. The articulation of the Hollywood Question in these publications envisioned a rootless ethnic sensibility invading the rooted, autonomous neighborhoods – neighborhoods that before modernization had somehow seemed to capture the essence of American identity.

By the time of the Great Depression and Roosevelt's New Deal, however, a new way of talking about American identity had emerged. As articulated by Will Hays, head of the film industry's trade organization, the melting pot rather than the grid served as an operative metaphor speaking to this American identity. One could interpret the act of moviegoing – indeed, any enjoyment of mass entertainment – as the harbinger of a new kind of America. In this new paradigm, mass entertainment would welcome yet subsume cultural differences in a way that served idealized national interests. Ever flexible, however, the Hollywood Question still responded to such shifting paradigms. Throughout the 1930s, theater owners and various other religious and community groups articulated the Hollywood Question in both overt and covert forms. Rather than envisioning Hollywood as fulfilling a new American ideal, these groups affirmed a vision of the autonomous American small town. Hollywood allegedly existed as a trust whose monopoly extended, not just over the film industry, but over American morality as well. In more overt fashion, such views appeared in more marginal expressions of anti-Semitism. Though located at the margins of discourse, however, hostility toward Jews operated within the mainstream as well. Covert though it was, this hostility nonetheless came to operate within the film industry itself. Thus, one can read the Production Code Administration as both an informal and a formal encoding of Hollywood Question anti-Semitism.

A whole way of speaking about Hollywood ethnic intent emerged from depression-era American popular culture. The movie mogul stereotype served as the most visceral example of this discourse, even manifesting itself in children's literature. This way of speaking appeared in both the "factual" accounts of bystanders and the fictional accounts of popular literature. Whether fact or fiction, each rendering appeared to give added weight to a remarkably cohesive body of observation.

The Hollywood Question could abut a range of political positions. Whether left or right, positions concerning anti-Semitism, Nazism, Communism, and entry into World War II served as conduits through which the Hollywood Question could be channeled. Within the terms of the Question, one could dismiss the importance of anti-Semitism. Overt reference to Jewish control could thus appear to operate at the margins while covert mention of Jewish ethnic intent still operated within popular culture. Film industry executives could respond to the Hollywood Question by censoring certain film narratives. Of course, these executives could just as easily produce narratives that responded to the Question covertly. The Hollywood Question could also define the terms within which one articulated anti-Communism. Ever flexible, these terms could in fact drive anti-Communist discourse long after this discourse omitted overt mention of Jews. Finally, the Hollywood Question could consolidate powerful discourses of both antitrust and isolationism, implicating the film industry in an alleged scheme to push the country into a war of foreign concern.

Just as the Hollywood Question could penetrate a range of positions, so it could elicit a range of responses. Often failing to confront the Question's terms and sometimes even consistent with these terms, these responses suggest a powerful and influential process of negotiation at work. Some, like Archibald MacLeish and *Fortune* magazine, sought to allay fears of anti-Semitism through asserting its marginal status. Within Hollywood, however, the Hollywood Question raised responses in a variety of communications, from confidential memos to an entire film genre like the biopic. Authors such as Nathanael West, Budd Schulberg, and F. Scott Fitzgerald replied to the Hollywood Question in a particular way. While deferring ethnic difference to a cohesive national identity, the specificity of Jewish ethnic intent in these narratives speaks to a range of universal American traits. The Jewish stereotype thus operates as a critique of American culture and identity. The work of Leo Rosten codified this fictional view, using the "lens of social science" to formalize the subjugation of ethnic difference. In his response to the Hollywood Question, Rosten articulates a vision that simultaneously challenges the Question's proposition and leaves its assumptions intact.

The most overt discussion of the Hollywood Question arose in relation to controversy over the United States's entry into World War II. Powerful enough to galvanize the isolationist movement, the Question also helped to bring about the movement's downfall. By the time the Propaganda Hearings of 1941 had opened on Capitol Hill, the anti-Semitism that had covertly mobilized opposition to Roosevelt had also worked to thoroughly discredit the movement as being out of step with a new paradigm for national ideals. As the public discourse following the hearings shows, the failure to engage anti-Semitism openly marked the triumph of a particular vision of America. No longer the loose confederation of decentralized, smaller communities, America now epitomized a global presence, a modernizing and industrializing society, and a culturally diverse population in which cohesion subsumed difference. At the same time, however, the Hollywood Question remained flexible enough to address the postwar concerns of this new American paradigm, capturing the anxieties of both antitrust and anti-Communism in the national security state. The Hollywood Question continues to operate to this day, driving a multitude of articulated fears about political correctness, racism, and cultural diversity. Its persistence ultimately marks the strange place of anti-Semitism within American popular culture: its overt manifestations lurk at the cultural margins, while its covert forms continue to drive a host of responses to changing cultural conditions.

Notes

1 Evan Carton, "The Self Besieged: American Identity on Campus and in the Gulf," *Tikkun* 6.4 (1991): 40.

2 Neal Gabler, "Jews, Blacks and Trouble in Hollywood," *New York Times*, 2 Sept. 1990 (late ed.), H7; Neal Gabler, *An Empire of Their Own: How the Jews Invented Hollywood* (New York: Crown, 1988).

3 Gabler, "Jews, Blacks and Trouble," H7.

4 "Manifest Destiny," *Encyclopædia Britannica Online*, accessed 20 Oct. 1999.

5 Gabler, H7.

6 Ibid., *Time*, 14 Feb. 1994, 17 (On-Line Expanded Academic Index); Douglas Century, "Hollywood Scuffle: Turning Moguls into Monsters," *Forward*, 16 Dec. 1994, 1 (Ethnic NewsWatch).

7 "Jewish Supremacy in Motion Picture World," *The Dearborn Independent*, 19 Feb. 1921.

8 Stephen Jay Gould, *The Mismeasure of Man* (New York: Norton, 1981).

9 Donald S. Strong, *Organized Anti-Semitism in the United States: The Rise of Group Prejudice during the Decade 1930–40* (Washington, DC: American Council on Public Affairs, 1941; rpt. Westport, CT: Greenwood Press, 1979), 19.

10 Michael E. Birdwell, *Celluloid Soldiers: The Warner Bros.' Campaign against Nazism* (New York: NYU Press, 1999), 2–3.

11 Stanley Fish, "The Empire Strikes Back," *There's No Such Thing as Free Speech . . . And It's a Good Thing, Too* (New York: Oxford University Press, 1993), 54.

12 Edward W. Said, *Orientalism* (1978; New York: Vintage-Random, 1979), 3, 94; original emphasis.

13 Sander L. Gilman, *Difference and Pathology: Stereotypes of Sexuality, Race, and Madness* (Ithaca: Cornell University Press, 1985), 23; Sander L. Gilman, *Jewish Self-Hatred* (Baltimore: Johns Hopkins University Press, 1986), 3.

14 Gilman, *Jewish Self-Hatred*, 2, 120.

15 Raymond Williams, *Marxism and Literature* (Oxford: Oxford University Press, 1977), 88; Richard Dyer, "White," *Screen* 29.4 (1988): 44–64.

16 Said, *Orientalism*, 7; Dick Hebdige, *Subculture: The Meaning of Style*, New Accents(London: Methuen, 1979), 16.

17 James Carey, "A Cultural Approach to Communication," *Communication as Culture: Essays on Media and Society*, Media and Popular Culture (Boston: Unwin, Hyman, 1989), 29.

18 John Higham, *Strangers in the Land* (New Brunswick, NJ: Rutgers University Press, 1955), 13.

19 William Shakespeare, *The Merchant of Venice*, dramatis personae, 4.1.

20 Ra Page and Michael Stodnick, "The Wandering Jew: Romantic Approaches," *Manuscript* 1.1 (1995), online, University of Manchester English and American Studies Department, Internet, 18 Dec. 1998, available http://www.art.man. ac.uk/english/ms/ramiconf.htm.

21 Higham, *Strangers in the Land*, 8; Morton Borden, "Alien and Sedition Acts," *Academic American Encyclopedia*, 1993 ed. (database on UTCAT PLUS system).

22 Douglas T. Miller, "Know-Nothing Party," *Academic American Encyclopedia*, 1993 ed.

23 Higham, *Stranger in the Land*, 14, 16, 17–18, 114; "The South and Immigration," *Harper's Weekly* 21 (June 1913): 3.

24 Samuel Joseph, *Jewish Immigration in the United States*, Studies in History, Economics and Public Law 59.4 (New York: Columbia University, 1914), 174.

25 Ibid., 91–92, 164, 174, 175, 186.

26 Editorial, *The National Economist*, 3 Jan. 1891: 252.

27 Daniel De Leon, "The Anti-Immigration Howl," *The People*, 22 March 1910; rpt. in "Daniel De Leon on Racism and Immigration," *The People*, 16 May 1992, 4S, pt. 5 of a series.

28 Higham *Strangers in the Land*, 47; John D. Mason, letter, "The South and Immigration," *Harper's Weekly*, 12 July 1913, 5; Monroe Royce, *The Passing of the American* (New York: Thomas Whittaker, 1911), 45.

29 Will Herberg, *Protestant–Catholic–Jew*, rev. ed. (1955; Garden City, NY: Anchor-Doubleday, 1960) 117; Higham 276.

30 Joseph, *Jewish Immigration* 189; "Jew versus Non-Jew in New York Finance," *The Dearborn Independent* 13 Nov. 1920; rpt. in *Jewish Activities in the United States*, The International Jew, vol. 2 (N.p.: n.p., 1921), 31.

31 Henry Aaron Yeomans, *Abbott Lawrence Lowell, 1856–1943* (Cambridge, MA: Harvard University Press, 1948; New York: Arno Press, 1977), 209–12.

32 Gregory D. Black, *Hollywood Censored: Morality Codes, Catholics, and the Movies*, Cambridge Studies in the History of Mass Communications (Cambridge: Cambridge University Press, 1994), 156; A. Lawrence Lowell, letter to Sol A. Rosenblatt, 13 Dec. 1933, rpt. in United States, Office of National Recovery Administration, Division of Review, "The Motion Picture Industry" by Daniel Bertrand, Work Materials 34, February 1936, 90–91.

33 Peter Pulzer, *The Rise of Political Anti-Semitism in Germany and Austria*, rev. ed. (1964; London: Halban, 1988), 286–87; Gould, *Mismeasure of Man*, 68–69.

34 Higham, *Strangers in the Land*, 22.

35 Paul Michael Rogin, *Ronald Reagan, the Movie* (Berkeley: University of California Press, 1987), 236.

36 Herberg, *Protestant–Catholic–Jew*, 15; Higham, 85; Gustavus Myers, *History of Bigotry in the United States* (New York: Random House, 1943), 268–69.

37 "Russianized America," *The National Economist*, 21 Feb. 1891, 360.

38 Gordon Clark, *Shylock: As Banker, Bondholder, Corruptionist, Conspirator*, (Washington, DC: n.p., 1894).

39 *The Talmud Jew* (New York: Titus, 1892), 7.

40 Royce, *The Passing of the American*, 7.

41 William T. Hornaday, *Awake! America* (New York: Moffat, Yard, 1918), 106–7, 118.

42 Emerson Hough, *The Web* (Chicago: Reilly and Lee, 1919), 12.

43 Woodrow Wilson, "Patriotism and the Sailor," address at the unveiling of the statue of Commodore John Barry, 16 May 1914; rpt. in *Selected Addresses and Public Papers of Woodrow Wilson*, ed. Albert Bushnell Hart (New York: Boni and Liveright, 1918), 30, 31; Theodore Roosevelt, *Fear God and Take Your Own Part* (New York, 1916); quoted in Rodney Minott, *Peerless Patriots* (Washington, DC: Public Affairs Press, 1962), 56.

44 John W. Baer, "The Strange Origin of the Pledge of Allegiance," *Propaganda Review*, Summer 1989, online, The Electronic Frontier Foundation, Internet, 20 Dec. 1998, available http://www.eff.org/pub/CAF/civil-liberty/pledge.history.

45 Hough, *The Web*, 36.

46 United States, Chamber of Commerce, Committee on Subversive Activities, *Combating Subversive Activities in the United States* (Washington, DC: Chamber of Commerce, 1934), 26, David O. Selznick Archives, Harry Ransom Humanities Research Center, Austin; emphasis added.

47 *Talmud Jew*, 54, 58, 60.

48 Telemachus Thomas Timayenis, *The Original Mr. Jacobs* (New York: Minerva, 1888), 74–75, 80, 211, 215.

49 Ibid., 76, 280–81.

50 Ibid., 232, 235–36, 280–81.

51 Ibid., 74–75, 80, 211, 215.

52 I[gnatius] D[onnelly], "New York Times Sold," *The Representative*, 5 Sep. 1894: 5.

53 I[gnatius] D[onnelly], "The Jews: An Explanation," *The Representative*, 12 Sep. 1894: 2.

54 Patricia Marks, "Life," in *American Literary Magazines: The Eighteenth and Nineteenth Centuries*, ed. Edward E. Chielens, Historical Guides to the World's Periodicals and Newspapers (New York: Greenwood Press, 1986), 213.

55 The American Jewish Archives in Cincinnati has a collection of these caricatures. American Jewish Archives, Hebrew Union College, Cincinnati, OH.

56 *Watson's Magazine* 21 (1915): 293; quoted in Higham, *Strangers in the Land*, 186; *Atlanta Journal*, 15 March 1914: 5–6; quoted in Dinnerstein, *The Leo Frank Case* (New York: Columbia University Press, 1968), 95; Dinnerstein, 116.

57 Quoted. in Julian Mack, letter to Louis Marshall, 19 March 1914; quoted in Dinnerstein 92; Pierre Van Paassen, *To Number Our Days* (New York: Scribners, 1964), 237–38, quoted in Dinnerstein, 158.

58 "Religiously Political," *Bob Shuler's Free Lance* 1.5 (1917): 126–27; "The Mighty Roman Parade," *Bob Shuler's Magazine* 5.6 (1926): 136.

59 Clark, *Shylock*, 90.

60 Sander L. Gilman, "Salome, Syphilis, Sarah Bernhardt, and the Modern Jewess," in *The Jew in the Text: Modernity and the Construction of Identity*, ed. Linda Nochlin and Tamar Garb (London: Thames & Hudson, 1995), 97–120, and Carol Ockman, "When Is a Jewish Star Just a Star? Interpreting Images of Sarah Bernhardt," in Nochlin and Garb, 121–39.

61 [James] Metcalfe, "The Sad State of Affairs," *Life*, 12 May 1898, 404; ibid., 404; James Metcalfe, review, "Mr. Daly's 'The Merchant of Venice,' " *Life*, 1 Dec. 1898, 432.

62 Metcalfe, "Sad State of Affairs," 404.

63 Ibid., 404 James S. Metcalfe, "Is the Theatre Worth While?" *The Atlantic Monthly* 96.6 (1905): 729.

64 Metcalfe, "Is the Theatre Worth While?" 729.

65 Joseph Smith, "The Deadhead," *Life*, 28 April 1898, 366, 377.

66 Henry Berkowitz, letter to the editor, *Life*, 31 Oct. 1901, 354; Richard Scheiner, letter to the editor, *Life*, 17 Oct. 1901, 314.

67 Response to Scheiner, *Life*, 17 Oct. 1901, 314.

68 Ibid., 314.

69 Scheiner, letter to the editor, 314.

70 Response to Berkowitz, *Life*, 31 Oct. 1901, 354.

71 W.I.W., letter to the editor, *Life*, 7 Nov. 1901, 368.

72 Ibid.

73 Higham, *Strangers in the Land*, 280.

74 Boris L. Brasol, *The World at the Cross Roads* (Boston: Small, Maynard, 1921), 1.

75 Ibid., 2, 396–97.

76 Ibid., 398.

77 *The Protocols and World Revolution* (Boston: Small, Maynard, 1920), 17–18, 39–40. Unless otherwise noted, all emphasis is original.

78 *Protocols*, 40, 41, 42.

79 Ibid., 42.

80 Ibid., 18, 43–44.

81 Ibid., 43.

82 Ibid., 44–45, 46.

83 *The Jewish Peril* (London: Eyre, Spottiswoode, 1920); quoted in *The Protocols and World Revolution* (Boston: Small, Maynard, 1920), 146.

84 Robert Singerman, "The American Career of the *Protocols of the Elders of Zion*," *American Jewish History* 71.1 (1988): 66, 70.

85 Department of Research and Education, Federal Council of the Churches of Christ in America, report, *The Public Relations of the Motion Picture Industry* (New York: by the author, 1931), 54; Frank Walsh, *Sin and Censorship: The Catholic Church and the Motion Picture Industry* (New Haven, CT: Yale University Press, 1996), 7.

86 Kristin Thompson and David Bordwell, *Film History: An Introduction* (New York: McGraw-Hill, 1994), 34–35; Patricia Erens, *The Jew in the American Cinema* (Bloomington: Indiana University Press, 1984), 52.

87 The Municipal Committee, The Cleveland Chamber of Commerce, *Shall the Movies Be Censored?* (Cleveland, OH: by the author, 1922), 5, 6.

88 U.S. House, Committee on Education, *Hearings on the Proposed Federal Motion Picture Commission*, 69th Cong., 1st sess., H. R. 4094 and 6233 (Washington, DC: GPO, 1926), 19.

89 *Fox Film Corp. v. Turnbull*, 7 Fed. (2) 715, abstract in Dennis Hartman, *Motion Picture Law Digest*, 2d ed. (Los Angeles: n. p., 1947), 50.

90 P. B. Wells, letter to Morris Newfield, 27 April 1918; photocopy courtesy of Leah Hagedorn.

91 U.S. House, *Hearings on the Proposed Federal Motion Picture Commission*(1926), 21.

92 Ibid., 20.

93 Ibid.

94 Municipal Committee, *Shall the Movies Be Censored?* 9.

95 Robert Sklar, *Movie-Made America*, updated ed. (New York: Vintage-Random House, 1994), 78.

96 Robert Sobel, *The Manipulators* (Garden City, NY: Anchor-Doubleday, 1976), 111; Gerald S. Schatz, "Will H. Hays and the Motion Picture Industry," *Historical Society of Southern California Quarterly* 43.3 (1961): 318; Sklar, 83; Douglas Gomery, ed., *A Guide to the Microfilm Edition of the Will Hays Papers*, Cinema History Microfilm Series (Frederick, MD: UPA, 1986),5 iii.

97 Gomery, xi.

98 Lea Jacobs, *The Wages of Sin: Censorship and the Fallen Woman Film, 1928–1942* (Madison: University of Wisconsin Press, 1991), 18–22.

99 U.S Congress, Senate, Temporary National Economic Committee, Bertrand, Evans, and Blanchard, *The Motion Picture Industry – A Pattern of Control*, 65.

100 Gomery, v.

101 Kenneth G. Crawford, *The Pressure Boys: The Inside Story of Lobbying in America* (New York: Julian Messner, 1939), 90.

102 Ibid., 91.

103 U.S. House, Committee on Education, *Hearings on the Proposed Federal Motion Picture Commission*, 69th Cong., 1st sess., H.R. 4094 and 6233 (Washington, DC: GPO, 1926), 24; " 'Fatty' Plus Hays and the American Public," *Bob Shuler's Magazine* 1.12 (1923): 191.

104 Department of Research and Education, Federal Council of the Churches of Christ in America, *The Public Relations of the Motion Picture Industry* (New York: by the author, 1931), 106–7.

105 Ibid., 147.

106 Ibid., 106.

107 Wilbur F. Crafts, *National Perils and Hopes: A Study Based on Current Statistics and the Observations of a Cheerful Reformer* (Cleveland, OH: Barton, 1910), 65–69.

108 Ibid., 34, 38.

109 Ibid., 66, 101.

110 Ibid., 65–69.

111 Ibid., iii–iv.

112 Charles Matthew Feldman, *The National Board of Censorship (Review) of Motion Pictures, 1909–1922* (Ph.D. diss., University of Michigan, 1975; New York: Arno Press, 1977), 67–68.

113 U.S. House, Committee on Education, *Hearings on the Federal Motion Picture Commission*, 64th Cong., 1st sess., HR 456 (Washington, DC: GPO, 1916); rpt. in Aspects of Film series (New York: Arno Press, 1978), 15.

114 *Hearings on the Federal Motion Picture Commission* (1916), 144.

115 Ibid., 145.

116 "Censorship Is Truly Silly," editorial, *The Searchlight*, 4 March 1922, 4.

117 "Klansmen Halt Chaplin Film at Walla Walla," *The Searchlight*, 14 April 1923, 1.

118 *Hearings on the Proposed Federal Motion Picture Commission* (1926), 25.

119 "Canon Chase, Episcopalian Defends Klan," *The Searchlight*, 9 Dec. 1922, 6.

120 ADL, B'nai Brith F. F. files roll no. 96; William Sheafe Chase, *Catechism on Motion Pictures in Inter-State Commerce*, 3d ed. (Albany: New York Civic League, 1922), cover, back cover.

121 Sklar, *Movie-Made America*, 124; U.S. House *Hearings* (1926) 128; Chase, addendum to 160; rpt. in United States, *Commission Hearing* (1926), 398.

122 Chase cover.

123 Chase 2.

124 Ibid.

125 Ibid., 57.

126 Gomery, *Will Hays Papers*, viii.

127 U.S. House, *Commission Hearing* (1926), 398.

128 Chase 115, 118.

129 Ibid., 119.

130 U.S. House, *Hearings* (1926), 83.

131 Close-Up, "Mirrors of Hollywood," Part 2 of a series, *Sunset Magazine*, August 1923, 58, in 1923 Correspondence, Folder 6, Adolph Zukor Collection, AMPAS, Beverly Hills, CA.

132 B. P. Schulberg, letter to Adolph Zukor, 7 Aug. 1923, ts., 1923, Correspondence Folder 6, Zukor Collection.

133 B. P. Schulberg, letter to Charles K. Field, 7 Aug. 1923, ts., 1923 Correspondence Folder 6, Zukor Collection.

134 Charles K. Field, letter to *Jewish Times and Observer*, 13 Aug. 1923, ts., 1923, Correspondence Folder 6, Zukor Collection.

135 U.S. House, *Commission Hearings* (1926), 24, 25.

136 Ibid., *Commission* (1926), 27.

137 Ibid., *Commission* (1926), 51.

138 Ibid., 66.

139 Ibid., *Commission* (1926), 408–9.

140 U.S. House, Committee on Interstate and Foreign Commerce, *Hearing on Federal Motion Picture Commission*, 73d Cong., 2d sess., H. R. 6097 (Washington, DC: GPO, 1934), 10.

141 Ibid., *Commission* (1934), 10.

142 Ibid., *Commission* (1934), 26, 28–29, 52.

143 Walsh, *Sin and Censorship*, 19.

144 Francis R. Walsh, " 'The Callahans and the Murphys' (MGM, 1927): A Case Study of Irish-American and Catholic Church Censorship," *Historical Journal of Film, Radio and Television* 10.1 (1990): 40.

145 "Dublin Paper Condemns Irish Hearts," *The Gaelic American*, 18 June 1927, 1.

146 "Irish Hearts Is Too Vile for Revision," *The Gaelic American*, 9 July 1927, 1.

147 "Dublin Paper Condemns Irish Hearts," *The Gaelic American*, 18 June 1927, 1.

148 James A. O'Gorrman, Jr., letter to Devoy, rpt. in "New Photo-Play to Replace Caricatures of the Irish Race," *The Gaelic American*, 6 Aug. 1927, 2.

149 "Roughhouse Play Caricatures the Irish," *The Gaelic American*, 16 July 1927, 1.

150 "The Stage Irishman Has Come Back," *The Gaelic American*, 23 July 1927, 1.

151 *Irish World and Independent Liberator*, 13 Aug. 1927; quoted in Walsh, *Sin and Censorship*, 43.

152 "Caricatures of the Irish on the Stage Are Again Prevalent," *The Gaelic American*, 30 July 1927, 1.

153 A. Reader, letter to the editor, *The Gaelic American*, 10 Dec. 1927, 4.

154 Jeremiah F. O'Carroll, letter to the editor, *The Gaelic American*, 26 Nov. 1927, 4.

155 Editorial, "Rotten-Egg the Stage Irishman," *The Gaelic American*, 6 Aug. 1927, 4.

156 *Irish World and Independent Liberator*, 13 Aug. 1927, quoted in Walsh, "The Callahans and the Murphys," 40; *Gaelic American*, 24 Sept. 1927, quoted in Walsh, 40; editorial, "Rotten-Egg the Stage Irishman," *The Gaelic American*, 6 Aug. 1927, 4.

157 Walsh, *Sin and Censorship*, 42.

158 *1939–1940 Motion Picture Almanac*, 726.

159 Erens, *The Jew in the American Cinema*, 72.

160 Joseph Levenson, "Censorship in the Movies," *Forum* 69 (1923); rpt. in issue on state censorship of motion pictures, *The Reference Shelf* 2.1 (1923): 90.

161 "M'Kee Bill Is Now Before General Welfare Committee of Board of Aldermen, New York," *The Gaelic American*, 5 May 1928, 2.

162 Mort Kass, memo to Sol Kolack, 29 Aug. 1961; in ADL no. 276 *King of Kings* (1961). MGM eventually remade *King of Kings* in 1961 as a big-budget epic directed by Nicholas Ray. The making of this film prompted a query to the ADL about the controversy surrounding the original *King of Kings*.

163 Alfred M. Cohen, letter to Carl E. Milliken, 21 Dec. 1927, photocopy courtesy of Francis R. Walsh.

164 Kass, memo to Sol Kolack, 29 Aug. 1961.

165 Arthur H. DeBra, resumé of activities, 20 March 1938, Motion Picture Producers and Distributors Association Papers, Margaret Herrick Library, Academy of Motion Picture Arts and Sciences, Los Angeles; C[arl] E. M[illiken], letter to W[ill] H. H[ays], 24 Sept. 1928, Motion Picture Producers and Distributors Association Papers, Margaret Herrick Library, Academy of Motion Picture Arts and Sciences, Los Angeles.

166 C[arl] E. M[illiken], memo, 19 Sept. 1928, Motion Picture Producers and Distributors Association Papers, Margaret Herrick Library, Academy of Motion Picture Arts and Sciences, Los Angeles.

167 Kirk [Russell], letter to Jason S. Joy, 12 April. 1927, Motion Picture Producers and Distributors Association Papers, Margaret Herrick Library, Academy of Motion Picture Arts and Sciences, Los Angeles.

168 Albert Lee, *Henry Ford and the Jews* (New York: Stein and Day, 1980), 14.

169 David E. Nye, *Henry Ford, "Ignorant Idealist,"* Series in American Studies (Port Washington, NY: Kennikat Press, 1979), 89–91.

170 David E. Nye, *Henry Ford, "Ignorant Idealist,"* Series in American Studies (Port Washington, NY: Kennikat Press, 1979), 92.

171 John L. Spivak, "Coughlin and Ford," *New Masses*, 12 Dec. 1939, 3.

172 Jonathan Norton Leonard, *The Tragedy of Henry Ford* (New York: G. P. Putman's Sons, 1932), 60.

173 *PM Magazine*, 20 Sept. 1940, rpt. in Lee, 100–1.

174 "Does This Explain Jewish Political Power?" *The Dearborn Independent*, 18 Sep. 1920, 8.

175 "How Jews Capitalized on a Protest against Jews," *The Dearborn Independent*, 22 Jan. 1921; rpt. in *Jewish Activities in the United States*, The International Jew, vol. 2 (N.p.: n.p., 1921), 110.

176 "Jewish Supremacy in Motion Picture World," *The Dearborn Independent*, 19 Feb. 1921; rpt. in *Jewish Activities*, 130.

177 "How Jews Capitalized," 114–15.

178 Ibid., 127–28; "Jewish Control of the American Theater," *The Dearborn Independent*, 1 Jan. 1921; rpt. in *Jewish Activities*, 93.

179 "Are You Going to the Movies?" *The Dearborn Independent*, 18 Sep. 1920: 4; "Jewish Jazz Becomes Our National Music," *The Dearborn Independent*, 6 Aug. 1921, rpt. in *Jewish Influences in American Life*, The International Jew, vol. 3 (N.p.: n.p., 1921), 65; "The Jewish Aspect of the 'Movie' Problem," *The Dearborn Independent*, 12 Feb. 1921; rpt. in *Jewish Activities*, 124.

180 "How Jews Capitalized," 109; " 'Movie' Problem," 126.

181 " 'Movie' Problem," 124; "Jew Versus Non-Jew in New York Finance," *The Dearborn Independent*, 13 Nov. 1920, rpt. in *Jewish Activities*, 31.

182 " 'Movie' Problem," 119; "American Theater," 89.

183 "The Jewish Element in Bootlegging Evil," *The Dearborn Independent*, 31 Dec. 1921; rpt. in *Aspects of Jewish Power in the United States*, The International Jew, vol. 4 (N.p.: n.p., 1922), 39–40.

184 "Angles of Jewish Influence in American Life," *The Dearborn Independent*, 21 May 1921, rpt. in *Jewish Power*, 50–51; "Candid Address to Jews on the Jewish Problem," *The Dearborn Independent*, 7 Jan. 1922, rpt. in *Jewish Power*, 225; "American Theater," 89, 94; original emphasis.

185 "Gigantic Jewish Liquor Trust and Its Career," *The Dearborn Independent*, 24 Dec. 1921, rpt. in *Jewish Power*, 29; "Jewish Jazz," 65.

186 "Does Jewish Power Control the World Press?" *The Dearborn Independent*, 11 Sep. 1920, 9; original emphasis.

187 "Motion Picture World," 125, 127; "World Press?" 8–9; "American Theater," 89–90.

188 "An Address to 'Gentiles' on the Jewish Problem," *The Dearborn Independent*, 14 Jan. 1922, rpt. in *Aspects of Jewish Power*, 242; "Angles of Jewish Influence," 47–48.

189 Leo P. Ribuffo, "Henry Ford and *The International Jew*," *American Jewish History* 69.4 (1980): 463, 465.

190 Ibid., 466–69.

191 Burton J. Hendricks, *The Jews in America* (Garden City, NY: Doubleday, Page, 1923), 123.

192 Ibid., 124.

193 Miles Kreuger, ed., *Souvenir Programs of Twelve Classic Movies, 1927–1941* (New York: Dover, 1977), 6.

194 Ibid., 17.

195 Quoted in Leonard, *The Tragedy of Henry Ford*, 208.

196 Victor H. Bernstein, "Ford Empire Played Both Sides in War," *Technocracy Digest* (1945), online, Technocracy, Internet, 9 July 1998, available http://www.technocracy.org/periodicals/social-trends/126/ford.html.

197 Will H. Hays, *See and Hear: A Brief History of Motion Pictures and the Development of Sound* (N. pl.: Motion Picture Producers and Distributors of America, 1929), 3–4, rpt. *Screen Monographs II*, Literature of Cinema (New York: Arno Press – New York Times, 1970).

198 Ibid., 4.

199 Ibid., 4.

200 Ibid., 6–7.

201 Jack Richmond, *Hollywood* (Los Angeles: by the author, 1928), 6.

202 Quoted U.S. House, Committee on Interstate and Foreign Commerce, *Motion Picture Films (Compulsory Block Booking and Blind Selling)*, 76th Cong., 3d sess., S. 280, pt. 1 (Washington, DC: GPO, 1940), 34.

203 Hays, *See and Hear*, 35.

204 Kenneth G. Crawford, *The Pressure Boys: The Inside Story of Lobbying in America* (New York: Julian Messner, 1939), 95.

205 *Message from the President of the United States Transmitting Recommendations Relative to the Strengthening and Enforcement of Antitrust Laws*, S. Doc. 173, 75th Cong., 3d sess., quoted in David Lynch, *The Concentration of Economic Power* (New York: Columbia University Press, 1946), 2, 8.

206 Lynch, 8.

207 United States, Office of National Recovery Administration, Division of Review, "The Motion Picture Industry" by Daniel Bertrand, Work Materials 34, February 1936, 39; "The Movie Code and the Independents," editorial, *The Christian Century*, 1 Nov. 1933, 1358.

208 United States, National Recovery Administration, *Report Regarding Investigation Directed to Be Made by the President in His Executive Order of November 27, 1933, Approving the Code of Fair Competition for the Motion Picture Industry*, made by Sol A. Rosenblatt to Gen. Hugh S. Johnson, 7 July 1934, 8.

209 Bertrand, "Motion Picture Industry," 49.

210 A. Lawrence Lowell, letter to Sol A. Rosenblatt, 13 Dec. 1933, reprinted in Bertrand, 90–91.

211 U.S. Senate, Subcommittee of the Committee on Interstate Commerce, *Hearings on Compulsory Block-Booking and Blind Selling in the Motion Picture Industry*, 74th Cong., 2d sess., S. 3012 (Washington, DC: GPO, 1938), 10–11.

212 Garth Jowett, Ian C. Jarvie, and Kathryn Fuller, *Children and the Movies: Media Influence and the Payne Fund Controversy*, Cambridge Studies in the History of Mass Communications (New York: Cambridge University Press, 1996).

213 Douglas Gomery, ed., *A Guide to the Microfilm Edition of the Will Hays Papers*, Cinema History Microfilm Series (Frederick, MD: UPA, 1986), xi; Crawford, *The Pressure Boys*, 95.

214 Crawford 96.

215　Ibid., 100; U.S. Senate, Committee on Interstate Commerce, Subcommittee on S. 280, *Hearings on Anti "Block-Booking" and "Blind Selling" in the Leasing of Motion-Picture Films*, 76th Cong., 1st sess., S. 280 (Washington, DC: GPO, 1939), 502.

216　U.S. Senate, *Hearings on Compulsory Block-Booking and Blind Selling*, 57.

217　Ibid., 44, 47, 54, 55.

218　F. J. Daugherty, letter to The Allied States Association of Motion Picture Exhibitors, 28 March 1939; rpt. in U.S. Senate, *Hearings on Anti "Block-Booking,"* 107.

219　U.S. Senate, *Hearings on Anti "Block Booking,"* 501.

220　James C. Quinn, letter to Abram F. Myers, 28 March 1939; rpt. in ibid., 593.

221　Ibid., 503–4.

222　Ibid., 501.

223　U.S. House, *Motion Picture Films*, 89–90.

224　Crawford, *The Pressure Boys*, 98.

225　U.S. House, *Motion Picture Films*, 23.

226　Ibid., 24.

227　Ibid., 27.

228　"Population, 1924" and "Population, 1952," in *The People's Chronology, Microsoft Bookshelf*, 1995 ed., CD-ROM (Redmond, WA: Microsoft, 1995).

229　Edward S. Shapiro, "The Approach of War: Congressional Isolationism and Anti-Semitism, 1939–1941," *American Jewish History* 74.1 (1984): 47; *Cong. Rec.*, 29 May 1933, 4539, 4540.

230　Shapiro, 47; *Cong. Rec.*, 29 May 1933, 4539, 4540.

231　*Cong. Rec.*, 15 June 1933, 6226.

232　Ibid., 6225–26, 6227.

233　Ibid., 6227.

234　Ibid., 6225, 6226, 6227.

235　*Cong. Rec.*, 31 May 1933, 4711–12, quoted in Shapiro, 48; Shapiro, 48.

236　"Fortune Quarterly Survey," *Fortune*, 3d in series, 13.1 (1936): 16.

237　Donald S. Strong, *Organized Anti-Semitism in the United States: The Rise of Group Prejudice during the Decade 1930–40* (Washington, DC: American Council on Public Affairs, 1941; rpt. Westport, CT: Greenwood Press, 1979), 30.

238　*New York Times*, 21 Feb. 1939, quoted in August Raymond Ogden, *The Dies Committee: A Study of the Special House Committee for the Investigation of Un-American Activities 1938–1943* (Washington, DC: Murray, Heister, 1943), 114.

239　Christine Ann Colgan, "Warner Brothers' Crusade against the Third Reich: A Study of Anti-Nazi Activism and Film Production, 1933 to 1941" (Ph.D. diss., University of Southern California, 1986), 140.

240　"A Proclamation," rpt. in Ogden, *The Dies Committee*, 2354.

241　Ogden, 2367–68.

242　Richard Lamparski, *Whatever Became of . . . ?* (New York: Crown, 1967), 12–13.

243　Strong, *Organized Anti-Semitism*, 63, 65.

244　Alan Brinkley, *Voices of Protest* (New York: Knopf, 1982; New York: Vintage-Random House, 1983), 108.

245　John L. Spivak, "Coughlin and Ford," *New Masses*, 12 Dec. 1939, 8.

246 Charles E. Coughlin, radio address, "A Chapter on Intolerance," 11 Dec. 1938; rpt. in *Am I an Anti-Semite?* (N.p.: n.p., 1939), 104.

247 Charles E. Coughlin, radio address, "Persecution – Jewish and Christian," 20 Nov. 1938; rpt. in *Am I an Anti-Semite?* 45; idem, radio address, "Let Us Consider the Record," 27 Nov. 1938, rpt. in ibid., 64; idem, radio address, "A Christmas Message," 25 Dec. 1938, rpt. in ibid., 133.

248 Opinion Research Corporation Polls conducted in September 1939 and April 1940, quoted in Charles Herbert Stember et al., *Jews in the Mind of America* (New York: Basic Books, 1966), 113.

249 Charley Orbison, " 'Fighting Bob' Shuler: Early Radio Crusader," *Journal of Broadcasting* 21.4 (1977): 460, 461, 462, 470; Kevin Starr, *Material Dreams, Americans and the California Dream* (New York: Oxford University Press, 1990), 136, 137.

250 "My Jew Brethren," *Bob Shuler's Magazine* 3.4 (1924): 358.

251 "Comment and Opinion," *Bob Shuler's Magazine* 3.7 (1924): 426.

252 "The 'Extra,' " *Bob Shuler's Magazine* 6.1 (1927): 21.

253 Orbison, " 'Fighting Bob' Shuler," 467.

254 Leo P. Ribuffo, *The Old Christian Right* (Philadelphia: Temple University Press, 1983), 80–81, 88.

255 "Companionate Marriage," *Defender Magazine* 2 (Jan. 1928): 3; quoted in Ribuffo, 91; Ribuffo, 84–85.

256 *Defender Magazine*, quoted in Ralph Lord Roy, *Apostles of Discord* (Boston: Beacon Press, 1953), 29; "Babbitt Wins," *Defender Magazine* 5 (Feb. 1931): 4; quoted in Ribuffo, 91; Gerald B. Winrod, *The Great American Home* (Wichita, KS: Defender, 1935), 9–10, quoted in Ribuffo, *Old Christian Right*, 91.

257 Ribuffo, 98, 109, 117, 119–23; L. M. Birkhead, *The Religion of a Free Man* (Girard, KS: Haldeman-Julius, 1929), 22–23; 30; quoted in Ribuffo, 85.

258 Ribuffo, 25–26, 29, 31–43.

259 J. R. Silverman, memo to HB, 11 May 1946; in ADL, Roll no. 385, Pelley file.

260 Jay Robert Nash and Stanley Ralph Ross, *The Motion Picture Guide*, pt. 2 (Chicago: Cinebooks, 1987), 2255; Ribuffo, *Old Christian Right*, 45–46, 49–52.

261 Strong, *Organized Anti-Semitism*, 51–53.

262 Sander A. Diamond, *The Nazi Movement in the United States, 1924–1941* (Ithaca, NY: Cornell University Press, 1974), 244.

263 *Liberation*, 14 June 1939, cover.

264 Ribuffo, *Old Christian Right*, 53–54, 57; William Dudley Pelley, *Nations-in-Law* (Asheville, NC: by the author, 1935), 46, 312; William Dudley Pelley, *The Door to Revelation*, IS (Asheville, NC: Foundation Fellowship, 1936), 215; advertisement, *Liberation*, 21 Oct. 1940, 10.

265 Pelley, *Door to Revelation*, 118–19, 215.

266 "All I Know Is What I Don't Read in the Papers," *Liberation* 7.3 (1937): 11; advertisement, *Liberation*, 21 Oct. 1940, 10; "What Our Jewspapers Don't Report," *Liberation* 21 March 1939, 8; Pelley, *Door to Revelation*, 290; "Three Letters That Tell a Significant Story," *Liberation*, 7 July 1938, 6; "Liberty Magazine Dishonors Itself . . . ," *Liberation*, 21 March, 1940, 12.

267 "Lest We Forget," *Liberation*, 21 Aug. 1939, cover.

268 "Sick Movies," *Liberation*, 14 July 1940, 5.

269 "What the Liberation Movement Must Fight to a Show-Down," *Liberation*, 21 March 1940, 9; "How to Bilk a People and Make Them Like It," *Liberation*, 28 July 1939, 5; "They Would Nullify the First Amendment," *Liberation*, 7 Nov. 1939, 3.

270 Pelley, *Door to Revelation*, 120, 126–27, 221.

271 "Hollywood's Slaves Bend to the Lash," *Liberation*, 14 Dec. 1938, 2; Pelley, *Door to Revelation*, 126, 127.

272 Pelley, *Door to Revelation*, 121, 184.

273 *Liberation*, 14 Dec. 1938, 1; "Why America's Leading Jews Aren't Worried by Depression," *Liberation*, 7 May 1939, 5; Pelley, *Door to Revelation*, 127.

274 "Judah's Big Sit-Down before Judah's Walkout," *The New Liberation* 7.6 (1937): 14; Kenneth Alexander, "Who's Who in Hollywood – Find the Gentile!" *Liberation*, 14 Aug. 1938, 6.

275 Alexander, 8.

276 Alexander, 6–7, 8.

277 "All I Know," *The New Liberation* 7.3 (1937): 11; Roy, *Apostles of Discord*, 63–64.

278 Danae Clark, *Negotiating Hollywood: The Cultural Politics of Actors' Labor* (Minneapolis: University of Minneapolis Press, 1995), 65–66.

279 "Code of Fair Competition for the Motion Picture Industry," rpt. in Louis Nizer, *New Courts of Industry: Self-Regulation under the Motion Picture Code* (New York: Longacre Press, 1935), 299–300.

280 Gomery, ed., *Guide to the Microfilm Edition of the Will Hays Papers*, ix.

281 Ibid., x.

282 U.S. Senate, Hearing on *Anti "Block Booking,"* 503–4.

283 *The Churchman*, 29 June 1929, 1; quoted in Richard Maltby, "The Production Code and the Hays Office," *Grand Design: Hollywood as a Modern Business Enterprise, 1930–1939*, ed. Tino Balio, History of the American Cinema 5 (New York: Scribner's-Macmillan, 1993), 45–46.

284 U.S. House, *Motion-Picture Films*, 201.

285 Fred Eastman, "Who Controls the Movies?" *The Christian Century*, 5 Feb. 1930; 173, pt. 4 of a series; John B. Newlin, "Have Faith in Will Hays!" letter, *The Christian Century*, 26 Feb. 1930, 276.

286 "A Jew Speaks to the Jews of Hollywood," *The Christian Century*, 19 Aug. 1931, 1036; quoted in Neal Gabler, *An Empire of Their Own: How the Jews Invented Hollywood* (New York: Crown, 1988), 278.

287 "Harrison Says Hays Must Go," editorial, *Christian Century*, 21 March 1934, 381.

288 Richard Ginder, *With Ink and Crozier: A Biography of John Francis Noll, Fifth Bishop of Fort Wayne and Founder of Our Sunday Visitor* (N.p.: n.p, n.d. [1953]), 250; James M. Skinner, *The Cross and the Cinema: The Legion of Decency and the National Catholic Office for Motion Pictures, 1933–1970* (Westport, CT: Praeger, 1993), 19.

289 Ginder, 249.

290 Frank Walsh, *Sin and Censorship: The Catholic Church and the Motion Picture Industry* (New Haven, CT: Yale University Press, 1976), 86.

291 Cantwell, letter to Archbishop McNicholas, 17 July 1933, Archives of the Archdiocese of Los Angeles; quoted in Walsh, 84.

292 Walsh, 150; John J. Cantwell, letter to John T. McNicholas, 1 Sept. 1936, quoted in Walsh, 150.

293 Walsh, 87.

294 John J. Cantwell, "Priests and the Motion Picture Industry," *The Ecclesiastical Review* 90.2 (1934): 142–43.

295 Walsh, 88–89.

296 Walsh, 90; *Hollywood Reporter*, 12 March 1933, quoted in Walsh, 89.

297 Quoted in Walsh, 90.

298 Paul W. Facey, *The Legion of Decency: A Sociological Analysis of the Emergence and Development of a Social Pressure Group* (Ph.D. diss., Fordham University, 1945), Dissertations on Film Series of the Arno Press Cinema Program (New York: Arno Press, 1974), 60.

299 Stephen S. Wise, letter to Samuel H. Goldenson, TS, 17 Dec. 1934, Central Conference of American Rabbis (CCAR), 16/12, American Jewish Archives (AJA), Cincinnati, OH.

300 Sidney Mallach (?), letter to Samuel H. Goldenson, TS, 5 April 1934, CCAR, 16/12, AJA.

301 Gregory D. Black, *Hollywood Censored: Morality Codes, Catholics, and the Movies*, Cambridge Studies in the History of Mass Communications (New York: Cambridge University Press, 1994), 36–37.

302 Gomery, *Guide to . . . Hays Papers*, x.

303 Black, *Hollywood Censored*, 38–39.

304 Walsh, *Sin and Censorship*, 84.

305 Quoted in ibid.

306 Joe Breen, letter to Msgr. Lamb, undated, Archives of the Archdiocese of Philadelphia; quoted in Walsh, 101–2.

307 Report, 13 March 1934, Hays Papers; quoted in Leonard J. Leff and Jerold L. Simmons, *The Dame in the Kimono* (New York: Grove Weidenfeld, 1990), 49.

308 United States Department of Commerce, *Biennial Census: 1937, Motion Pictures*, Jan. 1939; quoted in Leo C. Rosten, *Hollywood: The Movie Colony, the Movie Makers* (New York: Harcourt, Brace, 1941), 373.

309 Stuart Berg Flexner, *Listening to America: An Illustrated History of Words and Phrases from Our Lively and Splendid Past* (New York: Simon and Schuster, 1982), 422.

310 Victor Appleton, *Tom Swift and His Talking Pictures*, The Tom Swift Series (New York: Grosset and Dunlap, 1928), 9, 175, 178, 180, 181, 197, 202.

311 Ibid., 12–13, 176–77.

312 *1939–1940 Motion Picture Almanac* (New York: Quigley), 726.

313 Patricia Erens, *The Jew in America Cinema*, Jewish Literature and Culture (Bloomington: Indiana University Press, 1984), 90, 99.

314 Ibid., 133–34.

315 Ibid., 134–35.

316 Perley Poore Sheehan, *Hollywood as a World Center* (Hollywood, CA: Hollywood Citizen Press, 1924), 80, 82.

317 Ibid., 80–81.

318 Homer Croy, *How Motion Pictures Are Made* (New York: Harper, 1918), 97, 104.

319 Jay Robert Nash and Stanley Ralph Ross, "Homer Croy," in *The Motion Picture Guide* (Chicago: Cinebooks, 1987).

320 Tay Garnett, *Tall Tales from Hollywood* (New York: Liveright, 1932), 9–10, 41, 69.

321 Ray had been a highly successful film star. Beginning as a bit player in 1912–13 Thomas H. Ince films, he had achieved critical and financial success in the 1920s. At one time, Mary Pickford, Douglas Fairbanks, Sr., Charles Chaplin, and D. W. Griffith considered asking Ray to join United Artists. Ray's most popular films – *The Old Swimmin' Hole* (Charles Ray–Associated First National, 1921) and *The Girl I Loved* (Charles Ray–United Artists, 1923) – adapted source material like a James Whitcomb Riley narrative poem, took place in countrified settings, and featured a lovable bumpkin as the main character. "These country boys are the very spine of the nation," Ray told novelist Katherine Anne Porter in 1920. "They come to town full of hopes and plans, and they grab at life like a pup grabbing at a thistle, and they don't let go when it stings. They just grab harder." Ray himself was a victim of Hollywood's vicissitudes. In 1923, he produced the costume drama *The Courtship of Miles Standish*. At the time, costume dramas were in vogue, but the film proved a costly failure, bankrupting the actor-producer. Throughout the 1930s and 1940s, Ray starred in minor roles, but he never regained his original stature. By 1942, he declared bankruptcy again, and died within the year.

322 Charles Ray, "Sans Tarte," in *Hollywood Shorts* (Los Angeles: California Graphic Press, 1935), 26–27.

323 Ray, "Tarzan Clutches," in *Hollywood Shorts*, 56; Ray, "It Stinks," in ibid., 82, 91.

324 Harry Carr, *Los Angeles, City of Dreams* (New York: Grosset and Dunlap, 1935), 290–91, 292–93.

325 Jan Gordon and Cora Gordon, *Star-Dust in Hollywood* (London: George G. Harrap, 1930), 71, 249.

326 Ibid., 68, 118.

327 R. J. Minney, *Hollywood by Starlight* (London: Chapman, Hall, 1935), 131, 136, 138.

328 J. B. Priestley, *Midnight on the Desert* (New York: Harper, 1937), 43, 170, 182.

329 *1939–1940 Motion Picture Almanac*, 726–27.

330 Edward Said, *Orientalism* (1978; New York: Vintage-Random, 1979), 229.

331 George Randolph Chester and Lilian Chester, *On the Lot and Off* (New York: Harper, 1924), 1.

332 Ibid., 37.

333 Ibid., 39.

334 Ibid., 33–34.

335 Ibid., 34–36.

336 Adela St. Johns, *The Skyrocket* (1924; New York: Cosmopolitan, 1925), 10, 51, 52, 115, 296–97, 316.

337 Ibid., 316.

338 Carl Van Vechten, *Spider Boy* (New York: Knopf, 1928), 126, 193, 260.

339 Anne Gardner, *Reputation* (New York: A. L. Burt, 1929), 151.

340 Haynes Lubou, *Reckless Hollywood* (New York: Amour Press, 1932), overleaf, 111; John Gorman, *Hollywood's Bad Boy* (Hollywood, CA): Eugene V. Brewster, 1932), 58–59, 159; Jack Hanley, *Star Lust* (1934; New York: Grayson, 1949), 197–98, 199, 225.

341 Horace Wade, *To Hell with Hollywood* (New York: Lincoln Mac Veagh – Dial Press, 1931), 39, 113, 204, 295.

342 Ibid., 113, 219, 249, 275.

343 Ibid., 55, 118, 247, 264, 274.

344 "Beasts of Berlin," *Motion Picture Guide*, 1985 ed.

345 Shepard Traube, *Glory Road* (New York: Macaulay, 1935), 127, 145–46, 170, 195, 208, 211.

346 Ibid., 195, 211.

347 Cromwell Gibbons, *Murder in Hollywood* (New York: David Kemp, 1936), 8.

348 August Raymond Ogden, *The Dies Committee: A Study of the Special House Committee for the Investigation of Un-American Activities 1938–1943* (Washington, DC: Murray, Heister, 1943), 42.

349 Hadley Cantril, ed., *Public Opinion, 1935–1946* (Princeton, NJ: Princeton University Press, 1951), 108, 164.

350 Keith Sward, *The Legend of Henry Ford* (New York: Rinehart, 1948), 159.

351 Editors of *Fortune, Jews in America* (New York: Random House, 1936), 73.

352 Albert Kuhn, letter, "Was John an Anti-Semite?" *The Christian Century* 17, Feb. 1937, 219.

353 Fred Eastman and Edward Ouellette, *Better Motion Pictures*, Learning for Life (Boston: Pilgrim Press, 1936), 33, 35.

354 Breen, memo to Lord, 5 Dec. 1937, 3, 4; quoted in Stephen Vaughn, *Ronald Reagan in Hollywood: Movies and Politics* (Cambridge: Cambridge University Press, 1994), 44.

355 Martin Quigley, *Decency in Motion Pictures* (New York: Macmillan, 1937); Moving Pictures: Their Impact on Society (N.p.: Ozer, 1971), 47; Martin Quigley to Joe Breen, 10 Jan. 1939, Quigley Papers (1:3); quoted in Leonard Leff and Jerold L. Simmons, *The Dame in the Kimono* (New York: Grove Weidenfeld, 1990), 65.

356 Joseph Breen, letter to Jack Warner, 18 June 1936, *Black Legion* file, PCA-AMPAS.

357 I. Auster, memorandum, "*Black Legion* Story," 19 June 1936, ts., *Black Legion* file, PCA-AMPAS.

358 Joseph I. Breen, Production Code Reports, *Black Legion* file, PCA-AMPAS.

359 Yellow work sheet, n.d., *Three Comrades* file, PCA-AMPAS.

360 Joseph I. Breen, letter to Jack L. Warner, TS, 30 Dec. 1938, 1, *Confessions of a Nazi Spy* file, PCA-AMPAS.

361 Karl Lischka, memorandum, no date, *Confessions of a Nazi Spy* file, PCA-AMPAS.

362 Luigi Luraschi, letter to Joseph Breen, 10 Dec. 1938, *Confessions of a Nazi Spy* file, PCA-AMPAS.

363 Ibid.

364 Ruth Inglis, "Self-Regulation in Operation," *The American Film Industry*, ed. Tino Balio, rev. ed. (Madison: University of Wisconsin Press, 1985), 378.

365 Joseph Breen, letter to Sol Lesser, 25 Nov. 1936, *The Mad Dog of Europe* file, PCA-AMPAS.

366 Douglas Fairbanks, Jr., *The Salad Days* (New York: Doubleday, 1988), 309; Fairbanks quoted in Richard R. Lingeman, *Don't You Know There's a War On? The American Home Front 1941–1945* (New York: Putnam's, 1970), 172.

367 Fairbanks, 366.

368 "Timely British Sea Epic Exceptional," review of *Convoy*, *The Hollywood Reporter*, 28 March 1941, *Convoy* file, PCA-AMPAS.

369 Review of "Confessions of a Nazi Spy," *Variety*, 28 April 1939, *Confessions of a Nazi Spy* file, PCA-AMPAS.

370 Upton Sinclair, *Money Writes* (New York: Albert and Charles Boni, 1927), 74.

371 Greg Mitchell, *The Campaign of the Century* (New York: Random House, 1992), 303–4.

372 Ibid., 424.

373 "Films and Politics," *The New York Times*, 4 Nov. 1934; quoted in Upton Sinclair, "The Movies and Political Propaganda," *The Movies on Trial*, comp. and ed. William J. Perlman (New York: Macmillan, 1936), 193.

374 H. L. Sacks, letter to Louis B. Mayer; rpt. in *Epic News*, 5 Nov. 1934; quoted in Mitchell, *Campaign of the Century*, 510.

375 Max Knepper, *Sodom and Gomorrah* (Los Angeles: End Poverty League, 1935), 12, 26, 49.

376 Ibid., 46–47, 97.

377 Ibid., 174, 178.

378 David Welch, *Propaganda and the German Cinema, 1933–1945* (Oxford: Clarendon–Oxford University Press, 1983), 15–16.

379 "Hollywood to Give German Jews Work," *New York Times*, 3 July 1933; rpt. in *The New York Times Encyclopedia of Film: 1929–1936*, ed. Gene Brown, vol. 2 (New York: Times Books, 1984), n.p.; Carl Laemmle, letter to David O. Selznick, 9 Nov. 1938, Selznick Collection, HRC-UT; Howard Suber, "Politics and Popular Culture: Hollywood at Bay, 1933–1953," in *The Jews of the West*, ed. Moses Rischin (Waltham, MA: American Jewish Historical Society, 1979), 137–38; "Senate Isolationists Run Afoul of Willkie in Movie 'Warmonger' Hearings," *Life*, 22 Sept. 1941, 21.

380 Carl Laemmle, letter to Leon Lewis, 30 Dec. 1935, ts., Carl Laemmle file, Community Relations Council (CRC), Box 1, Part 1, UA-CSUN.

381 Stephen Vaughn, *Ronald Reagan in Hollywood: Movies and Politics* (Cambridge: Cambridge University Press, 1994), 34.

382 Fred S. Meyer, letter to Leon Lewis, 28 Dec. 1936, ts., Fred S. Meyer file, CRC, Box 1, Part 1, UA-CSUN.

383 Leo C. Rosten, *Hollywood: The Movie Colony, the Movie Makers* (New York: Harcourt, Brace, 1941), 140–41.

384 Luft, "Holocaust," *Davka* 5.3 (1975): 20.

385 Leonard H. Freiberg, letter to Walter L. Barsky, ts., 12 April 1937, Records of B'nai B'rith District no. 2, American Jewish Archives, Cincinnati, Ohio.

386 W. E. Weilert, letter to Will H. Hays, 27 May 1940, *Mortal Storm* file, PCA-AMPAS.

387 " 'Bloc[k]ade' Protest by New Haven," *Knights of Columbus Hollywood Council Bulletin* 12 (1938): 2, *Blockade* file, PCA-AMPAS.

388 August Raymond Ogden, *The Dies Committee: A Study of the Special House Committee for the Investigation of Un-American Activities 1935–1943* (Washington, DC: Murray, Heister, 1943), 134.

389 Ibid., 3.

390 *Cong. Rec.* 10 May 1938, 6562, quoted in Ogden, 43.

391 Richard Lamparski, *Whatever Became of . . . ?* (New York: Crown, 1967), 32.

392 U.S. House, Special Committee to Investigate Un-American Activities and Propaganda in the United States, *Report*, 76th Cong., 1st sess. (Washington, DC: GPO, 1939), 9, quoted in Ogden, *Dies Committee*, 48.

393 U.S. House, Special Committee on Un-American Activities, *Hearings on the Investigation of Un-American Propaganda Activities in the United States*, vol. 3 of 12, 75th Cong., 3d sess. (Washington, DC: GPO, 1939), 1717.

394 Ibid., 2041.

395 John R. Poe, Jr., "Martin Dies: The Development of a Southern Anti-Communist" (M.A. thesis, University of North Carolina, Chapel Hill, 1973), 2.

396 Lamparski, *Whatever became of . . . ?* 32.

397 *Un-American Propaganda*, 2366, 3027.

398 Ogden, *Dies Committee*, 116.

399 U.S. House, Special Committee on Un-American Activities, *Investigation of Un-American Propaganda Activities in the United States*, Hearings on H. Res. 282, 76th Cong., 1st sess., vol. 5 of 12 (Washington, DC: GPO, 1939), 3581.

400 Dennis Kay McDaniel, *Martin Dies of Un-American Activities: His Life and Times* (Ph.D. diss., University of Houston, 1988; Ann Arbor, MI: UMI, 1989), 432–33.

401 Kenneth G. Crawford, *The Pressure Boys: The Inside Story of Lobbying in America* (New York: Julian Messner, 1939), 115.

402 U.S. House, *Investigation of Un-American Propaganda*, 3: 2128–29.

403 Jack Peyton, letter, 11 March 1937, in ibid., 3: 2379–80.

404 John McClafferty, report, 6 June 1939, Martin P. Quigley Papers, Special Collections Division, Georgetown University Library, Washington, DC, quoted in Francis R. Walsh, *Sin and Censorship: The Catholic Church and the Motion Picture Industry* (New Haven, CT: Yale University Press, 1996), 158.

405 Martin Dies, "The Reds in Hollywood," *Liberty*, 17 Feb. 1940, 48, pt. 1 of a series.

406 *Los Angeles Daily News*, 22 Aug. 1940, 6; quoted in Rosten, *Hollywood*, 145.

407 Rosten, 145, 147.

408 Ibid.

409 Robert Stripling, interview by McDaniel, 10 March 1988; quoted in McDaniel, *Martin Dies*, 455–56.

410 *Los Angeles Examiner*, 16 Aug. 1940, 1, 8; quoted in Rosten, 148.

411 *San Francisco Examiner*, 20 Aug. 1940, quoted in McDaniel, 451–42.

412 George Gallup and Claude Robinson, "American Institute of Public Opinion–
Surveys, 1935–38," *Public Opinion Quarterly* 2 (1938): 388.

413 Ogden, *Dies Committee*, 114.

414 Wayne S. Cole, *Roosevelt and the Isolationists, 1932–45* (Lincoln: University of
Nebraska Press, 1983), 212–13; Alan Brinkley, *Voices of Protest* (New York:
Knopf, 1982; New York: Vintage-Random, 1983), 45.

415 Ibid., 479–80.

416 *U.S. Statutes at Large*, 55: 31.

417 *1939–1940 Motion Picture Almanac* (New York: Quigley, 1939), 1191; Crawford, *The Pressure Boys*, 98.

418 Wayne S. Cole, "And Then There Were None! How Arthur H. Bandenberg
and Gerald P. Nye Separately Departed Isolationist Leadership Roles," *Behind
the Throne: Servants of Power to Imperial Presidents, 1898–1968*, ed. Thomas J.
McCormack and Walter La Feber (Madison: University of Wisconsin Press,
1993), 236.

419 *Cong. Rec.*, 24 April 1941: 3280.

420 Ibid., 3279–80.

421 Edward S. Shapiro, "The Approach of War: Congressional Isolationism and
Anti-Semitism, 1939–1941," *American Jewish History* 74.1 (1984): 49.

422 Burton K. Wheeler and Paul F. Healy, *Yankee from the West: The Candid,
Turbulent Life Story of the Yankee-Born U.S. Senator from Montana* (New York:
Octagon, 1977), 302.

423 John Donald Cameron, *Burton K. Wheeler as Public Campaigner, 1922–1942*
(Ph.D. diss., Northwestern University, 1960; Ann Arbor, MI: UMI Press,
1962), 11–12, 14.

424 Ibid., 15–16.

425 Ibid., 46–47.

426 Ibid., 104–5; Press Release no. 67, LaFollette-Wheeler Progressive Campaign
Headquarters, *LaFollette-Wheeler Campaign Scrapbook of 1924*, Division of Man-
uscripts, Library of Congress, Washington, DC; quoted in Cameron, 106.

427 Wheeler and Healy, *Yankee from the West*, 303.

428 Lamparski, *Whatever Became of . . . ?* 144–45.

429 Wheeler and Healy, 422.

430 Ibid., 423–24.

431 Ibid., 420.

432 Shapiro, "Approach of War," 51; "Wheeler Warns of Dictator Here," *The New
York Times*, 14 Feb. 1938, 6.

433 Crawford, *The Pressure Boys*, 98.

434 Cameron, *Burton K. Wheeler*, 144.

435 Cole, "And Then There Were None!" in McCormick and LaFeber, *Behind the
Throne*, 233.

436 "English Propagandists Again Defeated," *The Gaelic American*, 10 July 1926, 1.

437 Crawford, *The Pressure Boys*, 211; Wayne S. Cole, *Senator Gerald P. Nye and
American Foreign Relations* (Minneapolis: University of Minnesota Press, 1962),
84.

438 Gregory P. Pavlik, "Introduction," in *Forgotten Lessons: Selected Essays of John*

T. Flynn, ed. Gregory P. Pavlik (Irvington-on-Hudson, NY: Foundation for Economic Education, 1996), 3.

439 John T. Flynn, "Forgive Us Our Debts," *Collier's*, 25 Sept. 1937, rpt. in Pavlik, ed., *Forgotten Lessons*, 26.

440 John T. Flynn, ADL Roll no.177, Anti-Defamation League (ADL), New York.

441 Cole, in McCormick and LaFeber, *Behind the Throne*, 241.

442 Ibid., 238.

443 Ibid., 241.

444 See Pavlik, ed., *Forgotten Lessons*.

445 Cole, in McCormick and LaFeber, 237.

446 Wheeler and Healy, *Yankee from the West*, 21–22.

447 Michelle Stenehjem Gerber, *An American First: John T. Flynn and the America First Committee* (New Rochelle, NY: Arlington House, 1976), 13–14.

448 Ibid.

449 Anne Morrow Lindbergh, *War Within and Without* (New York: HBJ, 1980), 188–89; Gerber, *An American First*, 122.

450 Gerber, 122–23; *Cong. Rec.*, 4 June 1941, 4726–27

451 Shapiro, "Approach of War," 61, 62; *Tupelo Journal*, 7 June 1941, quoted in Shapiro, 63.

452 Cole, *Roosevelt and the Isolationist*, 480.

453 Reinhold Niebuhr, Union for Democratic Action press release, 24 May 1941, 1-29-16, Americans for Democratic Action Papers, State Historical Society of Wisconsin, Madison, Wisconsin; quoted in Robert Pierce Clayton, *Liberals and the Cold War: Union for Democratic Action and Americans for Democratic Action* (Ph.D. diss., University of Wisconsin, 1979) (Ann Arbor, MI: University Microfilms, 1979), 79–22832, 32–33.

454 U.S. House, Special Committee on Un-American Activities, *Hearings on the Investigation of Un-American Propaganda Activities in the United States*, vol. 4 of 12, 75th Cong., 3d sess (Washington, DC: GPO, 1939), 2360.

455 Ibid., 2359.

456 Charles Edwin Silcox and Galen M. Fisher, *Catholics, Jews and Protestants: A Study of Relationships in the United States and Canada* (New York: Institute of Social and Religious Research – Harper Bros., 1934), 47.

457 Ibid., 47.

458 Ibid., 57.

459 Ibid., 341.

460 "Roper, Elmo (Burns, Jr.)," *Encyclopædia Britannica Online* <http://www.eb.com> (accessed April 2, 1999).

461 "Fortune Quarterly Survey," *Fortune*, 3d in series, 13.1 (1936): 46, 157.

462 "Jew Shoot," *Time*, 24 Aug. 1936, 40–41.

463 John Slawson, preface, *Jews in the Mind of America*, ed. Charles Herbert Stember et al. (New York: Basic Books, 1966), ix.

464 Scott Donaldson, *Archibald MacLeish: An American Life* (Boston: Houghton, Mifflin, 1992), 231–32, 242–43.

465 Ibid., 38, 186, 230–32.

466 Ibid., 244.

467 Ibid.
468 Quoted ibid., 243.
469 Ibid.
470 Editors of *Fortune*, *Jews in America* (New York: Random House, 1936), 9.
471 Ibid., 12, 98.
472 Ibid., 15.
473 Ibid., 12–13.
474 Ibid., 11.
475 Ibid., 25.
476 Ibid., 30–31.
477 Ibid., 34.
478 Ibid., 31–32.
479 Ibid., 24–25.
480 Ibid., 10.
481 Ibid., 39–40.
482 Ibid., 43.
483 Ibid., 76–78.
484 Ibid., 59–60.
485 Ibid., 60–61.
486 Ibid., 61–62.
487 Ibid., 78–79.
488 Seymour Stern, "The Bankruptcy of Cinema as Art," in *The Movies on Trial*, ed. William J. Perlman, 253.
489 Ibid., 117.
490 Harry Alan Potamkin, "The Jew as Film-Subject," *The Jewish Tribune*, 2 May 1930, 6.
491 Ibid., 10.
492 Harry Alan Potamkin, *The Eyes of the Movie*, International Pamphlets 38 (New York: International Pamphlets, 1934), 10.
493 Ibid., 4, 5, 23; Joseph Goebbels, address, 28 March 1933; quoted in Erwin Leiser, *Nazi Cinema*, trans. Gertrud Mander and David Wilson (New York: Collier-Macmillan, 1974), 10; 23–24.
494 "Luis Trenker," *Microsoft Cinemania 97*, CD-ROM (Redmond, WA: Microsoft, 1996).
495 Douglas W. Churchill, "Everything Happens to Hollywood," *New York Times*, 23 Feb. 1936, 5.
496 Welford Beaton, editorial, "To the Jews Who Control the Films," *Hollywood Spectator*, 26 Nov. 1938, 3–4.
497 Silvia Schulman, letter to William Koch, 14 May 1936, TS, Selznick 156.2, HRC-UT, Austin; Sol Lesser, letter to David [O. Selznick], 15 Jan. 1937, TS, Selznick 166.6, HRC-UT, Austin 2.
498 D[avid] O. S[elznick], letter to George Backer, 4 May 1936, TS, HRC-UT, Austin.
499 [Maurice] Red Kann, "Notes to You from Red Kann," *Boxoffice*, 10 June 1939, 14.
500 "Injects Religious Issue into 'Spy,' " *Boxoffice*, 20 May 1939, 9.
501 Ivan Spears, "Spearheads," *Boxoffice*, 2 April 1938, 23.

502 Patricia Erens, *The Jew in American Cinema*, Jewish Literature and Culture (Bloomington: Indiana University Press, 1984), 19.

503 Michael Rogin, *Blackface, White Noise: Jewish Immigrants in the Hollywood Melting Pot* (Berkeley: Centennial – University of California Press, 1996), 209.

504 Christine Ann Colgan, "Warner Brothers' Crusade against the Third Reich: A Study of Anti-Nazi Activism and Film Production, 1933 to 1941" (Ph.D. diss., University of Southern California, 1986), 95.

505 "Give the Facts," *Hollywood Now*, 19 May 1939, 3.

506 "Memorandum of Meeting Held at Hillcrest Country Club," 13 March 1934, 1, TS, 1934 Minutes file, CRC Box 1, Part 1, CRC-UA, CSU, Northridge.

507 Rothman and Rothman, "Statement of Cash Receipts and Disbursements," 29 Nov. 1935, TS, Financial Records file, CRC Box 1, Part 1, CRC-UA, CSU, Northridge.

508 Cyrus Adler, letter to Harry A. Hollzer, 22 June 1934, 1, TS, Harry A. Hollzer file, CRC Box 1, Part 1, CRC-UA, CSU, Northridge.

509 "Memorandum of Meeting Held at Hillcrest Country Club," 13 March 1934, 2, TS, 1934 Minutes file, CRC Box 1, Part 1, CRC-UA, CSU, Northridge; "N.2. Confidential Report," 10 April 1936, TS, Henry Herzbrun file, CRC Box 1 Part I, CRC-UA, CSU, Northridge.

510 Leon Lewis, "Memorandum from Louis Greenbaum over Telephone," 23 June 1934, TS, Louis Greenbaum file, CRC Box 1, Part 1, CRC-UA, CSU, Northridge.

511 Harry Warner, transcript of speech, 15 Dec. 1937, reel 3: 2, American Committee for Christian Refugees file, Harry M. Warner papers, JLW-USC; quoted in Colgan, "Warner Brothers' Crusade," 166.

512 Selznick 154.14, HRC-UT, Austin 1; George Gallup, Public Reaction to *The Great Dictator*, poll, 24 June 1942, Selznick 3738, HRC-UT, Austin.

513 Advertisement for Ross Federal Research Corporation, *1939–1940 International Motion Picture Almanac* (New York: Quigley, 1939), 6.

514 Louis Greenbaum, letter to Leon Lewis, [April 1934], TS, Louis Greenbaum file, CRC Box 1, Part 1, CRC-UA, CSU, Northridge.

515 Leon Lewis, letter to Fred Pelton, 27 May 1936, 1, TS, Fred Pelton file, CRC Box 1, Part 1, CRC-UA, CSU, Northridge.

516 Mrs. Leo Straus, letter to L. A. Rose, 5 Aug. 1936, Henry Herzbrun file, CRC Box 1, Part 1, CRC-UA, CSU, Northridge; T. Keith Glennan, memo to Henry Herzburn, 17 Aug. 1936, TS, Henry Herzbrun file, CRC Box 1, Part 1, CRC-UA, CSU, Northridge.

517 U.S. Congress, House, *Un-American Propaganda*, 345.

518 "An American Born," letter to Jack [L.] Warner, 1 Jan. 1939, TS, Warner Bros., Film and Television Archives (WB), Doheny Library, University of Southern California, Los Angeles; T. Haesle, letter to Jack [L.] Warner, 6 Sept. 1939, MS, WB, Doheny–USC, Los Angeles, 1–4; Ruth Herrimann, letter to William Hayes [*sic*], 3 Feb. 1939, WB, Doheny–USC, Los Angeles; J. J. Bone, letter to Jack L. Warner, 14 July 1939, TS, WB, Doheny–USC, Los Angeles, 2; J. P. Thompson, letter to Warner Bro[ther]s, 28 June 193[9], MS, WB, Doheny–USC, Los Angeles.

519 Charles Chaplin, dialogue continuity for *The Great Dictator*, reel 3, sec. B, PCA-AMPAS, Beverly Hills, 2.

520 David O. Selznick, memo to Lowell V. Calvert, 2 April 1936, Selznick 154.12, HRC-UT, Austin; D[avid] O. Selznick, memo to [Henry] Ginsberg 23 April 1936, TS, Selznick 156.2, HRC-UT, Austin.

521 [John Hay] "Jock" Whitney, telegram to [David O.] Selznick, 2 June 1936, TS, Selznick 3739, HRC-UT, Austin; D[avid] O. S[elznick], letter to John Hay "Jock" Whitney, 1 June 1936, TS, Selznick 3739, HRC-UT, Austin 2.

522 D[avid] O. S[elznick], letter to Herbert Bayard Swope, 1 June 1936, Selznick 3739, HRC-UT, Austin.

523 "Warners, MOT, Public Battle over Nazi Pic," *Daily Variety*, 22 Jan. 1938, 4, *March of Time "Nazi" Film vs. Warners Scrapbook*, Harry M. Warner Papers, JLW-USC, quoted in Colgan, "Warner Brothers' Crusade," 154; Colgan, 157.

524 Harry Warner, letter to Henry R. Luce, 2 Nov. 1938, Correspondence 1938 file, Harry M. Warner Papers, JLW-USC, quoted in Colgan, 235.

525 Harry Warner, *United We Survive, Divided We Fall!* pamphlet, 6–7, Harry M. Warner Speeches and Interviews file, Harry M. Warner Papers, Box 56, JLW-USC.

526 Leon L. Lewis, letter to Eddie Cantor, 13 Jan. 1937, TS, Eddie Cantor file, CRC Box 1, Part 1, CRC-UA, CSU, Northridge.

527 Leon Lewis, letter to David Blumberg, 2 Nov. 1933, TS, David Blumberg file, CRC Box 1, Part 1, CRC-UA, CSU, Northridge.

528 Morris D. Waldman, letter to David O. Selznick, 29 April 1936, TS, Selznick 155.15, HRC-UT, Austin; D[avid] O. S[elznick], letter to Morris D. Waldman, 6 May 1936, TS, Selznick 155.15, HRC-UT, Austin; D[avid] O. S[elznick], letter to Laudy L. Lawrence, 20 May 1942, TS, Selznick 303.17, HRC-UT, Austin.

529 Morris D. Waldman, letter to Walter S. Hilborn, 26 Feb. 1941, TS, Selznick 168.12, HRC-UT, Austin.

530 D[avid] O. S[elznick], letter to George Backer, 25 June 1937, TS, Selznick 166.8; George Backer, letter to David O. Selznick, 8 July 1936, TS, Selznick 166.8, HRC-UT, Austin 1.

531 David O. Selznick, notes, 16 May 1942, TS, Selznick 3739, HRC-UT, Austin 1; Phil Berg, letter to David [O.] Selznick, 19 May 1942, TS, Selznick 3739, HRC-UT, Austin 1.

532 Selznick, notes, Selznick Papers, HRC-UT, Austin 3.

533 Berg, letter to Selznick, 19 May 1942, 1, 2.

534 Mendel B. Silberberg, letter to Maurice Wertheim, 29 May 1942, TS, Selznick 303.7, HRC-UT, Austin 1–2.

535 Norman Salit, letter to David O. Selznick, 8 Dec. 1944, TS, Selznick 3744, HRC-UT, Austin.

536 *1939–1940 Motion Picture Almanac* (New York: Quigley, 1939), 726.

537 Colgan, "Warner Brothers' Crusade," 111.

538 Frances Selditz, letter to James Wingate, 29 Nov. 1933; Joseph Jonah Cummins, letter to Harry Brand, 22 Nov. 1933; Darryl F. Zanuck, letter to Will H. Hays, 27 Dec. 1933, 1; all transcribed in *The House of Rothschild* file, PCA-AMPAS, Beverly Hills.

539 James Wingate, letter to Darryl Zanuck, 2 Dec. 1933, TS, *The House of Rothschild* file, PCA-AMPAS, Beverly Hills.

540 Joseph I. Breen, letter to Will H. Hays, 11 Dec. 1933, 2, TS, in ibid.

541 Frederick L. Herron, letter to James Wingate, 7 Dec. 1933, TS, in ibid.

542 Joseph I. Breen, letter to Frederick L. Herron, 12 Dec. 1933, TS, in ibid.

543 Darryl F. Zanuck, letter to James Wingate, 4 Dec. 1933, TS, in ibid.

544 Joseph I. Breen, telegram to Will H. Hays, 14 Dec. 1933, TS, in ibid.

545 Will H. Hays, letter to Darryl Zanuck, 21 Dec. 1933, TS, in ibid.

546 Darryl F. Zanuck, letter to Will H. Hays, 27 Dec. 1933, TS, in ibid.

547 Darryl F. Zanuck, letter to Will H. Hays, 27 Dec. 1933, 1–2, TS, in ibid.

548 Darryl F. Zanuck, letter to Joseph I. Breen, 24 Feb. 1934, TS, in ibid.

549 Joseph I. Breen, memo to Will H. Hays, 6 March 1934, TS, in ibid.

550 Joseph Jonah Cummins, letter to Darryl F. Zanuck, 16 March 1934, TS, in ibid.

551 Darryl F. Zanuck, letter to Joseph I. Breen, 24 March 1934, TS, in ibid.

552 20th Century Pictures, Inc., Souvenir Booklet for *The House of Rothschild* ([Hollwyood]: by the author, [1934]), in ibid.

553 Joseph I. Breen, memo to Will H. Hays, 6 March 1934, TS, PCA-AMPAS, Beverly Hills.

554 Joseph I. Breen, 1 March 1934, in ibid.

555 Joseph Breen, letter to Jack Warner, 2 Feb. 1937, 3, TS, *The Life of Emile Zola* file, PCA-AMPAS, Beverly Hills.

556 Joseph I. Breen, letter to Walter Wanger, 4 Jan. 1938, 1, TS; Breen, letter, 3 Feb. 1937, 2, TS.; Breen, letter, 22 Feb. 1937, 1, TS, *Blockade* file, PCA-AMPAS, Beverly Hills.

557 Derek B. Mayne, report to Albert Deane, 30 June 1939, TS., PCA-AMPAS, Beverly Hills.

558 Colgan, "Warner Brothers' Crusade," 275.

559 Gradwell Sears, letter to Jack Warner, 10 April 1939, Gradwell Sears file, box 9, JLW-USC, quoted in Colgan, 276.

560 Ivan Spear, "Spearheads," *Boxoffice*, 2 April 1938, 23.

561 Norman Burnstine [Burnside], letter to Henry Blanke, 27 July 1938, *The Story of Dr. Ehrlich's Magic Bullet* file, WBC-USC, quoted in Colgan, 534. According to Colgan, Burnstine changed his name to Burnside in October 1939.

562 "Literature, 1791," *The People's Chronology*, Microsoft *Bookshelf 1996–97* CD-ROM (Redmond, WA: Microsoft Corporation, 1996).

563 Arthur Duff-Cooper, "The United States Risk Losing Freedom of Speech Because of Fear of Propaganda," *Paris Soir*, 17 March 1940, trans. Harold Smith, in Harold Smith, letter to Joseph I. Breen, 18 March 1940, *Dr. Ehrlich's Magic Bullet* file, PCA-AMPAS, Beverly Hills.

564 "O.K. to Use Word 'Syphilis' in Movie," in Joseph I. Breen, letter to Charles Einfeld, 20 Nov. 1939, TS, *Dr. Ehrlich's Magic Bullet* file, PCA-AMPAS, Beverly Hills.

565 Production Code Administration, letter to Jack L. Warner, 20 Dec. 1939, TS, in ibid.

566 Joseph I. Breen, letter to Harold L. Smith, 15 April 1940, TS, in ibid.

567 Joseph I. Breen, letter to Will H. Hays, 15 April 1940: 4, TS, in ibid.

568 Hal Wallis, letter to Joe Breen, 30 Aug. 1939, TS, in ibid.

569 Ian Hamilton, *Writers in Hollywood* (New York: Harper-Burlingame, 1990), 158.

570 Ibid., 164, 165.

571 Nathanael West, *Day of the Locust*, in *The Complete Works of Nathanael West* (New York: Octagon–Farrar, Straus, Giroux, 1980), 275.

572 Ibid., 273.

573 Matthew J. Bruccoli, *"The Last of the Novelists"* (Carbondale: Southern Illinois University Press, 1977), 100.

574 F. Scott Fitzgerald, "A Man in the Way," in *The Hobby Stories*, The Stories of F. Scott Fitzgerald 3 (Middlesex: Penguin, 1983), 37.

575 Fitzgerald, "Boil Some Water – Lots of It," in ibid., 43–50.

576 Jonas Spatz, "Fitzgerald, Hollywood, and the Myth of Success," in *The Thirties*, ed. Warren French (Deland, FL: Everett Edwards, 1967), 35.

577 F. Scott Fitzgerald, *The Last Tycoon* (New York: Scribner's, 1969), 20–21; Spatz, 35.

578 Fitzgerald, *The Last Tycoon*, 54, 77.

579 Ibid., 58, 90.

580 John Dos Passos, "A Note on Fitzgerald," in F. Scott Fitzgerald, *The Crack-Up*, ed. Edmund Wilson (New York: New Directions, 1945), 338–45.

581 "Data for Bulletin of Screen Achievement Records," n.d., *A Star Is Born* file, PCA-AMPAS, Beverly Hills.

582 Hamilton, Writers in Hollywood, 155; Budd Schulberg, interview with Victor S. Navasky, in Victor S. Navasky, *Naming Names* (1980; New York: Penguin, 1981), 240.

583 Buddy Schulberg, "In Your Own Backyard," synopsis, 1932, in Catalogue of RKO Stories: Unproduced Material, vol. 1, 1 June 1936, 88, Selznick Papers, HRC-UT, Austin.

584 Patricia Erens, *The Jew in American Cinema*, Jewish Literature and Culture (Bloomington: Indiana University Press, 1984), 16.

585 Sander L. Gilman, *Jewish Self-Hatred* (Baltimore: Johns Hopkins University Press, 1986), 9; Virgil Lokke, *The Literary Image of Hollywood* (Ph.D diss., State University of Iowa, 1955), Doctoral Dissertation Series 14 (Ann Arbor, MI: UMI, n.d.), 125; Fred T. Marsh, review of *What Makes Sammy Run?* "Here Is an All-American Heel!" *New York Herald Tribune Books*, 30 March 1941, 2.

586 Navasky, *Naming Names*, 239; Schulberg, in Navasky, 240.

587 Schulberg, in Navasky, 239, 240, 242; Navasky, 240.

588 Budd Schulberg, *What Makes Sammy Run?* (1941 New York: Modern Library–Random House, 1952), 92.

589 Ibid., 211–212, 285, 303.

590 Ibid., 118–19, 220.

591 Ibid., 249.

592 Erens, *The Jew in American Cinema*, 19.

593 Philip J. Hartung, review of *What Makes Sammy Run?* by Budd Schulberg, *Commonweal*, 6 June 1941, 163.

594 Leo C. Rosten, *Hollywood: The Movie Colony, The Movie Makers* (New York: Harcourt, Brace, 1941), v.

595 Ibid., 31.

596 Ibid., vii, 30.

597 "Leo Rosten, RIP," *National Review* 24 March 1997, 18, *Academic Search Elite*, EBSCOhost, Indiana Unversity–Purdue University Fort Wayne Helmke Library, 29 June 1999, <*http://www.epnet.com/*>.

598 Louis Harap, *Dramatic Encounters*, Contributions in Ethnic Studies 20 (New York: Greenwood Press, 1987), 34.

599 Christine Ann Colgan, "Warner Brothers' Crusade against the Third Reich: A Study of Anti-Nazi Activism and Film Production, 1933 to 1941" (Ph.D. diss., University of Southern California, 1986), 716.

600 Finlay McDermid, memorandum to Roy Obringer, 12 June 1941, *All Through the Night* papers, WBC-USC, quoted in Colgan 717.

601 Clifton Fadiman, review of *Hollywood: The Movie Colony, The Movie Makers*, *New Yorker Magazine*, 29 Nov. 1941, 1250.

602 John Gassner, review of *Hollywood: The Movie Colony, The Movie Makers*, *Atlantic Monthly*, January 1941, 320.

603 Anthony Bower, review of *Hollywood: The Movie Colony, The Movie Makers*, *The Nation*, 6 Dec. 1941, 480.

604 Garth Jowett, *Film: The Democratic Art* (Boston: Little, Brown, 1976), 267.

605 Rosten, *Hollywood*, vii.

606 Ibid., vi.

607 Ibid., v.

608 Ibid., ix.

609 Ibid., 55.

610 Ibid., 3.

611 Ibid., vi.

612 Ibid., 5.

613 Ibid., 7.

614 Floyd L. Ruch, *A Research Memorandum on Methods of Studying Public Opinion in Relation to the War* (New York: Social Science Research Council, 1942), 8.

615 Rosten, *Hollywood*, 21.

616 Ibid., 77.

617 Ibid., 178.

618 Ibid., 16–17.

619 Ibid., 267.

620 Ibid., 23.

621 Ibid., 356.

622 Ibid., 162.

623 Ibid., 360.

624 Ibid., 151.

625 Ibid., 153.

626 Ibid., 142.

627 Ibid., 87.

628 Ibid., 5.
629 Ibid., 4–5.
630 Frederick Lewis Allen, *Lords of Creation* (New York: Harper, 1935), 84, quoted in Rosten, 8.
631 Rosten, *Hollywood*, 9.
632 Ibid., 9.
633 Ibid., 15, 269.
634 Ibid., 6.
635 Ibid., 67.
636 Ibid., 245.
637 Ibid., 67.
638 Ibid., 68.
639 Charles Herbert Stember et al., *Jews in the Mind of America* (New York: Basic Books, 1966), 121.
640 Ibid., 123.
641 *Knights of Columbus Hollywood Council Bulletin* 12 (1938), *Blockade* file, PCA-AMPAS, Beverly Hills.
642 Town Meeting, 3 March 1941, 16–17, quoted in Rosten, *Hollywood*, 1941, 154.
643 "Politicos Bait Pix, Radio," *Variety*, 6 Aug. 1941, 1.
644 Gerald P. Nye, "War Propaganda," radio address, St. Louis, 1 Aug. 1941; reprinted in *Vital Speeches of the Day*, 1 Sept. 1941, 721.
645 Nye, 720.
646 Ibid., 721.
647 J. C. White, letter to Henry Stimson, 27 May 1936, 1, TS, *The Charge of the Light Brigade* file, PCA-AMPAS, Beverly Hills.
648 K. R. M. Short, *Screening the Propaganda of British Air Power: From R.A.F. (1935) to The Lion Has Wings (1939)*, Studies in War and Film 6 (Wiltshire, UK: Flicks Books, 1997) 22–23, 41.
649 Ibid., 99–100; F[rancis] S. Harmon, telegram to Joseph I. Breen, 4 Dec. 1939, TS, *Lion Has Wings* file, PCA-AMPAS, Beverly Hills.
650 S. Person Crump, postcard to the Hays [PCA] Office, 8 Dec. 1939, TS, in ibid.
651 Nye, "War Propaganda," 720–21.
652 K. R. M. Short, "*That Hamilton Woman* (1941): Propaganda, Feminism and the Production Code," *Historical Journal of Film, Radio and Television* 11.1 (1991), *Academic Search Elite*, EBSCOhost Direct, Indiana University–Purdue University Helmke Library, Fort Wayne, 1 July 1999 <*http://www.epnet.com/*>.
653 Joseph I. Breen, memo to Will H. Hays, 11 March 1941, TS, *Man Hunt* file, PCA-AMPAS, Beverly Hills.
654 Nye, "War Propaganda," 721.
655 Ibid.; "Sen. Nye and the Movies; Accuses Morgan; Facts about Jewish Producers, Catholic Pressure," *In Fact*, 25 Aug. 1941, reprinted in AMPAS, *Press Clipping File Hearings*, Build-Up sec., G, PCA-AMPAS, Beverly Hills.
656 Nye, "War Propaganda," 721.
657 Ibid.
658 Ibid., 722.
659 Quoted in U.S. Congress, Senate, Subcommittee of the Committee on Inter-

state Commerce, *Propaganda in Motion Pictures*, 1942, 16; Robert Clayton Pierce, *Liberals and the Cold War: Union for Democratic Action and Americans for Democratic Action* (Ph.D. diss., University of Wisconsin–Madison, 1979; Ann Arbor, MI: University Microfilms, 1979), 21, 56. Wayne S. Cole lists Kingdon's affiliation as the University of Newark; see Wayne S. Cole, *Senator Gerald P. Nye and American Foreign Relations* (Minneapolis: University of Minnesota Press, 1962), 146. Shortly thereafter, Kingdon became head of the UDA. By May 1942, he was calling on behalf of the UDA for Americans to vote isolationists out of Congress. See Pierce, 57, and John Ehrman, *The Rise of Neoconservatism: Intellectuals and Foreign Affairs, 1945–1994* (New Haven, CT: Yale University Press, 1994); chap. 1 is available on the Internet.

660 Quoted in U.S., Congress, Senate, Subcommittee of Committee on Interstate Commerce, *Propaganda in Motion Pictures*, Hearings, 99th Cong., 1st sess., S. Res. 152 (Washington, DC: GPO, 1942), 9, 10.

661 Quoted in ibid., 10.

662 Wayne S. Cole, *Senator Gerald P. Nye and American Foreign Relations* (Minneapolis: University of Minnesota Press, 1962), 195.

663 Ibid., 84.

664 Larry Ceplair and Steven Englund, *The Inquisition in Hollywood* (Berkeley: University of California Press, 1983), 161.

665 Richard Lamparski, *Whatever Became of . . . ?* (New York: Crown, 1967), 22.

666 Ibid., 22.

667 Charles A. Lindbergh, transcript of radio address, 19 May 1940; in ADL roll no. 298 Lindbergh, ADL, New York; Charles A. Lindbergh, transcript of radio address, 17 June 1940, ADL, New York.

668 " 'British, Jews and Roosevelt Administration' Seek to Get U.S. Into War, Says Lindbergh," *St. Louis Star-Times*, 12 Sept. 1941, 6.

669 Quoted in [L. M. Birkhead], *Is Lindbergh a Nazi?* ([Kansas City: Friends of Democracy, Inc., 1941]), 2, 15.

670 "A Letter to a Fellow Jew" (N.p.: B'nai B'rith, [1941]).

671 Ibid.

672 Opinion Research Corporation Poll, October 1941; quoted in Stember et al., *Jews in the Mind of America*, 111.

673 Opinion Research Corporation and Gallup Polls, October 1941; quoted in Stember et al., 115; George H. Gallup, "Pro-and Anti-War Groups," *The Gallup Poll: Public Opinion, 1935–1971*, 25 Oct. 1941 (New York: Random House, 1972), 302–3.

674 Anne Morrow Lindbergh, *War Within and Without* (New York: HBJ, 1980), 220.

675 Ibid., 223.

676 Martin Quigley, introduction to *The 1941–42 International Motion Picture Almanac* (New York: Quigley, 1941), v.

677 Fiorello H. LaGuardia, letter to Ernest W. McFarland, 11 Sept. 1941, reprinted in James E. McMillan, ed., *The Ernest W. McFarland Papers: The United States Senate Years, 1940–1952* (Prescott, AZ: Sharlot Hall Museum Press, 1995), 48.

678 Burton K. Wheeler and Paul F. Healy, *Yankee from the West: The Candid,*

Turbulent Life Story of the Yankee-Born U.S. Senator from Montana (New York: Octagon, 1977), 323, 366.

679 U.S. Congress, Senate, Subcommittee of Committee on Interstate Commerce, Propaganda in Motion Pictures, Hearings, 1912, 1.

680 Ibid., 2.

681 Ibid.

682 Ibid., 2, 66–68; "Neutrality Act," *The Concise Columbia Encyclopedia* 3d ed. (New York: Columbia University Press, 1995), in *Microsoft Bookshelf '95*, Microsoft, CD-ROM.

683 "Says the Public Likes Propaganda in Their Films," *Motion Picture Herald*, 9 Aug. 1941, 26.

684 Floyd R. Ruch, *A Research Memorandum on Methods of Studying Public Opinion in Relation to the War* (New York: Social Science Research Council, 1942), 8.

685 John Thomas Anderson, *Senator Burton K. Wheeler and United States Foreign Relations* (Ph.D. diss., University of Virginia, 1982; Ann Arbor, MI: UMI, 1990), 239.

686 Ibid., 234.

687 U.S. Congress, Senate, *Propaganda in Motion Pictures*, Hearings, 1942, 418.

688 Ibid., 10.

689 Charles W. Tobey, letter to Judge Page, 29 April 1938, *Tobey Papers*, Box 78, quoted in Marjory Zoet Bankson, "The Isolationism of Senator Charles W. Tobey" (thesis, University of Alaska, 1971), 83.

690 *Propaganda*, Hearings (1942), 284.

691 Ibid., 35, 60, 81; "The Man I Married (1940)," *Microsoft Cinemania '96*, CD-ROM (Redmond, WA: Microsoft Corporation, 1995).

692 *Propaganda*, Hearings (1942), 329.

693 K. R. M. Short, "Hollywood Fights Anti-Semitism, 1940–1945," *Film and Radio Propaganda in World War II*, ed. K.R.M. Short (London: Croom, Helm, 1983), 154.

694 Georg Gyssling, letter to Joseph I. Breen, 31 Oct. 1938, TS, *The Great Dictator* file, PCA-AMPAS, Beverly Hills.

695 J. Brooke Wilkinson, telegram to Joseph I. Breen, 3 Feb. 1939, TS, *The Great Dictator* file, PCA-AMPAS, Beverly Hills.

696 Walter W. McKenna, letter to Robert R. Reynolds, 17 Feb. 1939, TS, in ibid.

697 Production Code Administration report, 22 Dec. 1941, *The Man I Married* file, PCA-AMPAS, Beverly Hills.

698 Richard Lamparski, *Whatever Became of . . . ?* (New York: Crown, 1967), 120–21.

699 Joseph I. Breen, letter to Jason S. Joy, 26 April 1940: 2, TS, *The Man I Married* file, PCA-AMPAS, Beverly Hills.

700 *Propaganda*, Hearings (1942), 42–43, 44, 46–47.

701 Christine Ann Colgan, "Warner Brothers' Crusade against the Third Reich: A Study of Anti-Nazi Activism and Film Production, 1933 to 1941," (Ph.D. diss., University of Southern California, 1986), 688.

702 " 'Fight for Freedom' Challenges Senate Probe of U.S. Films," *Christian Science*

Monitor, 9 Sept. 1941; reprinted in AMPAS, Build-Up sec., S, AMPAS, Beverly Hills.

703 Colgan, 688.

704 Ibid., 687.

705 Stephen Vaughn, *Ronald Reagan in Hollywood: Movies and Politics* (Cambridge: Cambridge University Press, 1994) 101.

706 *Propaganda*, Hearings (1942), 35.

707 Lowell Mellett, memorandum to Franklin D. Roosevelt, 27 Aug. 1941, Official Files 73, FDRL, quoted in Colgan, 688.

708 McMillan, *McFarland Papers*, 61.

709 Raymond Moley, *The Hays Office* (New York: Bobbs-Merrill, 1945), 121; Colgan, "Warner Brothers' Crusade," 690–91.

710 William R. Wilkerson, "Industry Finally Awakens," *Hollywood Reporter*, 3 Sept. 1941, 1.

711 Wheeler and Healy, *Yankee from the West*, 389.

712 McMillan, 62; Gerald P. Nye, audiotape, recorded 24 Oct. 1940, Herbert Hoover Library, SRT-75/227 (3 3/4 ips, 7" reel). I have not listened to the tape, but have gone on the description of it provided in the online database WorldCat.

713 *Propaganda*, Hearings (1922), 83; McMillan 62.

714 McMillan, 57.

715 *Propaganda*, Hearings (1942), 1, 5–6.

716 Wendell L. Willkie, letter to D. Worth Clark, 8 Sept. 1941, reprinted in United States 19; United States 17.

717 *Propaganda*, Hearings (1942), 7.

718 Ibid., 7, 11.

719 Ibid., 12, 17, 25.

720 Ibid., 47.

721 Ibid., 11, 37, 47.

722 Ibid., 47.

723 Ibid., 12, 15, 17.

724 Ibid., 12, 15, 16.

725 Ibid., 10, 11.

726 Ibid., 10, 11.

727 Ibid., 11.

728 Ibid., 23, 41.

729 Ibid., 38–39, 41.

730 Review of *The Great Commandment*, *Film Daily*, 5 Oct. 1939, in *The Great Commandment* file, PCA-AMPAS, Beverly Hills.

731 Ibid., review.

732 *Propaganda*, Hearings (1942), 8, 10–11; James K. Friedrich, letter to Gerald P. Nye, 11 Aug. 1941, reprinted in United States 50. Friedrich later changed his name to the less German-sounding Frederick.

733 Review of *The Great Commandment*, *Variety*, 21 Oct. 1942, in *The Great Commandment* file, PCA-AMPAS, Beverly Hills.

734 *Propaganda*, Hearings (1942), 212.

735 Ibid., 192–93.

736 Ibid., 95.

737 Ibid., 106.

738 Ibid., 25, 26–32.

739 Ibid., 213.

740 Ibid., 24.

741 Ibid., 11, 12, 37–38.

742 Ibid., 381–82.

743 Ibid., 69–70.

744 Ibid., 376.

745 Ibid., 62.

746 Ibid., 8, 40.

747 Ibid., 77–78.

748 AFC Bulletin no. 496, 16 Aug. 1941, in folder "America First Committee, Bulletins, 1941 August," Subject File, Wood Papers, quoted in Anderson 233.

749 *Propaganda, Hearings* (1942), 6–7. The 1951 Supreme Court decision on the *Miracle* case eventually gave film First Amendment protections.

750 Ruch, *A Research Memorandum*, 25.

751 Margaret Frakas, "Why the Movie Investigation," *Christian Century*, 24 Sept. 1941, 1172.

752 Colgan, "Warner Brothers' Crusade," 713.

753 "Die Staatsfeinde," *The Free American and Deutscher Weckruf und Beobachter* 18 Sept. 1941, reprinted and transcribed in AMPAS, Second Recess sec., BB, AMPAS, Beverly Hills.

754 McMillan, *McFarland Papers*, 28.

755 Ibid., 25.

756 Ibid., 49, 51.

757 Ernest W. McFarland, *Mac: The Autobiography of Ernest W. McFarland* (N.p.: by the author, 1979), 62.

758 Reprinted in McMillan, *McFarland Papers*, 53.

759 "The Skinny," *Tucson Weekly*, 5 Jan. 1995, Internet; *Propaganda*, Hearings (1992), 2, 5. Later McFarland was instrumental, as Senate Majority Leader, of setting the protection of "the public interest, convenience and necessity" as a priority for the Federal Communications Commission. See "KTVK Petitions FCC to Revoke Scripps Howard Licenses," *Satellite Journal International* 29 Sept. 1994, Internet.

760 Ceplair and Englund, *The Inquisition in Hollywood*, 161.

761 [Charles Butterworth], "Senate Isolationists Run Afoul of Willkie in Movie 'Warmonger' Hearings," *Life*, 22 Sept. 1941, 1, 22.

762 Sam O'Neal, "President Puts Movie Probers on the Pan," *St. Louis Star-Times*, 17 Sept. 1941 (evening ed.), 2.

763 Ibid., 2.

764 "Propaganda or History," *The Nation* 20 Sept. 1941, 241.

765 *Propaganda*, Hearings (1942), 209.

766 Ibid., 211, 212.

767 Ibid., 338–39.

768 Ibid., 423.
769 Ibid., 423.
770 Reprinted in ibid., 21–22.
771 Quoted in ibid., 18.
772 Reprinted in ibid., 19.
773 Reprinted in ibid., 19.
774 Reprinted in ibid., 21.
775 Ibid., 212.
776 Ibid., 410.
777 Ibid., 246.
778 Ibid., 372.
779 Ibid., 381.
780 Ibid., 340.
781 Ibid., 421.
782 Ibid., 208.
783 Ibid., 327. Hopkins was an advisor to Roosevelt.
784 Ibid., 340.
785 Ibid., 342.
786 Ibid., 339.
787 Ibid., 345.
788 Ibid., 358.
789 McMillan *Mac*, 56.
790 Vaughn, *Ronald Reagan in Hollywood*, 101.
791 McMillan, *Mac*, 55.
792 *Propaganda*, Hearings (1942), 52, 54–55.
793 Reprinted in ibid., 21–22.
794 Mark Thornton, "How Antitrust Ruined the Movies," *The Free Market* 14.6 (1996): 1.
795 *The Best Years of Our Lives*, directed by William Wyler, performed by Myrna Loy, Fredric March, Dana Andrews, and Teresa Wright, Goldwyn, 1946.
796 Review of *The Motion Picture Industry – A Pattern of Control, Fact and Fancy in the T.N.E.C. Monographs: Reviews of the 43 Monographs Issued by the Temporary National Economic Committee*, compiled by John Scoville and Noel Sargent, *The Right Wing Individualist Tradition in America* (New York: National Association of Manufacturers, 1942; New York: Arno Press New York Times, 1972), 783.
797 Ibid., 783.
798 Ibid., 783, 789.
799 U.S. Senate, Temporary National Economic Committee, *The Motion Picture Industry – A Pattern of Control* by Daniel Bertrand, Wilmoth Duane Evans, and Edna Lillian Blanchard, Temporary National Economic Committee Investigation of Concentration of Economic Power 43 (Washington, DC: GPO, 1941; New York: Arno Press, 1978), 56.
800 U.S. Senate, *The Motion Picture Industry*, ix.
801 Charles Herbert Stember, "The Recent History of Public Attitudes," in Stember et al., *Jews in the Mind of America* (New York: Basic Books, 1966), 80.

802 ADL roll no. 496, Upshaw file, ADL, New York.
803 John Howard Thomas, *Senator Burton K. Wheeler and United States Foreign Relations* (Ph.D. diss., University of Virginia, 1982; Ann Arbor, MI: UMI, 1990), 6, 333.

Bibliography

Allport, Gordon. *The Nature of Prejudice*. Boston: Beacon Press, 1954.

Anderson, John Thomas. *Senator Burton K. Wheeler and United States Foreign Relations*. Ph.D. diss., University of Virginia, 1982. Ann Arbor, MI: UMI, 1990.

Appel, John J. "Jews in American Caricature: 1820–1914." *American Jewish History* 71.1 (1981): 103–33.

Appleton, Victor. *Tom Swift and His Talking Pictures*. The Tom Swift Series. New York: Grosset and Dunlap, 1928.

Baer, John W. "The Strange Origin of the Pledge of Allegiance." *Propaganda Review* (Summer 1989). Online. The Electronic Frontier Foundation. Internet. 20 December 1998. Available http://www.eff.org/pub/CAF/civil-liberty/pledge.history.

Balio, Tino, ed. *The American Film Industry*. Rev. ed. Madison: University of Wisconsin Press, 1985.

   Grand Design: Hollywood as a Modern Business Enterprise, 1930–1939. History of the American Cinema 5. New York: Scribner's-Macmillan, 1993.

Bernstein, Victor H. "Ford Empire Played Both Sides in War." *Technocracy Digest* (1945). Online. Technocracy. Internet. 9 July 1998. Available http://www.technocracy.org/periodicals/social-trends/126/ford.html.

Bettelheim, Bruno, and Morris Janowitz. *The Dynamics of Prejudice*. New York: Harper, 1950.

[Birkhead, L. M.] *Is Lindbergh a Nazi?* Kansas City, MO: Friends of Democracy, 1941.

Birmingham, Stephen. *"The Rest of Us."* Boston: Little, Brown, 1984.

Birdwell, Michael E. *Celluloid Soldiers: The Warner Bros. Campaign against Nazism*. New York: NYU Press, 1999.

Black, Gregory D. *Hollywood Censored: Morality Codes, Catholics, and the Movies*. Cambridge Studies in the History of Mass Communications. Cambridge: Cambridge University Press, 1994.

Bordwell, David, Janet Staiger, and Kristin Thompson. *The Classical Hollywood Cinema: Film Style and Mode of Production to 1960*. New York: Columbia University Press, 1985.

Brasol, Boris L. *The World at the Cross Roads*. Boston: Small, Maynard, 1921.

Brinkley, Alan. *Voices of Protest*. New York: Knopf, 1982. New York: Vintage-Random, 1983.

Brown, Gene, ed. *The New York Times Encyclopedia of Film: 1929–1936*. New York: Times Books, 1984.

Brownlow, Kevin. *Behind the Mask of Innocence*. New York: Knopf, 1990.

Bruccoli, Matthew J. *"The Last of the Novelists."* Carbondale: Southern Illinois University Press, 1977.

Cameron, John Donald. *Burton K. Wheeler as Public Campaigner, 1922–1942*. Ph.D. diss., Northwestern University, 1960. Ann Arbor, MJ: UMI, 1962.

Cantril, Hadley, ed. *Public Opinion, 1935–1946*. Princeton, NJ: Princeton University Press, 1951.

Cantwell, John J. "Priests and the Motion Picture Industry." *The Ecclesiastical Review* 90.2 (1934): 136–46.

Carey, James. *Communication as Culture: Essays on Media and Society*. Media and Popular Culture. Boston: Unwin, Hyman, 1989.

Carr, Harry. *Los Angeles, City of Dreams*. New York: Grosset and Dunlap, 1935.

Century, Douglas. "Hollywood Scuffle: Turning Moguls into Monsters." *Forward* 16 (December 1994): 1. Ethnic NewsWatch.

Ceplair, Larry, and Steven Englund. *The Inquisition in Hollywood*. Berkeley: University of California Press, 1983.

Chase, William Sheafe. *Catechism on Motion Pictures in Inter-State Commerce*. 3d ed. Albany: New York Civic League, 1922.

Chester, George Randolph, and Lilian Chester. *On the Lot and Off*. New York: Harper, 1924.

Chielens, Edward E., ed. *American Literary Magazines: The Eighteenth and Nineteenth Centuries*. Historical Guides to the World's Periodicals and Newspapers. New York: Greenwood Press, 1986.

Clarens, Carlos. "Mogul – That's a Jewish Word." *Film Comment* 17.4 (1981): 34–36.

Clark, Danae. *Negotiating Hollywood: The Cultural Politics of Actors' Labor*. Minneapolis, MN: University of Minneapolis Press, 1995.

Clark, Gordon. *Shylock: As Banker, Bondholder, Corruptionist, Conspirator*. Washington, DC: n.p., 1894.

Cohn, Norman. *Warrant for Genocide*. 1967. Rev. ed. Brown Judaic Studies 23. Chicago: Scholars Press, 1981.

Cole, Wayne S. *Roosevelt and the Isolationists, 1932–45*. Lincoln: University of Nebraska Press, 1983.

———. *Senator Gerald P. Nye and American Foreign Relations*. Minneapolis, MN: University of Minnesota Press, 1962.

Colgan, Christine Ann. "Warner Brothers' Crusade against the Third Reich: A Study of Anti-Nazi Activism and Film Production, 1933 to 1941." Ph.D. diss., University of Southern California, 1986.

Coughlin, Charles E. *Am I an Anti-Semite?* N.p.: n.p., 1939.

Crafts, Wilbur F. *National Perils and Hopes: A Study Based on Current Statistics and the Observations of a Cheerful Reformer*. Cleveland, OH: Barton, 1910.

Crawford, Kenneth G. *The Pressure Boys: The Inside Story of Lobbying in America*. New York: Julian Messner, 1939.

Croy, Homer. *How Motion Pictures Are Made*. New York: Harper, 1918.

Curry, Richard O., and Thomas M. Brown, eds. *Conspiracy*. New York: Holt, Rinehart, Winston, 1972.

Davis, David Brion, ed. *Fear of Conspiracy*. Ithaca, NY: Cornell University Press, 1971.

Department of Research and Education. Federal Council of the Churches of Christ in America. Report. *The Public Relations of the Motion Picture Industry*. New York: by the author, 1931.

Desser, David. Review of: *Hollywood's Image of the Jew* by Lester D. Friedman; *From Hester Street to Hollywood: The Jewish-American Stage and Screen*, ed. Sarah Blacher Cohen; *Laughter through Tears: The Yiddish Cinema* by Judith N. Goldberg; and *Indelible Shadows: Film and the Holocaust* by Annette Insdorf. "The Return of the Repressed: The Jew on Film." *Quarterly Review of Film Studies* 9 (1984): 127.

Diamond, Sander A. *The Nazi Movement in the United States, 1924–1941*. Ithaca, NY: Cornell University Press, 1974.

Dies, Martin. "The Reds in Hollywood." *Liberty*, 17 Feb. 1940, pt. 1 of a series.

Dinnerstein, Leonard. *The Leo Frank Case*. New York: Columbia University Press, 1968.

Ed. *Anti-Semitism in the United States*. American Problem Studies. New York: Holt, Rinehart, Winston, 1971.

Dobkowski, Michael N. *The Tarnished Dream*. Contributions in American History 81. Westport, CT: Greenwood Press, 1979.

Donaldson, Scott. *Archibald MacLeish: An American Life*. Boston: Houghton, Mifflin, 1992.

Dos Passos, John. "A Note on Fitzgerald." In *The Crack-Up* by F. Scott Fitzgerald, ed. Edmund Wilson (338–45). New York: New Directions, 1945.

Dyer, Richard. "White." *Screen* 29.4 (1988): 44–64.

Eastman, Fred. "Who Controls the Movies?" *The Christian Century*, 5 Feb. 1930, pt. 4 of a series.

Eastman, Fred, and Edward Ouellette. *Better Motion Pictures*. Learning for Life. Boston: Pilgrim Press, 1936.

Editors of *Fortune*. *Jews in America*. New York: Random House, 1936.

Ehrman, John. *The Rise of Neoconservatism: Intellectuals and Foreign Affairs, 1945–1994*. New Haven, CT: Yale University Press, 1994.

Encyclopædia Britannica Online. <http://www.eb.com>.

Erens, Patricia. *The Jew in American Cinema*. Jewish Literature and Culture. Bloomington: Indiana University Press, 1984.

Facey, Paul W. *The Legion of Decency: A Sociological Analysis of the Emergence and Development of a Social Pressure Group*. Ph.D. diss., Fordham University, 1945. Dissertations on Film Series of the Arno Press Cinema Program. New York: Arno Press, 1974.

Fairbanks, Douglas, Jr. *The Salad Days*. New York: Doubleday, 1988.

Feldman, Charles Matthew. *The National Board of Censorship (Review) of Motion Pictures, 1909–1922*. Ph.D. diss. University of Michigan, 1975. New York: Arno Press, 1977.

Fiedler, Leslie. *The Jew in the American Novel*. Herzl Institute Pamphlet 10. New York: Herzl Press, 1959.

Fish, Stanley. *There's No Such Thing As Free Speech . . . And It's a Good Thing, Too*. New York: Oxford University Press, 1993.

Fitzgerald, F. Scott. *The Hobby Stories*. The Stories of F. Scott Fitzgerald 3. Middlesex: Penguin, 1983.

The Last Tycoon. New York: Scribner's, 1969.

French, Philip. *The Movie Moguls*. London: Weidenfeld and Nicolson, 1969.

Friedman, Lester. "The Conversion of the Jews." *Film Comment* 17.4 (1981): 39–48.

Hollywood's Image of the Jew. New York: Ungar, 1982.

Friedman, Norman L. "Hollywood, the Jewish Experience, and Popular Culture." *Judaism* 19 (1970): 482–87.

Friedrich, Otto. *City of Nets*. New York: Harper and Row, 1988.

Gabler, Neal. *An Empire of Their Own: How the Jews Invented Hollywood*. New York: Crown, 1988.

The Gallup Poll: Public Opinion 1935–1971. New York: Random House, 1972.

Gardner, Anne. *Reputation*. New York: A. L. Burt, 1929.

Garnett, Tay. *Tall Tales from Hollywood*. New York: Liveright, 1932.

Gerber, Michelle Stenehjem. *An American First: John T. Flynn and the America First Committee*. New Rochelle, NY: Arlington House, 1976.

Gibbons, Cromwell. *Murder in Hollywood*. New York: David Kemp, 1936.

Gilman, Sander L. *Difference and Pathology: Stereotypes of Sexuality, Race, and Madness*. Ithaca, NY: Cornell University Press, 1985.

Jewish Self-Hatred. Baltimore: Johns Hopkins University Press, 1986.

Ginder, Richard. *With Ink and Crozier: A Biography of John Francis Noll, Fifth Bishop of Fort Wayne and Founder of Our Sunday Visitor*. N.p.: N.p., n.d. [1953].

Goldberg, Nathan. "Occupational Patterns of American Jews II." *The Jewish Review* 3.3 (1945): 161–86.

Gomery, Douglas, ed. *A Guide to the Microfilm Edition of the Will Hays Papers*. Cinema History Microfilm Series. Frederick, MD: University Publications of America, 1986.

Gordon, Jan, and Cora Gordon. *Star-Dust in Hollywood*. London: George G. Harrap, 1930.

Gorman, John. *Hollywood's Bad Boy*. Hollywood: Eugene V. Brewster, 1932.

Gould, Stephen Jay. *The Mismeasure of Man*. New York: Norton, 1981.

Graumann, Carl F., and Serge Moscovici, eds. *Changing Conceptions of Conspiracy*. Springer Series in Social Psychology. New York: Springer-Verlag, 1987.

Hall, Stuart. "Cultural Studies: Two Paradigms." *Media, Culture and Society* 2 (1980):57–72.

Hamilton, Ian. *Writers in Hollywood*. New York: Harper-Burlingame, 1990.

Hampton, Benjamin B. *History of the American Film Industry from Its Beginnings to 1931*. 1931. New York: Dover, 1970.

Handlin, Oscar. "American Views of the Jew at the Opening of the Twentieth Century." *Publications of the American Jewish Historical Society* 40.4 (1951): 323–344.

"Reconsidering the Populists." *Agricultural History* 39.2 (1965): 68–74.

Hanley, Jack. *Star Lust*. 1934. New York: Grayson, 1949.

Harap, Louis. *Dramatic Encounters*. Contributions in Ethnic Studies 20. New York: Greenwood Press, 1987.

Hartman, Dennis. *Motion Picture Law Digest*. 2d ed. Los Angeles: n. p., 1947.

Hays, Will H. *See and Hear: A Brief History of Motion Pictures and the Development of Sound*. N.p.: Motion Picture Producers and Distributors of America, 1929. Rpt. *Screen Monographs II*. Literature of Cinema. New York: Arno Press–New York Times, 1970.

Hebdige, Dick. *Subculture: The Meaning of Style*. New Accents. London: Methuen, 1979.

Hendricks, Burton J. *The Jews in America*. Garden City, NY: Doubleday, Page, 1923.

Herberg, Will. *Protestant–Catholic–Jew*. Rev. ed. 1955. Garden City, NY: Anchor–Doubleday, 1960.

Higham, John. "American Anti-Semitism Historically Reconsidered." In Leonard Dinnerstein, ed., *Anti-Semitism in the United States*, 63–77. New York: Holt, Rinehart, Winston, 1971.

———. "Social Discrimination against Jews in America, 1830–1930." *Publications of the American Jewish Historical Society* 47.1 (1957): 1–Rpt. Philadelphia: Maurice Jacobs, n.d.

———. *Strangers in the Land*. New Brunswick, NJ: Rutgers University Press, 1955.

Hofstadter, Richard. *The Age of Reform*. New York: Knopf, 1955.

———. "The Paranoid Style in American Politics." In *The Paranoid Style in American Politics and Other Essays*. New York: Borzoi-Knopf, 1965, 3–40.

Hollingsworth, J. Rogers. Commentary. "Populism: The Problem of Rhetoric and Reality," *Agricultural History* 39.2 (1965): 81–85.

Hornaday, William T. *Awake! America*. New York: Moffat, Yard, 1918.

Hough, Emerson. *The Web*. Chicago: Reilly and Lee, 1919.

Howe, Irving. *World of Our Fathers*. New York: Harcourt, Brace, Jovanovich, 1976.

The International Jew. Vols. 1–4. N.p.: n.p., 1921–22.

Jacobs, Lea. *The Wages of Sin: Censorship and the Fallen Woman Film, 1928–1942*. Madison: University of Wisconsin Press, 1991.

Jew in the Text: The Modernity and the Construction of Identity. London: Thames & Hudson, 1995.

Joseph, Samuel. *Jewish Immigration in the United States*. Studies in History, Economics and Public Law 59.4. New York: Columbia University, 1914.

Jowett, Garth. *Film: The Democratic Art*. Boston: Little, Brown, 1976.

Jowett, Garth, Ian C. Jarvie, and Kathryn Fuller. *Children and the Movies: Media Influence and the Payne Fund Controversy*. Cambridge Studies in the History of Mass Communications. Cambridge and New York: Cambridge University Press, 1996.

Knepper, Max. *Sodom and Gomorrah*. Los Angeles: End Poverty League, 1935.

Koppes, Clayton R., and Gregory D. Black. *Hollywood Goes to War*. New York: Free Press, 1987; London: Tauris, 1988.

Kreuger, Miles, ed. *Souvenir Programs of Twelve Classic Movies, 1927–1941*. New York: Dover, 1977.

Lamparski, Richard. *Whatever Became of . . . ?*. New York: Crown, 1967.

Lee, Albert. *Henry Ford and the Jews*. New York: Stein and Day, 1980.

Leff, Leonard J., and Jerold L. Simmons. *The Dame in the Kimono*. New York: Grove Weidenfeld, 1990.

Leiser, Erwin. *Nazi Cinema*. Trans. Gertrud Mander and David Wilson. New York: Collier–Macmillan, 1974.

Lindbergh, Anne Morrow. *War Within and Without*. New York: Harcourt, Brace, Jovanovich, 1980.

Lippman, Walter. *Public Opinion, 1922*. New York: Macmillan, 1941.

Lokke, Virgil. *The Literary Image of Hollywood*. (Ph.D. diss., State University of Iowa, 1955; Doctoral Dissertation Series 14, Ann Arbor, MI: University of Michigan, n.d.)

Lowenthal, Leo, and Norbert Guterman. *Prophets of Deceit*. 1949. 2d ed. Palo Alto, CA: Pacific, 1970.

Lubou, Haynes. *Reckless Hollywood*. New York: Amour Press, 1932.

Lynch, David. *The Concentration of Economic Power*. New York: Columbia University Press, 1946.

Lyons, Matthew Nemiroff. "Parasites and Pioneers: Anti-Semitism in White Supremacist America." In *The Third Wave: Feminist Perspectives on Racism*, ed. Alarcon et al. New York: Kitchen Table – Women of Color Press, 1992.

May, Lary. *Screening Out the Past: The Birth of Mass Culture and the Motion Picture Industry*. New York: Oxford University Press, 1980.

May, Lary, and Elaine Tyler May. "The Jewish Movie Moguls: An Explanation in American Culture." *American Jewish History* 72 (1982): 6–25.

Mayo, Louise A. *The Ambivalent Image*. Sara F. Yoseloff Memorial Publications in Judaism and Jewish Affairs 1. Rutherford, NJ: Fairleigh Dickinson University Press, 1988.

McCormick, Thomas J. and Walter LaFeber, eds. *Behind the Throne: Servants of Power to Imperial Presidents, 1898–1968*. Madison: University of Wisconsin Press, 1993.

McDaniel, Dennis Kay. *Martin Dies of Un-American Activities: His Life and Times*. Ph.D diss., University of Houston, 1988. Ann Arbor, MI: University of Michigan, 1989.

McFarland, Ernest W. *Mac: The Autobiography of Ernest W. McFarland*. N.p.: by the author, 1979.

McMillan, James E., ed. *The Ernest W. McFarland Papers: The United States Senate Years, 1940–1952*. Prescott, AZ: Sharlot Hall Museum Press, 1995.

Microsoft Bookshelf 1996–97. CD-ROM. Redmond, WA: Microsoft, 1996.

Microsoft Cinemania 97. CD-ROM. Redmond, WA: Microsoft, 1996.

Minney, R. J. *Hollywood by Starlight*. London: Chapman, Hall, 1935.

Minott, Rodney. *Peerless Patriots*. Washington, DC: Public Affairs Press, 1962.

Mitchell, Greg. *The Campaign of the Century*. New York: Random House, 1992.

Moley, Raymond. *The Hays Office*. New York: Bobbs-Merrill, 1945.

The Municipal Committee. The Cleveland Chamber of Commerce. *Shall the Movies Be Censored?* Cleveland, OH: by the author, 1922.

Myers, Gustavus. *History of Bigotry in the United States*. New York: Random House, 1943.

Nash, Jay Robert, and Stanley Ralph Ross. *The Motion Picture Guide*. Chicago: Cinebooks, 1987.

Navasky, Victor S. *Naming Names*. New York: Penguin, 1981.

The 1941–42 International Motion Picture Almanac. New York: Quigley, 1941.

1939–1940 International Motion Picture Almanac. New York: Quigley, 1939.

Nizer, Louis. *New Courts of Industry: Self-Regulation under the Motion Picture Code.* New York: Longacre Press, 1935.

Nye, David E. *Henry Ford, "Ignorant Idealist."* Series in American Studies. Port Washington, NY: Kennikat Press, 1979.

Ogden, August Raymond. *The Dies Committee: A Study of the Special House Committee for the Investigation of Un-American Activities 1938–1943.* Washington, DC: Murray, Heister, 1943.

Page, Ra, and Michael Stodnick. "The Wandering Jew: Romantic Approaches." *Manuscript* 1.1 (1995). Online. University of Manchester English and American Studies Dept. Internet. 18 Dec. 1998. Available., http://www.art.man.ac.uk/english/ms/ramiconf.htm.

Pavlik, Gregory P., ed. *Forgotten Lessons: Selected Essays of John T. Flynn.* Irvington-on-Hudson, NY: Foundation for Economic Education, 1996.

Pelley, William Dudley. *The Door to Revelation.* Typescript. Asheville, NC: Foundation Fellowship, 1936.

  Nations-In-Law. Asheville, NC: by the author, 1935.

Perlman, William J., comp. and ed. *The Movies on Trial.* New York: Macmillan, 1936.

Perlmutter, Ruth. "The Melting Plot and the Humoring of America: Hollywood and the Jew." *Film Reader* 5 (1982): 247–56.

Pierce, Robert Clayton. *Liberals and the Cold War: Union for Democratic Action and Americans for Democratic Action.* Ph.D. diss. University of Wisconsin – Madison, 1979. Ann Arbor, MJ: University Microfilms, 1979.

Poe, John R., Jr. "Martin Dies: The Development of a Southern Anti-Communist." M.A. thesis, University of North Carolina–Chapel Hill, 1973.

Pollack, Norman. "Fear of Man." *Agricultural History* 39.2 (1965): 59–67.

  "Hofstadter on Populism: A Critique of *The Age of Reform*." *The Journal of Southern History* 26.4 (1960): 478–500.

  "Myth of Populist Anti-Semitism." *American Historical Review* 68.1 (1962): 76–80.

Potamkin, Harry Alan. *The Eyes of the Movie.* International Pamphlets 38. New York: International Pamphlets, 1934.

  "The Jew as Film-Subject." *The Jewish Tribune*, 2 May 1930.

Powdermaker, Hortense. *Hollywood: The Dream Factory.* Boston: Little, Brown, 1950.

Priestley, J. B. *Midnight on the Desert.* New York: Harper, 1937.

The Protocols and World Revolution. Boston: Small, Maynard, 1920.

Pulzer, Peter. *The Rise of Political Anti-Semitism in Germany and Austria.* 1964. Rev. ed. London: Halban, 1988.

Quigley, Martin. *Decency in Motion Pictures.* New York: Macmillan, 1937.

  Moving Pictures: Their Impact on Society. N.p.: Ozer, 1971.

Ramsaye, Terry. *A Million and One Nights.* 1926; New York: Simon and Schuster, 1964.

Ray, Charles. *Hollywood Shorts.* Los Angeles: California Graphic Press, 1935.

Ribuffo, Leo P. "Henry Ford and *The International Jew*." *American Jewish History* 69.4 (1980): 437–77.

  The Old Christian Right. Philadelphia: Temple University Press, 1983.

Richmond, Jack. *Hollywood*. Los Angeles: by the author, 1928.

Rogin, Michael. *Blackface, White Noise: Jewish Immigrants in the Hollywood Melting Pot*. Berkeley: Centennial-University of California Press, 1996.

Ronald Reagan, the Movie. Berkeley: University of California Press, 1987.

Rose, Arnold. "Anti-Semitism's Root in City Hatred." *Commentary* 6 (1948): 374–78.

Rosten, Leo C. *Hollywood: The Movie Colony, The Movie Makers*. New York: Harcourt, Brace, 1941.

Roy, Ralph Lord. *Apostles of Discord*. Boston: Beacon Press, 1953.

Royce, Monroe. *The Passing of the American*. New York: Thomas Whittaker, 1911.

Ruch, Floyd L. *A Research Memorandum on Methods of Studying Public Opinion in Relation to the War*. New York: Social Science Research Council, 1942.

Rutland, James Richard. *State Censorship and Motion Pictures*. Reference Shelf 2.1. New York: H. W. Wilson, 1923.

Said, Edward W. *Orientalism*. 1978. New York: Vintage-Random, 1979.

Schatz, Gerald S. "Will H. Hays and the Motion Picture Industry." *Historical Society of Southern California Quarterly* 43.3 (1961): 316–29.

Schatz, Thomas. *The Genius of the System: Hollywood Filmmaking in the Studio Era*. New York: Pantheon, 1988.

Schulberg, Budd. *What Makes Sammy Run?* 1941. New York: Modern Library–Random House, 1952.

Scoville, John, and Noel Sargent, comps. *Fact and Fancy in the T.N.E.C. Monographs: Reviews of the 43 Monographs Issued by the Temporary National Economic Committee*. The Right Wing Individualist Tradition in America. New York: National Association of Manufacturers, 1942. New York: Arno Press–New York Times, 1972.

See, Carolyn Penelope. *The Hollywood Novel: An Historical and Critical Study*. Ph.D. diss. University of California–Los Angeles, 1963. Ann Arbor, MI: UMI, 1984.

Seligman, Ben B. "They Came to Hollywood; How Jews Built the Movie Industry." *Jewish Frontier* 20 (1953): 19–29.

Shakespeare, William. *The Merchant of Venice*. In *The Complete Works of William Shakespeare*, ed. W. J. Craig. London: Oxford University Press, 1914. Bartleby.com,2000.www.bartleby.com/Access/Aug.2000.

Shapiro, Edward S. "The Approach of War: Congressional Isolationism and Anti-Semitism, 1939–1941." *American Jewish History* 74.1 (1984): 45–65.

Sheehan, Perley Poore. *Hollywood as a World Center*. Hollywood, CA: Hollywood Citizen Press, 1924.

Short, K.R.M. "Hollywood Fights Anti-Semitism, 1945–1947." In *Feature Films as History*, ed. K.R.M. Short London: Croom, Helm, 1981.

Screening the Propaganda of British Air Power: From R.A.F. (1935) to The Lion Has Wings (1939). Studies in War and Film 6. Wiltshire, UK: Flicks Books, 1997.

"*That Hamilton Woman* (1941): Propaganda, Feminism and the Production Code." *Historical Journal of Film, Radio and Television* 11.1 (1991). *Academic Search Elite*. EBSCOhost Direct. Indiana University–Purdue University Helmke Library, Fort Wayne, IN, 1 July 1999 <http://www.epnet.com/>.

Silcox, Charles Edwin, and Galen M. Fisher. *Catholics, Jews and Protestants: A Study of Relationships in the United States and Canada*. New York: Institute of Social and Religious Research – Harper Bros., 1934.

Sinclair, Upton. *Money Writes*. New York: Albert and Charles Boni, 1927.

Singerman, Robert. "The American Career of the *Protocols of the Elders of Zion*." *American Jewish History* 71.1 (1981): 48–78.

Skinner, James M. *The Cross and the Cinema: The Legion of Decency and the National Catholic Office for Motion Pictures, 1933–1970*. Westport, CT: Praeger, 1993.

Sklar, Robert. *Movie-Made America*. 1975. Updated ed. New York: Vintage-Random House, 1994.

Slide, Anthony. "Hollywood's Fascist Follies." *Film Comment* 27.4 (1991): 63–67.

Sobel, Robert. *The Manipulators*. Garden City, NY: Anchor Press-Doubleday, 1976.

Spatz, Jonas. "Fitzgerald, Hollywood, and the Myth of Success." In *The Thirties*, ed. Warren French. Deland, FL: Everett Edwards, 1967.

Spivak, John L. "Coughlin and Ford." *New Masses*, 12 December 1939.

St. Johns, Adela. *The Skyrocket*. 1924. New York: Cosmopolitan, 1925.

Starr, Kevin. *Material Dreams*. New York: Oxford University Press, 1990.

Stember, Charles Herbert, et al. *Jews in the Mind of America*. New York: Basic Books, 1966.

Stenehjem, Michele Flynn. *An American First*. New Rochelle, NY: Arlington House, 1976.

Strong, Donald S. *Organized Anti-Semitism in the United States: The Rise of Group Prejudice during the Decade 1930–40*. Washington, DC: American Council on Public Affairs, 1941. Rpt. Westport, CT: Greenwood Press, 1979.

Suber, Howard. "Politics and Popular Culture: Hollywood at Bay, 1933–1953." In *The Jews of the West*, ed. Moses Rischin, 133–49. Waltham, MA: American Jewish Historical Society, 1979.

Sward, Keith. *The Legend of Henry Ford*. New York: Rinehart, 1948.

Szajkowski, Zosa. *Jews, Wars and Communism*. Vol. 1. New York: KTAV Publishing, 1972.

The Talmud Jew. New York: Titus, 1892.

Thomas, John Howard. *Senator Burton K. Wheeler and United States Foreign Relations*. Ph.D. diss., University of Virginia, 1982. Ann Arbor, MI: UMI, 1990.

Thompson, Kristin, and David Bordwell. *Film History: An Introduction*. New York: McGraw-Hill, 1994.

Thornton, Mark. "How Antitrust Ruined the Movies." *The Free Market* 14.6 (1996). Ludwig von Mises Institute. www. mises. org. Accessed 25 Aug. 2000.

Timayenis, Telemachus Thomas. *The Original Mr. Jacobs: A Startling Exposé*. New York: Minerva, 1888.

Traube, Shepard. *Glory Road*. New York: Macaulay, 1935.

20th Century Pictures, Inc. Souvenir Booklet for *The House of Rothschild*. [Hollywood]: by the author, [1934].

Unger, Irwin. "Critique of Norman Pollack's 'Fear of Man.'" *Agricultural History* 39.2 (1965): 75–80.

U.S. Chamber of Commerce. Committee on Subversive Activities. *Combating Subversive Activities in the United States*. Washington, DC: Chamber of Commerce, 1934.

U.S. Congress. House. Committee on Education. *Hearings on the Proposed Federal Motion Picture Commission*, 69th Cong, 1st sess., H. R. 4094 and 6233. Washington, DC: GPO, 1926.

House. Committee on Education. *Hearings on the Federal Motion Picture Commission*, 64th Cong., 1st sess., HR 456. Washington, DC: GPO, 1916. Aspects of Film series. New York: Arno Press, 1978.

House. Committee on Interstate and Foreign Commerce. *Hearings on Federal Motion Picture Commission*. 73d Cong., 2d sess., H. R. 6097. Washington, DC: GPO, 1934.

House. Committee on Interstate and Foreign Commerce. *Motion-Picture Films (Compulsory Block Booking and Blind Selling)*. 76th Cong., 3d sess., S. 280, pt. 1. Washington, DC: GPO, 1940.

House. Special Committee on Un-American Activities. *Hearings on the Investigation of Un-American Propaganda Activities in the United States*. 12 vols. 75th Cong., 3d sess.–78th Cong., 2d sess. Washington, DC: GPO, 1939.

Senate. Committee on Interstate Commerce. Subcommittee on S. 280. *Hearings on Anti "Block-Booking" and "Blind Selling" in the Leasing of Motion-Picture Films*, 76th Cong., 1st sess., S. 280. Washington, DC: GPO, 1939.

Senate. Subcommittee of the Committee on Interstate Commerce. *Hearings on Compulsory Block-Booking and Blind Selling in the Motion Picture Industry*. 74th Cong. 2d sess., S. 3012. Washington, DC: GPO, 1938.

Senate. Subcommittee of the Committee on Interstate Commerce. *Propaganda in Motion Pictures*. Hearings, 77th Cong., 1st sess., S. Res. 152. Washington, DC: GPO, 1942.

Senate. Temporary National Economic Committee. Daniel Bertrand, Wilmoth Duane Evans, and Edna Lillian Blanchard. *The Motion Picture Industry – A Pattern of Control*. Temporary National Economic Committee Investigation of Concentration of Economic Power 43. Washington, DC: GPO, 1941. New York: Arno Press, 1978.

U.S. National Recovery Administration. *Report Regarding Investigation Directed to Be Made by the President in His Executive Order of November 27, 1933, Approving the Code of Fair Competition for the Motion Picture Industry*. Made by Sol A. Rosenblatt to Gen. Hugh S. Johnson, 7 July 1934.

U.S. Office of National Recovery Administration. Division of Review. "The Motion Picture Industry" by Daniel Bertrand. Work Materials 34, February 1936.

Urquhart, Ronald Albert. *The American Reaction to the Dreyfus Affair*. Ph.D. Diss., Columbia University, 1972. Ann Arbor, MI: UMI, 1985.

Vaughn, Stephen. *Ronald Reagan in Hollywood: Movies and Politics*. Cambridge: Cambridge University Press, 1994.

Vechten, Carl Van. *Spider Boy*. New York: Knopf, 1928.

Wade, Horace. *To Hell with Hollywood*. New York: Lincoln MacVeagh–Dial Press, 1931.

Walsh, Francis R. " 'The Callahans and the Murphys' (MGM, 1927): A Case Study of Irish-American and Catholic Church Censorship." *Historical Journal of Film, Radio and Television* 10.1 (1990): 33–45.

Sin and Censorship: The Catholic Church and the Motion Picture Industry. New Haven, CT: Yale University Press, 1996.

Wanamaker, Mark. "History of the Jewish Presence in Hollywood – From Cowboy to Corporate Leader." *Legacy* 1.1 (1987): 5–64.

Weingarten, Irving. "The Image of the Jew in the American Periodical Press." Ph.D. diss., New York University, 1980.

Welch, David. *Propaganda and the German Cinema, 1933–1945*. Oxford: Clarendon–Oxford University Press, 1983.

Wells, Walter. *Tycoons and Locusts*. Crosscurrents–Modern Critiques. Carbondale: Southern Illinois University Press. London: Feffer and Simons, 1973.

West, Nathanael. *Day of the Locust*. In *The Complete Works of Nathanael West*. New York: Octagon–Farrar, Straus, Giroux, 1980.

Wheeler, Burton K., and Paul F. Healy. *Yankee from the West: The Candid, Turbulent Life Story of the Yankee-Born U.S. Senator from Montana*. New York: Octagon, 1977.

Whitfield, Stephen J. "Our American Jewish Heritage: The Hollywood Version." *American Jewish History* 75 (1986): 322–40.

Williams, Raymond. *Marxism and Literature*. Oxford: Oxford University Press, 1977.

Wilson, Woodrow. *Selected Addresses and Public Papers of Woodrow Wilson*. Ed. Albert Bushnell Hart. New York: Boni and Liveright, 1918.

Winokur, Mark. "Improbable Ethnic Hero: William Powell and the Transformation of Ethnic Hollywood." *Cinema Journal* 27.1 (1987): 5–22.

Wyman, David S. *Paper Walls*. 1968. New York: Pantheon, 1985.

Yeomans, Henry Aaron. *Abbott Lawrence Lowell, 1856–1943*. Cambridge, MA: Harvard University Press, 1948. New York: Arno Press, 1977.

Zierold, Norman. *The Moguls*. New York: Coward-McCann, 1969.

Index